D1621590

PUBLIC SPEAKING TODAY

2ND EDITION

DIANA CARLIN

University of Kansas

JAMES PAYNE

Blue Valley High School

National Textbook Company

a division of NTC/CONTEMPORARY PUBLISHING COMPANY

Lincolnwood, Illinois USA

Cover design:
Ophelia M. Chambliss

Front cover photos:
David Young-Wolff/PhotoEdit
Bob Daemmrich/The Image Works
Myrleen Ferguson Cate/PhotoEdit

Back cover photos:
Jeff Ellis

Published by National Textbook Company, a division of NTC Publishing Group.
© 1995, 1989 by NTC Publishing Group, 4255 West Touhy Avenue,
Lincolnwood (Chicago), Illinois 60646-1975 U.S.A.

Manufactured in the United States of America.

Library of Congress Catalog Card Number: 93-86239

7 8 9 0 QB 9 8 7 6 5 4

Preface

Since the first edition of *Public Speaking Today* was published, many public speakers have added compelling words and images to the closing decade of the twentieth century. Think of a few of the speeches that linger in our minds:

- President George Bush addressing the nation, announcing that American forces had begun an invasion of Iraq.
- Generals Norman Schwarzkopf and Colin Powell updating the American people on the progress of the Persian Gulf war.
- Presidential candidate Bill Clinton, appearing on MTV, appealing to a new generation of voters.
- Russian President Boris Yeltsin, speaking from a tank, facing down the threat of a government overthrow.
- Mary Fisher, founder of the Family AIDS Network, telling the audience at the 1992 Republican National Convention about living with AIDS and HIV.
- Nelson Mandela, leader of the African National Congress, freed after years in prison, promoting the cause of equality in South Africa by addressing a joint session of the U.S. Congress.
- H. Ross Perot recruiting millions of supporters in his 1992 bid for the presidency with his own brand of plain talk.

But when you think of the speeches given during the past few years, think also of the many speakers who were not famous. The impact of speeches given daily all over the world is often stronger than the impact of the speeches given by the famous. Consider:

- The sermon given by a local minister.
- The election speech of a local candidate for the school board.
- The sales talk presented by a regional manager for a computer manufacturer.
- The lecture delivered by a high-school history teacher.
- The speech on AIDS given to a community group by a local doctor.

All of these speeches, both the famous and the not-so-famous, are moments in our lives when someone says the right words at the right time and makes a difference. Public speaking is, after all, about making a difference. Public speakers hope that an audience will change after hearing their speech. The urge to make a difference motivates speakers. The hope that people can make a difference also motivates an audience to listen and to value public speaking.

The Importance of Studying Public Speaking

Public Speaking Today will teach you the public speaking skills that can help you make a difference. As you study public speaking, you are preparing for many of the speaking situations faced by presidents, generals, business leaders, celebrities, and reformers. You are also preparing for the more common situations faced by teachers, sales people, ministers, and others who want to make things better for themselves and their community.

As you study, you will find the challenges of public speaking both interesting and intimidating. Public speaking is interesting because it asks you to come to a better understanding of human nature and human communication. It asks you to know more of yourself and your audience. Public speaking is intimidating because it asks you to take a risk, to put yourself in a situation where you can succeed or fail in your effort to make a difference.

How *Public Speaking Today* Is Organized

This book introduces you to the skills that will make you a better speaker and a better listener. Unit 1, "What Is Public Speaking," explores your relationship to public speaking and why public speaking is so valuable to learn. The first unit also defines public speaking as a process and shows your role in the process as both a speaker and a listener.

Unit 2, "Public Speaking Fundamentals," identifies the primary methods and tools that speakers use to increase their effectiveness, including voice, nonverbal delivery, language, audience analysis, topic selection, speech delivery, and speech evaluation.

Unit 3, "Preparing Speeches," builds your skills in preparing speeches by discussing different types of support materials, research methods and strategies, speech organization, and the role of argumentation in public speaking.

Finally, Unit 4, "Presenting Speeches," brings together the skills learned in the first three units and applies them to specific types of speeches, from speeches to inform to speeches to entertain and speeches to persuade.

Special Features

Each chapter in *Public Speaking Today* begins with a list of objectives and key terms, which help you focus your reading and studying. Each chapter ends with exercises that test your knowledge of the material in the chapter and ask you to apply what you have learned, both individually and in groups.

A variety of special features are found throughout the text:

- *Spotlight on Speaking* boxes provide checklists and other information that can help you apply the skills outlined in the book to your own speech preparation.

- *Speaking about Speaking* boxes supply additional viewpoints about public speaking events or situations.

- *Sample Speeches* are models of excellent speeches from a variety of speakers in many different situations.

- *Voices* features provide a historical perspective on critical issues throughout time.

As speech teachers, we would like to be with each of you so we could explain how important public speaking is. We would like to talk about the skills detailed in this book. We would like to watch as you gain confidence and competence as public speakers. Since we can't be with you, we hope this book, together with your teacher's sound instruction and your own dedication, will help you become an effective public speaker. Now and in the future, you will be the ones giving the historically significant speeches and the day-to-day speeches that make a difference in our world.

Diana Carlin
James Payne

Contents

◆ *UNIT 4* ◆   **Presenting Speeches 310**

UNIT

1

What Is Public Speaking?

CHAPTER

·1·

Key Terms

Adrenalin

Communication apprehension

Democracy

Stage fright

Chapter Objectives

After studying this chapter, you should be able to:

1. Explain why public speaking is important in your world.
2. List three ways that public speaking can help you in other courses.
3. List three opportunities for public speaking you are likely to have.
4. Explain some of the benefits of public speaking.
5. Explain what communication apprehension is and what causes it.
6. Explain two techniques for controlling communication apprehension.

Public Speaking and You

Opportunities for Public Speaking

Many students ask why they should learn to give speeches. They often argue that they don't plan to be politicians, members of the clergy, or company presidents. Students who think that those are the only careers that require public speaking overlook the fact that most of the thousands of speeches delivered every day are given by average people. The coach who explains and demonstrates the right way to make a lay-up is giving a speech. So are the police officer who speaks to second graders about not talking to strangers and the parent who reports to the PTA on an upcoming school fundraiser.

If you think about it, you've given and listened to more speeches than you realize. Because speech-making is such an important part of your daily life, it only makes sense to study how to do it well. Most good speakers learned their skills; they weren't born with them. What is more, there are listening techniques that will help you get more out of the speeches you hear.

You never know when you'll have the opportunity to present a speech or to listen to one. By learning good speech-making techniques now, you can take advantage of opportunities at school, on the job, and as a citizen in a democracy. You'll also learn how to get the most from the speeches you hear.

Opportunities at School

As a student, you listen to class lectures every day. You also hear student speakers at assemblies or other school activities. While those situations are the most obvious, they are not the only ones.

You have been in school long enough to know that school provides many opportunities to speak in public. Students who give reports in English, take part in group discussions in history, and participate in extracurricular organizations express their ideas through public speaking. Many students who take advantage of speaking opportunities become school leaders and achievers because of their ability to communicate their ideas to others.

During the years ahead, you will have more opportunities to speak. You'll be able to improve your grades by giving speeches or oral reports about class projects. In addition, you can have an impact on school affairs as you learn to voice your opinions.

If you go on to college or vocational school, you'll find that some courses rely heavily on oral reports. Even if you understand the subject matter, your grades may suffer if you can't share your under-

School presents many opportunities for public speaking, from giving reports in English class to giving a speech at graduation.

standing with others. You will also discover that you can learn from other students' reports or speeches. As you become a better listener, your understanding of a variety of topics will grow.

School is an excellent training ground for good public speakers because all students can participate, not just a select few. Find out what classes offer you opportunities to speak, and take advantage of them. Your future success may be influenced by these opportunities.

Opportunities on the Job

When you train for a job, you learn the skills necessary to do that job. Unfortunately, many people forget that public speaking and communication skills are also important in most jobs. Several recent studies have revealed that businesses want employees who not only know their field but also can communicate. In fact, promotions may be based upon an employee's ability to communicate effectively with groups.

As a result, many businesspeople must make presentations within their own companies and must participate in community functions that require speaking and listening skills. Many large insurance agencies require all new employees, not just salespeople, to take a speech course. Many companies spend thousands of dollars annually on

Learning good communication skills is important for success at work since most jobs involve some public speaking.

workshops to improve employees' speaking and listening skills. Some companies pay tuition for employees who enroll in college courses in public speaking.

The number of speaking opportunities in business and industry shows why speech training is so important. When a crew chief or a supervisor meets with a ten-person crew, that is an opportunity for public speaking. When a salesperson demonstrates how a product works to potential customers, public speaking skills are essential. A sales meeting, a banquet, and a staff meeting are opportunities for employees to advance their careers through public speaking.

Because public speaking is so much a part of the business world, you will also find yourself on the listening end. By listening well, you will learn more quickly and handle your job more effectively.

Regardless of the type of job you have after leaving school, you will communicate with others. Even if you talk to only one person at a time, the skills of organization and clear speaking that you learn in a public speaking class are essential. Even in a highly technological society, people still need to communicate with each other. The methods for transmitting and receiving human communication may change, but it is doubtful that machines will reduce the need for public speaking.

| SPEAKING ABOUT SPEAKING | # First Amendment of the United States Constitution |

"Congress shall make no law respecting an establishment of religion, or prohibiting the free exercise thereof; or abridging the freedom of speech, or of the press; or the right of the people peaceably to assemble, and to petition the Government for a redress of grievances."

When the founders of our country added the Bill of Rights to the Constitution in 1791, the First Amendment guaranteed the rights listed above. Why were the rights concerning freedom of expression considered so important? What responsibilities must citizens accept in exercising these rights? What examples can you think of that illustrate how Americans exercise the rights listed in the First Amendment?

Opportunities in a Democracy

Winston Churchill, British Prime Minister during World War II, told the British House of Commons that, "The United States is a land of free speech. Nowhere is speech freer." The Constitution of the United States recognizes the importance of speech in a free society, and, in the First Amendment, it protects your right and freedom to speak. The founders of this country knew that in a **democracy,** where people govern themselves, they must have the right to speak out and must have free access to information. The roots of today's public speaking are found in the ancient Greek democracy of Athens. The relationship between government by the people and public speaking is a long-standing one. Appendix C gives you more insight into this tradition.

In a democracy, citizens have many opportunities to speak out on political issues, even if they don't run for public office. School board and city council meetings offer built-in opportunities for ordinary citizens to express their positions on local issues. State legislatures and the U.S. Congress hold hearings to learn the pros and cons of proposed laws, and those testifying are often ordinary citizens. In state capitals and in Washington, D.C., the steps of public buildings are scenes for speeches. Citizens use these symbols of democracy as a backdrop to speak out on such issues as the environment, urban problems, human rights, and peace.

As a citizen, you have the opportunity and the responsibility to make your opinions known through public speaking.

As a citizen in a democracy, you have the right and the responsibility to make your opinions known. Elected officials need to know the political positions of those they represent. You will find many opportunities to express your ideas at town meetings and other forums that allow open, public discussion.

The spoken word is a powerful tool for influence. Throughout this book you will be given examples of speeches and speakers who have made a difference in history. Adolf Hitler, the German leader who posed a great threat to democracy in this century, wrote in his book, *Mein Kampf:*

> I know that one is able to win people far more by the spoken word than by the written word, and that every great movement on this globe owes its rise to the great speakers not the great writers.

Hitler used his speaking ability to rally people to his cause. History has recorded the devastating results. Since people can be moved for both good and bad by a powerful speaker, you need to learn how to listen to a speech. Preserving a democracy depends on both those who speak and those who listen carefully. Listen carefully, and apply the lessons you learn throughout this book to analyze what you hear.

The Benefits of Public Speaking

You've read about the importance of public speaking in school, on the job, and in a democracy. As you continue in this class, you will find that the benefits of public speaking go beyond learning how to express yourself orally. This section explains some of the added benefits of learning how to make speeches.

Organizational Skills

As you read this book, you'll discover that organizational skills are an important part of composing a speech—in fact, the ability to organize ideas is a skill you will employ before you ever write a speech. The same is true for writing. You will also discover that the organizational skills so necessary in composing speeches carry over to other areas that require outlining and planning, such as organizing notes or reporting on science experiments.

Writing Skills

Many of the skills you use to compose good speeches are the same as those you need to write well. The practice you gain preparing speeches will improve your ability to express your ideas on paper. You will learn how to get your audience's attention, how to organize clearly, and how to support your ideas. These skills will benefit you when you write compositions in English class, essay questions on tests, and reports on the job. There is no substitute for practice when it comes to building speaking and writing skills, and practice in one carries over to the other.

Critical Thinking Skills

In the past few years, several studies have examined what is right and what is wrong with the American educational system. Many of these reports have indicated that this country's schools do not do enough to teach students to think and to analyze. Public speaking skills and related listening skills provide valuable tools for the critical analysis of ideas. By studying the use of supportive materials and persuasive strategies, you'll learn how to find an argument's weak points. You will learn to ask questions about the claims speakers make. By learning to think critically, you will be better able to solve job-related problems and to fulfill your duties as a citizen.

Research Skills

Often, when students are asked to prepare a report, they go to an encyclopedia and summarize the contents of an article. As a public-speaking student, you will be introduced to a variety of research materials. Knowing how to conduct research will be useful to you in a wide range of school and job-related activities.

Listening Skills

Speaking and listening go hand in hand. Whenever someone gives a speech, there is an audience to listen to it. By learning good speaking techniques, you'll prepare speeches that are easier for an audience to listen to and understand. You will also learn how to listen to other speakers in order to hear all the key points. By sharpening your listening skills as you analyze your classmates' speeches, you'll improve your listening skills in every other listening situation. Because listening is such a key part of the public speaking process, this text includes a separate chapter on it.

Self-Confidence

Giving a speech to a group of people involves a great deal of risk. Those risks are discussed later in this chapter. However, it is true that by learning how to give a speech in front of a group, your self-confidence will grow. Each speech will be easier to give.

As you become more confident as a public speaker, you'll gain confidence in your ability to communicate in general. It will become easier to speak out in class or in small groups. Interviews will become easier because you have learned techniques to prepare and present information about yourself.

To a large extent, success in life depends on your ability to feel good about yourself. Succeeding as a public speaker can give your self-confidence a tremendous boost and will carry over to other classes and on the job.

The Risks of Public Speaking

Thus far, you have learned about the opportunities for public speaking experiences and their benefits. To be honest about public speaking, there are also risks involved. There are very few enjoyable or profitable experiences in life that don't have risks, and public speaking is no exception.

Speakers have some real concerns—fear of failure, forgetting what to say, or having their ideas rejected by an audience. Many also fear being in front of a group. Most of these fears and risks are related and fall under the broad heading of communication apprehension.

Communication Apprehension

Communication apprehension, or **stage fright** as it is often called, is being fearful about participating in some form of communication with others. The degree to which people experience apprehension ranges from mild nervousness before beginning to speak to a total inability to say anything. Very few individuals suffer from the more serious form; however, it is safe to say that almost everyone experiences some form of nervousness. Even experienced speakers and actors get butterflies before a presentation.

Apprehension before a performance is not unusual. If you are a musician or an athlete, you have probably experienced nervousness before a concert or game. You also know that once you begin performing or playing, you forget your fears and lose yourself in what you are doing. The same is true for most speakers.

Anyone who thinks he or she is the only one in class worried about getting up and giving a speech is wrong. Research has shown that adults fear public speaking more than anything else. In fact, they are more afraid of public speaking than they are of death, snakes, and heights. Why? Perhaps they believe they can avoid some of the other fears. After all, if you fear snakes, you can avoid places where they live. It's different with public speaking. There are so many opportunities to speak at school, on the job, and in a democracy that few people can avoid giving a speech. Public speaking may be the number one fear because it is so necessary and because so few people are trained for it. By understanding why you fear public speaking, you can better deal with your fears.

Causes of Communication Apprehension

Before giving an oral report, do you feel nervous? Does your heart beat faster and more loudly? Do your palms sweat? Is your throat dry? Do you get butterflies in your stomach? These feelings are natural physical responses to any situation in which you risk something.

You can understand these physical sensations if you remember how an animal responds to a frightening situation. The animal has two responses—fight or flight. It must either defend itself or run away. Either action requires great physical energy, and the animal's body prepares itself. A substance called **adrenalin** is released into the bloodstream and stimulates the heart. The heart rate goes up. Breathing rate increases. Perspiration increases. The animal's senses are heightened because the fight-or-flight response has changed its body chemistry to prepare it for whatever happens.

The same thing happens to you when you feel fear. Stage fright is not imaginary. The feelings are definitely real, but they are not all negative. As athletes and performers know, nervousness can give you an edge. It may provide the something extra you need for a good performance. Some actors and speakers worry if they aren't nervous. They know their performance will be better when the adrenalin is flowing.

So, if you experience stage fright, you're perfectly normal. No one wants to fail or to be laughed at, and that's what stage fright is really about. With practice, you can learn to control your stage fright and use it to sharpen your performance.

Controlling Your Fears

The best solution for overcoming fear of speaking is preparation. If you've done your homework, have written a good speech, and have practiced it, you'll feel more confident. Confidence is a key to controlling stage fright. If you feel you're in control of the situation, you have less reason to be fearful.

It is also important to set realistic expectations for yourself. Your first few speeches won't be perfect. No one expects them to be, and you shouldn't either. After each speech, study the evaluation you receive, determine areas you need to work on, and set clearly defined goals for improvement. Take public speaking one step at a time, just as you would any other skill.

When the time comes to deliver your speech, don't rush to begin speaking as soon as you get to the front of the room. Get organized, take a deep breath, and begin speaking slowly. Once you get the first few words out, you'll think less about yourself and more about your subject.

Remember that the audience is not your enemy. It shares your fears. Seldom, if ever, does an audience laugh at a speaker, especially an inexperienced one. Your classmates all feel the same way you do, and they probably admire you for getting through the experience.

SPOTLIGHT ON SPEAKING

Controlling Stage Fright

Following these guidelines will help you control your stage fright:

1. Select a topic that the audience will find interesting.
2. Research your speech thoroughly.
3. Prepare the material in an organized and interesting fashion.
4. Practice—and then practice some more.
5. Take deep breaths before beginning; pace and practice if you can.
6. Get organized at the podium, and take a deep breath before beginning.
7. Incorporate movement into your speech.
8. Don't expect a perfect performance—set realistic goals for yourself.
9. View the audience as your friends.

Pausing, saying the wrong word, dropping notes, or making other mistakes will seem worse to you than to your audience. Your classmates are pulling for you to be successful. If you succeed, they know they can, too.

Finally, try to burn up some of your nervous energy before you start speaking. Take deep breaths to relax. Clench your fists and relax them several times while you are waiting to speak. If you are backstage or out of the audience's view, pace and practice your opening lines. Try to incorporate physical activity into the speech itself. Don't be afraid to use gestures or to move about if it is natural to do so. Use visual aids, or write on the board. Often, one of the first major speech assignments is a demonstration speech, which requires the speaker to actually show how to do something. This assignment is usually given first because it provides a speaker with a natural outlet for nervousness.

Perhaps the most important points to remember are that fear is natural and that you can use it to your advantage. While we have had many students who, like the adults in the survey, feared giving a speech more than they feared dying, we have not lost a student yet!

VOICES OF

FREEDOM

The Birth of America

When this country fought for its independence, a new group of speakers was needed to justify and explain the beliefs of Americans. While we had many, none are better known for their speeches than two Americans, Patrick Henry and George Washington, and one Englishman, Edmund Burke.

Best known for his "Liberty or Death" speech, Patrick Henry spoke out more than once for America's liberty. His speeches stirred the people of Virginia from a decade before the Revolution until a decade after it.

While better known as a general and a statesman, George Washington was also one of the country's most important speakers. His speeches helped guide the new nation and set many of the traditions for American presidents.

While these two leaders were thinking about a war of independence against England, England's finest orator, Edmund Burke, was trying his best to heal the wounds between the two countries. Although his eloquence didn't prevent the war, it was evidence that the American quest for liberty had its supporters, even in England.

WORDS TO REMEMBER

Patrick Henry

Caesar had his Brutus; Charles the First his Cromwell; and George the Third ["Treason!" cried the Speaker of the House of Burgesses]—*may profit by their example*. If *this* be treason, make the most of it.

Speech on the Stamp Act, 1765

I am not a Virginian, but an American.

Speech in the First Continental Congress, 1774

George Washington

The time is now near at hand which must probably determine whether Americans are to be freemen or slaves. . . . The fate of unborn millions will now depend, under God, on the courage and conduct of this army. . . . We have, therefore, to resolve to conquer or die.

Address to the Continental Army before the Battle of Long Island, 1776

If men are to be precluded from offering their sentiments on a matter which may involve the most serious and alarming consequences that can invite the consideration of mankind, reason is of no use to us; the freedom of speech may be taken away, and dumb and silent we may be led, like sheep to the slaughter.

Address to officers of the Army, 1783

The preservation of the sacred fire of liberty, and the destiny of the republican model of government, are justly considered as deeply, perhaps as finally staked, on the experiment entrusted to the hands of the American people.

First Inaugural Address, 1789

Edmund Burke

Reflect how you are to govern a people who think they ought to be free, and think they are not.

First Speech on Conciliation with America, 1774

Young man, there is America—which at this day serves for little more than to amuse you with stories of savage men and uncouth manners; yet shall, before you taste of death, show itself equal to the whole of that commerce which now attracts the envy of the world. . . .

It is not, what a lawyer tells me I *may* do; but what humanity, reason, and justice tell me I ought to do.

Second Speech on Conciliation with America, 1775

15

Opportunities for making speeches surround you at school, on the job, and in your democratic society. Since it is impossible to avoid making a speech at some point in your life, approach the study of public speaking with a positive outlook. The benefits of public speaking are as numerous as are the opportunities to speak. You will develop communication skills and self-confidence to help with your school work and in your career. You will also have numerous opportunities to listen to speeches. By studying public speaking, you will become a better listener.

While there are risks as well as benefits involved in giving speeches, the risks are relatively few. Being apprehensive about speaking is natural, and through practice you can learn to control your fear and use it to your advantage.

◆ Check Your Understanding

1. Explain why public speaking is important at school, on the job, and in a democracy.

2. List three skills you can learn or develop from public speaking practice that will help in other courses.

3. List three opportunities to give a speech that you can take advantage of in the near future.

4. List the benefits derived from public speaking.

5. Explain communication apprehension and its causes.

6. Explain two things you can do to control or reduce stage fright.

◆ Apply Your Understanding

1. Read your local newspaper and make a list of all the references to speeches reported. Identify the speaker, his or her position or occupation, the topic, and the audience. What conclusions can you reach about the importance of public speaking in your community, the nation, and the world?

2. Examine the help wanted listings in the classified section of a major newspaper. How many positions require good communication skills? What types of positions require such skills? What communication-related skills are mentioned? Make a list of all communication terms. What can you conclude about the importance of communication skills in the workplace? How will the study of public speaking help you learn the skills listed in the ads?

3. Conduct a survey of the members of your class to learn:
   a. How many class members have given a speech?
   b. What was the occasion? Make a list of all responses.
   c. How many class members have heard a speech in the last month? The last year? Make a list of the situations involved.

◆ Thinking Critically about Public Speaking

1. In a history text, find an example of a speaker or a speech considered important in history. Write a brief explanation of the situation, the speaker, and why the speech was important.

2. Listen to and watch a speech. Did the speaker appear confident? What did the speaker do with his or her voice, posture, and other nonverbal delivery to suggest confidence or a lack of it?

◆ Speak Out!

1. The class will divide into pairs. Each student should spend approximately ten minutes interviewing the other. Find out about the person's interests, place of birth, family, and hobbies. Also find out what subjects the person would like to learn more about by listening to speeches in class. Take notes. Have each student introduce his or her partner to the class.

2. The class will divide into groups of five or six. Think of a situation in which you were frightened. Share your story with the group, describing your physical reactions. Compare the experiences shared in your group. What did each individual do to reduce fear? What effect did it have?

◆ Speech Challenge

The First Amendment guarantees freedom of speech. Often, however, controversy arises regarding what limitations should be placed on freedom of speech. Freedom of speech has also been broadened to mean *freedom of expression,* which would include wearing buttons or special clothing, silent demonstrations, and other forms of *symbolic speech.* Compile a list of Supreme Court cases involving freedom of speech. Review the cases and choose one as a speech topic. In your speech, summarize both sides of the case: the side supporting freedom of expression and the side supporting limits to freedom of expression. At the end of your speech, reveal the Court's decision and offer your own view of the decision.

CHAPTER ·2·

Key Terms

Channel (medium)

Communication

Communication model

Context

Feedback

Feedback loops

Interference

Interpersonal
communication

Intrapersonal
communication

Mass communication

Message

Nonverbal communication

Process

Public speaking

Receiver

Sender

Small group communication

Verbal communication

Chapter Objectives

After studying this chapter, you should be able to:

1. Define *communication*.

2. Explain what a communication model is.

3. List and explain the components of the communication
   process.

4. Explain the five levels of communication and tell how
   they resemble and how they differ from one another.

5. Define *public speaking*.

6. List and explain the components of the public speaking
   process.

7. Explain feedback loops in the public speaking process.

The Process of Public Speaking

Communication Basics

You hear the term *communication* frequently. Because it's a common term, people assume that everyone knows what it means. But that's not necessarily true. For many, communication is simply talking or exchanging some type of message. While message exchange is a part of communication, there's more to it than that. In simple terms, **communication** is the process of creating understanding through the exchange of messages. In other words, simply talking is not communicating unless the person with whom you are talking understands or shares your message's meaning or intent.

As you will learn in studying the communication process, there are many reasons why understanding and sharing are difficult to achieve. Communication is seldom perfect. Just as it's important to know how a 35 mm camera operates before you can use it, it is equally important to understand how communication works before you can become a better communicator.

Communication Is a Process

When someone says communication is a **process,** he or she means it's an ongoing activity. It has no clear beginning or ending. When you open your mouth to begin a speech, that isn't the speech's beginning point. All the thought, preparation, and practice that precede the actual performance are part of the communication process. When you conclude your speech, communication doesn't end. The audience talks about the speech, and you reflect on what happened. A process is ongoing, and communication is a process.

The communication process also involves sending and receiving messages simultaneously. In other words, a speaker may send a message during a speech, but at the same time he or she is receiving information from the audience in the form of facial expressions, nods, or applause. The audience's reactions should affect how the speaker delivers the rest of the speech. In so doing, the speaker sends another message to the audience, telling them that their reactions are being taken into account. For instance, if you want to explain to your parents how the dining room window was broken, you will tell your story much differently than if you explain the same thing to your best friends. If your parents frown, raise their eyebrows, or give other signs of disbelief, you'll probably alter what you're saying or the way you tell the story. You and your audience are interacting.

The give and take between speaker and audience suggests another important characteristic of a process: All the parts are interrelated. One part affects the others and is affected by the others. For instance, in a public-speaking situation, the people who make up the audience affect the speaker's choice and treatment of the topic. The speaker's words then have an impact on the audience. The way in which the audience reacts to the message triggers a response in the speaker, who may or may not adjust the message, depending upon the audience's responses.

If this all sounds complex, that's because it is. Communication isn't a simple process, but by breaking it down into parts, you'll be able to understand how those parts relate to each other and how the process as a whole functions.

The Elements of Communication

Every subject has its own vocabulary. Mechanics talk about alternators and universals. Computer people refer to hardware and DOS. Communication is no different. In order to understand the process, you need to know several terms. You'll understand them best by examining how they fit into the communication process.

One of the best ways to examine the process is to visualize it. You may find it somewhat difficult to picture a process. The use of a **communication model,** or a diagram, explaining how the parts of the communication process work and relate to one another, may make it easier to understand what takes place when someone communicates.

A model of the communication process begins with its most basic parts—a sender and a receiver. The **sender** is the person who has a message to communicate. The **receiver** is the person or persons to whom the message is addressed, whether the speaker is talking to one person or to a large audience. The **message** is the idea the sender wants the receiver to understand. So, a model of the foundation of the communication process looks like Figure 2.1.

Figure 2.1
The Foundation of
the Communication
Process

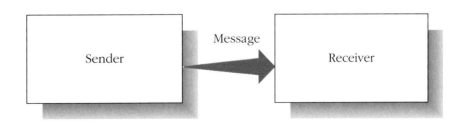

This diagram has problems, however. It suggests that communication starts and stops at specific points. The model also overlooks the way messages are sent and received simultaneously. In order to demonstrate that communication is a process, the model must have another component—feedback. **Feedback** occurs when a receiver responds either verbally or nonverbally to a message. **Verbal communication** is any communication, spoken or written, that uses words. **Nonverbal communication,** by contrast, is communication that doesn't use words. Instead, people communicate through facial expressions, gestures, vocal inflection, head movement, laughter, or silence. If your school's basketball team makes a basket, you may yell out, "All right!" That is verbal communication. If you clap, laugh, or thrust your fist into the air, you are using nonverbal communication.

Feedback makes communication a circular process that has no beginning or end. To illustrate this process, the model must look like the one in Figure 2.2.

This model is more accurate than the first one, but some important parts are still missing. One of those is the context of the speech. **Context** means the physical, social, psychological, and time elements in which communication takes place.

Figure 2.2
Feedback in the
Communication
Process

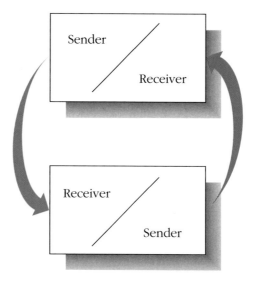

The place where a speech is given is the physical element of context. The social aspect includes the relationships between the people involved in the communication process, both the speaker and the members of the audience. The roles people assume or the acceptable behaviors for a particular situation also form part of the social aspect. The psychological dimension includes the attitudes and behaviors of those involved. Are the participants friendly or hostile? Is the occasion serious or humorous? Is the atmosphere formal or casual? Do the participants agree with one another or disagree? The time dimension includes the actual time the communication occurs. It also refers to the point in history or the stage in a relationship when communication occurs.

Add the element of context to the communication model and it looks like the one in Figure 2.3.

Generally, people communicate through the five senses: seeing, hearing, touching, tasting, or smelling. When included in the communication model, the **channel** (or method of communicating)

Figure 2.3
Context in the
Communication
Process

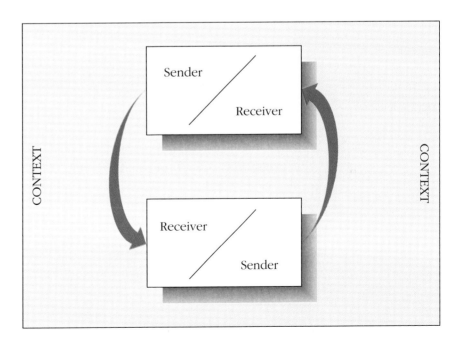

Figure 2.4
Channel in the
Communication
Process

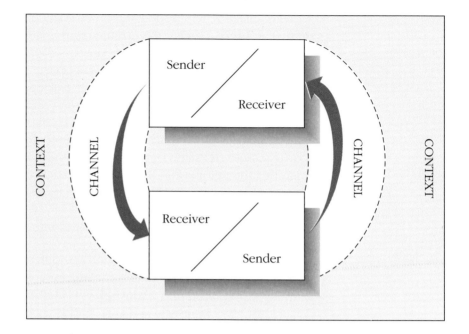

encloses the message, and both channel and message are enclosed within the context. This structure demonstrates the interrelationship between the parts. Method is affected by context, and both method and context affect the structure of the message and how it is treated (see Figure 2.4).

The model now looks much more complete, but one important part is still missing: interference. Communication is not perfect. Receivers don't always understand messages the way senders intend. **Interference** is anything that prevents effective communication. It can occur at any point in the process. Either the sender or the receiver (or both) can be a cause. If the sender doesn't prepare a clear message or doesn't speak clearly, there is interference. If a receiver doesn't pay attention, communication is disrupted.

Interference can also arise because of some element in the speech's context. Perhaps a poor sound system prevents audience members from hearing. The time of day can affect audience members' attention spans. The relationship between the sender and the receiver or the receiver's attitude about the message can also interfere with communication.

Figure 2.5
A Complete Model of
the Communication
Process

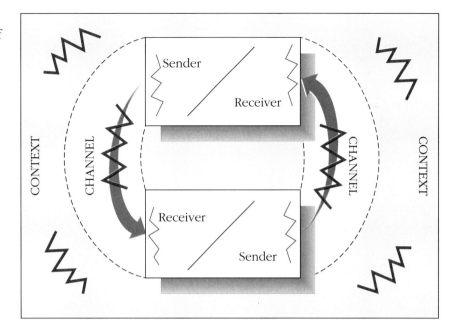

Distortions can also occur within the channel. Speakers who use visual aids rely on the audience's ability to see to communicate the message. If the aids are too small, the audience won't be able to see them and the message won't be communicated effectively. Everyone involved in the communication process must anticipate interference. By doing so, senders and receivers can compensate for many of the causes.

When the unavoidable element of interference is added to the model, its completed design looks like Figure 2.5.

The Public Speaking Process

The definitions and models you have seen apply to all types of communication, not just public speaking. To understand how the basics of communication apply specifically to public speaking, you need to back up and consider the situations in which communication takes place. People who study these situations often refer to *levels,* since each of the five levels is progressively more complex.

The Five Levels of Communication

The simplest form of communication takes place within yourself. This level is known as **intrapersonal communication.** Although you may actually talk to yourself out loud on occasion, most of your intrapersonal communication is in the form of thinking. This level is basic to all the others and is especially important in public speaking. Much of the preparation for a speech involves intrapersonal communication—that is, the time you spend thinking about what you want to say and how to say it. As you present your speech, the judgments about nonverbal feedback from the audience also require communication within yourself. Later in this chapter, you'll study three feedback loops. The first, *prespeech,* is actually intrapersonal communication.

The second level of communication is **interpersonal communication,** or communication between people. This level involves two or three people. It can be very informal, such as when you talk to a friend during lunch period, or very formal, such as when you discuss a job opening with a personnel manager. Level two is more complex than level one because level two involves senders *and* receivers, so the possibilities for interference increase.

The third level is **small group communication,** which involves interaction among four to twelve individuals. Small group communication is often used for problem-solving sessions or for meetings. When you and your friends get together to talk about an assignment in one of your classes or the new classmate who just moved to town, you are involved in small group communication.

The fourth level is the one this book examines—public speaking. **Public speaking** can be defined as one person communicating with many. It involves a continuous presentation by one individual in a face-to-face situation with an audience. Public speaking differs from small group communication because the size of the audience is too large to allow one person to interact with the others. Unlike the second and third levels, where there is constant give and take between senders and receivers, in public speaking, most of the feedback from the audience is nonverbal. There also can be delayed feedback in the form of questions and answers at the speech's conclusion.

The final communication level is **mass communication.** Here, electronic and print technologies send messages to large numbers of people, often at the same time. Television, radio, newspapers, magazines, and compact discs are all forms of mass communication. If a speech is delivered via television and radio and is printed in news-

Interpersonal communication involves only two or three people.

papers, communication takes place on two levels. For the people in the audience hearing the speech where it is given, it's public speaking. For those watching the speech on television or hearing it on the radio, the event falls under the heading of mass communication.

A Public Speaking Model

Now that you understand where and how public speaking fits into the larger framework of communication, you'll find it much easier to understand the public speaking process. A model of this process would not look much different from the model of the communication process in general. The primary difference is that the receiver is now the audience (see Figure 2.6 on page 28).

The change from receiver to audience marks a clear distinction between the roles of speaker and audience. While both are sending and receiving messages, the continuous presentation from the speaker alters the nature of the model.

Figure 2.6
A Model of the Public
Speaking Process

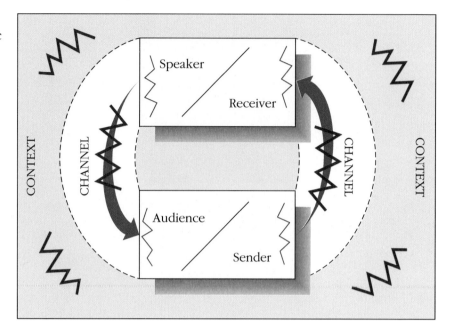

One other aspect of public speaking requires more explanation, and that's the feedback process. In essence, the feedback process involves three stages, all called **feedback loops:** prespeech, presentation, and postspeech. All three reinforce the idea that communication has no distinct beginning or ending—the process is continuous (see Figure 2.7).

The prespeech loop incorporates intrapersonal communication and relies heavily on the speaker's perceptions of the people he or she will be speaking to. The second loop—the presentation of the speech itself—involves both intrapersonal and public speaking levels. Speaker and audience react, sending feedback to one another. The postspeech loop can involve interpersonal or small group feedback, as well as intrapersonal communication. Members of the audience will think about the speech. They will talk to one or two friends or discuss it in small groups. To analyze the success or failure of the speech, the speaker considers all four elements of the classical model (message, channel, interference, and feedback). And because of the circular nature of the communication process, postspeech feedback analysis often becomes the starting point for a future speech.

Figure 2.7
Feedback Loops

Prespeech
The speaker anticipates the audience's response and creates a speech that will be clear and effective.

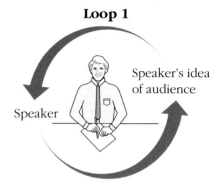

Loop 1

Speaker's idea of audience

Speaker

Presentation
The speaker presents the speech. As the audience responds, the speaker alters the speech to improve effectiveness.

Loop 2

Audience

Speaker

Postspeech
The speaker judges the effectiveness of the speech by observing the audience's behavior and listening to comments. The speaker uses the observations to help construct future speeches.

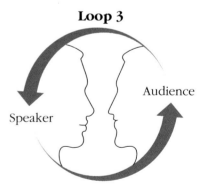

Loop 3

Audience

Speaker

Chapter 2 Summary

Communication is a complex, ongoing process that involves sending and receiving messages simultaneously. The basic components of communication—sender, receiver, message, channel, feedback, and interference—are involved in the communication process, whether you're communicating with yourself or with millions of others through the mass media.

Communication models enable people to visualize the process of communicating so they can better understand what they must do to be more effective communicators. Feedback loops show how the audience affects the preparation, presentation, and evaluation of a speech.

◆ Check Your Understanding

1. Using your own words and the explanations from this chapter as guidelines, define *communication*.

2. Explain what a communication model is, and identify and define the parts of the communication models presented in this chapter.

3. List and explain the five levels of communication. Describe how they are alike and how they differ. Explain how one level may incorporate another.

4. Define *public speaking*.

5. Explain how the public speaking process is similar to the communication process in general.

6. List and explain the three types of feedback loops that take place in the public speaking process.

◆ Apply Your Understanding

1. Prepare a list of nonverbal messages that audience members can send to a speaker. Compile a list based on ideas from the entire class. As a class, discuss how a speaker might interpret the messages: what a speaker's response to each message might

be, how messages might be misinterpreted, and what a speaker can do to verify his or her interpretations of messages audience members send.

2. Examine the communication model on page 28, and prepare a list of potential causes of interference at each step of the model. Suggest ways the speaker can adjust the speech to reduce each cause.

3. List intrapersonal communication questions a speaker should ask during the three feedback loops in the public speaking process.

◆ *Thinking Critically about Public Speaking*

Study one of the speeches in the text or Appendix B. What were the physical, social, psychological, and time contexts in which the speech was given? What did the speaker do to adapt to each?

◆ *Speak Out!*

Give a short presentation (one to two minutes) describing a humorous incident that resulted from some form of communication interference—for example, a misunderstanding between you and a friend, a misinterpretation of a word, or mishearing something.

◆ *Speech Challenge*

Divide into groups of five or six students. Prepare your own model of the public speaking process. Draw the model on the board or distribute copies to other class members. Explain the model to the class.

CHAPTER

3

Key Terms

Audience

Method

Purpose

Situation

Chapter Objectives

After studying this chapter, you should be able to:

1. Identify the four basic variables of speech planning and analysis.

2. Use situation, purpose, audience, and method to analyze speeches.

3. Use the terms *situation, purpose, audience,* and *method* to further understand speech preparation and delivery.

The Basics of
Public Speaking

SPAM Model of Public Speaking

The model of communication that we described in Chapter 2 can be applied to any acts. However, we can refine and simplify the model to make it more strictly applicable to public speaking. When we do this, we come up with a model of public speaking that has four variables: **s**ituation, **p**urpose, **a**udience, and **m**ethod—SPAM, for short.

Situation

In thinking about the first variable, remember that all communication (including public speaking) happens in a certain place at a certain time—the **situation.** Consider Abraham Lincoln's Gettysburg Address. When we read them now, Lincoln's words remind us that the speech was given at a specific point in time:

> Four score and seven years ago . . .

> Now we are engaged in a great civil war . . .

Lincoln's words also remind us of where the address was given:

> We are met on a great battlefield of that war . . .

But Lincoln understood much more about his situation than its physical time and place. First, he knew that the entire history of the United States was the background for his speech. He summarized this history when he said that the country was "conceived in liberty and dedicated to the proposition that all men are created equal." Second, he realized that the Battle of Gettysburg was a severe test of the Union. Finally, he knew that he had been severely criticized for the war and for his role as commander-in-chief. In sum, Lincoln recognized that the Civil War would have a profound impact on the country's future. All this knowledge that Lincoln brought to his speech was part of the situation. Thus, as you can see, Lincoln knew far more about his speaking situation than where and what time. In much the same way, you must understand more about the situation for a speech you give than where and what time you must give it.

As an example of the importance of situation, consider all the different factors that might affect a coach's pep talk to a basketball team at half-time:

- Is the team ahead or behind at the end of the half?
- Is anyone on the team in foul trouble?

SAMPLE SPEECH

Address Delivered at the Dedication of the Cemetery at Gettysburg, 19 November 1863
Abraham Lincoln

Four score and seven years ago our fathers brought forth on this continent, a new nation, conceived in Liberty, and dedicated to the proposition that all men are created equal.

Now we are engaged in a great civil war, testing whether that nation, or any nation so conceived and so dedicated, can long endure. We are met on a great battle-field of that war. We have come to dedicate a portion of that field, as a final resting place for those who here gave their lives that that nation might live. It is altogether fitting and proper that we should do this.

But, in a larger sense, we can not dedicate—we can not consecrate—we can not hallow—this ground. The brave men, living and dead, who struggled here, have consecrated it, far above our poor power to add or detract. The world will little note, nor long remember what we say here, but it can never forget what they did here. It is for us the living, rather, to be dedicated here to the unfinished work which they who fought here have thus far so nobly advanced. It is rather for us to be here dedicated to the great task remaining before us—that from these honored dead we take increased devotion to that cause for which they gave the last full measure of devotion—that we here highly resolve that these dead shall not have died in vain—that this nation, under God, shall have a new birth of freedom—and that government of the people, by the people, for the people, shall not perish from the earth.

- Is one player on the opposing team being particularly successful?
- Has the coach's team played well or poorly?
- Is the coach's game plan working?
- How did the coach's team do against the same team the last time the two teams played?
- Is the coach's team on a winning streak or a losing streak?
- What is at stake in the game?

Of course, there are many more factors that might affect this situation, but even this partial list shows that situation involves more than time and place.

What happens if you as a public speaker do not understand the situation? It is likely that you will miss many opportunities. For instance, if the coach of our imaginary team does not understand the situation completely, his or her pep talk may not have the information, the spirit, or the motivation the team needs.

Purpose

The second variable in the SPAM model is **purpose,** which refers to the goal a speaker hopes to achieve with his or her speech. In other words, public speaking is purposeful because a speaker expects his or her speech to have results. The coach wants the team to play better. A politician wants votes. A teacher wants learning. Each of these speakers would have a specific purpose for speaking.

Determining the purpose of a speech arises from an understanding of the situation. Lincoln's understanding of the situation at Gettysburg gave him a clearer purpose. The other people who spoke that day at Gettysburg believed they had only one purpose in speaking: to dedicate a portion of the battlefield as a cemetery. Lincoln shared that purpose, but he also had a grander purpose: to rededicate the Union to the belief that "a government of the people, by the people, and for the people, shall not perish from the earth."

Perhaps you have listened to a speaker who didn't seem to have a purpose. You probably found yourself wondering, "What is she talking about?" or "What's the point?" Chances are the speaker didn't prepare the speech with a firm understanding of purpose.

Our basketball coach has several purposes in mind when talking to the team. The coach's general purpose is to encourage the team to play better, to win. More specifically, however, the coach may want to motivate the team to pass better, to play tighter defense, and so on. You can see how essential it is for the coach to understand the purpose of the pep talk so that he or she can decide what to say and how to say it.

Audience

Audience is the easiest of the four SPAM variables to understand. Unfortunately, it is also the variable that many beginning speakers overlook because they are worried about what to say, how to say it, how to fill the time requirements, and so on. What beginning speakers often don't understand is that all these concerns—and many more—depend on the audience.

The **audience** is the people to whom a speech is directed. Thus, the audience is part of the situation. And the purpose of the speaker is to affect the audience in a planned way. It is the audience's response to a speech that ultimately determines whether that speech

The audience is the group of people to whom a speech is directed. As a speaker, you must adapt your speech to fit the needs of your audience.

succeeds or fails. As you can see, situation, purpose, and audience are interrelated.

Good speakers analyze their audiences and adapt their speeches to them. For example, if you stayed in, say, an American history teacher's room all day, you would see how that teacher's presentation changes from one period to the next. Even though the situations each period are roughly the same (except for time of day), and the teacher's purpose is the same for each class of students, the audience is different in each class. Much of the teacher's presentation will be the same, but some of his or her comments, examples, techniques, and strategies will differ because the audiences differ.

In the Gettysburg Address, Lincoln seemed to have several audiences in mind. One audience was the people attending the ceremony, of course, but Lincoln knew that most of them had come to hear another speaker. Another audience was the nation as a whole; people would learn of the speech through newspaper articles. Finally, when we read the speech after more than 130 years, we get the feeling that he might have been speaking to yet another audience—namely, future Americans. We feel that perhaps he was justifying all that had happened and was going to happen in the Civil War.

For another example, consider the coach giving the half-time pep talk. Who is his or her audience? Clearly, the audience is the players. Now consider the differences between a pep talk given to a high-school team and one given to a professional team. Would the coach use the same emotion? The same vocabulary? The same strategies? There might be similarities, but a coach speaking to a group of high-school athletes would likely give a different speech than he or she would give to a group of professional athletes.

Method

Once a speaker knows the situation (when and where) and has determined his or her particular purpose (why) with an audience (who), only one variable remains to be considered: what **methods** (what) will best accomplish the purpose. A speaker must select the methods that he or she thinks will work best.

In considering method, a speaker knows that there are an almost infinite number of choices to be made about a speech: what kind of language to use; how to organize the speech; what mood to convey; how to begin and end; and so on. There are different methods that

Figure 3.1
The Many Methods
Available to Speakers

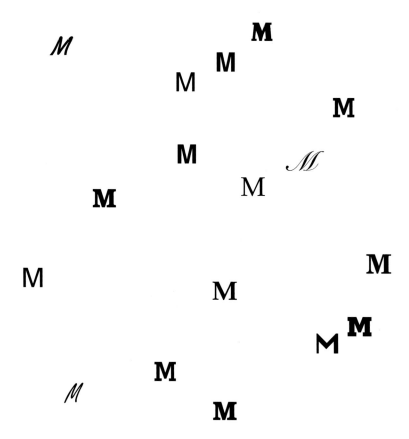

can be used for each of these variables. In choosing what kind of language to use, for example, a speaker may decide that his or her audience would prefer formal language rather than informal, colloquial language. We can represent these different methods with the letter *M* (see Figure 3.1). Each *M* is different because each represents a different method. To select appropriate methods, a speaker must understand the situation, develop a purpose, and read the audience. These three variables become anchors in the search for appropriate methods.

Figure 3.2 shows that a speaker chooses certain methods and excludes others based on his or her understanding of situation, audience, and purposes, which leads to the conclusion that some methods will likely work, but others will not. Similarly, a coach selects methods (strategies, tools, ideas, language, emotions, examples) to use in a pep talk based on situation, purpose, and audience. And

Figure 3.2
Using Situation,
Purpose, and
Audience to Choose
Appropriate Methods

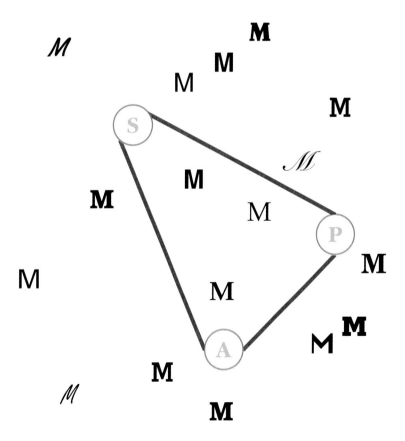

Lincoln selected his methods in the Gettysburg Address based on his understanding of situation, audience, and purpose. To understand Lincoln's choice of methods, consider these questions. Why did Lincoln start by reminding his audience of the nation's founding? Why did he use imagery of birth (*conceived, dedicated*) at the commemoration of a cemetery? Why did he state that it was beyond his "poor power" to bring honor to this cemetery? Why did he end the speech commemorating a cemetery with a call for the nation's recommitment to liberty? The methods Lincoln used in the Gettysburg Address were tied directly to the situation as he understood it, the audience he spoke to, and the purpose he had in mind.

Which Comes First?

Although the SPAM model starts with consideration of situation, that may not be the case when you prepare a speech. You may start to understand the speaking situation by looking first at the audience and then at purpose and situation. If you are assigned a specific speech that is supposed to accomplish a specific purpose, you would start with purpose and then consider situation and audience.

Even though you may consider situation or purpose first, you should remember that audience is always the most important of the four variables. It is the audience, after all, who will determine if your speech succeeds or fails. A speaker's purpose is always based on a consideration of the audience, and a speaker's situation includes the audience. In other words, a speaker can never forget that his or her speech is intended for an audience.

SPAM and You

Where do you—as a public speaker—fit into the SPAM model? One of the advantages of this model is that it can give you a new way to look at yourself as a public speaker. After all, aren't you and your speech going to become part of the situation? Don't you ultimately decide what you want the speech's purpose to be based on what you want to accomplish (or what you think you can accomplish)? Doesn't your relationship with the audience become clearer when you think about situation and purpose? When you choose the methods you want to use in your speech, you are making the choices based on all these variables.

If you have a hard time remembering the SPAM model, try to put it in the context of a simple act of communication, such as asking your parents for a favor.

Situation: You need to borrow the car. Your own car is in the shop because you had an accident. You are seventeen years old. Your grades are coming out in two weeks.

Purpose: To persuade your parents to let you have the car for an evening.

Audience: Your parents.

Method: What should you do? Promise to be responsible? Promise that your grades are good? Promise to pay if there is an accident? Promise to be home at a certain time? Throw a tantrum? Cry?

SPAM and Speech Analysis

You can also use the SPAM model to analyze another speaker's speech. Such analysis is really very simple. What follows is a quick analysis of a famous speech by Patrick Henry, "Speech before the Virginia House of Burgesses," given on 23 March 1775.

Situation

When you want to understand or analyze a particular speech, you must place it in a particular situation. For example, to realize the full impact of the famous quotation from Patrick Henry's speech ("Give me liberty, or give me death"), you need to know that the speech was given as the colonies prepared to make war to gain their independence from England. The House of Burgesses was contemplating going to war against Britain, the world's greatest power in 1775. Knowing this situation will help you understand the significance of the quotation.

Purpose

You must also consider Henry's purpose, which may not be immediately evident. Why did Henry give the speech? What did he hope to accomplish? In this case, Henry was trying to convince his listeners that dying in the fight for liberty would be better than living under Britain's oppression. Knowing Henry's purpose helps you understand the emotion throughout the speech—the emotion that underlies, "Give me liberty, or give me death!"

| SPEAKING ABOUT SPEAKING | Comparing Communication Models |

This book offers two ways of viewing communication: the SPAM model, which is based on classical rhetoric, and the contemporary communication model outlined in Chapter 2. The two models were developed for different reasons and at different times. The classical (SPAM) model came out of a need to describe public speaking. The contemporary model applied communication theory that was developed at the same time as computers and other forms of electronic communication. Both models share basic elements. In some ways, they describe the same process using different emphases and a different vocabulary.

SPAM Model

Situation: The "when and where" a speech is given. Specifically, situation is time and place. Complete understanding of situation, however, means looking into what was happening before, during, and after the speech—the "history" leading up to a speech and the results that followed it. Viewed generally, the situation contains the problem the speaker is addressing.

Purpose: The speaker's intent; what he or she wants to accomplish with the audience. The answer to the question, "Why is the speech being given?"

Audience: The audience is the people intended to hear the speech and respond to it. Sometimes, there may be an unintended audience, as is the case when a speech is heard by someone not included in the speaker's plans.

Contemporary Communication Model

Context: The physical, social, psychological, and time elements in which communication takes place.

Message: In the contemporary communication model, purpose is not identified. Purpose is implied in the arrow in Figure 2.1 labeled *message*. The message is the idea, feeling, or information that exists in the sender (the speaker). The sender wants the receiver to understand. This desire within the sender is the purpose.

Receiver: The receiver in the communication model (see Figure 2.1) is the same as the audience. The model, which is based on one-to-one communication, simplifies the process of public speaking by displaying the audience

Methods: The methods a speaker uses are any of the choices he or she makes to adapt the message to the audience. Methods include word choice, gestures, organizational patterns, proof, quotations—any of the subjects covered in this book.

as a single person. A public speaker realizes that an audience is made up of individuals who will react differently to a message, but public speaking requires a message that can be understood by many individuals.

Channel: The channel is the means for communicating a message. Narrowly, a channel would be the specific means: written word, spoken word, pictures, or gestures. Generally, the channel is any of the means: word choice, gestures, organizational patterns, proof, quotations, or any of the methods covered in this book.

Interference: When a message is sent through an electrical system or through the air on radio waves, the message may be disrupted by interference. In the model of communication developed from the study of information exchanged electronically, *interference* became the term for anything that causes a message to break down. The rhetorical model has no exact counterpart. While classical speech teachers knew that speakers frequently were misunderstood or unsuccessful, the notion of *interference* was not used. Instead, the classical rhetorician would have looked at what methods were used and why they weren't successful.

Feedback: The audience's response to a message was certainly important to classical rhetoric, but it was not called *feedback.* Still, in either model of communication, the audience's reaction is the only way of knowing if a speech has been a success.

Patrick Henry addressing the Virginia House of Burgesses on 23 March 1775.

Audience

Remember, a speaker's purpose is determined by a consideration of the audience. When Henry prepared his speech, he knew he would be speaking to the members of the House of Burgesses, colonial Virginia's legislature. He knew that the members were all educated, relatively wealthy men who understood the issues. He knew also that his audience would be risking a great deal in a war with England. Thus, after considering his audience, Henry clearly saw that he had a difficult task and that he would have to use reason *and* emotion.

Method

Henry had to decide what he could do to convince the House of Burgesses (the audience) to prepare for war with England (the purpose) as the colonies' discontent with English rule grew (the situation). If you consider these same variables in analyzing Henry's speech, you will be able to determine whether the methods he chose were successful.

Henry's speech was much longer than the famous line, of course, but consider why he said, "Give me liberty, or give me death!" He was in the midst of a truly desperate crisis. The greatest power in the world was threatening the colonists' freedom, so the colonists, no more than a handful of brave people, were considering war. The members of the House of Burgesses knew that war might cost them their positions and wealth. In turn, Henry knew that convincing the members to go to war would require more than reasoning or listing the abuses of the king of England. He saw that he had to mention the ultimate risk—death. His defiant promise of "liberty or death" showed the members that the risks were not as great as the rewards.

VOICES OF

THE CLASSICS

Greek and Roman Speakers

The two great classical cultures—Greece and Rome—provided the origins of the study of speech. Both the Athenian democracy and the Roman Republic fostered the freedom of expression needed for the development of the art of oratory. Three classical orators whose names are still familiar today are Pericles, Demosthenes, and Cicero.

Pericles was a Greek statesman in about 400 B.C. Due in large measure to his abilities in public speaking, he helped govern Athens for thirty years. Pericles' Athens has been called the "cradle of democracy," and it might also be called the "cradle of free speech." Political speech was common in the city, but few speakers could equal Pericles.

A hundred years later, Athens produced another celebrated speaker, Demosthenes. Called the greatest of the Greek speakers, Demosthenes supposedly copied by hand great speeches to learn the speakers' styles and strategies. In addition, the legend is that he overcame a speech difficulty by placing pebbles in his mouth and speaking against the roar of the ocean.

Cicero was a Roman who lived about 100 B.C. According to historians, he was the greatest orator Rome ever produced. His speeches were powerful enough to make many friends and many enemies. In addition to speaking, he wrote about the theory of speech, and many of his ideas are still commonly referred to.

WORDS TO REMEMBER

Pericles

Our constitution is named a democracy, because it is in the hands not of the few but of the many.

But the bravest are surely those who have the clearest vision of what is before them, glory and danger alike, and yet notwithstanding go out to meet it.

Fix your eyes on the greatness of Athens as you have it before you day by day, fall in love with her, and when you feel her great, remember that this greatness was won by men with courage, with knowledge of their duty, and with a sense of honor in action.

Funeral Oration, 430 B.C.

Demosthenes

Every advantage in the past is judged in the light of the final issue.

First Olynthiac, 341 B.C.

Nothing is easier than self-deceit. For what each man wishes, that he also believes to be true.

Third Olynthiac, 341 B.C.

Two things, men of Athens, are characteristic of a well-disposed citizen: . . . In authority, his constant aim would be the dignity and preeminence of the commonwealth; in all times and circumstances, his spirit should be loyal.

On the Crown, 338 B.C.

Cicero

If a man aspires to the highest place, it is no dishonor to halt at the second, or even at the third.
The freedom of poetic license.

Orator ad M. Brutum

Then what happiness will you enjoy, with what delight will you exult, in what pleasure will you revel, when in so numerous a body of friends you neither hear nor see one good man!

First speech against Catiline, 63 B.C.

47

There are four basics of speech preparation and analysis: situation, purpose, audience, and method (abbreviated SPAM). The *situation* involves the time, place, and other background information that relates to a speech. The *purpose* is the goal a speaker hopes to achieve. The *audience* is the people to whom a speech is directed. Once a speaker understands situation, purpose, and audience, he or she is ready to make decisions about what to say and how to say it. Those decisions are the *methods* used by the speaker. The methods are the tools or strategies a speaker uses to accomplish his or her purpose. A speaker can begin with an understanding of situation, purpose, or audience, but he or she must understand all three before making good choices about methods.

When you are analyzing a speech given by someone else, you can use SPAM to understand and evaluate the speech. Try to understand the speaker's analysis of situation, purpose, and audience. Evaluate the speaker's methods by combining what he or she knew with what you know. This strategy will help you understand why speakers make the choices they do.

◆ *Check Your Understanding*

1. List and define the four basic variables of speech planning and analysis.

2. Explain how you would use situation, purpose, audience, and method to analyze speeches. Use the SPAM model.

3. Explain why audience is the most important variable in the SPAM model.

◆ *Apply Your Understanding*

1. Here are some lines from Henry's speech. Can you use situation, purpose, and/or audience to determine why he used the methods in each of the quotations?

"This is no time for ceremony."

"The question before the House is one of awful moment to this country. For my own part, I consider it as nothing less than a question of freedom or slavery."

"[Keeping back my opinions would be] an act of disloyalty toward the Majesty of Heaven, which I revere above all earthly kings."

"We are apt . . . [to] listen to the song of that siren till she transforms us into beasts." (This is a reference to the *Odyssey*.)

2. Working in groups of four to five, develop a short skit in which one character has to persuade the group members to do something. Plan the skit using the SPAM model. Perform the skit for the class. Following the skit, help the class understand the methods your character used. Explain the skit in terms of the SPAM model.

◆ *Thinking Critically about Public Speaking*

1. Write a few paragraphs in which you defend or oppose the chapter's assertion that audience is the most important of the variables of public speaking.

2. Select an ad from a magazine. Analyze the ad (using SPAM) as if you were the head of an advertising agency who was trying to convince your client that this ad was a good one.

3. Read the opening to Thomas Paine's pamphlet *Common Sense,* which was produced about the same time as Henry's speech. The situation was the same, but the audience was very different. Describe the audience for Paine's pamphlet and use the difference in audience to explain the difference in method.

4. Select three magazines. Photocopy the table of contents for each. Using the titles of articles and features, determine whom the editors see as the magazines' audiences.

5. Select a speech from a source suggested by your teacher. Analyze the speech using the SPAM model. Explain whether you think the speech was successful or not.

◆ *Speak Out!*

Use question 2, 4, or 5 above as the basis for a two- to five-minute speech. You may use a visual aid.

◆ *Speech Challenge*

Most of us will never have the chance to give a speech like Patrick Henry's at such an important occasion in history. Assume that you are at an important moment in history: arguing before the Supreme Court, presenting a bill to Congress, addressing the nation on television, or speaking to the President and advisors. Select a topic that might be appropriate. Compose a speech that addresses the audience about an important issue. In your speech, outline the situation as you understand it. Suggest a course of action for your audience to take.

Key Terms

Critical listening

Empathy

Hearing

Listening

Precision

Retention

Selective listening

Chapter Objectives

After studying this chapter, you should be able to:

1. Explain the difference between listening and hearing.
2. Explain how listening is part of the public speaking process.
3. Explain why listening is an important skill to master.
4. Understand the levels of listening.
5. Explain at least three causes of poor listening.
6. Explain and put into practice at least three strategies to improve listening skills.

Learning
to Listen

The Listening Process

Along with speaking, reading, and writing, listening is one of the four basic communication skills. Despite the fact that you listen each day more than you speak, read, or write, listening is the least understood and the least taught skill.

Listening and Hearing Are Different

It's possible to *hear* someone speak without *listening* to what he or she is saying. **Hearing** is the sense through which sound is received. This physical process is the first step in the listening process. Actual **listening** involves concentrating on the sounds you hear, interpreting them, and reacting to them. Listening is a mental process that requires the receiver's active participation. Hearing, on the other hand, is a passive process. No one has to think to hear.

For example, many people like background "noise" from a radio, tape, stereo, or television when they work around the house. If someone asked, however, most people would be hard-pressed to identify the last song or statement they heard. This happens because they were hearing sounds rather than listening to them.

In a classroom, students frequently are aware that their teacher is giving a lecture. They hear sounds—words and phrases—but when called upon to answer a question, they often have to have the question repeated. If the students were actually *listening* to the teacher and not just *hearing,* they would be able to answer right away.

Listening and Public Speaking

During speeches, the audience can hear the speaker but may not listen to the message. As both an audience member and a speaker, you should be concerned about listening. By developing good listening habits, audience members not only get more out of a speech, they also give more back to the speaker through their feedback during and after the speech.

Chapter 2 described the communication process in general and the public speaking process in particular. Feedback is an important element in the process. Listening is one of the key factors in audience feedback. Good listeners provide far more clues to a speaker's success or failure than poor ones.

By concentrating on what is said and how it is said, audience members hear more than words. They also hear the emotions and the emphasis that lie behind the words and that add to their meaning. As a result, both nonverbal and verbal feedback are more complete. Good listeners also gain more from a speech. They not only understand more, but they're likely to remember the content longer.

The Importance of Listening

Public speaking isn't the only area where good listening skills improve the communication process. These skills are also important for success in interpersonal relationships and on the job. Many businesses realize this fact. Sperry was one company that believed so strongly in the importance of listening that it required all of its employees to receive listening training. The company also sponsored a series of advertisements promoting listening skills in national magazines. One of the ads pointed out that if each worker in the United States committed a ten dollar listening error, the total business loss would be one-billion dollars every year.

You can probably think of times in your own life when listening errors have been costly. Think about the points you lost on tests because you didn't listen carefully or take good notes. Think of the time you wasted doing something incorrectly because you didn't listen carefully.

Fortunately, listening is a skill you can improve through study and practice. Participating in public speaking activities as both a sender and a receiver is an excellent way to improve and apply your listening skills. This chapter explains how.

Levels of Listening

Listening is a skill, and just like other skills, it involves levels of difficulty. If you've taken swimming lessons, you probably advanced through several classes. The first level taught the basics—floating, breathing, and paddling. More advanced swimming classes taught specific strokes or perhaps even special skills required for racing or lifesaving.

Listening to music
is listening
for enjoyment.

No matter what level of class you were in, however, the course's purpose or goal affected the level of its difficulty. The same is true with listening. It is the particular purpose and situation that determine the level of concentration and skills required of you.

When you listen to speeches, the level of concentration you must exert is affected by the speech situation, purpose, audience, or method. For instance, if a speech is given outdoors, the people in the audience must concentrate more, simply to block out distracting noises around them. When you hear a speech to inform, you must listen for main ideas and for details more carefully than if you hear a speech to entertain.

If the audience is generally opposed to the speaker's ideas, you'll need to listen more carefully than usual to how the speaker supports those ideas. The speaker's method can also affect the way you approach your task as a listener. Some speeches require the audience to be more actively involved than others. When listening to a speech, consider the speaker's situation, purpose, audience, and method, and adjust accordingly. Keep the following levels of listening in mind as you work to improve your skills.

Listening to a lecture in class is listening for information.

Listening for Enjoyment

When you listen to an after-dinner speech or to an amusing story or joke, you're listening for enjoyment. You also use this listening level for music, television, a movie, or a play. The easiest of the five levels of listening, listening for enjoyment requires only momentary concentration, but not long-term memory. You don't need to take notes because you listen for general ideas, not for specifics. Listening for enjoyment does require paying attention, however. You should sit where you can see and hear and where noise and other distractions are at a minimum.

Listening for Information

When you listen to an informative speech, you're listening for information. This level requires more concentration than listening for enjoyment. You need to learn the speaker's main idea. Note words and phrases that preview important details supporting the main idea. A lecture in a history class is a good example of listening for information. Taking notes may improve your listening skill because those notes will help you remember most of the lecture for a test. Other examples that require listening for information are listening to instructions, directions, and descriptions of people, places, and things. Two-way communication is important at this level. Listeners can ask the speaker questions to clarify ideas.

Critical Listening

Critical listening involves listening for information and evaluating that information. This skill will help you determine how information you hear in a speech can affect you. Don't confuse the word *critical* with *criticism*. You aren't listening just to find fault or weaknesses. You also listen to determine strengths and to find ideas you support. Most importantly, you listen to understand how the speaker's information may affect you.

When you listen to a persuasive speech, you must listen critically. Do the facts lead to a particular conclusion? If a salesperson promises a great warranty on a new stereo, you listen critically to the explanation to see if the warranty is as good as the salesperson promises. If a speaker asks you to vote for a candidate, you evaluate the candidate's stands on the issues to decide if they are similar to yours.

Critical listening is an active process. As such, it requires feedback. It is important to take notes and to question the speaker about his or her ideas.

Precision Listening

Precision refers to exactness or to the ability to distinguish clearly. Listening with precision gives clues to a speaker's emotions and meanings. Listening for changes in how quickly a speaker talks or for changes in the volume of the speaker's voice can help determine what is most important to a speaker.

Musicians use this level of listening as they tune their instruments. So do mechanics who detect problems by listening for unusual sounds. You and your classmates have probably used precision listening when you've had problems with your parents to determine how serious or how angry they are. Precision listening enables people to hear more than just words. This listening level gives added clues to meaning.

Empathic Listening

Empathy is the ability to put yourself in another's place. It enables you to understand why a person feels, believes, or acts in a certain way. You do not necessarily come to share the person's views or feelings, but you do understand them. Critical listening is an important first step in becoming an empathic listener.

When you listen to speakers, it's often important to understand why they express certain ideas. Such understanding will help you evaluate the information you hear more completely. Empathy will also help you respect a speaker, even if you disagree with what he or she says. To achieve this level of listening, you must listen for information, you must evaluate it critically, and you must listen to emotions as well as to words. Empathic listening is the most difficult level to master. It requires not only great concentration but also good feedback skills.

Causes of Poor Listening

Listening isn't an easy skill to master. Even good listeners recall only 50 percent of what they hear. **Retention,** the ability to remember and recall information, decreases about 20 to 25 percent after a few days. So no matter how well you listen in class, you're always going to have to refresh your memory before a test!

Unfortunately, many people have poor listening habits, and most people have had little listening training. To improve your listening skills, it's important to understand what causes poor listening. Most listening problems can be classified as physical or mental. Physical problems are the easiest to identify, and, in most situations, the easiest to correct. Mental barriers require more work, but with practice you can reduce them.

Physical Barriers

The most obvious physical barrier is an actual hearing problem, such as partial hearing loss. Hearing aids and, in some cases, surgery can correct hearing loss. However, most people don't suffer from that type of barrier.

For most people, noise or other physical distractions—even things they see—create barriers to good listening. Some speakers hinder their listeners' ability to hear by speaking too softly or by not speaking clearly. Microphones help, but they can also be distracting if they don't project well or if they produce electronic feedback or distortion.

If it's difficult to see a speaker, or if there's something more interesting to look at, your listening ability is affected. A speaker's facial expressions or gestures can add emphasis to the speech, so if you can't see the speaker, your ability to hear will be affected.

The final physical cause of poor listening is the listener's physical condition. If you're tired, uncomfortable, or ill, you can't concentrate as deeply as when you're well. Which times during the school day can you listen to a teacher most easily? They probably don't fall at the beginning or the end of the school day. Your physical condition at those times makes it more difficult to concentrate—you're not quite awake, or you're waiting to go home.

Mental Barriers

Mental conditions can also reduce listening effectiveness. The most common problem is a wandering mind, or inattention. If you find it difficult to concentrate solely on what a speaker is saying, there's a good reason. The mind processes information much faster than a speaker can speak. The brain can process over 500 words per minute, while the average speaker talks at a rate of 125 to 250 words per minute. That means your mind can hear what's being said and can think about something else at the same time.

Attitudes can also interfere with good listening. If you have a negative attitude about the speaker or the topic, you'll find it difficult to listen attentively. Hostile or captive audiences often have more difficulty listening than do favorable or voluntary ones.

A third mental barrier is related to the level of the listener's knowledge. If a speaker speaks over the heads of an audience, the listeners may find it difficult to concentrate. Speakers who use unfamiliar words or who use incomplete explanations make it more difficult to listen. Speakers who talk down to audiences, failing to acknowledge what the audience already knows, also create mental blocks.

A final mental barrier is **selective listening.** When people listen selectively, they simply block out what they don't want to hear. For instance, many people have habits that are dangerous to their health, such as smoking. However, they often choose to block out what a speaker says about health risks. They may listen to a speech and think that the speaker's message applies to other people, not them. In other words, they hear what they want to hear and ignore what they don't want to hear.

Improving Listening Skills

Did you recognize any of the descriptions of poor listening habits? If you did, you're not alone. Everyone has weaknesses as a listener. To work on your listening skills, set reasonable goals. Work first at becoming an adequate listener. First, remove some of the most common barriers, such as simple distractions around you. Then, with additional concentration and practice, you can begin to develop the skills necessary for the higher listening levels. Remember, good listening is active listening.

You should also keep in mind that you need to use different listening strategies for different situations. Review the levels of listening, and determine which is required for each listening situation. The following suggestions should help you, regardless of your purpose.

Concentrate

The best way to improve listening skills is to work at them. Block out distractions, and think about what you're hearing. Mind over matter is the key to beginning your improvement.

Practice

Use every opportunity you can to concentrate on what you hear. Watch newscasts and other informational programs on TV that you might not normally take time to watch. Spend quiet time concentrating on the sounds around you. See if you can hear sounds you had not noticed before, such as the buzzing of lights.

Prepare to Listen

Sit where you can see and hear the speaker. If you're going to listen to a speech on a subject you know little about, do some preliminary

You can improve your listening skills by learning to concentrate and taking notes on what you hear.

reading, or ask questions before the presentation. If you're given program notes, read them carefully, including information about the speaker. Always read your text before a class lecture to get the most benefit. The more familiar you are with the material, the easier it will be to concentrate.

Listen for Key Words

Speakers often give you clues about what is important. Numbering ideas is a sign that what follows is important. Listen for phrases such as, *the most important thing, my next point is,* or *in other words.* Those phrases all indicate that you should pay particular attention to what follows.

Take Notes

When you take notes, it isn't necessary to write down every word. Outline the major ideas. Listen for key words and phrases, and summarize what follows. Develop your own shorthand, and learn to abbreviate words. Make notes about any examples speakers use to explain or illustrate their ideas, because examples will often help you remember information more completely.

Checklist for Listeners and Speakers

Once you know the ways in which people listen, keep them in mind when you write a speech. Good speakers know the listening habits of their audiences, and they take pains to counteract bad listening habits in order to get their messages across. The lists below compare your two tasks in this class and in any public speaking situation—whether you're the listener or the speaker. ⸰

Listener	**Speaker**
1. Be prepared to listen. Make sure you're ready to hear and understand what's being said.	**1.** Don't begin your speech until the audience is ready to listen. Wait until their attention is focused on you.
2. Sit where you can see the speaker. You'll be more likely to understand the speech.	**2.** Make sure you're visible to as much of the audience as possible. Establish eye contact.
3. Listen for the main idea and for key words and phrases that explain that idea. When the speaker says, "In other words," you know you are going to hear an explanation.	**3.** Use key words and phrases. Don't be afraid to tell the audience what is important and what you are doing.
4. Concentrate on the speaker. Try not to be distracted.	**4.** Provide sufficient variety in your voice, physical expressions, and materials so the presentation promotes listener concentration.
5. Take notes.	**5.** Organize your presentation to make it easy for the audience to take notes.

Chapter 4 Summary

Listening is a skill that you can learn. First, you must understand that listening isn't just hearing sounds—it is concentrating on sounds and interpreting them. Good listeners adapt their listening behavior to fit particular situations, because some situations require more concentration and active participation than others. There are five general levels of listening: listening for enjoyment, listening for information, critical listening, precision listening, and empathic listening. Know when you need to take notes and to ask questions to improve your retention.

Good listeners reduce physical and mental barriers. Physical barriers are hearing loss, outside distractions, the inability to see the speaker, and the listener's physical condition. Mental barriers are inattention, the listener's attitudes, the listener's level of knowledge, and selective listening.

To improve listening skills, you should concentrate, practice, prepare for listening, note key words and phrases, and take notes. In the end, good listeners are those who practice listening, not just hearing.

◆ *Check Your Understanding*

1. Explain the difference between listening and hearing.

2. Explain how listening is an important part of the public speaking process.

3. Give three reasons why listening is important in your daily life.

4. Explain the levels of listening and how to use them when you listen to speeches.

5. Explain the difference between physical and mental barriers to effective listening. Give three examples of barriers.

6. Explain at least three ways to improve listening skills, and outline your plans for improving your skills.

◆ *Apply Your Understanding*

1. Listen to the evening news, take notes, and explain two news stories to a member of your family.

2. List three errors you made or misunderstandings you had because of poor listening skills. In your list, include examples

from home, school, and work. Explain what happened because of your errors. Did they cost you time or money?

3. List the five levels of listening. For each level, describe a situation in your home, work, and school life that requires you to use that level.

4. Listen to a tape recording of a speech, and make a list of the key words and phrases the speaker used to indicate important information would follow.

◆ *Thinking Critically about Public Speaking*

Listen to a speech or a class lecture, and outline the content. Compare your notes with other members in the class. What did you miss that others didn't? What did you have that others missed? What could account for the differences?

◆ *Speak Out!*

Divide into groups of three. Select one important school or social problem for each person to discuss. The first person should explain his or her opinions or feelings on the issue. Before the next person can speak, he or she must explain the previous person's comments. The speaker must say the summary is accurate before the next person can state his or her own ideas.

◆ *Speech Challenge*

Your teacher will either read you an editorial or opinion piece from a newspaper or play a video or audiotape of a broadcast commentary. You are to listen to the commentary, which will be read or played only once, take notes, and prepare a response. Your response should not only present the other side, but should analyze weaknesses in the author's use of facts and support for his or her arguments. Present your commentary to a group of five or six classmates. After each of you has completed your oral presentation, compare notes about the differences in your responses and determine how you might have listened to the original opinion differently.

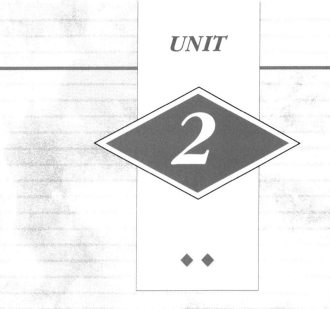

UNIT

2

Public Speaking Fundamentals

CHAPTER

·5·

Key Terms

Articulation
  (Enunciation)

Emphasis

Framing

Inflection

Intensity

Pause

Pitch

Resonation

Respiration

Speech rate

Vibration

Volume

Chapter Objectives

After studying this chapter, you should be able to:

1. Identify the four steps in the process of voice production.
2. Explain ways of improving articulation.
3. Explain how volume, intensity, and emphasis improve vocal effectiveness.
4. Explain how rate, pause, and framing improve vocal effectiveness.
5. Explain how pitch and inflection improve vocal effectiveness.
6. List guidelines for using the microphone.

Voice

Voice Production

Because speech is such a natural and important part of everyday life, people take their voices for granted. Every time you speak, you're operating a truly amazing machine, one that coordinates many parts of your body to produce intelligible sounds. You control the components of this "voice machine," so you should know how the machine works. There are four stages of voice production: respiration, vibration, resonation, and articulation.

Respiration

Voice production requires air pressure that comes from the diaphragm—the same large band of muscle, just below the rib cage, that enables you to breathe. When you inhale, air rushes into the nose and throat and on to the lungs until the air pressure in the lungs equals the air pressure outside the body. Another name for this process is **respiration.** When the diaphragm expands, the chest cavity is enlarged, creating a sort of vacuum. When you control the diaphragm during speech, you release air gradually. The quantity of air exhaled helps determine both the length of a phrase or sentence and the loudness of your voice. Since voice production begins with respiration, breath control is important to good vocal control.

Vibration

By itself, rushing air makes little sound. Listen to yourself whisper. This is the sound of your voice if you don't use your vocal cords (the folds contained in your larynx), or your voice box. Expelled air must pass over the vocal cords to produce loud sounds. Sound production is the stage of voice production called **vibration.** Air passing over the tightened vocal cords produces sound much like that made by a rubber band when you stretch it and blow vigorously across it. The size of the larynx differs with an individual's age, size, and sex. Consequently, the sound differs from person to person. See Figure 5.1.

Resonation

Like a vibrating rubber band, your vocal cords would sound flat and lifeless without **resonation,** which is the amplification and enrichment of the voice. The parts of your body responsible for this stage of the process—the resonators—allow the sound to echo, just as the box of a guitar allows the sounds of the strings to echo.

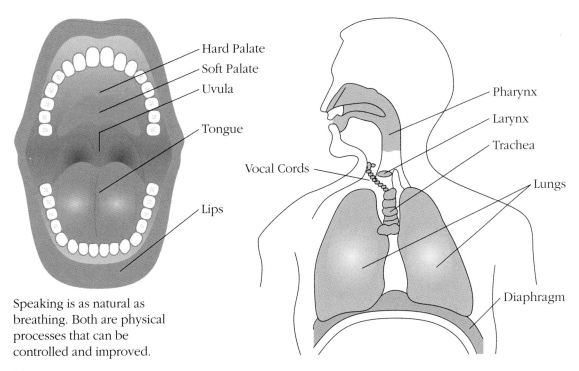

Speaking is as natural as breathing. Both are physical processes that can be controlled and improved.

Figure 5.1
The Physical Process of Speaking

To understand resonation, think about the way your voice sounds when you sing in a bathroom. Your voice sounds fuller because it "bounces around," or echoes off the walls and ceilings. If you stretch a rubber band over a small box, resonation will produce a louder, fuller tone.

Your voice's resonators are the throat, skull, sinuses, and chest cavity. Even the bones of the skull build and develop sound from the larynx. This process gives your voice much of its character. To learn how your voice sounds without some of your resonators, remember how you talk when a cold clogs your sinuses or when you pinch your nose shut. Why does your voice sound differently when you speak than when you hear it on recording tape? You usually hear your voice from the inside, without the same resonance that people outside hear.

Articulation

Producing a full, rich sound is not the end of the voice production process. You must shape the sound into intelligible speech. The production of language's various sounds is called **articulation.** You use two kinds of articulators, fixed and movable.

Fixed articulators are those you can't alter voluntarily. The most obvious example is your teeth. You use your teeth (in combination with other articulators) to produce many of the common sounds in English words: the *th-* in *thirty* and *three;* the *l-* in *lollipop;* the *f-* in *favorite;* the *v-* in *valve;* or the *z-* in *zero.* You probably don't remember how hard it was to say words like these after you had lost your front teeth, but you may know how braces change your ability to articulate. Another fixed articulator is the hard palate, which is the bony structure on the roof of your mouth that extends from behind your front teeth to about halfway back.

Move your tongue back along the roof of your mouth until you reach the end of the hard palate, then you will feel the soft palate. The soft palate gives with pressure of your tongue. This structure, along with the tongue, jaw, and lips, is in the second category of articulators—movable articulators. You use them in combination with your teeth and hard palate to create understandable, meaningful sounds. Since movable articulators are under your control, guard against lazy or sloppy use. Poor articulation makes it difficult for your audience to understand you.

Although the voice machine may seem complicated, you *can* control it. Use your diaphragm, vocal chords, resonators, and articulators to create a voice that's uniquely yours and that's clear and expressive. Learning to control your voice takes practice and exercise.

Voice Quality

Perhaps you've heard of voice prints. Like fingerprints, the voice prints of two speakers are never alike. Even the cleverest impressionist can't duplicate another person's voice exactly.

At each stage of voice production, you can improve the quality of your voice. While some aspects of your voice can't be changed (such as your fixed articulators), others can. Here are some weak qualities that detract from a public speaker's voice:

breathy (the speaker seems out of breath)

raspy (the speaker sounds as though he or she has a sore throat)

shrill (the speaker's voice is on the verge of breaking)

nasal (the speaker seems to be talking through his or her nose)

denasal (the speaker seems to have a cold)

husky (the speaker's voice is "trapped" in the throat)

There is no one perfect speaking voice, but most audiences agree that a pleasant, expressive voice has certain pleasing qualities. Mostly, this means the speaker avoids the weak qualities just listed.

Audiences like voices that are firm, rich, and resonant. That means they like speaking voices produced with sufficient air pressure from the diaphragm, they like speakers who relax their throats and vocal cords to avoid shrillness, and they like speakers who speak using all their resonators without overusing or underusing the nose and sinuses. In other words, they like speakers who articulate well.

Tools of Vocal Expression

Your voice has three basic sets of controls: volume, rate, and pitch. By handling these controls, you express a wide range of ideas and feelings. Almost without thinking, you communicate anger, fear, disappointment, sorrow, excitement, surprise, and countless other emotions.

If you already use volume, rate, and pitch, why study them? Unfortunately, speaking in public isn't as easy as talking casually with a friend. When you stand in front of a group, your voice may lose its natural liveliness and expression. This loss can make your speech ineffective. Variety in volume, rate, and pitch keeps an audience attentive, builds your personal appeal, and helps sell your message.

Volume, Intensity, and Emphasis

Successful speakers know they use great amounts of physical energy when they give a speech. Even though it may look like a speaker just has to stand up there and talk, even a five-minute speech can be tiring. It takes energy to control your diaphragm to produce the vibration that results in your voice. Expending this energy produces volume, intensity, and emphasis.

Volume **Volume** is the measure of how loud or soft your voice is. This characteristic should be your first concern, because if you speak too softly, no one in the audience will hear anything you say. Your speech won't be effective, no matter how good it is. Listening to a speaker who talks too softly is a strain. An audience soon grows tired of concentrating so hard just to hear what's being said. Above all, your speech should be audible—which means it should be loud enough to be heard.

If you're sure your speech is audible, you can vary your volume. Increasing or reducing the volume of certain syllables, words, or phrases adds meaning to your speeches. Imagine that you're giving a speech about an exciting concert you attended. Your voice is at normal volume as you tell about buying the tickets and moving

Public speakers can vary the volume and intensity of their voices to give emphasis to what they are saying. Storytellers use volume and intensity to convey the action and meaning of their stories.

inside to your seat. As you tell about waiting for the music to begin, your volume is softer, reflecting your anticipation. When you describe the climax of the event, your voice becomes bolder and louder. Without these volume cues, your audience might not sense changes in subject and mood that make your speech interesting.

Intensity Volume isn't the only way to draw attention to words and phrases. Your delivery can be intense without being too loud. Even a whisper can be intense. Like volume, intensity is increased by forcing more air out of the diaphragm. **Intensity** is a way of communicating your emotional message. A speech about a day in the park requires little intensity as you describe the park's general appearance. Your intensity will increase when you explain why the experience was important to you—how you truly saw the beauty for the first time, or how a mugger destroyed a perfect afternoon.

Emphasis Varying volume and intensity allows a speaker to give **emphasis** to key words or phrases. Think about the words people usually emphasize when they quote Abraham Lincoln's famous

Sound Check: Using a Microphone

Often, speakers must use a microphone. If you speak in a large room or in front of a large group, you should use a microphone to be sure you're heard. When you use a microphone, follow these guidelines:

1. Try to practice with the microphone you will actually use. Even if you can't go through your whole speech, a brief rehearsal will help you feel at ease.

2. Find out if there is an off/on switch and learn how to work it—before you speak.

3. Adjust the microphone to suit your height. This is especially important if the speaker who talks before you do is taller or shorter than you are.

4. When it's time for you to speak, don't blow on the microphone or tap it to see if it's working. That just annoys an audience. If you know that the microphone is on, there is no need to test it. If you don't know whether it is on or not, begin with a simple remark or the first line of your speech.

5. Find out how close you must be so your voice will be picked up and amplified but the normal noises aren't audible.

6. Guard against electronic feedback—the screeching sound caused by a loudspeaker that's located too close to the microphone. If there is a problem, stop speaking momentarily to halt the noise. Then adjust your distance from the microphone and your volume. If the results aren't satisfactory, the microphone, loudspeaker, or volume level may have to be adjusted.

phrases, "of the people, by the people, and for the people." Consider Franklin Roosevelt's famous line, "the only thing we have to fear is fear itself." If you read the words without increasing your volume, the key words lose their impact.

One of the most dramatic speakers of the twentieth century was General Douglas MacArthur. His farewell speech to Congress, after fifty-two years in the U.S. Army, was an emotional, exciting speech. His conclusion is famous. MacArthur didn't shout. Instead, he relied on variety in volume, intensity, and emphasis to draw his audience into his speech's emotion. How would you deliver his conclusion?

Where would you be loud? Soft? How intense would you be? Which words or phrases would you emphasize?

> I am closing my fifty-two years of military service. When I joined the army, even before the turn of the century, it was the fulfillment of all my boyish hopes and dreams.
>
> The world has turned over many times since I took the oath on the plain at West Point, and the hopes and dreams have long since vanished, but I still remember the refrain of one of the most popular barracks ballads of that day which proclaimed most proudly that old soldiers never die; they just fade away.
>
> And like the old soldier of that ballad, I now close my military career and just fade away, an old soldier who tried to do his duty as God gave him the light to see that duty. Good-bye.

Managing Volume, Intensity, and Emphasis   One mistake that speakers commonly make (especially debaters and contest speakers) is to begin a speech with so much volume and intensity that they can't increase either quality. As a result, their speeches are frequently delivered at one volume: loud. It's a fact that if every word is emphasized, it's as if no words are emphasized, because none stand out. With no way to add variety in volume, intensity, or emphasis, speakers lose three of the tools of vocal expression.

Rate

The speed at which you talk is your **speech rate,** and your rate communicates much to your audience. A very rapid rate can mean such things as anger, confusion, and impatience. A slow rate might show caution, fatigue, hopelessness, or sincerity.

When you're at ease, your speech rate usually takes care of itself. When you're nervous, however, you may begin to speak rapidly without knowing it. Many inexperienced speakers prepare a five-minute speech only to find that it lasts only three minutes in front of an audience! If you speak too rapidly, you may speak unclearly or mispronounce words. Speed makes it easy to skip a syllable or slur a word or phrase. Try reading this paragraph aloud—first slowly, then rapidly. What changes take place in the clearness of your voice? In the mood you convey?

Pause   Speaking too rapidly can also deprive speakers of one of their most important tools—the **pause.** The silences a speaker uses between words, phrases, and sentences add drama and meaning to a speech. Beginning students may have the most difficulty learning the value of silence. They can be as afraid of saying nothing as they are of saying something. Think about your favorite comedian. That person's success often rests on the ability to pause and deliver punch lines at the right time. You've probably heard speakers who knew precisely when—and how long—to pause to set up a word or phrase. Even a pause at the beginning of a speech, before you say a word, may set a strong mood.

Framing   One particularly effective use of the pause is called **framing,** which is pausing slightly before and after a word or phrase. Read these sentences without framing: "Have you ever read one of Poe's short stories? They may be scary even to you." Now read them again, but frame the phrase *even to you.* Do you notice the difference? Framing gives the sentences drama—even a bit of playfulness.

Using Rate   As you rehearse your speeches, practice variety in rate as well as pausing and framing. If you use an outline, listen to yourself to make sure you don't miss opportunities to vary your speech rate. If you speak from a manuscript, you have an extra advantage. Pauses are often indicated by periods, commas, semicolons, and dashes. You can also mark pauses on the manuscript, if there's no punctuation where you want to pause.

Ex-President Ronald Reagan was called the Great Communicator. Many of his speeches contained moving, inspirational examples of heroism. In this speech, given on 24 October 1985, to celebrate the United Nations' fortieth anniversary, see how the punctuation helps plan pauses. Where else would pauses be effective?

> America is committed to the world, because so much of the world is inside America. After all, only a few miles from this very room is our Statue of Liberty, past which life began anew for millions, where the peoples from nearly every country in this hall joined to build these United States.
>
> The blood of each nation courses through the American vein, and feeds the spirit that compels us to involve ourselves in the fate of this good Earth. It is the same spirit that warms our heart in concern to help ease the desperate hunger that grips proud people on the African continent.
>
> It is the internationalist spirit that came together last month when our neighbor, Mexico, was struck suddenly by an earthquake. Even as the Mexican nation moved vigorously into action, there were heartwarming offers by other nations offering to help and glimpses of people working together, without concern for national self-interest or gain.
>
> And if there was any meaning to salvage out of that tragedy, it was found one day in a huge mound of rubble that was once Juarez Hospital in Mexico City.

| *SPEAKING ABOUT SPEAKING* | Planning Vocal Variables |

Knowing that you *can* control your voice isn't much use unless you use that control. The best way to develop variety is to rehearse your speech out loud. Students often try to rehearse a speech by going over it "in their heads"—never actually saying the words until they're in front of their audience. This is a bad technique for beginners. If you rehearse aloud, you'll hear some of what the audience hears. You can vary the way you say a phrase to find out how you want it to sound. Try to test your speech on a friend. He or she may hear things that you don't.

If you are using a manuscript, you can plan your variables by marking up the copy. Underline words or phrases to indicate places where you want to increase or reduce volume. Put a line or two to remind yourself about where to put long and short pauses. You can even note where pitch changes would be helpful. What follows is an example of a manuscript marked for a reading. Note how the speaker has tried to build the scene to a climax with changes in volume, rate, and pitch. What vocal variety would you plan?

/ = pause
underline = intensity

Start slow
|
build

louder

The takeoff of a hot air balloon is a slow,/steady build to a climax of great beauty./The crew unrolls the balloon,/a limp,/lifeless object that's about as inspiring as an old sleeping bag.//A large fan breathes life into the loose/cloth bag./Air rushes into the opening in what seems to be a pointless battle to inflate the balloon.//Then,/unexpected by the observers,/the gas jets are lit,/and with a <u>whooshing</u> roar/the hot air is <u>shot</u> into the body of the now-swelling balloon./As the hot air builds,/the balloon begins to <u>strain</u> against the efforts of the ground crew to keep it stable./Men and women are dwarfed/as it grows and raises itself to the sky./With the basket attached and the hot flames shooting into the

pick up → speed

interior of the balloon,/the ground crew gives up the struggle,//and the spirited,/colorful balloon triumphantly rises overhead.//Spectators crane their necks,/and amid shouts and applause,/the balloon soars overhead/ seeking the air currents that will take it on its journey.///The crowd

decrease volume

watches until the balloon is a speck on the horizon./Their role is over,/ but the beauty of the sight lingers in their sighs and quiet comments.

A week after that terrible event and as another day of despair unfolded, a team of workers heard a faint sound coming from somewhere in the heart of the crushed concrete. Hoping beyond hope, they quickly burrowed toward it.

And as the afternoon light faded, and racing against time, they found what they had heard and the first of three baby girls—newborn infants—emerged to the safety of the rescue team.

And let me tell you the scene through the eyes of one who was there. "Everyone was so quiet when they lowered that little baby down in a basket covered with blankets. The baby didn't make a sound, either. But the minute they put her in the Red Cross ambulance everybody just got up and cheered."

Well, amidst all the hopelessness and debris came a timely—and timeless—lesson for us all. We witnessed a miracle of life.

Pitch

The most important aspect of voice quality to control is pitch. **Pitch** refers to the highness or lowness of your voice. Think of pitch as notes on a musical scale. Just as a melody moves up and down the scale, speaking also uses variety in pitch to express meaning.

You learn to use pitch very early in life. Even small children know that if they ask a question they must end the sentence with a rise in pitch. The words *have a nice day* can be a question or a statement, depending on what you do with pitch when you say the word *day*.

Naturally, your pitch is determined in part by your speaking voice. Whether your voice is quite low, high, or somewhere in between, you must work on developing variety within your natural range.

Altering the pitch of your voice is called **inflection.** Vocal inflection is an important way to maintain audience attention. Without inflection, your voice becomes a monotone; you use a flat, droning delivery that gets boring very quickly.

Articulation

As defined, articulation is how clearly and precisely you speak. Another word for articulation is **enunciation.** An audience relies on you to speak clearly. A reader who tries to read a blurred text becomes frustrated and quits reading. Similarly, a listener trying to understand a speaker who doesn't articulate clearly often becomes frustrated and quits listening. In many cases, improving articulation is simply a matter of replacing bad habits with good ones. The most common problems in articulation are really quite easy to correct.

Improving Articulation

Consider the following guidelines to improve your articulation:

1. Are you delivering your speech with your head up, or are you talking to the podium? It is difficult for an audience to follow a speaker when the sound is directed away from them.

2. Can the audience see your face? Not only will this help the sound of your voice, but the audience will see your lips move and will understand you better.

3. Are you opening your mouth? Because they feel nervous, some speakers barely move their jaws and lips. Since you can control the articulators, use them.

4. Are you keeping your hands away from your face? Even speakers with good articulation can muffle their voices by putting their hands in front of their faces.

5. Have you rehearsed your speech aloud? You'll be better prepared for all the words and phrases in your speech if you're very familiar with them.

6. Have you looked up unfamiliar words in a dictionary? If you aren't quite sure how to pronounce a word, it's always better to look it up or to ask someone who knows.

Dropping Word Endings

Sometimes, out of habit or laziness, people drop *-ed, -ing,* or some other word ending. "Going" becomes "goin'." "Chased" becomes "chase." Although dropped endings probably don't bother your friends in casual conversation, they're unacceptable in public speaking. Your audience expects you to pronounce words fully.

Running Words Together

Because of speed, nerves, or both, some speakers run their words together. "Going to" becomes "gonna." "I don't want to go" becomes "Idoewannago." Running words together makes it almost impossible for an audience to understand whole sections of your speech.

Substituting Sounds

Even though they may not realize it, some speakers substitute one sound for another in words. Instead of "for," they say "fer." Instead

Speech therapists can help those with articulation problems overcome their speaking difficulties.

of "to," they say "tuh." "Computers" comes out "compuders." Instead of "secretary," they say "secutary." Some audiences will think this problem indicates the speaker lacks education or manners.

Adding Sounds

Rarer, but still too common, is the problem of adding sounds. Some people who know the correct pronunciation of "library" still say "liberry." "Cabinet" becomes "cabinent." Such mispronunciations detract from a public speaker's appeal.

Solving Common Voice Problems

You may wonder if you have any vocal delivery problems that you don't know about. To find out, keep in mind the three feedback loops discussed in Chapter 2. Anticipate your audience's expectations and the situation you'll be speaking in. As you practice, adjust your volume, rate, and pitch. While you are speaking, watch your audience's responses to determine if the audience is having difficulty understanding you. If necessary, adjust your voice during the speech until you have positive audience feedback. Finally, review your speeches, and listen carefully to evaluations. While some speech difficulties require work with a speech pathologist (someone trained to help people with speech disabilities), you can solve most of your problems with practice.

Chapter 5 Summary

The elements of voice production are respiration, vibration, resonation, and articulation. By understanding the anatomy of your "voice machine," you can have better control over your speaking voice. Effective vocal control produces variety in volume, intensity, emphasis, speech rate, and pitch. Effective pauses can also build speech effectiveness. As you work on your speeches, say your words clearly and precisely. Avoid dropping word endings, running words together, or substituting or adding sounds to words. The best way to develop good vocal control is to prepare well. Rehearse out loud. Remember that often your natural speaking voice will be amplified by a microphone. Use the microphone correctly, or it can hurt your presentation more than help it.

♦ Check Your Understanding

1. Summarize the four stages of voice production.

2. Explain how you can improve articulation.

3. Explain the differences between volume, intensity, and emphasis. Be able to illustrate each aloud.

4. Read a paragraph from a speech to illustrate changes in rate, use of pauses, and framing.

5. Explain the terms *pitch* and *inflection*.

6. List guidelines for using a microphone.

♦ Apply Your Understanding

1. Practice one of the tongue twisters below to improve your articulation. Say the phrase slowly at first, then build speed.

   toy boat (repeat rapidly ten times)
   rubber baby buggy bumpers
   Shall she sell sea shells?
   Ten tiny trumpeters tunefully tuning their ten tiny trumpets.
   She thrust three thousand thistles through the thick of her thumb.

2. Collect a list of words or phrases that are commonly articulated poorly. Share the list with the class. Refer to the chapter to describe the articulation problem for each word or phrase.

3. Refer to the four stages of voice production. Speculate on how stage fright might affect the voice in each of the stages.

◆ *Thinking Critically about Public Speaking*

1. Select a famous radio, TV, or film personality with a recognizable voice. Listen to the voice and write a short description of it. Use these categories in your description/analysis: volume, rate, pitch, variety, voice quality, and bad habits.

2. As a class or in a small group, discuss the evaluations made in the previous exercise. Debate the merits of the voices of the famous people you've evaluated. Determine the criteria for selecting the best voice.

3. Record your own voice as you read a passage from a textbook. Listen to the recording for at least five minutes, using the criteria you developed in the previous exercise to evaluate your own voice. Describe the voice you hear on tape.

◆ *Speak Out!*

Select a passage from a speech in this book or from one approved by your teacher. Find a passage that conveys some feeling or emotion, like the examples in this chapter. Make a script of the passage by photocopying, typing, or writing it out. Mark the following: volume increases and decreases, changes in intensity, emphasis of words and phrases, changes in rate, pauses, and framing. Practice the piece aloud. Present the piece to the class. Use a two- to four-minute time limit.

◆ *Speech Challenge*

Frequently, speech students give all speeches in one location, probably their classroom. Seldom do public speakers in the real world give speeches in one location only. Prepare a short speech based on any of the exercises at the end of this chapter. The speech needs to be only two to four minutes long. You will need to give this speech in an auditorium. The purpose of this speech is to experiment with voice. During your speech, your classmates should be spread out through the auditorium. Begin the speech with a microphone; experiment with the distance the microphone is from your mouth. If possible, use more than one kind of microphone. For part of your speech, use no microphone, and see if you can make yourself heard by all your classmates. After the experiment, discuss the experience with classmates to see what you've discovered.

CHAPTER

Key Terms

Descriptive gestures

Emphatic gestures

Eye contact

Gestures

Movement

Multi-channelled

Paralinguistics

Posture

Chapter Objectives

After reading this chapter, you should be able to:

1. Explain why nonverbal delivery is important.
2. Explain the relationship between verbal and nonverbal delivery.
3. Identify and explain the seven major elements of nonverbal delivery.
4. List strategies for improving nonverbal delivery.

Nonverbal
Delivery

The Importance of Nonverbal Delivery

In 1960, a series of historic debates took place between presidential candidates Senator John Kennedy, the Democratic nominee, and Vice President Richard Nixon, the Republican. The debates were carried on television and radio. After the first debate, many who had watched the debates on television felt that the lesser-known Kennedy was the winner. Kennedy looked energetic, self-confident, and in command of the situation. Nixon, on the other hand, looked tired and drawn (he had recently been in the hospital). He seemed to lack the energy Kennedy displayed.

Radio listeners, on the other hand, were more likely to select Nixon as the winner. On the basis of Nixon's words and voice, not his appearance, he seemed better prepared and more knowledgeable. Kennedy won that election. It may be that nonverbal communication helped shape the nation's history.

Chapter 2, which introduced the basics of the communication process, explained that the means of communicating fall into two categories: verbal communication, which uses words, and nonverbal communication, which doesn't. In every speech, a sender uses both verbal and nonverbal channels to communicate ideas. Such communication is said to be **multi-channelled.** By using both verbal and nonverbal channels, a speaker has a greater impact on the audience, for several reasons.

Most Communication Is Nonverbal

If you've ever tried to talk with someone who doesn't speak English or any other language you know, you probably discovered that you could still communicate to some degree. Through nonverbal communication, you could make some fairly good guesses about the other person's message. Even when you're communicating with someone in the same language, you still rely heavily on nonverbal cues.

Some researchers suggest that less than ten percent of a message's impact comes from verbal communication. While you listen to a speaker's words, whether you realize it or not, you're also influenced by the way the speaker talks as well as by the speaker's actions. The fact that nonverbal communication has such a strong influence on the way people interpret messages emphasizes an important rule about communication—it is impossible *not* to communicate. Even when you're silent, you're communicating. Before you begin to speak, when you pause, or when you leave the speaker's stand, you're still sending messages to your audience.

Nonverbal communication, including facial expressions and gestures, often says more than verbal communication.

Nonverbal Reinforces Verbal

One reason that nonverbal communication influences interpretation is that it reinforces what's being said. It can make the audience trust—or distrust—a speaker. If a speaker says, "I'm delighted to be here today," and actually smiles and looks and sounds energetic, you'll think the person is sincere. On the other hand, if another speaker says the same thing but looks solemn and unhappy, you'll probably think the statement isn't true.

Nonverbal Can Replace Verbal

An old saying points out that a picture is worth a thousand words. Often, speakers present nonverbal "pictures" with their facial expressions or body stance. Those pictures can say more than words. Effective speakers know that sometimes a look alone is all they need to communicate. When speakers use visual aids to explain something, nonverbal communication replaces verbal. If you watch comedians on television or have seen a comedian in person, you know how much nonverbal communication can get laughs. Speakers can communicate messages successfully without words.

Nonverbal Can Contradict Verbal

People who study nonverbal communication have learned that when a verbal message says one thing and a nonverbal message says another, audiences tend to believe the nonverbal. For instance, the speaker who said, "I am delighted to be here" but didn't look enthusiastic, sent contradictory messages. Because people have less control over their nonverbal messages than their verbal messages, listeners tend to believe how they act rather than what they say. Audiences rely on their interpretation of nonverbal messages to determine a speaker's sincerity, honesty, or overall credibility.

There's no doubt that verbal and nonverbal communication complement one another. Words alone can't communicate a speaker's knowledge of the subject matter. Nonverbal elements must also play a part by reinforcing or replacing ideas.

The Elements of Nonverbal Delivery

Facial expressions, diagrams or drawings, and vocal variables such as those discussed in Chapter 5 are all examples of nonverbal delivery. This section will discuss these tools and others.

Posture and Stance

The way you stand (your **posture**) has a lot to do with how you sound as well as how you look and move. Without erect posture, you won't be able to breathe properly. Without adequate breath control, you won't be able to project your voice well. You'll have to take more breaths, which will make your delivery choppy.

Erect posture also communicates that you're interested in your topic and enthusiastic about your speech. Someone who slumps over the speaker's stand or shifts from one foot to another appears uninterested or nervous. Stand with both feet firmly planted. Distribute your weight evenly on both feet. Avoid standing with your feet parallel (see Figure 6.1a). If you stand this way, you may rock back and forth or sway. It's better to spread your feet apart slightly, positioned so you can move easily (see Figure 6.1b). The stance in Figure 6.1b gives you better balance and reduces distracting movements.

Appearance

While it isn't necessary to dress up to give a speech in class, be aware that your appearance can add to your message or detract from it. Your clothes should be neat and shouldn't distract the audience in

Your posture affects how you sound when you speak. Without erect posture, you can't breathe properly, so you won't be able to project your voice.

any way. If you're wearing a T-shirt with a cute picture or saying, your audience may pay more attention to your shirt than to your ideas. Avoid wearing jewelry that you might be tempted to play with without knowing it. Also, avoid wearing caps or other accessories that might draw attention away from what you have to say.

When giving a speech somewhere besides the classroom, wear clothes that fit the occasion. Obviously, if you're speaking at a formal dinner, you should wear a suit or dress, not blue jeans and a T-shirt.

Figure 6.1
Stance while
Speaking

(a) Standing this way makes it easy to sway or rock. Avoid this stance if possible.

(b) This stance gives you a firmer footing. It's also easy to move from this position.

When giving a speech, wear clothes that fit the occasion.

Women should choose reasonably conservative clothes. Bold and bright prints or unusual styles can be distracting.

Your appearance communicates a great deal about you and your attitude about the event you're attending. Part of your job as speaker—analyzing the situation—includes identifying the appropriate dress for the occasion. You want to dress in a way that's fitting for your age and position, but you should also be aware of how formal the situation is.

If you speak to the school board, you'd probably dress more formally than you do for class. If you were going to talk to a group of elementary students, however, your school clothes might be perfectly acceptable.

Movement

Speech students often think that speakers stand behind a podium and never move. But think about some speakers who have captured and held your attention. Did they move around? More than likely, they did. And as they moved, they displayed an energy that enhanced their credibility.

Movement, actually moving your entire body from one spot to another, tells an audience several things. First, it says that you're moving to a new point of discussion. Second, it helps you get closer to the audience. This makes the audience feel as if you're really communicating with each of them. Third, movement keeps the audience from getting bored. When you move, audience members shift their focus. This keeps them alert. Movement also benefits the speaker. Moving around uses up some nervous energy and provides a positive way to release natural tension.

While movement can help you emphasize a point or get closer to an audience, you can move too much. If a speaker paces or moves unnecessarily, the audience thinks the speaker is nervous. When a speaker is nervous, the audience often feels restless and uneasy.

In general, movement is a positive characteristic, but only if it's natural. Don't plan when you're going to move. When speakers program their movements, the movements don't match up with the words, so the movements look awkward. Contest speakers have a tendency to program their movements, which can distract judges from what's being said. Movement is effective only if it complements your verbal delivery.

If you're using a microphone, you must be careful about your movements. As you learned in Chapter 5, a microphone may pick up sound only if the speaker talks directly into it. Other microphones allow some movement, but it's usually limited. Check out the microphone you'll be using ahead of time so you know how it will restrict you. Ideally, if movement is an important part of your delivery style, try to secure a lavaliere microphone, which is a small mike that clips to your clothing.

Gestures

Gestures express emotions through the movement of your limbs, body, or head. Many beginning speakers worry about what to do with their hands. Although you are probably unaware of your hands when you talk to your friends, your arms and hands may seem larger than life when you're standing in front of a roomful of people. Suddenly you can feel as if you look like Popeye! This feeling is quite natural. To see how most people are affected, read the boxed feature on pages 90–91, which describes the problems former President Ford had with his hands.

While gestures can be a source of frustration to the beginning speaker, they can also be a real asset to a speech. Gestures can be divided into two types. **Emphatic gestures** allow a speaker to provide emphasis for the spoken word. **Descriptive gestures** help a speaker describe something.

SPEAKING ABOUT SPEAKING	# Fingers Fumble Gesture of Goodwill ### *Bill Vaughn*

I thought Gerald Ford did very well in his little television chat in which he gave us the good news that he was planning a tax rebate and the bad news that it was going to cost more to stay warm and mobile.

The style was new. Informal, warm. We open on the star standing behind the desk, he walks around the desk and eventually sits behind the desk. And he is watching a prompter instead of reading from a manuscript.

That's the technique advised by all the close students of public speaking. Think what a smash Abraham Lincoln would have made at Gettysburg if he hadn't read the Address off the back of an envelope.

But I think the White House communications staff is going to have to add another specialist. The President needs a handperson.

It struck me, anyway, that Mr. Ford had everything under control, except what to do with his hands.

Now anybody who has ever tried to inflict a message upon a group of people knows that the hands are the big problem.

Professors who teach such matters say that men should not talk with their hands in their pockets, although it never seemed to hinder Will Rogers much. It has always seemed to me natural for a man to put his hands, or one of them anyway, in his pockets or pocket while talking. I mean you can't just have one or more hands dangling at your side.

I don't know about women. Would they feel more comfortable speaking if they put their hands in their purse? Maybe we'll find out when we have a woman president.

Anyway, Jerry, as he is sometimes called, kept his hands busy in an understandable but distracting manner.

Speakers who are exciting to watch use many emphatic gestures. They stab the air with a finger, shrug their shoulders, nod their head, or pound on the podium. Gestures like these show that a speaker is excited and involved. They add to the speaker's believability.

Descriptive gestures help the audience visualize what the speaker is talking about. They create mental images by indicating the size or shape of something. Descriptive gestures are also used to explain the location of a person, place, or thing.

You can enrich your speeches by using one or both types of gestures. The best way to learn to use such gestures is to let them

A friend who was present during the telecast said that the President looked to him like a third base coach who had been signaling: "Take two and hit to right."

This friend, a staunch Republican, said, "The administration is in trouble if the Democrats steal the signals."

The President also did something which is pretty risky. That is to use gesture to illustrate the meaning of his words.

It is an easy trap to fall into.

Like you say, "There are three important things to remember," and you hold up three fingers. The risk here is that you may discover that you have held up the wrong number of fingers, from one to five. It leads to untoward giggling among the audience.

Also, there is the danger that you may promise three points and only be able to deliver two, which leaves you gazing at a remaining finger in some astonishment.

At one point the President held his hands close together to indicate short-term plans and farther apart for long-term ones. It was very effective, but you have to get it coordinated, or you wind up looking like an accordion player while trying to get your short and long terms sorted out.

As I have said, I thought it worked nicely. It gave the ordinary citizen a warm feeling that he had a President who had no more idea of what to do with his hands than anybody else who gets up in public.

For the long term (hands wide apart), however, I think the best course is to stay behind the lectern, which gives you something to hold onto and, if the need should arise, hide behind.

develop naturally. If you select a topic you're truly interested in, and if you practice your speech, gestures will come easily. Think about your speech, not about your body. As you become more experienced, you'll find yourself using gestures without giving it much thought.

To free your hands, don't grasp the sides of the podium or hold your notes with both hands. (Many beginning speakers do both.) Remember, movement of any kind uses up whatever anxious energy you may have. If you can release that energy through gestures and movement, you'll do better.

A speaker uses emphatic gestures to emphasize what he or she is saying. Such gestures help convey the speaker's emotion.

Eye Contact

We all like to have the feeling that a speaker is actually talking to us alone. In our culture, we tend to think a person is more trustworthy if he or she looks us in the eye; this is maintaining **eye contact.** A speaker who doesn't look at us through most of a speech loses not only our attention but also our belief and trust. So, when you give speeches, you need to look at your audience.

The key to good eye contact is knowing your material. If you know your material, you'll rely less on your notes. If you practice impromptu delivery, you will increase your skill in establishing eye contact with the audience. How you put your notes together can also affect your eye contact. Later chapters discuss strategies that make it easier to watch both your notes and the audience.

Chapter 2 presented three feedback loops. Loop 2 described the interaction between speaker and audience during a speech. Since much of the feedback from the members of the audience is nonverbal, you must look at them. That's the only way you'll receive nonverbal clues about their interest, understanding of the topic, or agreement with the content. Speakers who watch their audiences can adjust their speeches when necessary. For instance, if you notice that your audience is straining to hear or see, you can speak more loudly or move closer.

You should direct your eye contact to all parts of the audience. It's all too easy to find one or two friendly faces and then look at no one else. But all audience members need to be addressed. That doesn't mean you must move your head constantly. In fact, you can switch eye contact with only a slight head movement. If you practice your speech in front of friends or family members, don't let them sit together. If they sit far apart, it will force you to look in more than one direction.

Facial Expressions

Facial expressions communicate a great deal. Turn off the volume on a television set and watch the actors' faces. More than likely, you'll be able to figure out their moods and the attitudes they are conveying. Look around any classroom, and you can tell by their faces which students are interested and which are bored and daydreaming.

Good storytellers use more than their voices to read or tell a story. They also use facial expressions. As with gestures, facial expressions should be natural. Unfortunately, you have the least control over this aspect of nonverbal delivery. Furthermore, you know the least about what your facial expressions are. The best way to find out if you have a lively face is to make a videotape of one of your speeches and watch yourself. If you're interested and involved in your topic, your face will communicate that to the audience.

Paralinguistics

Paralinguistics are vocal clues, such as volume, rate, or inflection, that tell a receiver how to interpret spoken words. Chapter 5 described many aspects of paralinguistics. These techniques are an aspect of nonverbal delivery, rather than verbal delivery, since the messages they send rely as much on how something is said as what is said. Paralinguistics add to a lively delivery. Combined with facial expressions, gesture, and movement, they help maintain audience interest and enrich understanding.

VOICES OF

THE FRONTIER

American Originals

As the United States expanded to fill a continent, new voices with new accents were constantly being drawn into the American forum. The speakers who came from the frontier brought freshness, originality, and challenge to American debate. Not all the messages from the frontier were happy, but they were all proof of how freedom of speech welcomes everyone to participate in democracy. Three speakers give us insight into the American frontier: Ralph Waldo Emerson, Abraham Lincoln, and Chief Joseph of the Nez Perce.

Born and reared in Massachusetts in the 1800s, Emerson was a man of the pulpit and the university, not the wild frontier. Still, in 1837, many Europeans looked on America as barely civilized. America had not yet proven she could stand on her own intellectually. In his famous speech "The American Scholar," Emerson settled once and for all the dispute about whether this "wilderness" could produce great thinkers. This speech has been called "the declaration of American intellectual independence."

Abraham Lincoln was a true frontiersman. He was a rail-splitter who spent much of his early life in the woods of Illinois. From this frontier, he emerged to become one of the greatest—if not *the* greatest—American speakers of all time. Lincoln himself contrasted his plain, simple style with the more extravagant styles of his contemporaries. As a voice from the frontier, he helped the country through the darkest days of the Civil War.

Chief Joseph of the Nez Perce is another voice from the frontier—the voice of the Native American. His short, direct speech shows the eloquence that the frontier gives to American public address.

WORDS TO REMEMBER

Ralph Waldo Emerson

If the single man plant himself indomitably on his instincts, and there abide, the huge world will come round to him.

This time, like all times, is a very good one, if we but know what to do with it.

The American Scholar, 1837

Abraham Lincoln

No man is good enough to govern another man without that other's consent.

Speech at Peoria, Illinois, 1854

The ballot is stronger than the bullet.

Speech at Bloomington, Illinois, 1856

"A house divided against itself cannot stand." I believe this government cannot endure permanently half slave and half free.

Speech at the Republican State Convention, 1858

. . . government of the people, by the people, and for the people, shall not perish from the earth.

Gettysburg Address, 1863

Chief Joseph

Our chiefs are killed . . . The old men are all dead . . . The little children are freezing to death. My people, some of them have run away to the hills and have no blankets, no food. No one knows where they are, perhaps freezing to death. I want to have time to look for my children and see how many of them I can find. Maybe I can find them among the dead. Hear me, my chiefs. My heart is sick and sad. From where the sun now stands, I will fight no more forever.

Speech to the Nez Perce tribe after surrendering, 1877

Chapter 6 Summary

Giving a speech requires more than just speaking. The nonverbal elements of delivery—what the audience sees and the way something is said—help communicate the speaker's message by reinforcing or replacing words. Sometimes nonverbal messages contradict verbal ones.

Good posture and an appropriate stance help your vocal delivery and provide you with a solid footing so you can move without being awkward. Your appearance can add to or detract from your message. Movement can signal transition points in a speech and can help place you closer to the audience. Gestures can provide emphasis and description. Eye contact helps your listeners feel that you are speaking to each one of them. It also enables you to watch the audience for valuable feedback. Facial expressions complement your vocal delivery and add life to your speech. Your appearance can tell the audience you are serious about your topic. Your paralinguistic or vocal clues add meaning to your words.

Verbal and nonverbal delivery go hand in hand. Through practice, both will become natural.

◆ Check Your Understanding

1. List three reasons why nonverbal delivery is important in speech-making.

2. Discuss two reasons why verbal and nonverbal delivery are closely related.

3. Identify the seven major elements of nonverbal delivery, and explain how each can enhance your effectiveness as a speaker.

4. List at least three things you can do to improve your nonverbal delivery.

◆ Apply Your Understanding

1. Play charades. Then discuss why some clues were easy to understand and others weren't. Determine how much of the degree of difficulty had to do with the topic and how much with the nonverbal messages.

2. Select five or six pictures of people from magazines or newspapers. Write captions for each based on facial expressions, stance, or other nonverbal communication.

3. Your teacher will supply you with a list of nonverbal messages, such as frowning, moving hands rapidly, and speaking loudly. Working in groups, write several meanings for each. How would verbal clues help you to interpret the nonverbal clues?

◆ Thinking Critically about Public Speaking

1. Watch a videotape of a speaker with the sound turned off. Write an analysis of the speaker's nonverbal delivery. Would you expect this speaker to be effective? Watch the speech a second time with the sound turned on. What is your opinion of the speaker's effectiveness? How much is or is not due to nonverbal communication?

2. Watch a videotape of one of your speeches. Which aspects of your nonverbal communication are effective? Which need improvement? What can you do to improve?

◆ Speak Out!

1. Give a one- to two-minute speech describing a common object but not telling what it is. Use descriptive gestures and movements to help the audience visualize your subject. When you're finished, have audience members write down what they think you described. How many were correct?

2. Select a poem or short story with your teacher's approval. Read a part of your selection three times. Each time you read it, change the tone or meaning by changing the rate, volume, emphasis, or inflection.

◆ Speech Challenge

To determine how your nonverbal communication affects how an audience receives your speech, try this experiment. Give a speech from the assignments above. You will need to create two short videotapes. One videotape will be of your shoulders and head only; the other will be a "full body" shot. (You can either give the speech twice or, if you have two cameras, give the speech once with two different camera shots.) Show the speech to two different groups of people. Your speech class could be divided into two sections to provide different audiences. Have each audience critique the speech. Note in their critiques how their perceptions differ.

CHAPTER ·7·

Key Terms

Alliteration
Allusion
Antithesis
Appropriate language
Assonance
Clarity
Connotation
Denotation
Dialect
Economy
Ethics
Figure of speech
Grace
Hyperbole
Inversion
Irony
Jargon
Metaphor
Parallelism
Parenthesis
Pronunciation
Repetition
Rhetorical question
Simile
Style
Syntax
Tone
Vocabulary

Chapter Objectives

After reading this chapter, you should be able to:

1. Explain why appropriate language selection depends on situation, purpose, and audience.
2. Define *style*.
3. List the three elements of style.
4. Define *denotation* and *connotation*.
5. Recognize and name common stylistic methods.
6. Define *tone*.

Language

Effective Use of Language

When you speak, you should use all the skills at your disposal to increase your effectiveness. Students frequently concentrate most of their efforts on voice. As a result, they sometimes overlook one of the most important, effective tools they have: language. The words you choose and the order you put them in can make the difference between success and failure. Never assume that effective language use is only important in English class. It's important every time you communicate with others.

Whole books are devoted to effective use of language. As you read this chapter, please remember that situation, purpose, and audience will determine what effective use of language means. What is effective in one situation may not be effective in another. This chapter will focus on the characteristics of language that prove to be effective in most situations.

Effective language is important any time you talk to others.

Ethics and Language

People can use language ethically or unethically. **Ethics** are principles of right and wrong. The function of language is to create meaning with words. As a public speaker, you must decide how to create meaning. You can use language to lie, distort, and mislead. You can make things that are bad sound good, and vice versa. What will you do? Using language to hide the truth or to create an untruth is unethical. Even though you may hear and read deceptive language every day, you must decide if you'll use deceptive language yourself. The choice is a very important one.

What can happen when you choose to use language to deceive? Think about these possibilities: Your deception is likely to be discovered and challenged. If your deception is discovered, your audience is not only unlikely to be persuaded by your speech, but you are less likely to be believed the next time you speak. You will have sacrificed the trust you need from an audience. Your credibility as a speaker will be reduced. Far from accomplishing your purpose, you may hurt not only your speech but also the cause for which you speak.

What about using language to manipulate? That is a tougher question. As a speaker, you will want to change people's opinions and attitudes. You will want them to be somewhat different after your speech than before. Is it ethical to use language to gain your ends? Certainly we all recognize that using language to persuade others is acceptable. A politician who wants a citizen's vote can even do the country a valuable service by expressing ideas in clear, persuasive language. But when does language stop being persuasive and start being manipulative?

A speaker's language goes from being persuasive to being manipulative and deceptive when the speaker uses language that leads an audience away from what the speaker thinks is true. Even if a speaker thinks that he or she is deceiving or manipulating for a good cause, the speaker is still using language in an unethical way.

Appropriate Language

Appropriate language is language that's suited to situation, purpose, and audience. Language is one of the means of persuasion available to you when you give speeches. By analyzing the situation, purpose, and audience of your speech, you'll be able to choose the

| SPEAKING ABOUT SPEAKING | # Different Situations, Different Language |

How can you know when language is appropriate or inappropriate? As with most things in public speaking, you know by considering your situation, purpose, and audience. Choose language that suits the situation. Make sure the language is consistent with your purpose, and try to forecast how your audience will react to your language. Consider the SPAM aspects of the following two passages from speeches by Lyndon Johnson:

Passage 1

This is a sad time for people. We have suffered a loss that cannot be weighed. For me it is a deep personal tragedy. I know that the world shares the sorrow that Mrs. Kennedy and her family bear. I will do my best. That is all I can do. I ask for your help and God's.

S: 22 November 1963. Johnson had just become President, following the assassination of John Kennedy. The speech was delivered on television.

Passage 2

Unfortunately many Americans live on the outskirts of hope—some because of their poverty, some because of their color, and all too many because of both. Our task is to help replace their despair with opportunity.

S: Johnson was giving his first State of the Union message, a traditional speech that the President gives to Congress at the start of each year. He was beginning a long campaign to pass civil rights legislation. Civil rights was a very important issue to the American people. This speech was televised.

most effective language, or method, you can use. Consider the two passages by President Lyndon Johnson in the Speaking about Speaking box above.

As those examples show, appropriateness is relative. It depends on situation, purpose, and audience. There are, however, some general guidelines regarding language that apply to almost all speeches. See the Spotlight on Speaking box on page 104.

P: Johnson needed to assure the nation that, despite the tragedy, the government was secure. He needed to express the nation's grief.

P: Johnson wanted to arouse support in the Congress and among the American people for his civil rights proposals. He wanted to persuade Congress and the people to support his views.

A: The television audience was millions of shocked, grieving people. They looked to Johnson for leadership in this crisis.

A: The Congress and the American people were very supportive of their new President. All the members of Congress and most of the American people were aware of recent protests and marches for civil rights. There was, however, some opposition to the legislation that Johnson was supporting.

M: President Johnson used simple and direct language. Stark statements ("I will do my best. That is all I can do.") were dignified and calm. The language is plain. Johnson apparently felt short, declarative sentences would best assure and calm the audience, while convincing them that he was firmly in charge of the government. He spoke as an individual (using the first-person pronoun "I").

M: The President's language was less simple, less stark. He chose more colorful, more elaborate phrases ("some because of . . . , some because of . . . , all too many because of . . . "). He spoke for the people ("Our task is . . .") rather than for himself.

Dialect

No matter where you live, you speak a **dialect,** a type of speech characteristic of a region or group. Most of the time, dialects don't present a problem for speakers. Often the audience and the speaker both speak the same dialect—in fact, an audience usually expects the speaker to "talk as they do." Then, too, many audiences enjoy

Appropriate Language

When deciding what sort of language to use, consider the following guidelines:

1. Standard usage is preferred to nonstandard. Standard usage is language that's acceptable everywhere. (You probably use standard English when you talk with your teachers or your employer.) Nonstandard usage is acceptable only in some conversations, but not in front of an audience.

2. Since slang is nonstandard, it is inappropriate in public speaking.

3. Any words that might offend or embarrass the audience are inappropriate.

4. Poor grammar is inappropriate in public speaking.

listening to a speaker with a slight accent. Sometimes, however, dialect is a problem. If it's too unfamiliar to the audience, the speaker must accommodate the audience by minimizing dialect.

Pronunciation

The most obvious language difference between one part of the United States and another is **pronunciation,** the way a word is said. A person from the Midwest, for example, may pronounce *roof* using the *oo* sound in *took.* In the East, the same word is pronounced with the *oo* sound in *boot.* In the South, vowels are drawn out. *My* is pronounced with an *ab* sound, for instance. These pronunciations are all correct. The differences are slight and will cause few audience problems. What about pronouncing *creek* like *crick,* as happens in some parts of the country? This pronunciation is more of a problem, because although the dictionary lists *crick* as acceptable, it's not the dialect that most Americans speak.

Vocabulary

Another problem arises with dialect. People from different parts of the country use various words to indicate the same thing. In other words, different people may use different **vocabularies.** What do you call a carbonated soft drink that comes in bottles and cans? Many people call such drinks *sodas.* In some places, however, the word *soda* indicates a carbonated drink with ice cream in it. These people may call a carbonated soft drink *pop*. Although this particular word may not present you with a problem, you may use other words that a large audience wouldn't readily understand. How about the various words for a sofa: *couch, divan, davenport,* and *chesterfield?* Do you see the potential problems?

Syntax

The way that words and phrases are put together to form sentences is called **syntax;** it is another part of dialect. For the most part, American dialects retain standard syntax. Sometimes, however, differences in syntax can create confusion. A speaker must always be aware of the audience's reaction to his or her manner of speech. For example, most audiences expect a speaker to say something such as, "He is coming to town for the summer." The nonstandard, "He be coming to town for the summer" would cause confusion. While the second sentence may be acceptable in some dialects, it isn't appropriate in standard English.

Using Dialect

When you are speaking to people who use the same dialect as you, you probably don't worry that you might sound different. Sometimes, however, public speakers are concerned that a regional dialect may be a problem when they speak to an audience from another part of the country. Recent experience shows that dialect is not a block to effective public speaking. In the Democratic national primaries of 1992, one candidate was from Massachusetts, one from Arkansas, one from Iowa, one from Virginia, and so forth. None seemed to be hurt by dialect. Of our last eight presidents, you could identify four as southerners from their speech. The Kennedys' Boston accents seemed to go naturally with their eloquence. In the 1992 presidential elections, all three candidates (Bush, Clinton, and Perot) lived in the South, and one (Bush) had connections to the Northeast.

The lesson? These dialects and others do not necessarily cause communication problems. In fact, many audiences find dialect charming or distinguishing.

Style

Style is the way something is said or done, rather than what is said or done. Consider this example: People can choose from a large number of car models. Almost all will do what cars should—provide reliable transportation. Why, then, are there so many different kinds?

It's true that different cars (sports cars, station wagons, pick-ups) serve different functions. More important, people see cars as a means of self-expression. Color, body shape, and extras all help make cars more or less appealing. And the kind of car a person drives tells a lot about the kind of person he or she is.

By the same token, the words you choose for a speech tell an audience a lot about you. Your style with words will influence your audience. Even a brief look at a famous quotation shows that the way in which something is said is often as important as what is said. At the beginning of the Gettysburg Address, Abraham Lincoln could have said "Eighty-seven years ago . . ." instead of "Four score and seven years ago. . . ." Which is more memorable? Thomas Jefferson could have ended the Declaration of Independence with "We are totally committed." Instead he said, "We pledge our lives, our fortunes, and our sacred honor." That's the phrase that went down in history.

Why does one speech live on in the minds of an audience and another fail to keep an audience's attention for five minutes? The answer is often style. The elements of style are clarity, economy, and grace. When a speech has these characteristics, it's described as eloquent. Eloquence is more than just speaking; it's speaking well. The British poet and playwright Ben Jonson drew the same distinction: "Talking and eloquence are not the same: to speak, and to speak well are two things. A fool may talk, but a wise man speaks." How can your speech have clarity, economy, and grace?

Clarity

If you speak with **clarity,** you state your ideas in a clear, understandable way. Clarity is the most important element of style, because an unclear message leads to confusion and misunderstanding.

Clarity depends on specific, understandable words (vocabulary) in an understandable order (syntax). When you are considering style, always consider clarity first. Why? If your speech isn't clear, nothing else will matter. Unclear speech confuses and tires an audience. Even if you have what you think is a beautifully worded speech with carefully composed sentences, if it lacks clarity, your message won't get through.

Despite the many successful speeches given in his political career, President George Bush was often criticized for unclear speech. Sometimes, Bush's speech seemed rambling and unfocused. During his campaign for reelection in 1992, Bush was speaking in New Hampshire about the economy, which was then in a recession.

Here's what he said:

> The guy over at Pease—a woman actually—she said something
> about a country-western song, you know, about a train, a light at
> the end of the tunnel. I only hope it's not a train coming the other
> way. Well, I said to her, well, I'm a country music fan, I love it, al-
> ways have. Doesn't fit the mold of some of the columnists—of what
> they think I ought to fit in, but I love it. . . . But nevertheless I said
> to them, you know there's another one the Nitty Ditty Nitty City—
> that they did. And it says if you want to see a rainbow, you've got
> to stand a little rain. We've had a little rain. New Hampshire has had
> too much rain. A lot of families are hurting.

To be fair, not all of President Bush's comments were so confusing.
Still, these kinds of passages from his speeches limited the effectiveness of some of his presentations. The use of the song might have
been a good idea, so might the comment on the columnists and the
references to the person at Pease. But all in the same hundred-plus
words? In addition, he interrupted himself several times and changed
pronouns from *her* to *them*. A clearer, simpler statement might have
been more effective.

> It's true the economy has suffered somewhat and a lot of families
> are hurting, but better times are coming. They say if you want to
> see a rainbow, you've got to stand a little rain. We've had the rain;
> we're ready for the rainbow.

Run-ons   Running ideas together is one of the common enemies
of clarity. Speakers often link sentence after sentence together with a
series of *ands*. Here are two explanations of how a compact-disc
player works. The first passage is marred by run-on sentences:

Unclear
In a series of little pits impressed into the disc are all the sounds of
a song and the disc is read by lasers which shine on the pits and
then the music is the result of the disc player which translates the
pits into sound and the sound is very good.

Clear
All the sounds in the song are recorded as little pits in the disc itself. As the disc spins, the lasers in the disc player "read" the little
pits, translating each pit into a digital language made up of zeros
and ones. The player then reads this code. The result is clear, sharp,
undistorted sound.

Many fields or hobbies, such as computers, have their own specialized words, which are known as jargon. Use jargon in a speech only if you are certain your audience will be familiar with the terms.

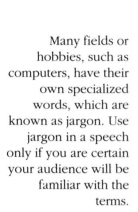

Jargon **Jargon** is the specialized, technical words of a specific job, hobby, or social group. If you know a lot about computers, you probably know many words that sound like Greek to other people—words such as *bit, byte, user-friendly, floppy disk, boot,* or *WYSIWYG.* If you use these terms when you speak to an audience that is also knowledgeable about computers, there won't be any problems. But will a general audience understand you? Probably not. Your message will be unclear, and your audience will become confused and bored.

As you prepare a speech, remember your audience's need for clear, precise language—the first element of style. After all, the audience doesn't know as much about your subject as you do. The audience shouldn't have to guess your meaning.

Denotation and Connotation Speakers should always be concerned about an audience's reaction to particular words. One thing to remember is the difference between a word's denotation and connotation. The **denotation** of a word is its direct meaning, the meaning in the dictionary. A word's **connotation** is the meaning that a word suggests, the meaning people may associate with it. You must be aware of both the denotative and connotative meaning of words. Otherwise, you may say one thing, but your audience may hear something else.

Politicians always have trouble with the word *taxes*. It's easy to understand why. People really don't enjoy paying more taxes from their wages and salaries. The denotation of *taxes* is simple: money collected by the government for public purposes. The connotation is far from simple. What do people associate with the word *taxes?* Some think of waste; some think of big government; some think of tax audits and paperwork; some just think of having less money. The word doesn't really suggest to many people the benefits that might come from taxes: schools, fire departments, highways, social programs, and so on.

President Bush took advantage of the word's negative connotation when he expressed an important part of his economic plan in simple language: "Read my lips. No new taxes!" Because of the word's negative connotation and the firmness of Bush's language, this pledge became very popular. Bush—as well as presidents before and since—used other words as a substitute for *taxes*. One of the most popular in recent times is *revenue enhancement*. Note that the denotation is the same. *Revenue enhancement* is really money collected by the government for public purposes. Still, the term doesn't come with all the emotion that *taxes* does.

Economy

To speak with **economy** is to state your ideas briefly and concisely. No audience wants to listen to a speech filled with unnecessary words. In addition, as you become more experienced in public speaking, you'll value the time you have to deliver your speech. Right now you may think a ten-minute speech is very long. But you may find that ten minutes isn't enough time when your speech is about an important subject. In those ten minutes, you must make every word count.

What does it mean when someone says a statement is too wordy? Study these two examples:

Wordy
In today's modern society, the students of high-school age must add additional courses to their schedules if they are going to be fully prepared in a complete way for a successful career.

Economical
Today's high-school students must take more courses to prepare for successful careers.

What is the wordy speaker trying to do? If he or she is trying to impress the audience, do you think the attempt worked? Not when they realize the speaker took thirty-three words to say what could have been said in fourteen!

The economical speaker makes several important changes. Unnecessary repetition is reduced. *Today* and *modern* mean almost the same thing in this speech. So do the words *fully* and *complete*. The economical speaker also chooses the simple, direct expression *high-school students* instead of *students of high-school age*. If all of the wordy speaker's speech is written like this one sample, the speech could be almost twice as long as the economical speech. And it won't say any more.

Don't assume, however, that short speeches are always better than long speeches. It often takes time to make a point. Think of a lawyer speaking before a jury. Although the lawyer's speech shouldn't waste time, the lawyer can't shorten the speech just to save time. If a defendant is to have a fair trial, the lawyer must take enough time to explain the defendant's position. Remember two things: First, a speech written in an economical style isn't the same as a short speech. A twenty-minute speech can be as economically written as a two-minute speech. Second, clarity is more important than economy. A longer speech that is clear is better than a shorter speech that leaves the audience confused.

Grace

To speak with **grace** means stating your ideas in an appealing, skillful manner. Graceful language is easy to listen to. An audience remembers graceful words and phrases in which the language is beautiful, dramatic, or powerful. All speakers strive for clarity and economy, but those who are remembered use words or phrases that make their subjects come alive in the minds of the listeners.

Graceful speeches are remembered long after they're given. On 4 July 1826, America celebrated the fiftieth anniversary of the signing of the Declaration of Independence. On that same day, two former presidents, Thomas Jefferson and John Adams, died. A month later, one of America's most famous speakers, Daniel Webster, spoke at a memorial service for them both. His language was more than clear and economical; it was alive and beautiful. It captured the solemnity and nobility of the situation:

> Sink or swim, live or die, survive or perish, I give my hand and my heart to this vote [in support of the Declaration]. It is true, indeed, that in the beginning we aimed not at independence. But there is a divinity which shapes our ends. The injustice of England has driven us to arms; and, blinded to her own interest of our good, she has obstinately persisted, till independence is now within our grasp. We have but to reach for it, and it is ours. Why, then, should we defer the Declaration? Is any man so weak as now to hope for reconcili-

ation with England, which shall leave [n]either safety to the country and its liberties [n]or safety to his own life and his own honor?

Webster could have been more economical. He could have said, "No matter what the results, I support the Declaration. Even though we didn't start out trying to get independence, it was meant to be. All we need to do is fight for it." Had Webster been that blunt, his words wouldn't have outlived the moment. Instead, Webster transfixed his audience with his eloquent, graceful language.

Making Language Memorable

The graceful use of language involves more than using words that sound good. Speakers strive to use language that will stay with their listeners long after the speech is completed. A speaker usually can't talk to every audience member individually after the speech. By using memorable language, you can be sure your message isn't forgotten. There are many ways of making speeches memorable. But they all make use of stylistic devices.

Parallelism

Speakers use **parallelism** when they arrange sentences so words and phrases echo each other in length and structure. Nouns are linked with nouns, gerunds with gerunds, prepositional phrases with prepositional phrases. You can hear the parallel elements in Webster's speech:

> Is any man so weak as now to hope for a reconciliation with England, which shall leave [n]either <u>safety to the country and its liberties</u> [n]or <u>safety to his own life and his own honor?</u>

Webster repeats the same grammatical structure in the underlined phrases. Do you hear the structure's repetition? Use your "mind's ear" to hear parallelism, even if you don't read the sentences aloud. When you prepare your speeches, use your mind's ear first. Then rehearse aloud so you can hear sentences needing parallel structure.

Antithesis

Antithesis is like parallel structure except that words having opposite meanings are paired together. Note how Webster opens his speech with antithesis:

> Sink or swim, live or die, survive or perish . . .

Notice the neat and balanced sound of the paired opposites. John F. Kennedy's inaugural address contains two other famous examples of antithesis:

> Let us never negotiate out of fear, but let us never fear to negotiate.

> Ask not what your country can do for you, ask what you can do for your country.

Sentences such as these are memorable. They stay with an audience long after the speech is finished.

Rhetorical Question

If you ask a question during a speech but don't expect an answer, you're asking a **rhetorical question.** A rhetorical question is a way to make a statement or to make your audience think. You may or may not answer the question, depending on your purposes or goals. Webster didn't expect anyone to answer his rhetorical questions:

> Why, then, should we defer the Declaration? Is any man so weak as now to hope for reconciliation with England . . . ?

Interrupting for Emphasis

You may not think that interrupting parallel or antithetical statements is a good idea. It could destroy the balance you're trying to create. But good speakers use interruptions to their advantage. Webster used a brief interruption (called **parenthesis**) with the word *indeed.* It has no grammatical relationship to the rest of the sentence. Note how Ronald Reagan used an interrupter to emphasize a point in this speech on tax reform:

> After taking the basic deductions, the first tax rate of 15 percent would apply to each dollar of taxable income up to $29,000 on a joint return. The second rate, 25 percent, would apply—and only apply—to taxable income above $29,000 up to a maximum of $70,000.

Reagan's point might have been lost in all the numbers if he hadn't interrupted himself to reassert it.

Repetition

One of the easiest and most effective language devices is **repetition.** You simply repeat a sound, word, phrase, or idea. Glance through any newspaper or magazine and you'll see plenty of examples. In the

Gettysburg Address, Lincoln thought the phrase "the people" was important enough to say it three times: "that government of the people, by the people, and for the people shall not perish from the earth."

Repeating key words and phrases can serve an important function in public speaking. Unlike readers, listeners can't review material when they want to. Repeating key words and phrases builds clarity as well as grace.

Repeated Sounds   Alliteration is the repetition of consonant sounds. **Assonance** is the repetition of vowel sounds. If these repetitions are not irritating or overdone, they can help build speech effectiveness:

> **Alliteration**
> Sink or swim . . .

> **Assonance**
> . . . obstinately persisted, till independence is now within our grasp.

Repeated Words and Phrases   Sometimes a repeated word sounds just awful. If the speaker isn't careful, repetition becomes a problem instead of a benefit. Used correctly, however, repeated words can have a strong impact on listeners. One of the most famous examples of repetition is in Winston Churchill's radio address to the British people in the darkest days of World War II:

> You ask, what is our aim? I can answer in one word: Victory—victory at all costs, victory in spite of all terror, victory however long and hard the road may be; for without victory, there is no survival.

By repeating the word *victory,* Churchill affirmed his and his people's hope for the future.

Inversion

Altering normal word order is another way of increasing the effectiveness of your language. In the normal English sentence, the subject comes first, followed by the verb. A direct object or a complement may follow the verb. Sometimes, you can reverse the order and form a very effective structure. This is called **inversion.** Later in Webster's speech, he uses inversion and antithesis to create a striking sentence:

> The former she would regard as the result of fortune; the latter she would feel as her own deep disgrace.

In this sentence, Webster places the complements (*former* and *latter*) first, followed by the subjects (*she* and *she*). The word order then becomes complement-subject-verb—an inversion.

Inversion adds variety to a speech. Of course, no one likes to listen to an entire speech of inverted sentences. The successful speaker uses these techniques sparingly.

Allusion

An **allusion** is a reference to literature, religion, mythology, or history. Since the audience is expected to recognize the reference, sometimes a speaker won't even identify the allusion. For example, if a lot of students fail a big test, someone might say the test was their "Waterloo." The reference is to Napoleon's defeat at Waterloo. Webster uses an allusion in his speech when he says, " . . . there is a divinity which shapes our ends." The words are Shakespeare's, and they come from the play *Hamlet*. Webster expected his audience to recognize the allusion.

Metaphor and Simile

A **figure of speech** uses words or phrases in ways that expand their meanings beyond a literal sense. If you have ever heard someone say, "I'm so hungry I could eat a horse," you probably didn't think he or she meant exactly what was said. This is a figure of speech. When you strive for graceful language, you'll use many figures of speech.

Both metaphors and similes are comparisons between unlike things. A **simile** uses the words *like* or *as* to make a comparison. A **metaphor** doesn't use those words. Instead, a metaphor uses one word as a stand-in for another to make a comparison. For example, you might say, "My conscience was a lighthouse, warning me of approaching danger." You wouldn't really mean that your conscience *is* a lighthouse, but that your conscience is similar to a lighthouse. Similes and metaphors are vivid, memorable ways to make a point:

Simile
The wrath of God is like great waters. . . .

—Jonathan Edwards

Metaphor
Now is the time to lift our nation from the quicksands of racial injustice to the solid rock of brotherhood.

—Dr. Martin Luther King, Jr.

Remember, metaphors and similes must be fresh to work. A comparison that everyone has heard a million times is called *trite*. For instance, "the hands of a clock" is a metaphor. So is the saying "sharp as a tack." However, both are so familiar that no one would remember them if they occurred in a speech.

When a speaker develops a metaphor or simile into a more elaborate comparison, it becomes *extended*. Extended metaphors are common in public address. Perhaps you don't want to use elaborate, extended metaphors, but as a listener, you may be affected by them. One of the most famous is Martin Luther King, Jr.'s comparison of this country's Constitution and Declaration of Independence to a check or promissory note:

> . . . In a sense we have come to the capital to cash a check. When the architects of our republic wrote the magnificent words of the Constitution and the Declaration of Independence, they were signing a promissory note to which every American was to fall heir. This note was a promise that all men—black men as well as white men—would be guaranteed the unalienable rights of life, liberty, and the pursuit of happiness.
>
> But it is obvious today that America has defaulted on this promissory note insofar as her citizens of color are concerned. Instead of honoring this sacred obligation, America has given the Negro people a bad check—a check that has come back marked "insufficient funds." But we refuse to believe that the bank of justice is bankrupt. We refuse to believe that there are insufficient funds in the great vaults of opportunity in this nation.
>
> So we have come to cash this check. A check that will give us the riches of freedom and the security of justice.

King begins with a basic comparison. Then he builds a list of similar comparisons upon that foundation. The speech is built upon an extended metaphor.

Irony

Irony occurs when you say something that should mean one thing, but you intend it to mean the opposite. Good use of irony often depends on saying the word in a certain way so the audience hears that you do not mean the word to be taken literally. For instance, you could describe a boy you know by saying, "He's a real sweetheart." If you say it in a straightforward tone of voice, everyone will know you mean the boy is a nice person. But if you say it sarcastically, everyone will know you don't like the boy at all. You have used irony to convey meaning.

| SPEAKING ABOUT SPEAKING | # Eloquence and Effective Language |

We have a tendency to think that the age of graceful, eloquent speaking has long passed, that it belonged to the nineteenth century. That would be a mistake. Modern speakers also strive for eloquence. Each speaker achieves eloquence in his or her own way. When the Reverend Jesse Jackson appeared before the 1988 Democratic National Convention, he used the same kinds of speaking methods used by Daniel Webster over 150 years earlier. They are the same methods speakers will use 150 years from now. Here is a sample of some of the methods that he shared with Webster.

Parallelism

"*We are not a perfect party. We are not a perfect people.* Yet, we are called to a perfect mission: our mission, *to feed the hungry, to clothe the naked, to house the homeless, to teach the illiterate, to provide jobs* for the jobless, and *to chose the human race* over the nuclear race."

"If in my high moments, I have *done some good, offered some service, shed some light, healed some wounds, rekindled some hope,* or *stirred someone* from apathy to indifference, or in any way along the way helped somebody, then this campaign has not been in vain."

Antithesis

"But our healthy competition should make us *better, not bitter.*"

Rhetorical Question

"*How is he [Reagan] paying for these short-term jobs?* Reagan's economic recovery is being financed by deficit spending . . . "

Interrupting for Emphasis

"With all this confusion in this convention—*there is bright lights and parties and big fun*—we must raise up the simple proposition: If we lift up a program to feed the hungry, they will come running . . . "

Repeated Sounds

"My constituency is the <u>d</u>amned, <u>d</u>isinherited, <u>d</u>isrespected, and the <u>d</u>espised."

Repeated Words and Phrases

". . . just because you're born in a slum, does not mean the slum is born in you . . . I told them in every slum, there are two sides. When I see a broken window, *that's the slummy side.* Train that youth to be a glazier, *that's the sunny side.* When I see a missing brick, *that's the slummy side.* Let that child in the union and become a brick-mason and build, *that's the sunny side.* When I see a missing door, *that's the slummy side.* Train some youth to become a carpenter, *that's the sunny side.* When I see the vulgar words and hieroglyphics of destitution on the walls, *that's the slummy side.* Train some youth to be a painter, an artist, *that's the sunny side.*"

Inversion

"For friends who loved and cared for me, and for a God who spared me, and for a family who understood me, I am eternally grateful."

Allusion

"Leadership can *part the waters and lead our nation in the direction of the Promised Land.*"

Metaphor and Simile

"Our flag is red, white and blue, but *our nation is a rainbow*—red, yellow, brown, black, and white . . . America is not like a blanket—one piece of unbroken cloth, the same color, the same texture, the same size. *America is more like a quilt*—many patches, many pieces, many colors, many sizes, all woven and held together by a common thread."

Irony

"President Reagan says the nation is in recovery. Those 90,000 corporations that made a profit last year but paid no federal taxes are recovering."

Exaggeration

"In this world in which we live, we dropped the bomb on Japan and felt guilty. But in 1984, other folks also got bombs. This time, if we dropped the bomb, six minutes later, we, too, will be destroyed. *It's not about dropping the bomb on somebody; it's about dropping the bomb on everybody.*"

Detriments to Memorable Language

When you're striving for memorable language, avoid certain things:

1. Avoid clichés. Expressions such as "over the hill" or "solid as a rock" have been used so often that audiences are tired of them. Use fresh, original language in your speech.

2. Avoid language fads. Some words may be popular now among your age group, but will they suit all situations and all audiences?

3. Avoid weak verbs. Whenever possible, use strong verbs in your sentences. Strong verbs command attention and make sentences dynamic. Avoid passive verbs that contain a form of *be,* as in this sentence: "The speech was given by Joe." Passive verbs aren't as forceful as active verbs: "Joe gave the speech."

4. Don't forget your audience. No matter how good a sentence sounds to you, the audience is the ultimate judge of its effectiveness. Build memorable language with your audience in mind.

One of the most famous examples of irony in a speech was written by William Shakespeare for the play *Julius Caesar.* Caesar has been murdered. Brutus allows Antony to speak at Caesar's funeral only if Antony says nothing against Brutus and the others who killed Caesar. Antony lives up to his word. He calls Brutus and his friends "honorable" men, but note how the word comes to mean the opposite through irony.

> [Caesar] was my friend, faithful and just to me;
> But Brutus says he was ambitious,
> And Brutus is an honorable man.
> . . .
> When that the poor cried, Caesar hath wept;
> Ambition should be made of sterner stuff.
> Yet Brutus says he was ambitious,
> And Brutus is an honorable man.

How do you think Antony would say the word *honorable?* His tone of voice could easily communicate that he thought Brutus was anything but honorable.

Exaggeration

One way to call attention to your point is to exaggerate. This technique is called **hyperbole.** Webster used exaggeration to describe the Fourth of July holiday as he sees it in the future:

> Through the thick gloom of the present, I see the brightness of the future as the sun in heaven. . . . [Our children will] celebrate it with thanksgiving, with festivity, with bonfires, and illuminations. On its annual return, they will shed tears, copious, gushing tears. . . .

By exaggerating the emotional reaction of Americans on the Fourth of July, Webster underscores the intensity of the patriotism we feel for the day.

Tone

When all the elements of language combine, they create the tone of a speech. Used in this sense, **tone** means the author's attitude toward subject and audience. An audience listens to a speaker's language to determine the speaker's attitude. Is the speaker serious or joking? Does the speaker like the subject or not? Does the speaker care about the people in the audience? These are important questions. Audiences who think a speaker is uncaring, sarcastic, or arrogant probably won't be open to the speech.

A speaker's attitude toward a subject is revealed by his or her tone. Audiences may not listen if they don't feel that a speaker cares about the subject.

Language is composed of words. The speaker's responsibility is to use words appropriately and ethically. The way you write your speech and deliver it will be affected by your dialect. Dialect is made up of pronunciation, vocabulary, and syntax. Speakers must not let dialect interfere with communication. Style is the way in which a speaker presents ideas and is made up of three elements: clarity, economy, and grace. Clarity is hindered by run-on sentences, jargon, and dialect. Ignoring the connotations of words can make a speech unclear. Economy demands cutting away wordiness. Graceful language makes a speech eloquent. The speaker who achieves eloquence can make the message memorable. Some ways to achieve eloquence are parallelism, rhetorical questions, interruptions, repetitions, inversion, allusion, metaphor, simile, irony, and hyperbole. Finally, a speaker must know that the language used will be part of the tone of the entire speech.

◆ Check Your Understanding

1. Define *appropriate language*.

2. Define *style,* and list its three most important components.

3. List the three elements of style. Explain the meaning of each.

4. Define *denotation* and *connotation*.

5. Define the following terms and give an example of each: *parallelism, antithesis, rhetorical question, interruption, repetition, alliteration, assonance, inversion, metaphor, simile, irony,* and *hyperbole*.

6. Define *tone*.

◆ Apply Your Understanding

1. Collect examples of each of the following from newspapers and magazines: parallelism, antithesis, rhetorical question, interruption, repetition, alliteration, assonance, inversion, metaphor, simile, irony, and exaggeration. Share them with the class and decide if the stylistic devices were suitable to the situation, purpose, and audience.

2. Select a topic for class discussion. Have each student select a different tone from the list below. Carry on an organized dis-

cussion, with students choosing the kind of language that would create their particular tone:

sarcastic	certain	patient	arrogant
pleading	enthusiastic	hateful	hurt
apathetic	objective	frightened	cautious
angry	stubborn	amused	pushy
frustrated	bored	businesslike	childish
puzzled	relaxed	rational	stern

◆ *Thinking Critically about Public Speaking*

1. Select a speech from this text or from another source and have your teacher approve your selection. Evaluate the language used. Look for examples of these characteristics: appropriateness, clarity, economy, and grace. Provide words, phrases, or sentences from the speech to support your evaluation.

2. Use the same selection chosen above. Review the speech to determine if there are any grounds for challenging the ethics of the speaker. Select examples to show the speaker's questionable ethics or to show the speaker's ethical use of language.

3. To illustrate the difference between denotation and connotation, prepare a two- to three-minute explanation of how a particular word affects different people. Share your explanation in small groups. Select the best one and explain your choice to the rest of the class.

◆ *Speak Out!*

With a classmate, compose a three-minute speech on a topic of your choice, using as much acceptable current slang as possible. Then, write a nonslang translation of the speech. Present both to the class. Discuss possible audience reactions to the two versions.

◆ *Speech Challenge*

Compose and deliver a speech in which you use the techniques of language examined in the chapter. Specifically, include parallelism, antithesis, interruption, alliteration, inversion, metaphor, irony, and exaggeration. Your instructor will set the time limits. Before your speech, prepare a list of the techniques you used and present it to your instructor.

CHAPTER ·8·

Key Terms

Apathy

Attitude

Demographics

Ethnic group

Gender

Motive

Reading the audience

Chapter Objectives

After studying this chapter, you should be able to:

1. Explain what it means to read an audience.
2. Define *demographics* and understand their role in preparing speeches.
3. Identify the most important demographic characteristics of an audience.
4. Identify strategies for coping with audiences that agree with you, disagree with you, or aren't interested in your topic.
5. Demonstrate that you understand how to modify speeches to accommodate situational variables.

Analyzing Audience
and Situation

Matching Your Appeals and Your Audience

When you're asked to give a speech, you'll have to make several decisions. The situation often requires that you talk about a specific subject. The situation may also determine who will be in the audience. For example, how many parents would come to a speech about passing a driver's license test? Knowing about your audience will help define your purpose. Some audiences need information. Others need persuading. Your analysis of the audience and the situation will help you choose the most effective methods to use in your speech.

In Figure 2.7, page 29, we discovered that a public speaker depends on three kinds of feedback: (1) feedback before a speech (Loop 1), which is created by a speaker based on his or her understanding of what the audience will be like and how it will react to various speaking strategies; (2) feedback during a speech (Loop 2), which is feedback from the audience that lets a speaker know how the audience is reacting to a speech while it's being given; and (3) feedback after a speech (Loop 3), which lets a speaker know if a presentation was successful, and why. This chapter will focus on Loop 1—feedback before a speech. One key to becoming a good speaker is anticipating an audience's reaction to your speech and planning for the reaction desired.

Reading the Audience

When you begin your preparation, you must read the audience. **Reading the audience** means trying to understand the audience's background. Having this information enables you to put the audience at the center of the speech process.

The presidential debate between John F. Kennedy and Richard M. Nixon demonstrates the advantage that reading the audience gives a speaker. Both candidates began with opening speeches that illustrated how they read their audience. Both had the same purpose: to convince Americans to vote for them. The situation was this: In 1960, many Americans feared that the Soviet Union led the United States in science and technology—partly because of the launching of the Sputnik satellite three years earlier. Another campaign issue was what Kennedy called a "missile gap." Kennedy and Nixon had agreed to debate only about domestic issues. But Kennedy knew what Americans were worried about. His opening speech turned a domestic debate into a debate about competition with the Soviet Union. Kennedy's plan probably looked like this:

S: Americans' growing fear that the Soviets were ahead of the United States

P: to convince Americans to vote for Kennedy

A: the voting public, concerned with Soviet competition

Now, what methods did Kennedy use? First read Kennedy's speech below. After reading the text of Kennedy's speech, look at Speaking about Speaking (page 128) to see how Kennedy used his understanding of his audience and their concerns to help him build his speech.

SAMPLE SPEECH
The Kennedy-Nixon Debate of 26 September 1960
John F. Kennedy

Mr. Smith, Mr. Nixon: In the election of 1860 Abe Lincoln said the question was whether this nation should exist half slave or half free. In the election of 1960 and with the world around us, the question is whether the world will exist half slave or half free, whether it will move in the direction of freedom, in the direction of the road that we are taking or whether it will move in the direction of slavery. I think it will depend in great measure upon what we do here in the United States, on the kind of faith we build, on the kind of strength that we maintain.

We discuss tonight domestic issues, but I would not want any implication to be given that this does not involve our struggle with Mr. Khrushchev for survival. Mr. K is in New York and he maintains the Communist offensive throughout the world because of the productive power of the Soviet Union itself.

The Chinese Communists have always had a large population, but they are important and dangerous now because they are mounting a major effort within their country.

The kind of country we have here, the kind of society we have, the kind of strength we build in the United States will be the defense of freedom. If we do well here, if we meet our obligation, if we are moving ahead, then I think freedom will be secured around the world. If we fail, then freedom fails.

Therefore, I think the question before the American people is, are we doing as much as we can do? Are we as strong as we should be? Are we as strong as we must be if we are going to maintain our independence and if we are going to maintain and hold out the hand of friendship to those who look for assistance, to those who look to us for survival.

I should make it very clear that I do not think we are doing enough, that I am not satisfied as an American with the progress that we are making. This is a great country, but I think it could be a greater country; and this is a powerful country, but I think it could be a more powerful country.

I am not satisfied to have 50 percent of our industrial mill capacity unused. I am not satisfied when the United States had last year the least rate of economic growth of any major industrialized society in the world, because economic growth means strength and vitality.

It means we are able to sustain our defense. It means we are able to meet our commitments abroad. I am not satisfied when we have nine billion dollars worth of food, some of it rotting, even though there is a hungry world and even though four million persons wait every month for a food package from the government which averages five cents a day per individual.

I saw cases in West Virginia, here in the United States, where children took home parts of their school lunch in order to feed their families. I don't think we are meeting our obligations towards these Americans. I am not satisfied when the Soviet Union is turning out twice as many scientists and engineers as we are.

I am not satisfied when many of our teachers are inadequately paid or when our children go to school on part-time shifts. I think we should have an educational system second to none.

I am not satisfied when I see men like Jimmy Hoffa in charge of the largest union in the United States still free. I am not satisfied when we are failing to develop the natural resources of the United States to the fullest.

Here in the United States, which developed the Tennessee Valley and which built the Grand Coulee and the other dams in northwest United States, at the present rate of hydropower production, that is the hallmark of an industrialized society, the Soviet Union by 1975 will be producing more power than we are. These are all the things I think in this country that can make our society strong or can mean it is standing still.

I am not satisfied until every American enjoys his full constitutional rights. If a Negro baby is born, and this is true of Puerto Ricans and Mexicans in some of our cities, he has about one-half as much chance to get through high school as a white baby, he has one-third as much chance to get through college as a white student. He has about a third as much chance to be a professional man, about half as much chance to own a house. He has about four times as much chance that he will be out of work in his life as the white baby.

I think we can do better. I don't want the talents of any American to go to waste.

I know that there are those who say that we want to turn everything over to the government. I don't at all. I want the individual to meet his responsibility, and I want the states to meet their responsibilities. But I think there is also a national responsibility.

The argument has been used against every piece of social legislation in the last 25 years. The people of the United States individually cannot develop the Tennessee Valley, collectively they could have.

A cotton farmer in Georgia or a peanut farmer or a dairy farmer in Wisconsin or Minnesota, cannot protect himself against the forces of supply and demand in the marketplace, but working together in effective governmental programs he can do so.

Seventeen million Americans who are over sixty-five live on an average social security check of about $78 a month. They are not able to sustain themselves individually but they can sustain themselves through the Social Security System.

I don't believe in big government but I believe in effective governmental action, and I think that's the only way that the United States is going to maintain its freedom. It is the only way in which we are going to move ahead. I think we can do a better job.

I think we are going to have to do a better job if we are going to meet the responsibilities which time and events have placed upon us. We cannot turn the job over to anyone else. If the United States fails then the whole cause of freedom fails, and I think it depends in great measure on what we do here in this country.

The reason Franklin Roosevelt was a good neighbor in Latin America was because he was a good neighbor in the United States, because they felt that the American society was moving again. I want us to recapture that image.

I want the people in Latin America and Africa and Asia to start to look to America to see how we are doing things, to wonder what the President of the United States is doing and not to look at Khrushchev or look at the Chinese Communists. That is the obligation upon our generation.

In 1933 Franklin Roosevelt said in his inaugural that this generation of Americans had a rendezvous with destiny. I think our generation of Americans has the same rendezvous. The question now is, can freedom be maintained under the most severe attack it has ever known?

I think it can be, and I think in the final analysis it depends upon what we do here. I think it is time America started moving again.

You can find many more examples of Kennedy's speaking methods. Those listed here indicate how Kennedy thought out the development of his speech. First, he read his situation and audience. Then he selected appeals that would accomplish his purpose. Things like his quotations, examples, and statistics were the result of how he read the audience and situation. Kennedy even styled his gestures and voice to suit television. His biographer, Theodore Sorenson, said Kennedy's style "was ideally suited to this medium [TV]. His unadorned manner of delivery, his lack of gestures and dramatic inflections, his slightly shy but earnest charm . . . were exactly right for the living room."

You may never be involved in a presidential debate, but you still have to do what Kennedy did. What questions must you ask to analyze your audience?

1. Who is the audience?
2. What do the audience members know about the topic?

SPEAKING ABOUT SPEAKING

A Professional Speaker Reads an Audience

To understand how Kennedy used his understanding of audience to help him build his speech, consider how various passages responded to audience concerns.

What Kennedy knew of his audience	What Kennedy said	Why
The audience was concerned with Kennedy's age. If elected, he would be the youngest president ever elected.	"In the election of 1860, Abe Lincoln said . . . " "In 1933 Franklin Roosevelt said in his inaugural that this generation had a rendezvous with destiny."	Kennedy "borrowed" some of the respect he wanted by quoting two of America's most respected presidents.
The audience was concerned about Kennedy's wealth. He was a member of one of the nation's wealthiest families. Would he understand the problems of common people?	"I saw cases in West Virginia, here in the United States, where children took home parts of their school lunch in order to feed their families." "I am not satisfied when many of our teachers are inadequately paid . . . " "I am not satisfied until every American enjoys his full constitutional rights."	Kennedy's repeated use of examples of common people with common problems built Kennedy's identification with average people: teachers, the poor, and so on.
The 1950s had been a time of prosperity and growth. The Soviet Union launched Sputnik in 1957, which caused Americans to suspect that we were slipping, that we were no longer number one. Republicans had been in power for eight years. If voters concentrated on prosperity, Kennedy might lose the election.	"We discuss tonight domestic issues, but I would not want any implication to be given that this does not involve our struggle with Mr. Khrushchev [the leader of the Soviets] for survival." "I am not satisfied that the Soviet Union is turning out twice as many scientists and engineers as we are."	By understanding the fears that the Soviets were gaining on us, Kennedy was able to make people worry about the country's future. He was able to overcome the feeling that everything in America was fine and that people should automatically vote for the party that had been in power.

3. What do the audience members feel about the topic and speaker?

4. Why are these people together as a group?

You can answer these questions with four words: demographics, attitudes, knowledge, and situation. Considering these characteristics will help you become an effective speaker.

Demographics

How many students in your class have jobs? What is their average age? How many are female? Male? How many own portable CD players? How many listen to FM radio? How many see more than three movies a month?

The answers to these questions will help you know more about the average student in your class. Statistical information about groups of people is called **demographics.** Demographic data tells you about group characteristics, not individuals. From demographics, you can learn about these characteristics:

age	religion
gender	political background
occupation	ethnic or cultural background
educational background	social-economic status

You don't need to know about all these characteristics for every speech. However, the more you know about your audience, the easier it will be for you to prepare your speech. Knowing that 20 percent of your classmates know how to ride a horse won't help you prepare a speech on the Constitution. But if you're giving a speech about increasing recreational facilities for teens, that knowledge would be very useful. Some speakers should consider all demographic elements, however. Politicians often hire professional pollsters. Advertising people make demographics an important part of every project.

It's true that you'll never communicate with a group of people who are exactly alike. Still, most audience members have something in common. Otherwise, they wouldn't have joined together to hear your speech. Demographic information can help you decide how to use language, tone, arguments, examples, jokes—even how long you should talk.

Age

For many of your speeches, your audience will be your classmates. You probably know how your peers think. You know what kind of language appeals to them. You know what music they listen to. If your speech is about last summer's movies, you know what movies most of the group has seen. You probably know which were popular and which weren't.

Do you know as much about other age groups? What if you had to give a speech on teen movies to your classmates' parents? What changes would you have to make? Most of your audience wouldn't know very much about some of the movies. You'd have to summarize plots and explain why teens enjoyed the movies.

The age of the audience really makes a difference in how you prepare your speech. Age influences the amount of knowledge an audience has, as well as their attitudes, values, and interests. Stephen Joel Trachtenberg, the president of George Washington University, described how he chose his topic for a speech to a group of high-school students. He said to himself, "Look, Steve, these kids are *teenagers*. And one thing we know about teenagers is that they are given to questioning the values handed to them by adults." This thought helped Trachtenberg choose a topic that appealed to teens.

Gender

Gender is another word for classification according to sex. What percentage of the audience is male? What percentage is female? Today, very few topics are clearly men's or women's, but men and women still have different interests and attitudes. Women still play the major role in child care and housekeeping, whether they work outside the home or not. There still are more men than women in certain occupations. For the most part, however, speakers usually don't alter a speech just because of the gender of the audience. If there are any changes, they'll be minor.

Can you think of a topic that would force you to change your appeals because of the sex of your audience? How would you defend the law that says both men's and women's athletics must receive equal treatment in a public high school? In this case, the gender of your audience would affect your presentation. Women may be more sympathetic when they hear about sex discrimination, while men may be most concerned about the law's impact on men's sports. A mixed group will have multiple concerns. You have to take those differences into account as you plan your speech.

Don't assume, however, that you're supposed to say only what your audience wants to hear. You have to plan your appeals differently, not change your position. For instance, Elizabeth Cady Stanton was a tireless speaker on women's rights in the nineteenth century. In 1853, she was invited to speak before the New York State Legislature. Instead of her usual audience of women, she would be facing only men. Her conclusion shows how she structured her appeal to suit her audience:

> Would to God you could know the burning indignation that fills woman's soul when she turns over the pages of your statute books . . . "Do unto others as you would have others do unto you." This . . . is all we ask at your hands.

You can see that Stanton didn't change her beliefs at all. She only presented them differently to men than she would have to women.

Occupation

A person's occupation often influences his or her way of life, interests, and attitudes. For example, students who plan to go to college feel differently about tuition cutbacks than students who are going to get jobs after they graduate. The income level and social standing of a student's family also affect the student's interests and attitudes.

Politicians know they have to adapt their speeches to suit their audiences. During presidential primaries, candidates from a variety of backgrounds must campaign in many states for the votes of many different voters. Campaigners speak to farmers about farming, to textile workers about textiles, and to cattle breeders about cattle. That doesn't mean that the candidates are hypocrites. Farmers want to talk about farming, not about textiles. The candidate reads the audience and addresses them on the topics of concern to them.

Educational Background

For a minute or two, think about your classmates. Chances are, some students in your class have had geometry and others haven't. If you give a speech on how surveyors do their jobs, you'll have to decide how to handle geometry terms in your speech. In other words, the courses your classmates have taken determine what you can say and how you can say it.

Knowing the audience's educational background will help you avoid two big mistakes: talking down to an audience and talking over the audience's head. When a speaker talks down to an audience, the members of the audience think the speaker underestimates their intelligence. They won't be receptive to the speaker's message. When a speaker talks over the audience members' heads, they may feel the speaker is showing off. They may even feel the speaker is trying to make them feel ignorant. Understanding educational background helps the speaker decide upon the language and content of a speech.

Religious Background

Although religious beliefs are personal, you must consider them when you are reading an audience. Religious beliefs affect a person's views on topics such as divorce, war, drinking, and family. If you want to address these topics, you must consider your audience's religious beliefs. Most of all, you must avoid saying anything that might insult another person's religion.

Political Background

In the United States, there are two main political parties, Republicans and Democrats. If your topic is a political one, knowing your audience's political loyalties is essential. You also need to know the political positions of the two parties.

Knowing the political background of the audience includes knowing how they feel about specific issues. After all, not all Democrats or all Republicans agree.

Ethnic or Cultural Background

An **ethnic group** is a group of people who are tied together by religion, race, culture, or national origin. Demographics sometimes reveal an audience's ethnic or cultural identity. Some cities have large Polish, Italian, and Hispanic neighborhoods. Are there specific ethnic groups in your school?

How does this information affect how you prepare for a speech? You need to know the language, interests, and customs of your audience. Otherwise, you may build a speech that doesn't address the audience's concerns. You also must be sensitive to ethnic and cultural differences. Using common sense and courtesy, you can address an ethnic group without offending anyone.

President Kennedy provided a good example of a speech that used appeals directed at his audience's ethnic or cultural background. On 26 June 1963, Kennedy spoke in Berlin, West Germany. The Berlin Wall had gone up several years before. Kennedy's audience felt threatened by East Germany, and they were anxious to hear what Kennedy had to say. The famous conclusion to Kennedy's speech assured them of his determination to help them:

All free men, wherever they may live, are citizens of Berlin, and, therefore, as a free man, I take pride in the words "Ich bin ein Berliner [I am a Berliner]."

Speakers need to know the languages, interests, and customs of their audiences and must be sensitive to ethnic and cultural differences.

By ending his speech with a sentence in German, Kennedy assured his audience—in their own language—that he was committed to a free Berlin.

Social-Economic Background

Socioeconomic status is involved in many demographic categories. Sometimes you need to consider income and social groups as separate issues. Speakers who use this classification system believe that income and social group say a lot about audience attitudes and interests. The subgroups are numerous: blue-collar and white-collar; low-, middle-, and high-income; yuppies (young urban professionals); DINKs (double-income, no kids); and more.

Using Demography

You probably don't have access to a demographic chart of your speech class, but you probably don't need one, because you already know a lot about your classmates. Even when you speak to another class, you still know a great deal. But the further you go from your own age group and background, the more you'll need to study your audience's make-up.

Demographics are a statistical aid for a speaker, but they aren't a substitute for treating people as individuals. Don't treat your audience as a lump of statistics. Audiences who feel that you care for individuals will be far likelier to trust you. Use demographics to imagine an ideal audience so you can decide on effective speech strategies.

Knowledge

Demographics help you know what your audience already knows about a subject. An audience may have very little information about your subject. If this is true, you may need to inform the audience about the topic. If your audience already knows a lot about your topic, you'd only waste time talking about basic information.

Attitudes

Understanding demographics won't help you unless you understand attitudes. An **attitude** is a state of mind about something. It's the way someone feels or thinks about a person, a thing, an action, or an idea. Demographic studies try to find out about attitudes by gathering information about the audience's background.

Think of your own attitude toward something such as homework. Why do you hold this attitude? Is it because of your experience, age, and background? Does your attitude toward homework differ from semester to semester? Month to month? Week to week? A senior's attitude toward homework usually differs from a sophomore's. And students' attitudes certainly differ from teachers'. Knowing your audience's attitudes enables you to create an effective speech. Suppose you give a speech on Native American crafts to members of a craft club. They'd be more interested in the how-to of the craft itself than in the Native American lore and legend that accompanies it. If you give the same speech to the local historical society, however, it might not be well-received. To members of the historical society, Native American crafts aren't something to do; they're a way to learn about history. Think of the various attitudes you may encounter and how you might adjust your speech to take those attitudes into account.

An Agreeing Audience

Often, you'll have to address an audience that already agrees with you. Think of a basketball coach speaking to a school pep assembly. The students already know the coach, the team, the speech's purpose, and the time and place of the next game. So what's the coach going to talk about? It seems as if the speech makes little difference. Still, haven't you heard some pep speeches that were very inspirational and some that were disappointing? How can you adapt a speech to capture an agreeing audience?

First, you won't have to spend much time winning over the audience. You won't need a long introduction, and you won't have to provide background information. Your audience will listen and agree. You can concentrate on affirming what the audience knows and restating the audience's own beliefs. In this situation, your job is primarily to reinforce and inspire.

Second, be sure your speech touches all the bases. Since the audience already agrees with you, don't leave out information that the audience agrees with.

Third, state the purpose of your speech early, so the members of the audience can develop positive feelings early. If they know from the beginning of the speech that you agree with them, they'll become willing participants in the speech process.

Finally, express appreciation, gratitude, and admiration for the audience's attitude. After all, if the members of the audience already agree with you, that means they have thought about the topic and arrived at a reasonable conclusion.

On 14 November 1985, Ronald Reagan addressed an agreeing audience—the American people—on controlling nuclear weapons. Demographics told him that Americans favored arms control. In addition to touching all the bases, Reagan stated his purpose early and expressed his appreciation:

> My fellow Americans. Good evening. In thirty-six hours, I will be leaving for Geneva for the first meeting between an American President and a Soviet leader in six years. I know that you and the people of the world are looking forward to that meeting with great interest, so tonight I want to share with you my hopes and tell you why I am going to Geneva.
>
> Both Nancy and I are grateful for the chance you've given us to serve this nation and the trust you've placed in us. I know how deep the hope of peace is in her heart, as it is in the heart of every American and Russian mother.

A Disagreeing Audience

What can you do if your audience disagrees with you? From the beginning, you seem to be at a disadvantage. But there are some strategies that you can use to gain the attention and sympathies of a disagreeing audience.

Don't set your goals too high. You may not win over all—or even most—members of a disagreeing audience. Sometimes you should simply try to get them to think about what you've said or to question their own attitudes.

VOICES OF

ECONOMICS

"The Business of America Is Business"

Throughout the history of the United States, people have debated the role of business in our society. Should government control business? Can business accumulate too much power? Is business the most important part of the economy?

Beginning around the turn of the century, the debate became even more important. The "businessman" had largely replaced the explorer, the soldier, and the adventurer as the American hero. Certain businesses had grown so large and powerful that they were thought to control the government. Industries such as oil, steel, and railroads were known not only for their economic power, but also for the character of the individuals who ran them.

Theodore Roosevelt, Woodrow Wilson, and Calvin Coolidge entered into the debate on business as part of their campaigns for the presidency and as part of their governing in that office. Roosevelt was known as the "trustbuster" for his opposition to immensely powerful business. But like Coolidge, he too recognized the economic need of big business. Wilson came to the presidency from a background in education. Big business often mistrusted him. His policies toward business led to opposition from some businesspeople. When Wilson's term was over, American business was ready for a return to normalcy. Coolidge was thought to be a good President for business. "Silent Cal" was well-known for being brief and to the point, as his quotations on the next page reveal. All three Presidents helped shape the perceptions of the American people about big business during a time when it had become bigger than ever.

WORDS TO REMEMBER

Theodore Roosevelt

The biggest corporation, like the humblest private citizen, must be held in strict compliance with the will of the people.

Speech in Cincinnati, Ohio, 1902

I hold it to be our duty to see that the wage worker, the small producer, the ordinary consumer, shall get their fair share of the benefit of business prosperity. But it either is or ought to be evident to everyone that business has to prosper before anybody can get any benefit from it.

Address to the Ohio Constitutional Convention, 1 February 1912

Woodrow Wilson

We have witnessed in modern business the submergence of the individual within the organization, and yet the increase to an extraordinary degree of the power of the individual, of the individual who happens to control the organization. Most men are individuals no longer so far as their business, its activities or its moralities are concerned. They are not units but fractions.

Speech at Chattanooga, Tennessee, 31 August 1910

Business underlies everything in our national life, including our spiritual life. Witness the fact that in the Lord's Prayer, the first petition is for daily bread. No one can worship God or love his neighbor on an empty stomach.

Speech in New York City, 23 May 1912

Calvin Coolidge

Civilization and profits go hand in hand.

Speech in New York City, 27 November 1920

The business of America is business.

Speech before the Society of American Newspaper Editors, 17 January 1925

137

Find something that everyone *can* agree on. This is called establishing common ground. If you give a speech on later curfew hours to a group of parents who support the present curfew, how can you establish common ground? Maybe you could begin by saying, "Adolescence is a time when a person takes on more and more responsibility. That is what it means to be an adult." Since parents feel responsible for their children, and you are trying to be responsible, you have gotten the support of your audience. For this technique to work, the audience must perceive that you are sincere. Otherwise, the audience will feel manipulated and will lose trust in you.

You may want to wait until later in the speech to state your topic and point of view. By winning over the audience early with less controversial statements, you may get the message across. Too early a statement of topic and point of view can cause the audience to stop listening to you.

Speeches to a disagreeing audience must be carefully supported. Since the audience will disagree with many of your points, you must support your ideas with proof. While an agreeing audience supplies much of the proof, a disagreeing audience is likely to debate with you. If this happens, here is what you should do: (1) acknowledge the opposing point of view fairly; (2) state your own point of view; and (3) provide proof, support, or evidence of your point.

John Kennedy's campaign to become president gives a good example of a speaker addressing a disagreeing audience. In 1960, no Roman Catholic had ever been president. Kennedy, a Catholic, frequently was called upon to discuss his religion. In his most famous discussion of his religion and politics, Kennedy spoke before a group of ministers in Houston, Texas. His audience could be called disagreeing in that most members were Protestant ministers who had reservations about Kennedy's religion and how it might affect his role as president. Here is part of his introduction:

> I am grateful for your generous invitation to state my views.
>
> While the so-called religious issue is necessarily and properly the chief topic here tonight, I want to emphasize from the outset that I believe that we have far more critical issues in the 1960 election: the spread of Communist influence, until it now festers only ninety miles off the coast of Florida—the humiliating treatment of our President and Vice President by those who no longer respect our power—the hungry children I saw in West Virginia, the old people who cannot pay their doctor's bills, the families forced to give up their farms—an America with too many slums, with too few schools, and too late to the moon and outer space.

> These are the real issues which should decide this campaign. And they are not religious issues—for war and hunger and ignorance and despair know no religious barrier.

Note that Kennedy began by building common ground with his audience. He advanced a series of issues that all people could agree with: U.S. security, hungry children, health care, poverty, and so on. At the same time, Kennedy stressed the importance of these issues to diminish the importance of the religious issue. He also used his first sentence to thank his audience for the opportunity to express his views. Kennedy delayed asking for the group's unbiased judgment of his try for the presidency until halfway through the speech.

An Apathetic Audience

What can you do if your audience is apathetic? **Apathy** is simply an "I don't care" attitude. An apathetic audience doesn't seem interested in your topic. There are techniques to help you deal with this sort of audience.

Since first impressions are very important, develop a strong, interest-grabbing introduction. (Chapter 14 gives you some ideas on how to do this.)

You can show members of an apathetic audience how the topic affects them. Suppose you are giving a report on radar to a physics class. You might begin by saying, "Without the subject of my speech, you might not know how to dress for school tomorrow, you might never have gotten a speeding ticket, or you might have died in a plane crash." In one sentence, you have grabbed the audience's attention and shown how your topic affects everyone's life. Do you see how this kind of opening can overcome apathy and at least get your audience to listen to you?

To keep the attention of an apathetic audience, build a speech full of high-interest examples, stories, and statistics. So, even though your purpose may be to explain how radar works, you may want to include other interest-building information. For example, you could point out that radar operates in the same way as the homing system of a bat. While this doesn't explain how radar works, it is an interest-builder.

Apathetic audiences need to be entertained. Humor is one way to build and keep interest. So are stories related to the topic. One well-prepared story about someone's attempt to teach manners to a puppy can introduce some humor into a speech on dog training and win over the most apathetic listener.

Speakers at speech contests frequently face an apathetic audience. Contest judges don't know what topics they'll hear about. That means they aren't an agreeing or a disagreeing audience. This speech beginning, delivered by Gary Lillian of Shawnee Mission West High School, was judged the best in the nation a few years ago. Lillian worked at getting an apathetic audience interested in his topic: striking a balance between the needs for privacy and community:

> Let us begin by taking some time to compile a list. At the top of that list imagine, if you will, the name of your doctor . . . and right beside that, place the name of his or her spouse . . .
>
> If you have school age children, select one of them and picture the name of the child's teacher right below your doctor's name. If the teacher has any children, then think of their names also, and their ages if you remember them. . . .
>
> Now think of the place that you most often go to purchase groceries, and at the bottom of the list put the grocer's name and where he or she lives. . . .
>
> Is that list just a little vague? Perhaps a bit more than vague? That is the case for the majority of us who have lost touch with the other members of our community.

Even if Lillian's audience didn't care about the topic, chances are he won them over. He built credibility with good intentions. He showed the audience that the topic was about them. Building a mental list got the audience involved with seeing the people he was talking about.

Understanding Motive

The key to dealing with audience attitudes is understanding audience motives. A **motive** is a reason for acting or thinking a certain way. Why are the members of the audience angry? Why are they apathetic? Eager? Suspicious? If you know why an audience feels a certain way, you can create a speech that addresses the audience's needs. For example, if you know the audience is apathetic, you know that you must give a speech that creates interest. But if you know *why* the audience doesn't care, you can create a speech specifically for them.

Is the audience apathetic because they've heard many speeches on the same subject? If so, find a new angle for the speech. Find fresh information. Admit that others have spoken on the topic, but add that you have important new insights.

Is the audience apathetic because they don't think the speech is important? Demonstrate the importance of the subject to give the audience a reason to listen.

Are the audience members apathetic because they've listened to many speeches in a row? Contrast your speech with previous ones. Use visual aids or demonstrations. Stand in a different place than previous speakers. Establish a different tone.

Motive is something that demographics alone can't tell you. Being thoughtful involves far more than reading statistics. It's understanding why the audience feels as it does and constructing a speech with that audience in mind.

The Speaking Situation

To create an effective speech, view the audience as part of the speaking situation. Knowing why people have come to hear you speak is part of reading an audience. These questions will help you anticipate audience feedback:

1. What is the occasion of the speech?
2. What do the audience members have in common?
3. Where is the speech taking place?
4. How long should the speech be?
5. What comes before and after the speech?

If you combine answers to these questions with demographic data and attitude analysis, your speech will meet the audience's needs and interests.

Occasion

Speakers need to know why they're giving a speech, because the occasion affects the tone and content of a speech. Is the occasion a school assembly? The regular meeting of a club? Part of a holiday celebration? A business meeting? If your speech is part of a special event, such as a Fourth of July celebration, the subject and tone must fit the event. A speech describing Americans' commitment to freedom would be more appropriate than one about the growth of the American auto industry.

Common Interests

Audiences are composed of individuals, but they often share a reason for listening to your speech. If you're speaking to an organization, everyone in the audience is there because he or she is a member. Structure your speech to appeal to the loyalty the audience

A speaker who speaks at an organizational meeting generally faces an audience that has ties to that organization. Such a speaker should structure his or her speech to appeal to those common interests.

has to the organization. What would a meeting of the Humane Society expect a speaker to talk about? What should you have as the topic for a speech to a Drama Club?

When a famous speaker is featured at an assembly or gathering, he or she can assume that the audience chose to attend. When students attend a school assembly, however, they often have to be there. How does your attitude toward a required assembly or meeting compare to your attitude toward a concert or ball game? If you're facing an involuntary audience, you must plan a speech that will get the audience's attention—and keep it.

Location

Physical surroundings often influence how you prepare, practice, and deliver a speech. Knowing beforehand where you'll give your speech gives you a chance to create a speech that suits the place. A speech in a classroom in front of twenty-five people will be less formal than one given in an auditorium seating two thousand. Perhaps you would develop an intimate, low-key talk for a small group in a small conference room and a formal, forceful speech for a larger group in a large hall.

Knowing the location can also help you head off trouble. If you're giving a speech outdoors, expect noise and distractions from such things as passing airplanes and wind. You'll have to speak louder—you may even have to stop and wait for a moment. If the audience must stand during your speech, keep it short. If the speech is at a banquet, know when to begin so people won't have to listen and eat at the same time.

Length of Speech

Several factors determine the length of your speech. Are you the only speaker or one of several? Few audiences can listen to several long speeches in a row. If you're the featured speaker in a program, prepare a speech that's worthy of the honor. If your audience is uncomfortable due to such things as temperature, crowd size, or lack of a break, shorten your remarks.

Always ask the person who invited you to speak for a time estimate. Usually he or she knows how long the entire program will be and what the group expects. Then, be sure to stay within the limits set for you. If you speak too long, you may lose the audience's interest. You could even upset the timetable for the rest of the program.

In class, your teacher will give time limits, usually a maximum and a minimum. Observe them. The minimums are there to encourage you to develop the topic. The maximums are there to keep the class moving and to prevent anyone from talking too long.

Before and after Your Speech

It's good to know as much as possible about the events that come before your speech. Then you can refer to other events and speakers in your speech. You and other speakers may be able to coordinate your material so you don't repeat information. Are you going to follow a musical presentation or are you the first or last speaker? Adjust your speech accordingly.

When your speech is completed, be prepared for whatever follows. Will you answer questions from the audience? Will you listen to other speakers? Will you take part in a ceremony? Knowing these things in advance will reduce your fears about speaking in an unfamiliar situation.

Speakers must read an audience and a situation before and during speaking. Think of your audience demographically. Consider age, gender, occupation, educational background, religion, political background, ethnic or cultural background, and social-economic status. Try to understand common elements in the audience's attitudes. Above all, understand why the members of the audience hold certain attitudes.

Know the situation in which you will speak. Know the audience's reasons for being together, their expectations, the occasion, time restrictions, and the events that precede and follow your speech. Take care to prepare a speech that fits the situation.

◆ *Check Your Understanding*

1. What are demographics? How can you use demographics to help you read your audience as you prepare your speech?

2. List five important demographic characteristics of an audience, and suggest ways each might affect the topic you select or how you develop it.

3. Give three suggestions to a speaker who is going to talk to an agreeing audience.

4. Give three suggestions to a speaker who's going to talk to a disagreeing audience.

5. Give three suggestions for a speaker who's going to talk to an apathetic audience.

6. What are the five questions you should consider to understand the speaking situation?

◆ *Apply Your Understanding*

1. List ten topics that teenagers would find interesting and would agree with. List ten they would disagree with. List ten others that teens would be apathetic about. Explain why the audience would feel as they would; use terms from the chapter.

2. Use an almanac to develop a demographic report on your state. What is the average age of the residents? How many people are in your age range? Your parents'? What is the gender breakdown? What are the most prominent occupations? What are the major religious groups? What is the ethnic or cultural make-up? What is the socioeconomic breakdown?

◆ *Thinking Critically about Public Speaking*

1. One of the best ways to practice reading an audience is to prepare a speech for an audience you are not used to. Divide into groups and brainstorm the following questions: How would you develop a speech on current books (or music) for first-graders? Junior-high students? High-school seniors? A business club? A group of teachers? A church group?

2. Find a product (jeans, foods, computers, movies, and so on) that is sold to people of different ages. Find advertisements that are designed for the different age groups. Explain how the advertiser sees the potential buyers, based on the choices made by the advertiser.

◆ *Speak Out!*

Select an upcoming holiday. Prepare a two- to three-minute speech that relates to the holiday. Focus your preparation on being original and interesting without losing sight of the demands of the occasion. Discuss with your teacher what kind of audience you are preparing for: Are they your age; adults; senior citizens; children? When you give your speech, tell your class what kind of audience you have prepared for. After the speech, discuss the methods you chose and how effective they might have been with your chosen audience.

◆ *Speech Challenge*

This assignment requires you and your classmates to cooperate. For this speech challenge, select a controversial topic regarding school. Develop your speech for a disagreeing audience. (If your topic would be opposed by a group of students, plan your speech for those students. If your topic would be opposed by faculty members, plan your speech for them. If your topic would be opposed by the school board, plan for them.) When you give your speech, your classmates will play the role of the audience for whom you have planned. Allow them to interrupt you with questions or to challenge your ideas. They shouldn't heckle, but they should raise issues and confront you with their position. Your job will be to keep your poise, maintain your patience, respond to their challenges, and stay with your speech. Your teacher will set your time limits and referee, if needed.

CHAPTER

·9·

Key Terms

Categorical terms

Controlling purpose

Hidden agenda

Narrowing a topic

Occasion

Purpose statement

Speech to entertain

Speech to inform

Speech to persuade

Thesis statement

Chapter Objectives

After studying this chapter, you will be able to:

1. Identify the three basic purposes of public speaking.
2. Define and explain the role of *hidden agenda* in public address.
3. Contrast a thesis statement and a purpose statement.
4. Identify the characteristics of a good thesis statement.
5. Narrow a broad topic to a manageable speech topic.
6. Analyze audience and occasion to identify appropriate topics for public speaking.

Building a Topic

The Link between Purpose and Topic

Whenever you prepare a speech for any group, you must have a specific idea about your topic and purpose. Selecting your topic and identifying your purpose are closely related activities. If you don't know what you want to talk about, you can't figure out why you're speaking. On the other hand, if you don't understand why you're speaking, you'll have a hard time choosing a topic that suits your audience and occasion.

Speech purpose and topic selection depend on each other. Speakers don't simply *select* an idea—they *build* an idea by choosing a speech purpose, selecting a subject, and narrowing it to a suitable speech topic. That's why speech purposes and topic selection are combined in this chapter.

Speech Purposes

There's a saying, "If you don't know where you're going, you'll probably get somewhere else." In other words, to succeed, you have to know what your goals are. In this class, you need to know the purpose of a speech so you can set a goal for it.

The Speech to Entertain

A speech that simply tries to gain and keep the audience's attention is a **speech to entertain.** This speech doesn't necessarily present new information to the audience, and the speaker doesn't necessarily expect the audience's attitudes to change. Instead, the speaker wants the listeners to have a good time and to be amused or interested by the speech. If people in the audience enjoy themselves, the speech is a success. This is harder to achieve than it sounds. Think about how difficult it is to entertain your classmates during the last class on a Friday.

The most common kind of entertaining speech is a humorous speech. This type of speech is like any other except that its contents are chosen because they're funny. A humorous speech isn't a comedy routine; it's a *speech* that's humorous. Filled with colorful stories and jokes, humorous speeches are popular. Audiences enjoy a light, amusing speech that requires little more than listening and laughing.

Often, a humorous speech is given as an after-dinner speech, when the audience is in the mood to be entertained. Another type of humorous speech is the roast which is a collection of ironic remarks about a guest of honor, designed only to make people laugh. Everyone knows roasts aren't serious.

However, a speech to entertain isn't always humorous. Some are frightening or unusual—and also very entertaining. A lecture on a trip, while informative, is meant primarily to entertain. People attend such talks for recreation.

The Speech to Inform

You should be familiar with the **speech to inform.** By now you've probably heard many classroom lectures, which are a type of informative speech. Informative speeches are also important outside school. Nature programs on TV are informative speeches. Many business meetings are really a series of informative speeches.

In an informative speech, the audience learns about a new subject or hears new information about a familiar subject. Whatever you present should be new to your audience. Suppose you were to give an informative speech on stars to a group of astronomers and then to a student science club. How would the speeches differ? The astronomers would expect you to talk about the most recent research in astronomy. The science club, however, wouldn't expect—or understand—the information you gave the astronomers. Your speech would be much more general.

Informative speeches are quite varied, from lectures in school to nature talks at the beach. In informative speeches, the audience learns something new.

The Speech to Persuade

A speech that's intended to change the audience's attitudes or behavior is a **speech to persuade.** This type of speech is probably the most challenging kind of speech because it often is about controversial subjects that are important to both speaker and audience.

When you try to convince your parents, teacher, or employer to let you do something, you're giving an informal persuasive speech. Salespeople give many formal persuasive speeches in order to convince their audiences to buy a product.

Political speakers give the kinds of speeches that most people think of when they hear the word *persuasion.* Such speeches often promote a specific candidate. Sometimes, the goal is to persuade the public about issues that are controversial and emotional. Because of their length and importance, these speeches usually require more thought and preparation than others.

Overlapping Purposes

While people divide speech purposes into entertaining, informing, and persuading, it's unusual for a speech to fill only one purpose. Usually, all three purposes exist in a speech, although only one is the most important. The primary purpose of a speech is called the **controlling purpose.**

Suppose you want to persuade an audience to support a new community basketball program. You'll probably want to be entertaining enough that the audience will pay attention. In addition, you'll have to inform the audience about the subject. Otherwise, the

Figure 9.1
Ladder of Speech
Purpose

Ladder of Speech Purpose

Think of the speech purposes
in order. Entertainment is often
needed to get information
across. New information is
often necessary to persuade
an audience.

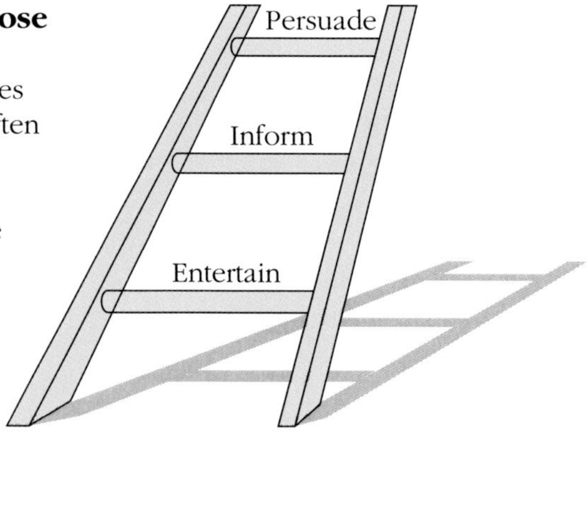

audience might not understand the importance of your proposal. But your primary purpose isn't to entertain or to inform. You want your audience to support the new program. The purpose of the entertainment and the information is to help persuade the audience.

The Hidden Agenda

Sometimes when you listen to a speech, you realize that its purpose isn't all that obvious. Speakers don't always identify their purposes clearly. Perhaps you've heard about "parties" that are supposedly given for entertainment. When the guests show up, they learn that the real reason for the "party" is to persuade them to join a group or to buy a product. When the purpose of a speech is intentionally unstated or hidden behind another purpose, the speech has a **hidden agenda.**

Sometimes the hidden agenda is to inform. This is especially true of speeches given to children. Even children's television shows often disguise informational programs as entertainment.

People hide their speech purposes for many reasons, but a hidden agenda gives rise to several problems. Your purpose may be so well hidden that the audience never understands what you are truly saying. If the members of the audience do perceive your hidden purpose, they may disregard it because you didn't emphasize it. Or—worst of all—they may feel you're trying to trick them and become angry.

Topic Selection

Selecting a purpose goes hand in hand with selecting a topic. Finding the right topic is one of the most important skills in successful public speaking. To find a topic, consider your own needs, the audience's needs, and the demands of the situation.

Suiting Yourself

Unless you're interested in your topic, your audience won't be. So you need to think about what you want to talk about. Usually, when a person is invited to give a speech, he or she knows something about the topic. A florist would expect to be asked to give a speech on flower arranging, for example, not on electrical repair.

Selecting a Speech Topic

When you need to select a speech topic, consider these guidelines:

Suiting Yourself

1. Are you interested in the topic?

2. Do you already have information through experience or study?

3. If you need further information, do you have the time and resources to find it?

4. Will you enjoy talking about this topic?

5. Are there other topics that suit your audience and occasion that you'd rather speak on?

6. Does the topic let you entertain, inform, or persuade? Which purpose do you want to accomplish?

Suiting Your Audience

1. Will the audience be interested in your topic?

2. Can you interest the audience in your topic?

3. Does the audience need to know about your topic?

4. Will your topic offend some members of your audience?

5. What does the audience already know about your topic?

6. Will this topic be fresh and original, or is it one the audience is tired of hearing about?

7. Will the audience expect to be entertained, informed, or persuaded? Does the topic allow you to meet these expectations?

Suiting the Occasion

1. Does the occasion have a special purpose?

2. Do the members of the audience have a special purpose for meeting together?

3. Does your topic fit the audience's expectations of what's appropriate for the occasion?

4. Are you comfortable speaking on this occasion?

5. Does the occasion require a serious tone or a light tone?

6. Does the occasion require a speech to entertain, to inform, or to persuade? Does the topic fit that speech purpose?

7. Can you give the speech in the time limit allotted?

Interest in a topic isn't enough, however. You must also be—or become—thoroughly informed about the topic. Why would anyone speak on an unfamiliar topic unless required to? Why would an audience listen to someone who didn't know anything about a topic? Would you listen to a speaker tell you how to administer CPR (cardiopulmonary resuscitation) if he or she had never had a CPR course? Probably not.

Remember, the effect you have on the audience is based on the audience's perception of your expertise, good intentions, and trustworthiness. Choose a topic that shows off your best points.

Suiting Your Audience

Whether you choose your topic or it's assigned to you, you must consider audience needs. As you narrow a topic, determine what the audience wants or needs to hear, using audience analysis skills from Chapter 8.

For classroom speeches, choose topics that you find interesting. Since your classmates are like you in many ways, they should be interested in those topics, too. But don't be afraid to talk about subjects your classmates know little about. After all, you can almost always make a topic interesting.

Along with audience interests, consider the group's knowledge of the topic. People usually listen to speeches to hear new information, so don't bore an audience with a speech they've heard many times before. For example, everyone has studied World War II, but how many people have heard a detailed description of the Battle of the Bulge? Even if an audience has general knowledge of your topic, you can narrow it to present new or more detailed information that will be unfamiliar to the audience.

Suiting the Occasion

An **occasion** is a specific event within the situation. The topic must suit the occasion. If you're giving a speech to the student council, why talk about your favorite sports team? If the occasion celebrates Thanksgiving, why talk about your hobbies? Common sense should help you select a topic that suits the occasion. For help in this process, see Chapter 8.

Expressing Your Purpose

The decision you make about your purpose is for yourself—it helps you design your speech. When you give your speech, you'll want to make your purpose clear to your audience. The two tasks are not the same. Purpose statements are written for the speaker's use. Thesis statements are written for the audience.

Purpose Statement

The **purpose statement** controls your speech preparation and narrows your topic. A good purpose statement has two important characteristics. It is phrased in terms of the audience, and it limits the speech by limiting the subject.

When you give your speech, how do you want the audience to react? What do you want them to feel? To think? To do? If you don't know what you want from the audience, you won't know what to say or how to say it. These examples show how to word a purpose statement:

> The purpose of this speech is to give a humorous review of the swimming season for team members and fans. (entertain)

> The purpose of this speech is to update the students on recent changes in school rules and policies. (inform)

> The purpose of this speech is to convince the junior class that selling calendars is a good way to raise money for the prom. (persuade)

Each purpose statement specifies the *audience* (swim team members and fans, students, the junior class), the *subject* (the swim season, the new school rules, selling calendars), and the desired *result* (humorous review, update, convince). In other words, each purpose statement clarifies the relationship between the audience and the subject by identifying the speaker's purpose.

When you prepare a speech, you must decide what you will and will not include—you must limit your subject. Without an idea of your purpose, you can't make good decisions. Suppose you're going to give an informative speech on cars to a drivers' education class. A purpose statement that's too broad is useless:

Broad Statement (Poor)
I'm going to tell the class about cars.

This statement doesn't limit the subject or help you prepare. Will you talk about gas mileage? Car care? Racing? All of these things? If you're unsure of the speech purpose, imagine the audience's confusion. An audience listening to a speech that includes so many subjects will begin to wonder what the point is. They'll question why they're listening. They may stop listening altogether.

A good purpose statement narrows the subject:

Narrow Statement (Better)
The purpose of this speech is to inform student drivers that simple car maintenance done at home can save money.

Now the speaker can make wise decisions. If gas mileage is related to home maintenance, it can be included in your speech. You won't discuss racing at all. It's easy to prepare a speech based on this purpose statement. You know exactly what to talk about and why.

Thesis Statement

Since the purpose statement would sound awkward in the speech, you must convert it to a thesis statement. A **thesis statement** is simply your point of view about the topic reduced to a single sentence. A thesis narrows your speech topic and states your position precisely so the audience knows what you plan to talk about. Note the differences between the purpose statement and the thesis statement.

Purpose Statement
The purpose of this speech is to convince the junior class that selling calendars is a good way to raise money for prom.

Thesis Statement
The junior class should sell calendars to raise prom money because calendars return high profits without a big investment of time and money.

A thesis statement is the one that summarizes the speaker's position. It is necessary for three reasons. First, the audience expects a thesis early in the speech. If the thesis is missing, you don't meet the audience's expectations.

Second, a thesis helps the audience follow your ideas. If you don't state your position early in the speech, some of your points might not make sense to the members of your audience. By preparing them, you help them listen. You let them know early to listen critically, to listen for information, or to follow some other listening strategy.

Third, a thesis shapes your audience's expectations. If your thesis is "Doing simple auto maintenance at home can save you money," your audience won't expect you to talk about the recent auto show or the Indianapolis 500.

Writing a Good Thesis

You can write a good thesis if you remember its four necessary qualities. It generates interest, it is precise, it is concise, and it doesn't contain categorical terms.

Generating Interest

When audience members hear your thesis, they should say, "Why do you think that?" "How do you know?" "What's your proof?" If the reaction is "So what," the thesis doesn't generate interest.

Dull Thesis
You can learn a lot from looking at people's trash.

Interesting Thesis
"Garbagology," the close examination of trash, is a new means of learning about the lives of people, both past and present.

Why is the second thesis more interesting? It uses a novel word—*garbagology*. It accurately describes the subject: close examination of trash, rather than simply looking at trash. It raises an interesting issue: How does trash tell us about the past? Placing a good thesis early in a speech helps build audience interest.

Being Precise

A good thesis uses exact words. In the example above, the dull thesis says "you learn a lot." The better thesis is more exact, saying you'll learn "about the lives of people, both past and present."

Imprecise
Taking pictures of people is hard.

Precise
Because capturing a person's character on film is so difficult, portrait photography requires a great deal of training.

The more precise statement tells the audience what you're going to talk about. It shows why taking pictures of people is hard. It tells the audience that you'll talk about a portrait photographer's training. Using the term *portrait photographer* tells the audience that you aren't going to talk about just taking snapshots.

Being Concise

A thesis statement doesn't contain any supporting material. Avoid beginning your thesis with *I believe* or *in my opinion*. If you say it, the audience will assume you believe it:

Wordy
In my opinion some of the television shows that young children watch, like cartoons on Saturday morning from 8:00 in the morning until noon, aren't nearly as good as the cartoons we used to watch when we were kids and would get up real early and turn on the TV and settle down with a bowl of crunchy cereal to watch Bugs Bunny and Popeye.

Concise
Current Saturday morning cartoons simply aren't as imaginative as the cartoons we watched when we were children.

The first example has some good elements: the examples, the colorful language. But they don't belong in a thesis statement. The second thesis states the speaker's position briefly. Examples and colorful language belong later in the speech.

No Categorical Terms

Categorical terms are words that don't allow exceptions—words such as *all, never,* and *none.* Terms such as these aren't very useful in a thesis. They make it more difficult to support. Use qualified terms instead:

Categorical
No one should ever learn to drive from a friend or relative.

Narrowing a Topic

If you aren't sure about how to develop your speech, this list of questions may help narrow your topic:

1. What is it? Define the subject.

2. What examples of (the subject) are there? (Be as specific as possible.)

3. Of these examples, which are most interesting? Most unusual? Most typical? Most controversial? Why?

4. What are the subject's parts or features? Can the subject be broken down into parts, groups, or other constituents?

5. Of the parts or features, which is most important? Most interesting? Most controversial? Why?

6. How is the subject like other things?

   A. Figurative similarities? (similes and metaphors)

   B. Literal similarities? (comparisons and analogies)

7. How is the subject different from other things in important ways?

   A. How is it different from items in 6A?

   B. How is it different from items in 6B?

   C. How is it different from items previously unlisted?

8. What is the nature of the subject?

   A. Is it a process, a series of stages or steps that yield a product?

   B. Is it the product of a series of stages or steps?

   C. Is it one of a series of stages or steps?

9. What causes the subject?

10. What are the results or consequences of the subject?

11. What have others said about the subject?

12. Does investigation into the subject reveal a need for a change? If so, why is a change needed?

13. What changes might solve problems identified in #12?

Qualified
Taking driving lessons from a qualified instructor is almost always better than trying to learn from a friend or relative.

The first thesis allows no exceptions, and someone in the audience can always think of an exception to a categorical thesis. The second one is better, because it allows for a reasonable exception.

Narrowing Your Topic

One of the biggest mistakes you can make is to fail to narrow a broad general topic. **Narrowing a topic** is a way to make the topic more manageable. Could someone give a ten-minute speech on World War II? Or a five-minute speech on scuba diving? Narrowing a topic allows you to address an aspect of the topic in depth. A general topic doesn't allow in-depth treatment.

Often, your common sense will help you narrow your topic. If you want to speak on monsters and other mysterious creatures, you know you can't talk about all of them in five minutes. Common sense tells you to limit this general topic to a narrow one: the Loch Ness monster, Bigfoot, or the Abominable Snowman. Most common sense narrowing is based on the type of development used in the speech. See the Spotlight on Speaking box on page 160.

When you select a type of development, you have taken the first step toward narrowing. For example, if you decide to compare the Loch Ness monster to legendary sea serpents, you've narrowed the topic. You won't talk about Bigfoot or other legendary land creatures. If you decide to inform your audience about the possible truth of these legends, you'll concentrate on the legends' believability.

| SPEAKING ABOUT SPEAKING | # How Methods of Development Narrow the Topic |

DESCRIPTION—detailed physical characteristics of a subject
Topic: Solar-powered cars
Narrowed Topic: What will the cars of the future look like?
Purpose Statement: The purpose of this speech is to inform the auto mechanics class about coming changes in car design as a result of new technology.
Thesis Statement: Because scientists are developing solar power to power cars of the future, the car you drive in twenty years may look like a science fiction writer's dream.

NARRATION—an account of some activity in story form
Topic: The Alamo
Narrowed Topic: The last days of the soldiers at the Alamo
Purpose Statement: The purpose of this speech is to persuade the history club that the Battle of the Alamo was one of our country's greatest examples of bravery.
Thesis Statement: The final days of the Battle of the Alamo provide many examples of inspiring heroism.

COMPARISON/CONTRAST—significant similarities and differences
Topic: Computers
Narrowed Topic: The differences between supercomputers and regular computers
Purpose Statement: The purpose of this speech is to inform the computer science class about the great progress that has taken place in building advanced computers.
Thesis Statement: America's new supercomputers are thousands of times more complex, more useful, and more amazing than the computers of just a few years ago.

DEFINITION—the meaning of a term or terms
Topic: Search and seizure
Narrowed Topic: The difficulty of defining *probable cause* in cases of police search and seizure
Purpose Statement: The purpose of this speech is to persuade the class that laws controlling police actions should be made clearer.
Thesis Statement: Every time the police investigate a crime, they are hindered by the cloudy definition of *probable cause,* a definition that should be clarified.

PROCESS ANALYSIS—the importance of the steps leading to a product
Topic: Hurricanes
Narrowed Topic: Preparing for a hurricane
Purpose Statement: The purpose of this speech is to inform the class of how people in the states on the Gulf of Mexico work together to survive a hurricane.
Thesis Statement: When hurricane forecasts come in, everyone in the community pulls together to protect lives and property in a process that is a yearly ritual.

CAUSE AND EFFECT—the relationship between cause and effect
Topic: Aquariums
Narrowed Topic: The causes of fish diseases in home aquariums
Purpose Statement: The purpose of this speech is to inform aquarium owners of the causes of fish diseases.
Thesis Statement: Since you control the environment of your fish, you should be aware of the typical causes of fish diseases in home aquariums.

CLASSIFICATION—dividing a subject into groups or categories
Topic: Diets
Narrowed Topic: Types of harmful diets
Purpose Statement: The purpose of this speech is to persuade the foods class that many diets can be harmful.
Thesis Statement: Harmful weight-loss diets come in three types: diets that supply too little nutrition, diets that don't provide a variety of nutrition, and diets that depend on drugs to reduce appetites.

You will probably want to use more than one type of development in your speech. For example, a speech developed primarily through description can include comparison-contrast. A speech developed primarily through narration may include description and definition. We will discuss speech development more in Chapter 12. The point to remember here is that selecting a primary type of development can help narrow your speech topic.

Chapter 9 Summary

There are three kinds of speech purposes: to entertain, to inform, and to persuade. Some speeches employ more than one purpose. A speech to entertain doesn't present new information or attempt to change people's minds. Its only intent is to entertain. A speech to inform presents new information. The type of information included depends on how much the audience already knows. A speech to persuade attempts to change the audience's ideas or behavior. Although you may use more than one purpose in a speech, the controlling purpose controls the overall development of the speech. If a speech has a hidden agenda, its stated purpose masks the controlling purpose.

A speaker writes a purpose statement for his or her own use. A good purpose statement limits the topic, specifies the audience, and sets out the desired result. A narrowed topic can be discussed within the time allowed for the speech. The thesis statement tells the audience what you are going to talk about. A well-written thesis generates interest, is precise, concise, and contains no categorical terms.

It's easier to give an interesting speech if the topic suits you and you are informed about it. A topic suits the audience if it meets the audience's needs. A topic suits the occasion if the speaker considers the occasion as part of the speech's situation.

◆ Check Your Understanding

1. List the three basic speech purposes.

2. Define and give an example of *hidden agenda*.

3. Explain the difference between a purpose statement and a thesis statement.

4. List the four qualities of a good thesis statement.

5. Explain the advantage of a narrow topic over a broad topic.

6. Explain why analyzing your audience is important to good topic selection.

◆ Apply Your Understanding

1. Select one of the following topics and write three different purpose statements for it—one for a speech to entertain, one for a speech to inform, and one for a speech to persuade. Remember, your topic must be narrower than the ones listed here:

sports	clothes	teen jobs	hobbies	teen stress
friends	videos	pets	homework	driving

2. Take the purpose statements written for the previous question and turn them into thesis statements.

3. Select the best topics for speeches before the groups listed below. Defend your selections in class. If there is no suitable topic, write your own.

a club for retired women

a class on safety

a group of small business owners

a local community service group

a group of war veterans

a group of tourists to your area

4. In small groups, brainstorm topics that would be appropriate for your class speeches. Keep a list of all suggested topics. Compile the group lists to make a class list. Evaluate each topic in terms of suitability to a classroom audience and educational setting.

◆ *Thinking Critically about Public Speaking*

1. Find a sample speech in this text, a speech anthology, or *Vital Speeches*. Evaluate the speaker's topic selection in relationship to audience and occasion.

2. Tape a local news broadcast. After viewing some of the news, weather, and sports, determine how the show's producers and journalists make sure the show is entertaining as well as informative. Discuss if the entertainment qualities of the show interfere with the informational qualities.

◆ *Speak Out!*

Prepare a three- to four-minute speech on a hobby or interest. The goal of the speech should be to interest (entertain) your audience.

◆ *Speech Challenge*

Speakers who are authorities in their fields are often faced with a very difficult task: they have to give a brief speech on a topic that they know a great deal about. Select a topic that you are an "authority" on. It could be anything from your basketball team's offense to rap. Prepare a short speech (three to four minutes). Your topic should be narrowed sufficiently to allow you to develop it in the brief time you have. For example, rather than talk about a team's offense, talk about how to set a screen.

163

Key Terms

Dynamism

Extemporaneous
    delivery

Fluency

Impromptu delivery

Manuscript delivery

Memorized delivery

Teleprompter

Transition

Chapter Objectives

After studying this chapter, you should be able to:

1. Identify and explain the four guidelines for effective delivery.

2. Identify and explain the four formats of speech delivery.

3. Explain the advantages and disadvantages of the four delivery formats.

4. Prepare appropriate notes for each method of delivery.

5. Employ effective practice techniques for each type of delivery.

6. Explain strategies for answering questions that might arise from an audience at the conclusion of a speech.

Delivery
Techniques

Guidelines for Effective Delivery

Good public speakers are made, not born. Very few speakers can give a stirring speech without preparation and practice. By studying public speaking techniques, you may not become a famous speaker. However, you will be able to get your message across clearly and completely.

So far, you've examined many elements involved in writing a speech. You've also studied the verbal and nonverbal elements of effective delivery. Now, you need to learn how to bring them all together. Essentially, there are four guidelines to follow in order to deliver a speech effectively.

Be Natural

Good speakers let their unique personalities shine through. They don't try to imitate other speakers. As you develop a speech, your interests and attitudes shape its content. As you deliver a speech, you'll communicate those same interests and attitudes to the audience through your verbal and nonverbal delivery. Because it isn't as natural to express yourself through public speaking as through conversation, you must be well-prepared. Preparation gives you the confidence that lets you be yourself.

Be Lively

No one wants to listen to a dull speaker. That doesn't mean you have to tell dozens of jokes or use gimmicks to hold an audience's attention. It does mean that your delivery must express your interest and enthusiasm for your topic and your audience. A speaker who has an energetic, lively, active, or assertive style is said to possess **dynamism.** Research has shown that dynamism is one element that establishes a speaker's **credibility**—the audience's willingness to trust the speaker's honesty. Lively delivery can help build the audience's perception of the speaker's credibility.

Be Appropriate

Good delivery is appropriate for the situation, the purpose, and the audience. A speaker presenting a tribute to someone who died would be expected to create a solemn, respectful mood through vocal techniques, posture, and facial expressions, as well as through the words selected. Of the four formats of delivery discussed in this chapter, some are more appropriate for certain situations than for others.

Pair Delivery and Message

Good delivery gives meaning to a speaker's message. Through appropriate vocal and nonverbal techniques, you can emphasize ideas or provide pauses that allow the audience to reflect on what has been said. For instance, if you read a somber quotation in a quiet and serious tone, you add to the meaning of the quotation. Likewise, using a gesture to indicate an object's size adds clarity to a description.

Some speakers believe delivery is so important that they don't allow their speeches to be printed after they give them. They believe that some part of their message is lost when their speeches are read and not heard. These people understand the relationship between content and delivery, even though they may overlook what others can learn about arrangement and style from studying manuscripts. Speeches are often more effective than written messages because speeches include a human element. When you prepare a speech, don't overlook the importance of the interrelationship of content and delivery.

The Formats of Delivery

Good speakers present speeches that have **fluency;** they flow without unnecessary interruption. Fluent speeches require a great deal of preparation and practice. In this section, the term *delivery* doesn't refer to the verbal and nonverbal presentation of the speech. Instead, *delivery* refers here to the method of presenting the speech. The final part of the preparation process is selecting a delivery format that best meets the needs of the audience, the situation, and the speaker. There are four common delivery formats: impromptu, extemporaneous, manuscript, and memorized.

Impromptu Delivery

The delivery format that requires the least preparation is **impromptu delivery.** Impromptu delivery isn't rehearsed and doesn't involve notes or prior planning. When a teacher calls on you in class, your response is impromptu. Even though you read the lesson, you probably didn't prepare answers to questions you thought the teacher would ask. By studying the material in advance, however, you prepared yourself for the possibility that you'd have to respond. Through intrapersonal communication, you interpreted the reading assignment and the teacher's question in order to give an answer.

Sometimes, someone has to give a speech without any advance warning or preparation. This commonly happens on special occasions, such as when a person receives an unexpected award. The answers you give to audience questions at the conclusion of a speech are also impromptu, even though you may have anticipated questions and thought about answers.

While impromptu speeches require the least amount of work, they're difficult to give well. An impromptu speech must be organized. It must have a clear message, even if you're only saying a simple "Thank you, I appreciate your thoughtfulness." To present a clearly organized impromptu speech, take a few seconds to form a thesis statement, just as you would for a prepared speech. Then, develop your statement with a few simple ideas supported by facts or examples, as you would in a prepared speech. An impromptu speech should be lively and maintain interest. The speaker's emotions often guide the words, making the delivery and the words complement each other.

Impromptu speeches are usually brief. Audiences don't expect them to be long since the speaker hasn't had time to prepare. Impromptu speeches aren't appropriate if the audience expects the speaker to give thought and preparation to the speech.

Extemporaneous Delivery

Extemporaneous delivery relies on an outline or on notes. Notes contain key words and phrases that remind you of your ideas. The major advantage of an outline is flexibility. You can adjust the speech's length, the number and type of examples, and the language to fit the situation and audience. By using an outline of general ideas, you can even address many groups on the same topic.

Outline delivery also lets you make changes right before you're scheduled to speak. If a previous speaker said something that applies to your topic, make a brief note on the outline to remind you to mention the new information. An outline can save preparation time and provide better organization than is possible in impromptu delivery.

In terms of both verbal and nonverbal delivery, extemporaneous delivery isn't as good as impromptu or memorized delivery, which is discussed later on. You have to find a way to manage your notes without losing eye contact with your audience or eliminating gestures and movement. If you're familiar with the outline and either place your notes on a stand or hold small note cards, you should have fewer problems. The key to effective extemporaneous delivery is practice. That's the only way to become familiar with your notes. Practice will also reduce the number of times you refer to your notes during a speech. With more practice, verbal delivery becomes more natural.

For beginning speakers, the outline is the best method. It provides a crutch without tying your attention to a manuscript for every word. For the experienced speaker, an outline allows a great deal of flexibility and a more natural delivery.

Manuscript Delivery

Manuscript delivery requires a speaker to write out every word of a speech. A manuscript is especially valuable when you must word your comments carefully. Public figures, business leaders, and political speakers use manuscripts for several reasons:

1. They need a record of what they said.
2. They need to make consistent public statements.
3. They need to supply copies of their comments to the news media.
4. They need to select language carefully.
5. They must fill a specific amount of time.

Public figures, however, aren't the only ones who need to prepare speeches word for word. Contest speakers use manuscripts so they can adjust to specific time limits, prepare speeches to memorize, and verify that their speeches are ones they wrote themselves.

Delivering a speech from a manuscript appeals to many beginning speakers. Right there on the pages is every word they want to say, so they don't worry about opening their mouths and having the

Manuscript delivery requires a speaker to write out every word of a speech and then read it to the audience.

| SPEAKING ABOUT SPEAKING | The Four Types of Delivery |

Impromptu: Delivery without prior preparation

When to use: When no preparation is possible; in response to a spontaneous event

Advantages:
1. No prior work involved
2. Speakers sound natural and sincere
3. Speeches are usually brief

Disadvantages:
1. Requires speaking experience
2. Must have a purpose and be organized immediately, with no preparation or planning

Extemporaneous: Delivery using notes

When to use: In most speaking situations

Advantages:
1. Allows speaker to adapt to different audiences and situations
2. Changes can be made up to and during the speech
3. Delivery sounds natural
4. Takes less time than writing a manuscript
5. Enables a speaker to organize ideas easily

Disadvantages:
1. Eye contact may suffer while looking at notes
2. Handling notes may interfere with gestures and movement

wrong words come out. However, it's difficult to write a speech that sounds natural. Your spoken vocabulary is much smaller than your written vocabulary. As a result, some words you might write in a manuscript don't sound natural to the ear, even though they look natural to the eye. Rules for spoken English aren't as strict as those for written English. If a speech is written as a formal essay, it may not necessarily sound natural to an audience.

In fact, it's so difficult to write a speech that sounds natural that professional speechwriters, who have mastered this art, can earn an

Manuscript: Delivery from a text in which every word of the speech is written out

When to use: In situations where a speech must be worded carefully or a record of the content is necessary

Advantages:
1. Assures exact wording
2. Holds to specific time limits
3. Preparation time allows for careful language when exact wording is essential

Disadvantages:
1. Difficult to write for spoken English; the speech often sounds awkward
2. Affected or stilted delivery
3. Requires a great deal of experience to prepare
4. Cannot be adapted to the situation and the audience during delivery
5. Requires a great deal of time to prepare

Memorized: A manuscript speech that's committed to memory

When to use: In contest situations; when you don't want notes to interfere with delivery and eye contact

Advantages:
1. Allows for a very polished delivery
2. Includes the advantages of a manuscript without losing eye contact or affecting delivery

Disadvantages:
1. Can be overrehearsed and sound unnatural
2. Speaker can forget portions of the speech
3. Suffers from all the disadvantages of manuscript delivery

excellent income. Their skills take time to acquire. As a beginner, you can't expect to write a natural-sounding manuscript the first time you try. To illustrate this point, read a paragraph or two from this book aloud. Now, explain the content in your own words. Is there a difference in word choice, sentence length, and style?

If you still want to give your speech from a manuscript, be prepared to revise. Very few speeches can be written once or even twice and sound good. Like English compositions, most speeches must be reworked.

Using a manuscript may also affect delivery. Often, you lose eye contact because you have to look at your pages for every word. Your gestures may be limited, simply because you have to turn pages all the time. If you lose your place during the speech, awkward pauses will mar your presentation.

There are times, however, when you may have to use a manuscript. Some speaking contests require a manuscript. If you need to prepare a manuscript, follow the guidelines found later in this chapter.

Memorized Delivery

The final format is **memorized delivery,** which requires preparing a manuscript and presenting it from memory. In classical times, memorized delivery was very common. Today, speakers seldom use this type of delivery.

Two situations that call for memorized delivery are contest speaking and professional speaking. Professional speakers often prepare a general speech on a topic with broad appeal, such as motivation or how to be successful. They then give the same speech to audiences across the country, with little or no adaptation.

As with the other formats, this method has its advantages. If you memorize your speech, you can concentrate on movement, gestures, and appealing vocal delivery. Often a memorized speech sounds and looks more like a dramatic performance than a conversational talk.

Depending on the speaker's purpose and audience, a dramatic approach can be effective. If your purpose is to entertain, for example, a well-rehearsed, memorized speech produces the best comic timing. If you write the original manuscript in a conversational style, your memorized speech will sound conversational. If the style isn't conversational, the speech will sound artificial or forced.

Speakers using memorized delivery can also have problems with physical delivery. Inexperienced speakers, especially, don't know what to do with their hands. Unless their situation requires a microphone, they don't have to stand behind a podium and even look unnatural doing so. Some contest speakers try to solve these problems by planning their gestures and movements, but the movements often look planned. They can distract more than help convey the message.

Another problem that can arise when you memorize a speech is forgetting part of the speech. This can create awkward pauses and can be especially upsetting to beginning speakers. If you must memorize a speech, remember that audience members aren't following along with a copy. If you don't say something exactly as you wrote it, no one will know. You should also work on memorization and vocal delivery and let gestures and movement develop naturally.

Perhaps the biggest disadvantage of a memorized speech is that it's inflexible. If your audience looks confused, it isn't easy to add another example. If your audience reacts negatively to an idea, it's difficult, if not impossible, to adapt without moving away from your memorized script. You may find it difficult to return smoothly to the prepared material.

Preparing Notes for Speech Delivery

The first step to being a fluent speaker is to know your material as well as possible. Research, planning, and practice will help you master your subject. The second step is having notes or a manuscript that is easy to use. Although each speaker needs to develop a system that works best for him or her, there are some helpful guidelines for preparing speaking notes, whether you use an outline or a written manuscript.

Preparing an Outline

You can write an outline on a set of note cards or on a sheet of paper. If you use note cards, the four-by-six-inch or five-by-eight-inch size lets you write more and write larger than you can on three-by-five-inch cards. Whether you use cards or sheets of paper, plan for enough white space (or blank areas) so you can see key words easily. White space also lets you add to your notes at the last minute without crowding. Skip three or four lines between items and have wide margins on the left and right.

Write out everything large enough so that it's easy to see when you put the cards on a speaker's stand. Many professional speakers use oversized type for notes. Most typewriters or word processors with changeable typing elements have one you can use for speech scripts. To see the difference between regular type and oversized type, try to read the following samples when you're standing two feet away from this book:

Advantages of an outline

ADVANTAGES OF AN OUTLINE

If you don't have access to oversized type, print large letters or use all capital letters on a regular typewriter.

You can write an outline in words and phrases or in complete sentences. It's best to use as few complete sentences as possible. A rule of thumb is to have a few words guide at least fifteen to thirty seconds of speaking. With the exception of your introduction and conclusion, don't write out most points in complete sentences or paragraphs. Even though you should write out introductions and conclusions, practice them so they're partially memorized.

A speech outline using the note-card method looks something like Figure 10.1.

Notice that on the first two cards, the entire introduction, including the thesis statement, is written out. Card 3 outlines one part of the speech, the description of the calendars. By placing a few words on each card explaining the calendars and the money-making potential, this speaker can easily see all the cues. It's helpful to include extra notes, such as a reminder to show the calendars, on the cards.

Since each card holds only a few words and phrases, practice the speech several times. Practice will help you select the explanations for each point and remember them.

Beginning speakers may want to include some complete sentences in their outlines. The sentences can serve as **transitions,** words and phrases that connect ideas in one part of a speech to those in another.

The example in Figure 10.2 of a partial outline includes transitions. This example is handwritten, rather than typed, and is prepared on sheets of paper rather than on cards.

Figure 10.1 Sample Note Cards
Card 1

Introduction: Everyone looks forward to prom night. It's a fairy

tale night. We trade in our jeans, T-shirts, and running shoes for

formal dresses and tuxedos. But it takes money and hard work to

turn the school gym into a garden paradise.

Card 2

We have only one year to raise money for our prom, and we need

to find a money-making project that will produce big profits with

a minimum of time. Selling school calendars is one of the best

money-making projects we could have. After I describe the

calendars and how much we can earn, I think you'll agree

with me.

Card 3

I. Description of school calendars

    A. They are for fundraising only

        1. Not found in stores

        2. Colorful pictures for each month

        3. Over 2,000 schools have sold them

Figure 10.2 Transitions

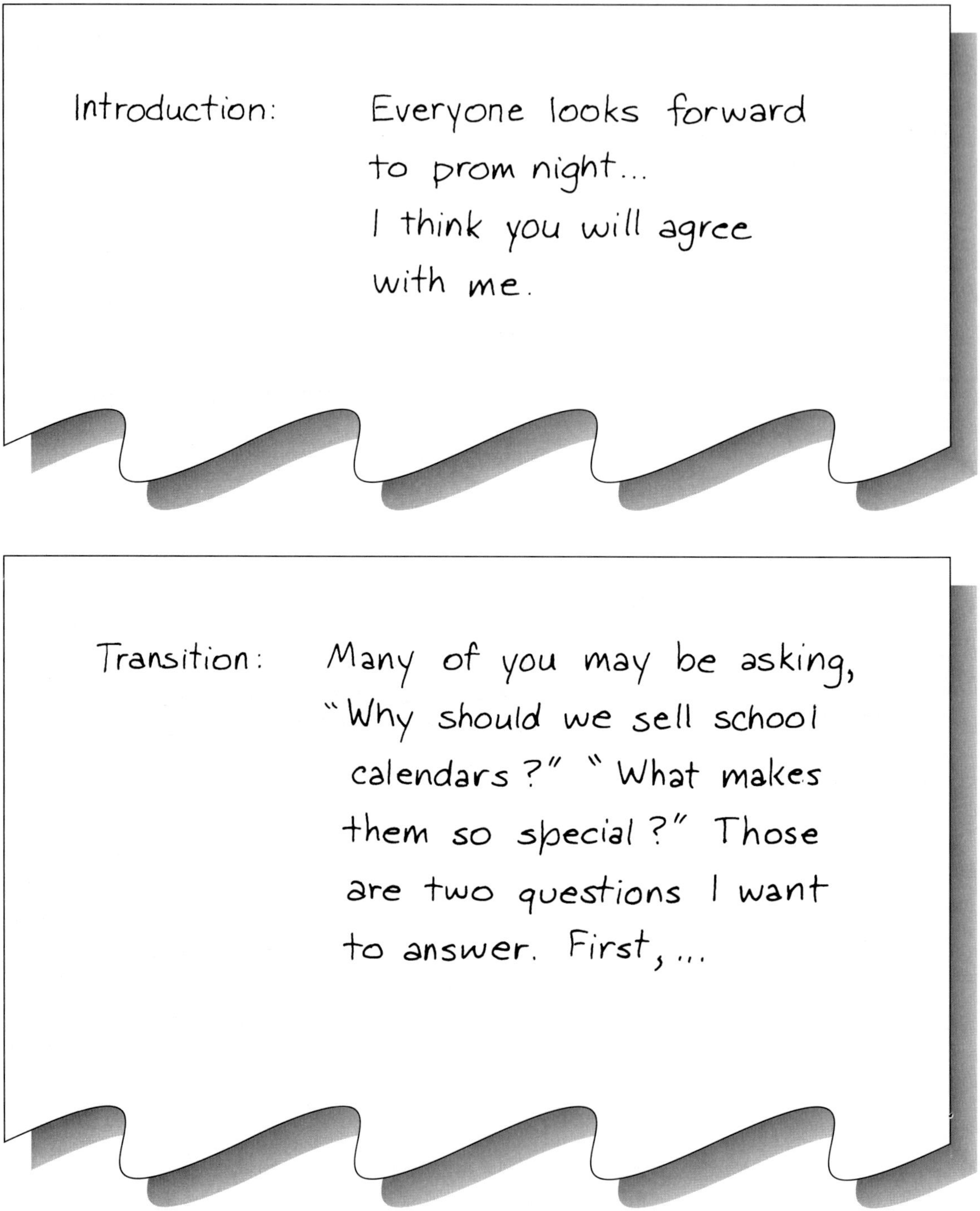

Introduction: Everyone looks forward to prom night...
I think you will agree with me.

Transition: Many of you may be asking, "Why should we sell school calendars?" "What makes them so special?" Those are two questions I want to answer. First, ...

A.   They are only for fundraising

1.   They are not found in stores

2.   Over 2,000 schools have
     sold them

Some speakers emphasize transitions with a colored highlighter. After you've prepared and given one or two speeches, you'll be able to develop your own system, which will make it easier to read your notes.

Giving a speech from an outline means that you must know how to outline. If you need work on this skill, see page 277 for a complete explanation.

Manuscript Preparation

Preparing a manuscript for a speech involves several steps. Begin with an outline. Once you complete it, talk through the speech. Tape-record your ideas, if possible. When you're ready to write, talk through each section of the speech before putting it down on paper. Write what you said. Read aloud the last sentence or two of what you've written; then talk through the next section and repeat the process.

Follow this system until you complete the speech. Read the whole text aloud several times, and smooth out the rough spots. Have someone else listen and tell you if the speech sounds natural. Be prepared to write several drafts of the speech. Each time you practice, you'll find a better way to phrase some sentences.

SPEAKING ABOUT SPEAKING

Evolution of a Speech Manuscript

Because it's so difficult to word a speech manuscript so that it sounds natural and is easy to read, most manuscripts require several drafts. Even professional speechwriters and experienced speakers rewrite their speeches. An examination of the files of President John Kennedy's speechwriter, Ted Sorenson, reveals the following revisions of the most famous line from President Kennedy's inaugural address. The changes aren't major, but they make a difference. Which version do you think is the most effective? Why?

From an early draft of the speech
"So ask not what your country is going to do for you. Ask what you can do for your country."

As the line appeared on the President's notes for delivery
"And so, my fellow Americans: ask not what your country will do for you—ask what you can do for your country."

As the President actually delivered the line
"And so, my fellow Americans: ask not what your country can do for you—ask what you can do for your country."

Once you have finished the manuscript, work up a clean copy that is easy to read. Once again, large type or writing and white space will help you see what's on the paper. If possible, use a typewriter or word processor rather than writing the speech out in longhand. A printed manuscript is easier to read.

It's also helpful to mark the script. Read through the speech to learn where you should pause or emphasize words. Underline words to emphasize, write volume and rate cues above words or in the margins, and use a slash (/) or other mark to indicate pauses. There's no right or wrong way to mark a speech manuscript. You'll have to develop your own system. The manuscript excerpt in Figure 10.3 uses a variety of techniques, including white space, speaking cues, and pause marks, to help the speaker prepare a lively delivery.

Figure 10.3
Manuscript
Excerpt

One morning last week when I sat down at the table for breakfast/my mother handed me the newspaper. She didn't say anything.//She just looked at me/and then/walked back to the range.

On the front page of the paper/was the picture of one of my best friends/—the victim of a drunken driver.

As teenagers,/we think/we're going to live forever. Death/is
SLOWER
for old people. But I went to my friend's funeral. He was only sixteen. He wasn't old,/but he was dead.

We all/like to think we are grown up enough to drink,/even if we aren't legally old enough. The driver who killed my friend/was old enough to drink. And/old enough to know better than to drink and drive.

Since my friend's death,/I've given a lot of thought to drinking and driving,/and I decided SOMETHING should be done about it. I don't want myself/or anyone else I know/to be the next victim. So I got involved in S.A.D.D.,/—Students Against Driving Drunk/—and I want to tell you about S.A.D.D./in hopes you'll also get involved.

Reading a Manuscript   As you read the manuscript, did you follow the speaking cues? Were they natural for you? If they weren't, don't be surprised. All of us speak differently. Each of us might emphasize some of the same words, but not all of them. The main thing to remember when you write and mark a manuscript is that the speech should sound as natural as possible.

For effective delivery of a manuscript speech, you'll have to deal with two major problems: reduced eye contact and unnecessary pauses to turn pages. Even experienced speakers have to practice with a manuscript before they can maintain good eye contact with their audiences. The President and many other political speakers, as well as television newscasters, often solve the eye contact problem by putting their speeches on a teleprompter—a device that carries the words of the speech. One type of teleprompter reflects the speech onto mirrors that look like clear glass. The speech is shown as if it were rolling from bottom to top. The speakers can see the words, but the audience can't. Since teleprompters are at eye level, the speaker doesn't have to look down. Another type of teleprompter looks something like a television screen.

Teleprompters are not foolproof. When President Bill Clinton addressed Congress on health-care reform in 1993, he got to the podium and saw the wrong speech on the screen. He had to ad lib for five minutes. He was able to do so because he knew his material well. Regardless of the type of speaking notes you have, nothing improves your delivery the way practice does.

The clear glass panel in front of President Bill Clinton is part of the teleprompter. The text of Clinton's speech is reflected onto the panels, so he can read his speech without having to look down at a manuscript on the podium. This allows him to have better eye contact with the audience.

SPEAKING ABOUT SPEAKING	**Prespeech Jitters Heard on Open Mike**

Associated Press

President Clinton upstaged himself Saturday night on his announcement of a military strike against a Baghdad intelligence site.

A few minutes before his hastily arranged speech to the nation, the President was heard rehearsing the opening lines of his address over an open microphone from the Oval Office.

Clinton's inadvertent speech preview was carried live on at least some national radio stations and in the White House press room.

As aides were heard scurrying around the room, the President cleared his throat, asked for some water, and asked worriedly: "Is there a teleprompter? What are we going to do about the teleprompter? How long are we going to have to wait?"

While this not-so-behind-the-scenes drama was unfolding, the start time of Clinton's speech was pushed back from 6:31 p.m. to 6:35 p.m. to 6:40 p.m.

When Clinton appeared on TV, he appeared cool and collected, giving no sign of the hectic last-minute preparations.

Teleprompters are expensive, and few individuals have access to one. Since you are unlikely to have one, you can make adjustments in a script to improve eye contact. One technique is to write or type the speech on no more than the top third of a sheet of paper. You'll use more sheets of paper, but you won't have to glance all the way down a page, lowering your head as you read.

There are two things you can do to avoid unnecessary pauses. To move from page to page smoothly, have two pages of your script showing at all times. Begin the speech with page one on the left and all remaining pages on the right, as is shown in Figure 10.4. In this way you can see both the first and second page. As you finish page one and begin page two, move page two to the left so pages two and three are visible. When you're finished, all pages will be in reverse order on the left.

A second technique to make reading smoother is to end each page with a complete sentence. You don't want to have to switch pages in the middle of a sentence.

Figure 10.4
Shifting Manuscript
while Speaking

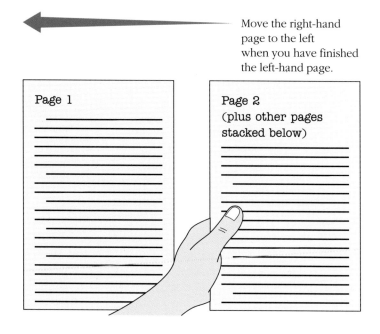

Move the right-hand
page to the left
when you have finished
the left-hand page.

Page 1

Page 2
(plus other pages
stacked below)

Memorizing a Speech

To deliver a memorized speech, you must first prepare a manuscript as just described. Practice talking through the speech several times to make sure the style is conversational and that you're comfortable reading it. As you begin memorizing, work on one paragraph at a time. As you recite a new paragraph, go back and pick up the previous paragraph. The process is a time-consuming one, but it will help you reinforce what you've already learned. As you memorize, try to see the words on the page.

Answering Questions

Speeches are often followed by a question-and-answer period. This time allows audience members to clarify ideas that the speaker presented or have the speaker expand on ideas. The speaker's answers are a type of impromptu speech, so these remarks should be brief and organized. The following guidelines will assist you in answering questions after a speech.

Anticipate Questions

Prepare for the question-and-answer period by trying to determine questions the audience might ask. Which points of your speech are likely to cause controversy? What parts of your speech might need more explanation than you can give during the allotted time? What other topics might the speech raise in a listener's mind? By asking yourself these and similar questions, you'll be better prepared to answer audience questions in an organized fashion. The questions you ask yourself are an important part of the prespeech feedback loop. The actual questions supply feedback for the presentation and post-speech loops.

Restate the Question

Always restate the question after it's asked, for three reasons. First, everyone in the audience may not have heard the question. Second, it's a way of ensuring that you heard the question correctly. If you haven't, let the questioner rephrase it. Third, restating the question gives you time to phrase a response.

Be Polite

Often, questions come from individuals who don't agree with what you said in the speech. If this happens, don't argue or debate with the questioner. Thank the questioner, and use the opportunity to compare your position with other points of view.

Relate to the Audience

Although some questions may seem to be important only to the questioner, find a way to relate your answer to your original comments and to the audience's wider interests. Don't make your answer a dialogue only with the questioner. If you do, you'll lose the rest of the audience.

Admit What You Don't Know

Every speaker is occasionally stumped by a question. If someone asks a question that you can't answer, admit it. Tell the audience you'll check into it if it's something that could be important in later speeches. In some cases, you can also offer to speak with the questioner after the formal conclusion of your speech. You can then arrange to research an answer and get back to the individual.

Chapter 10 Summary

Good delivery sounds natural, allowing the speaker's personality to come through. It's lively, and its tone suits the topic. Effective delivery results from thorough research, planning, and practice. It's also dependent on using the appropriate type of delivery for the audience and the situation.

The speech format used when the speaker has no time to prepare is an impromptu speech. In most cases, a speaker has prior warning. For speeches prepared ahead of time, there are three delivery formats to choose from: extemporaneous, manuscript, and memorized. Of the three, extemporaneous is the best for most situations. However, each type has its advantages and disadvantages, and these should be considered before selecting a format. Beginning speakers should avoid manuscript and memorized speeches unless they're doing contest speaking or are required to use them.

The question-and-answer session that follows some speeches calls for a type of impromptu speech. In preparation, try to anticipate questions. During the session, be polite, relate questions to the entire audience, and be honest if you do not know the answer to a question.

All speeches, regardless of format, should be organized, should have clear beginning and ending points, and should be fluent. Practice is essential for success. Even the impromptu speaker must have experience to perform well.

♦ Check Your Understanding

1. Explain the four guidelines for effective speech delivery.

2. List and describe the four types of delivery, and explain when it's most appropriate to use each format.

3. List at least two advantages and two disadvantages for each of the four types of delivery.

4. Explain how to prepare notes for the three formats requiring preparation.

5. Give at least one suggestion for practicing each type of speech delivery.

6. Give at least three strategies to follow in answering questions at the conclusion of a speech.

◆ Apply Your Understanding

Using one of the following topics, prepare speaking notes for an extemporaneous speech. Include transitions.

    a. What books would you want on a desert island and why?
    b. Why is volunteerism important?
    c. How would you change the school curriculum?
    d. What does your community need to do to support teens?

◆ Thinking Critically about Public Speaking

Work with a group of four or five other students. Using one of the speeches in Appendix B or a speech from *Vital Speeches of the Day,* prepare a manuscript copy for each group member. Working individually, mark the manuscript for emphasis and pauses as you would read it. Compare the markings of the group members. Take turns reading sections to one another. Do they sound natural? What rewriting or remarking would make them more natural?

◆ Speak Out!

1. Present a one- or two-minute impromptu speech on a topic assigned by your teacher. Topics should be similar to these:
    a. What is your favorite fast-food restaurant and why?
    b. What would you do with a $1,000 gift?
    c. If you could take an expense-paid trip anywhere, where would you go and why?
    d. What person has influenced you the most and why?

2. Prepare a short speech on one of the topics listed in Question 1. Memorize the speech and present it.

3. After giving an impromptu or extemporaneous speech, have a question-and-answer session with your classmates. Were you satisfied with your answers? What could you do to improve your answers?

◆ Speech Challenge

Tape-record an impromptu speech. Prepare a manuscript speech on the same topic. Present it and tape it. Compare the two presentations. Which was more fluent? Which was more natural? Which was more effective overall? Why? What changes can you make in the manuscript to be more natural?

CHAPTER ·11·

Key Terms

Artistic qualities

Criterion-referenced form

Ethics

Evaluation

Chapter Objectives

After studying this chapter, you will be able to:

1. Explain the benefits of speech evaluations for speakers and for listeners.
2. Explain three of the five bases for evaluation.
3. Explain the guidelines an evaluator should follow in making comments to a speaker.
4. Explain how to get the most benefit from the evaluations you receive.
5. Explain how purpose affects the evaluation of a speech.
6. Explain how to use each of the two major types of evaluation forms.
7. Describe strategies to evaluate your own speeches.

Speech Evaluation

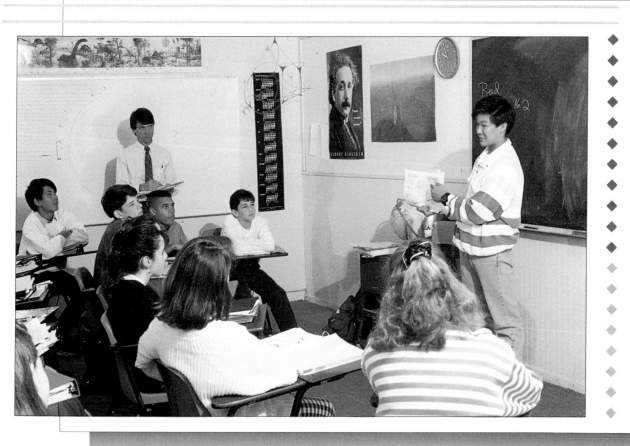

The Benefits of Evaluation

As you listen to a speech, you are also making judgments about it. This process is known as **evaluation.** What's the speaker's main idea? What claims is he or she making? Are the claims supported? Can you hear the speaker? Does the speaker make you feel that the topic is important? These questions and others form the basis of critical listening. Even when you're listening for enjoyment, you still evaluate. You may conclude that a joke wasn't funny or that the speaker wasn't lighthearted enough for a speech to entertain.

Sometimes, your evaluation is informal. You don't give the speaker written or oral comments. In a speech class, however, much of the evaluation is formal. For instance, after most speeches your teacher will give you a written evaluation form on which he or she comments on your strengths and weaknesses. Some teachers prefer oral comments. Some combine the two. Whatever the method, evaluation will help you improve as a speaker. It will also help you become a better audience member. Basically, there are four good reasons for learning how to evaluate speeches.

You can improve your speeches by evaluating the speeches of others.

Becoming a Better Speech Consumer

As consumers of speeches, all of us need to learn how to sort out valid information from invalid information, good ideas from bad. As you go through life, you'll listen to hundreds of speeches. Some speakers will present information honestly. Others will distort it. History is full of examples of people who were fooled by smooth speakers. Some followed corrupt leaders who were responsible for killing millions of innocent people. Others purchased worthless medicine from "doctors" in medicine shows. Through today's media, you're exposed to hundreds of sales pitches for products and ideas. There's no doubt that speeches are powerful tools of persuasion. You must learn to listen with a critical ear. By learning the basics of speech evaluation, you'll learn how to detect sound ideas.

Providing Feedback

You already know that speakers need feedback. They can then adjust their messages or alter their presentation methods to meet their purposes and the audience's needs. Feedback can come in the form of facial expressions, a teacher's written criticism, a grade, or a newspaper editorial.

As a speech-maker, you need to know how to improve. Whether you just want to pass this course or want to become a better speaker, a formal system of feedback will help you identify areas in which you need improvement.

Learning from Others

By evaluating others' speeches, you can improve your own speaking skills. By looking and listening attentively, you can see what works and what doesn't. Models, both good and bad, can serve as mirrors of your behavior as a speaker. For instance, your teacher may tell you that you need better eye contact. If you study a speaker who doesn't make eye contact and begin to think the speaker doesn't care about you, you'll understand why you need to correct your own technique.

A word of caution, however. You can learn from others' speeches, but you must develop your own style. Your personality needs to come through in your speaking. Don't try to imitate another speaker. Instead, identify effective techniques that you can adopt to become part of your own style.

Appreciating Speeches as Art

A final reason for studying speeches is to learn to appreciate them as art forms. A well-written, well-delivered speech can inspire, console, or even lead nations into battle. In English classes, you study poetry, short stories, and novels to appreciate the artful use of language and to understand the human condition. Studying speeches can also teach you about these things. Throughout this book are features on famous speakers. From those samples, you'll learn how speeches helped women get the vote, unified the nation after a political campaign, or praised someone who died. You can learn how speakers use language to achieve their purposes.

Oral communication has an ancient tradition. Some speeches live on long after the speakers who gave them. By learning how to evaluate speeches, you can better understand and appreciate why that's the case.

The Bases for Speech Evaluation

If you go out to buy a used car, you know you have to consider many factors, such as cost, mileage, appearance, condition, and age. To be an intelligent consumer of public messages, you also need a general set of guidelines for judging a speech. There are five general bases on which you can evaluate a speech: results, content, ethics, artistic qualities, or a combination of these.

Judging Results

You can evaluate a speech by results alone. To do so, you must determine what the speaker intended to happen and then decide if he or she was successful. This task seems simple, but it has one major difficulty. In a real public speaking situation, a speaker may try to persuade you to favor one side of a controversial issue. You may not be convinced. However, other members of the audience may be. When you evaluate a speech by results, you need to consider the entire audience's reaction, not just your own.

Judging Content

Judging a speech on the basis of its content is a common approach. In fact, many consider content the most important element of a speech. When judging on content, keep in mind the specific purpose of the speech you're evaluating. A speech to entertain should have content that keeps the audience's attention. A speech to inform should develop a topic with new and important information. A speech to persuade must include good reasons why a listener should favor the speaker's claims and point of view. Judging content also should include analyzing supporting materials, such as examples, statistics, or facts.

Judging Ethics

If you're judging persuasive speeches, one element you may want to consider is the speaker's ethics. **Ethics** are a set of beliefs about what is right and wrong. If a speech changes the listeners' minds, it should do so in an ethical manner. We all agree, for example, that a politician running for office shouldn't lie to gain votes. If you're an intelligent consumer of the spoken word, you will detect lies or half-truths. As Chapter 1 pointed out, speakers have the responsibility of using the freedom of speech properly. When judging ethics, the audience determines if a speaker is meeting that responsibility.

Judging Artistic Qualities

When judging **artistic qualities,** you consider the manner of delivery, the language, the organization, and the overall impact of the speech. You may comment on the speaker's enthusiasm or the way he or she worded the message. Personal tastes about what is pleasant or attractive play a role in this type of evaluation. Keep this fact in mind and explain that your comments are your own personal opinion.

Using a Combined Approach

In most instances, you'll judge a speech on the basis of more than one factor. The combined approach allows you to evaluate both content and delivery. Both factors are essential for a successful speech presentation. By using a combined approach, you can look at several or all aspects of speech-making.

Guidelines for Evaluating Speeches

Evaluation is an important part of the feedback loop discussed in Chapter 2. As an evaluator, your task is to be a helpful critic, not merely one who criticizes. In other words, look for strengths as well as weaknesses. Don't use evaluations as a way to get back at someone or to put a person down more. If your evaluation is to be beneficial to the speaker, keep several guidelines in mind.

Be Positive

It's important to say something positive about every speech. You'll find that every speech does have strong points, and every speaker has some effective elements of delivery. Encourage speakers by commenting on their strengths as well as on their weaknesses. You may say something as simple as, "This was an excellent topic for this

Questions to Consider When Evaluating Speeches

1. What is the speech's stated purpose?
2. How well does the speaker achieve the stated purpose?
3. What are the speaker's claims? Are they supported? Are they exaggerated?
4. How does the speaker want to change your attitudes or beliefs? Are you convinced to make the change?
5. Does the speech contain sufficient information to accomplish its goal?
6. Are the speaker's ideas consistent with what you already know?
7. Are new ideas and claims supported through research?
8. Does the speaker's position seem reasonable?
9. Does the speaker's delivery communicate enthusiasm? Sincerity? Honesty?
10. Does the speech seem well-prepared?
11. Is the material presented in an organized fashion?
12. Is the speaker's language clear and precise?
13. Is the speaker's language appropriate for the audience?

audience," "It was easy to hear your speech," or "I can tell you researched the topic."

Give Suggestions

If you observe a weakness, don't just identify it. Suggest ways for the speaker to correct the problem. It's always easy to criticize; it's more difficult to teach.

Here is a simple four-step method for making suggestions. First, make specific observations about the speaker's content or technique. Second, review the criteria for an effective speech. Third, determine if the observed content or behavior meets those criteria. Fourth, make suggestions for improving any weaknesses you observed.

Comments that teach as well as point out weaknesses would include: "Practice your speech by giving it to two or three people sitting in different parts of the room. That way you can work on maintaining eye contact with more people," or "Use more examples to explain your ideas. I wasn't always sure how this idea applied to everyday life," or "Be sure to tell the audience how many steps are involved in the process before explaining them. This makes it easier to know if we have caught them all."

Avoid Personal Comments

You may not like a speaker, or you may not agree with a person's beliefs. That's natural. However, when you evaluate a speech, you shouldn't attack the person or attack the ideas on a personal level. Tact is an important part of being a good evaluator. Examples of untactful personal comments would include: "Only someone with an IQ under 70 would believe something like that," or "Your dress is really ugly, and it kept me from concentrating on your speech." Tactful versions such as these will get your point across: "Not all your views are shared by others. When you present controversial information, try to at least acknowledge that there is another side," or "Remember to keep distractions to a minimum. This includes what you wear. The pattern in your dress is unusual, and people may concentrate on it and miss something important you're saying."

Be Fair

No speech is perfect, and beginning speakers can't be expected to do everything right the first few times. Set reasonable standards for your evaluations. With each new speech, it's reasonable to expect more, but be sure the standards fit the assignment, the purpose, the audience, and the speaker's level of skill.

Avoid Personal Opinions

If you can, keep your comments impersonal. Just because you don't like working on automobiles doesn't mean that the topic is a bad one. Criticize only elements in the speech that would be a problem to more listeners than just yourself, and refer to others who feel the same way. If your comment is a reflection of your personal taste, just say so.

Allow for Individuality

Let a speaker be an individual. Making comparisons to others can be pointless, as well as hurtful. We all do things somewhat differently, and what works for one person doesn't always work for another. This warning is especially important to remember when comparing relatives. No one wants to be told he or she isn't as fluent or persuasive as a brother or sister.

VOICES OF

THE ENVIRONMENT

Speaking for the Wolf

We are used to thinking of concern for the environment as a new issue. In fact, environmental issues have been important to American speakers for many years. Throughout the public debate of the proper treatment of the environment, there have been two main concerns. How do we use natural resources to grow economically? How can we save natural resources so that future generations can enjoy them? People who choose to speak in support of environmental protection risk the opposition of people who speak for economic development.

Native American speeches show an early understanding of how dependent we are on nature. In the tribal councils of some Native American groups, one member of the tribe was chosen to "speak for the wolf," to represent the voice of the wilderness in tribal discussions. In that tradition, such speakers as Chief Joseph of the Nez Perce tribe spoke wisely of how the environment should be regarded, even while most of our country was interested only in exploiting nature, thinking it would endure forever without change.

Theodore Roosevelt recognized the need for conservation. Because of his own regard for nature and the kind of life natural challenges imposed on people, he began to set aside special areas to be protected from development. These are what we now know as our national parks. It was Roosevelt's vision in the early part of the twentieth century that enables us on the verge of the twenty-first century to see parts of nature that might otherwise have been destroyed.

Recently, Vice President Albert Gore has become a leading speaker for environmental concerns. His speeches earned him names such as "ozone man" from his political opponents. In the 1980s and 1990s, when the United States economy was in recession and unemployment began to rise, Gore spoke of the need to continue environmental protection despite its possible impact on the economy.

WORDS TO REMEMBER

Chief Joseph

Do not misunderstand me, but understand me fully with reference to my affection for the land. I never said the land was mine to do with it what I chose. The one who has the right to dispose of it is the one who created it.

Theodore Roosevelt

The nation behaves well if it treats the natural resources as assets which it must turn over to the next generation increased, not impaired, in value.

Speech before the Colorado Live Stock Association, Denver, Colorado,
29 August 1910

Albert Gore, Jr.

For generations we have believed that we could abuse the earth because we were somehow not really connected to it, but now we must face the truth. The task of saving the earth's environment must and will become the central organizing principle of the post-Cold War world.

Acceptance Speech, Democratic National Convention, 16 July 1992

Many of us have come to believe as human beings that the ecological crisis is fundamentally a spiritual crisis. It is not an accident that in those countries where the environment has been the most devastated, human suffering is usually the worst. Where the human spirit has been pushed down and where hope has been abandoned, we see the erosion of the soil and cutting down of the forest and the poisoning of the water and the air.

Speech to the Global Forum of Spiritual and Parliamentary Leaders
on Human Survival, 5 June 1992

Be Specific

When possible, describe what you like or dislike about a speech in specific terms. You help a speaker very little by saying that the speech was good without explaining why. Comment on the positive aspects of delivery, the topic choice, or whatever made the speech good. If your evaluation is to help a speaker, you must include guidelines for improvement.

Be Realistic

Comment only about those things that the speaker can control. If the assignment is to give a five-minute speech, it does little good to tell the speaker to add material that will make the speech run ten minutes. Base your expectations on the assignment, the speaking situation, and the speaker's level of experience.

Learning to Accept Evaluations

When you are the one being evaluated, keep a positive attitude. View evaluations as tools for self-improvement. Very few speakers, even highly experienced ones, do everything right. The authors of this text have been giving speeches for over twenty years. They still welcome suggestions from audiences because they know they have yet to give the perfect speech. Even politicians and professional speakers, who give dozens of speeches each year, rely on advice from others to improve. They often practice before staff members and have someone help them rewrite their material in order to do the best job possible.

You'll receive evaluations from many sources. Give your friends and family a chance to comment on your practice runs. Your teacher will give you suggestions. Your classmates may also have a chance to comment. Often, you'll hear the same thing from several people. Sometimes, only one individual will comment on a strength or weakness. All this can be confusing. What do you accept? What do you reject? Who's right, and who's wrong? There is no easy answer, but you can make the most of criticism if you ask yourself the following questions:

1. Is the criticism consistent with what you've learned are good public speaking practices?
2. Is the criticism consistent with the comments of other listeners? Have you received similar comments on previous speeches?

3. Is the criticism related to something you can actually control and improve?

4. Is the criticism related to an external factor, such as the microphone or the length of the program? If so, what can you do in the future to avoid the problem?

5. Is the criticism a result of the evaluator's closed mind or is it a legitimate difference of opinion you should take into account in future speeches?

The Mechanics of Evaluation

While it's easy to set evaluation guidelines, it isn't as easy to actually evaluate a speech. Beginning critics learn it's difficult to listen to a speech, watch the speaker, and write comments all at the same time. The only way to master this task is through practice. However, your first attempts will be easier if you have a clear purpose in mind and if you have a good evaluation instrument to guide you.

Knowing the Purpose

Base your comments and the evaluation form you use on three things: the speaker's purpose for the speech, the use you'll make of the evaluation, and the use the speaker will make of the evaluation.

If the speaker's purpose is to entertain, you should be less concerned about the soundness of the ideas and more with results and artistic qualities. However, if you're listening to a persuasive speech, you may be more concerned with the soundness of the ideas, the speaker's ethics, and the results.

Your reason for doing the evaluation is also important. Are you trying to learn more about speech-making techniques in order to improve your own delivery? If so, study the speaker's artistic qualities. However, if you're more concerned with providing the speaker with feedback to help him or her improve, concentrate on observations that will benefit the speaker most.

In general, your teacher will grade your speeches for two reasons. First, the evaluation will provide constructive criticism to assist you as you prepare future speeches. Second, you'll receive a grade or score so you can compare your performance with an ideal standard or with other students' performances. The evaluation instruments discussed in the next section are designed to achieve both those purposes.

Evaluation Instruments

In most classrooms, a form is used to grade speeches. Generally, the form is divided into categories. The evaluator assigns a point value to each category, comments on strengths and weaknesses, and suggests ways to improve. Often, different forms are used for each speech assignment. This allows categories to be adjusted to the speech purpose.

Evaluation Categories   You've already read several guidelines for evaluating speeches. You've also seen a list of questions to ask as you listen to a speech. To simplify the process, evaluation forms are usually divided into categories.

Common categories are content, organization, use of language, delivery, and overall effect. Depending on the specific type of speech being evaluated, a category related to specific requirements for the speech may also be included. The *content* category usually includes the message itself, along with the forms of support and ethical proofs for ideas. *Organization* covers both the overall outline and use of transitions, previews, and summaries. *Use of language* refers to the language and stylistic devices used. *Delivery* covers both the verbal and nonverbal aspects of the presentation. The way a speaker uses notes is an important element of effective delivery. A speaker should have command of ideas, information, and notes, whether they are on note cards or on a teleprompter. The final category of *overall effect* refers to the speaker's ability to accomplish the speech's goal. Did the speech inform, persuade, or entertain? Did the speaker accomplish what was stated in the thesis? Was the speech interesting?

Types of Forms   Some evaluation forms are very simple. They contain only a few words to describe the evaluation categories. There's an explanation of each category and space to comment. Point values are assigned for each category, and you total them to determine the final score. Notice that questions serve as guidelines in each category. The evaluator is also asked to score each category. The sample form in Figure 11.1 has been filled out to serve as a model.

Other forms are more complex check sheets that require less writing but still point out specific areas of strengths and weaknesses. The example in Figure 11.1 is known as a **criterion-referenced form,** which lists specific behaviors a speaker should demonstrate to be effective. An evaluator assigns a rating in each of several categories. The criteria tell judges what to consider when they give a rating.

Whichever form you use, remember that you can't watch or listen to everything and write at the same time. Make quick notes as you listen. After the speech, take time to elaborate on your observations. Where possible, be sure you suggest ways the speaker can improve in addition to identifying weaknesses.

Self-Evaluation Strategies

Figure 11.1
Criterion-Referenced
Evaluation Form

Unless you're aware of your own weaknesses, it will be difficult to improve your speaking skills. Therefore, it is important to evaluate yourself as well as to study others' evaluations of your speech. Self-evaluate your work before, during, and after your speech.

EVALUATION FORM
GENERAL REQUIREMENTS

Name *Julia Anthony*   Evaluator *Carlin*

Rate each of the following areas on a scale of 1–5 using the following as guidelines: 1–poor, 2–fair, 3–good, 4–very good, 5–excellent.

1. CONTENT (Are the ideas well-explained and well-supported with a variety of supporting materials? Is the content consistent with the speaker's stated purpose?)

    Comments: *Excellent use of description and explanation - especially on the extent of the damage and how the solutions work. Your expert evidence needed to come from more than one source even though you did a good job of establishing his credentials. Your evidence supported your claims throughout.*
    Score *4*

2. ORGANIZATION (Is the organizational pattern suitable for the speech purpose and topic? Does the speech use appropriate transitional devices, internal summaries, etc.? Does the introduction include a thesis and forecast? Does the conclusion summarize?)

    Comments: *In general, a well organized speech. The problem - solution pattern was a good one for the topic. Be sure to forecast your major points - remember to "tell the audience what you are going to tell them." You needed a better transition to your problem section. Rather than saying "Now for the problems," you might have said something like, "As a result of the government's failure to enact environmental legislation, several problems have resulted." This serves*
    Score *3* *as a summary of your previous point as well as a lead in to your next. A good summary in your conclusion.*

3. DELIVERY (Does the speaker use effective oral and nonverbal delivery?)

Comments: *Good eye contact - much better than on your last speech. Volume was good, but try to use more variety for emphasis. Your quotation from Dr. West would have had more impact had you softened the last sentence. Rate and enunciation were good. Gestures looked natural. Using note cards has helped free your hands.*

Score __4__

4. USE OF LANGUAGE (Does the speaker use appropriate grammar? Is the language suitable for the audience? Is the language direct and clear?)

Comments: *No problems with grammar. You use several technical terms - "fluorocarbons," "toxics," micro-organisms" - without complete explainations. Be sure to define contextually or explain with examples. Good, detailed explanations of the solution. In general, you did an excellent job of using description to aid us in creating mental images of the problem.*

Score __4__

5. OVERALL EFFECT (Does the speech achieve its purpose?)

Comments: *The speech met the requirements for a persuasive speech. If you had used a variety of experts, your claims about the need for the solutions you suggested would have been stronger. Your use of two-sided arguments added to your credibility as being knowledgeable. Delivery was sincere and created an appropriate tone.*

Score __4__   Score __19/25__

Prespeaking Strategies

In order to do a self-evaluation before your speech, you have to practice. You can practice in front of friends or family members or alone. Regardless of your approach, use an evaluation form as a guide. It is best to use the type of form your teacher will use for your class presentation, such as Figure 11.2. Identify goals for improvement and know how to measure them. For instance, if you want to reduce the number of "you knows" and "and uhs" in your speech, have someone count them. Each time you practice, see if the number is smaller.

Chapter 10 contains suggestions for improving your delivery. If you watch yourself in a mirror or tape-record your speech, use an evaluation form afterwards to score yourself.

Figure 11.2 General Evaluation Form

Evaluator _Payne_

INFORMATIVE SPEECH

Name _Lisa Runyan_

Instructions: Each category will be rated on a scale of 1–5: 1–poor, 2–fair, 3–good, 4–very good, 5–excellent.

Within each category, individual requirements are to be rated with a + or –.

1. SPECIFIC ASSIGNMENT CRITERIA   1 2 3 (4) 5

   _+_ Speech met the 4- to 6-minute time limit. *about 20 seconds over.*

   _+_ Speech met criteria for an informative speech. *- you were able to take*
        a potentially persuasive
   _+_ Speech was presented in outline form. *yes* *topic and treat it only in*
        an informative manner
   _+_ Speech showed evidence of research. *yes-* *successfully. Good job!*
        but see
        notes below. 1 2 3 4 (5)

2. ANALYSIS

   _+_ Speech adhered to general and specific speech purposes. *yes*

   _+_ Speech was narrow to be fully developed and handled *yes-*
        adequately in time alloted. *your overtime was more a result of*
        delivery than content problems.
   _+_ Topic was appropriate for an informative speech. *see note above*

   _+_ Topic was appropriate for the audience. *This is a high interest topic*
        for students, and you were able to add new insights.

3. SUPPORTING MATERIALS   1 2 (3) 4 5

   _____ Speech utilized sufficient clarifying materials (i.e., examples, *Good on*
           illustrations, etc.) *stats and expert opinion- could have used*
           more illustration
   _____ Speech utilized a variety of supporting materials. *Statistics were good,*
           but add a few examples to make them more realistic.
   _____ Sources were identified where necessary. *Don't just say "expert report"*
           tell us who those experts are.
   _NA_   Visual aids, if used, were appropriate and used correctly.

4. INTRODUCTION AND CONCLUSION   1   2   3   4 ⑤

Introduction was properly developed:

___+___ Gained audience attention and created interest. *Excellent use of personal anecdote.*

___+___ Oriented audience to the speech. *yes – it was clear from the audience what the topic would be.*

___+___ Included a clear and precise thesis statement. *yes*

___+___ Major ideas were forecast. *Very good forecast*

Conclusion was developed properly:

___+___ Summarized the speech content. *Excellent*

___+___ Provided a link back to introductory comments. *Very well done*

___+___ Provided an idea for the audience to remember. *yes – the closing line was a nice play on words.*

5. INTERNAL ORGANIZATION   1   2 ③ 4   5

___+___ Organization of the speech (overall) was clear and easy to follow. *yes – good use of classification*

___–___ Transitions provided necessary links between ideas. *Vary your transitions – numbering is all right, but it became repetitive – look at the list of internal transitions in the book for suggested ways to vary.*

___+___ Speech utilized appropriate signposts and internal summaries. *you jumped from the second to third point without warning (see below)*

___+___ Organizational pattern was appropriate for topic and type of speech. *yes*

6. DELIVERY TECHNIQUES   1   2 ③ 4   5

___+___ Stance and posture were appropriate. *yes*

___+___ Eye contact was appropriate. *Good*

___+___ Facial expressions helped to convey/clarify ideas. *okay*

___+___ Gestures added emphasis and descriptions. *good, very natural*

Vocal delivery was effective:

___+___ appropriate volume *good*   ___–___ appropriate rate *– a little slow in spots – especially on the first point –*

___+___ conversational style   ___+___ enthusiastic

___+___ clear enunciation *good*   ___–___ used pauses correctly *– a few too many at first.*

___+___ vocal variety *okay once you relaxed*   ___–___ fluent delivery *– in-consistent – got better the last 2/3's. Practice will help.*

Seemed unsure of yourself at first. Be sure to practice aloud.

7. WORD USAGE/LANGUAGE   1   2   3 ④ 5

_____+_____   Language was direct and made the speaker's point clearly.   *–very good*

_____+_____   Words were used appropriately.

_____+_____   Grammar was appropriate.

_____+_____   Word pronunciations were correct.   *good job on several difficult words.*

_____+_____   Language was suitable for the audience.   *– yes – you explained new terms well.*

TOTAL SCORE _____ *27 / 35* _____

COMMENTS AND SUGGESTIONS FOR IMPROVEMENT:

You handled a difficult topic well. Your organizational pattern and supporting materials were very appropriate for an informative speech. In general, the speech was well structured. The transition to your last point would have been better had you summarized the second and drawn the relationship to the third point rather than just saying "Now, for my third and last point." Be sure to practice out loud – you seemed unsure of how to explain some ideas early on. Look over your notes before class begins.

Evaluating While Speaking

During the speech, use audience reactions to evaluate your effectiveness and try to adjust as necessary. If people appear to be straining to hear, speak up. If people look confused, add another example or explanation. You can't rewrite your speech on the spot, but you can make adjustments as you go along.

Postspeaking Evaluation

After the speech, look over your notes and indicate places that need more work. Make a list of delivery problems you noticed. Write any ways you can improve your performance. Equally important, determine what you did well and keep doing it. If possible, have someone record (either audio or video) your actual performance. Then, sit down with an evaluation sheet and score yourself. By combining self-evaluations with evaluations from your classmates, you should be able to improve with each speech you give.

Chapter 11 Summary

Feedback is an important part of the public speaking process. As an audience member, you provide feedback during a speech and afterwards. At times, your evaluations may even be written.

As you evaluate speeches, listen with a critical ear. Assess the soundness of the ideas presented, the achievement of a stated purpose, the speaker's ethics, and the artistic qualities of the content and delivery.

Base your evaluation on a speech's results, content, ethics, artistic qualities, or a blend of these. Your evaluation should have a positive focus. Present suggestions for improvement fairly, without inserting personal opinions or attacking the speaker personally. Be specific and realistic when you evaluate any speech.

When you judge a speech, concentrate on factors that serve the purpose of the evaluation. If the evaluation is for yourself, concentrate on observing effective speaking techniques, organization, or artistic qualities. If you're evaluating a speech to help the speaker, use an evaluation form.

A speaker can also evaluate his or her own speech. Judge practice sessions using the evaluation form you use in class. During the speech, be aware of audience feedback. Afterwards, think back over your speech and write down any problems you experienced.

◆ Check Your Understanding

1. Explain how both speakers and audience benefit from evaluating speeches.

2. Explain the five bases for evaluating speeches and describe when each would be most effective.

3. Give at least three guidelines a good evaluator should use to give the speaker fair and helpful feedback.

4. Explain what you can do when evaluators give you some conflicting advice.

5. Explain how purpose affects the way you evaluate a speech.

6. Explain the differences between the two major types of evaluation forms.

7. Describe ways in which you can evaluate your own speeches.

◆ Apply Your Understanding

Give several suggestions for evaluating yourself before, during, and after a speech.

◆ Thinking Critically about Public Speaking

1. Using the criteria listed on one of the evaluation forms in this chapter, listen to or watch a speech and evaluate it.

2. List five speeches you have heard in the last year. In each speech, was the speaker's purpose to inform, persuade, or entertain? Did the speaker achieve his or her purpose? Compare your lists with those of your classmates.

3. Select a speech from Appendix B. Write an analysis of the speech's artistic qualities.

4. As a class, watch a videotaped speech. Each class member should complete an evaluation form. Compare your class members' comments. On what areas did all or most of you agree? Where did you differ? Why? If you were the speaker receiving the comments, which would you accept, and why?

5. Select one of the speakers presented in the "Voices" features located throughout the text. Locate a complete speech given by that speaker using a source suggested by your teacher. Using the SPAM model from Chapter 3, evaluate the speech.

◆ Speak Out!

1. Record a speech (either audio or video) you give for your class. Using the evaluation form your teacher uses to grade you, evaluate your own speech. Make a list of suggestions for improvement. Describe a plan to improve your next speech and determine how you'll judge your success.

2. Listen to a classmate's speech in a practice session. Complete an evaluation form. Give your classmate the form and talk about the speech. Then present your speech to your partner and have him or her evaluate your presentation the same way.

◆ Speech Challenge

Speech criticism is the field of communication study that analyzes public address and attempts to define how it works. With the help of your speech teacher or a media specialist, find an example of speech criticism. Be sure to locate the speech as well. Read both and prepare a short lesson for your class on the speech and the critique you read. You may find speech criticisms in anthologies or in journals at college libraries. Many political speeches are critiqued by columnists.

Preparing Speeches

CHAPTER

Key Terms

Analogy

Claims

Comparison

Contrast

Data

Definition

Description

Development

Evidence

Example

Illustration

Incident

Paraphrase

Statistics

Support material

Technology

Testimony

Visual aids

Chapter Objectives

After studying this chapter, you will be able to:

1. Define *support material*.
2. Explain how situation, purpose, and audience help a speaker select support material.
3. Explain the difference between data and development.
4. List the three types of data.
5. Explain ways to use common methods of development.
6. Select and use appropriate visual aids.
7. Explain the new types of technology that can be used to augment public speaking presentations.

Using Support Materials

Supporting Your Thesis

You've already learned to write a purpose statement and a thesis statement for your speech. However, neither of these stands by itself. A thesis, for example, is a promise you make to your audience. If your thesis statement is, "The history of the American motion picture industry is short, but full of interesting and surprising information," you've promised your audience two things. They'll hear a speech on the history of the American motion picture industry, and they'll hear interesting and surprising information. How can you meet these promises? You must present information about American movies that really will be interesting and surprising. The information that makes up most of the speech comes in many forms, but its functions are always the same: to accomplish the speech's purpose, to support the thesis, and to maintain audience interest.

Defining Support Material

Information that helps you make a point is called **support material.** Think back to the speech purposes. When you speak to entertain, you must have something to say that's entertaining. When you speak to inform, you must have something to say that's new to the audience. When you speak to persuade, you must have something to say that will convince the audience. Support material is the *something to say* that makes your speech.

To understand the role of support material, consider your thesis. Remember, a thesis is a single statement that summarizes your position. Since your thesis includes no support material, you must explain why the thesis is valid. That requires **claims,** the conclusions or ideas you want your audience to accept. Claims are supported by **data,** which is also called **evidence.** When data needs further support, develop it with details and information. Note how the levels of support work in this example:

Thesis: Lincoln should be considered America's most important public speaker.

Claim #1: Lincoln's speeches addressed our country's most serious problems.

Data: Constitutional scholar and U.S. Senator Sam Ervin considered the Civil War during Lincoln's administration to be the most significant Constitutional crisis in our history.

Development: Even though other speakers gave eloquent speeches, their speeches are less important. For example, Theodore Roosevelt was a powerful speaker, but his speeches addressed less urgent difficulties than Lincoln's.

Claim #2: Lincoln's speeches lasted far beyond their immediate situation.

Data: Dictionaries of quotations contain far more quotations from Lincoln than from any other president.

Development: Think of just a few examples: "of the people, by the people, for the people," "with malice toward none, with charity for all," "this government cannot endure permanently half slave and half free."

Data: Lincoln's speeches have endured while those of others have not.

Development: People remember Lincoln's words and arguments in the Lincoln-Douglas debates of 1854. Douglas's have largely been forgotten.

Development: The Gettysburg Address is now honored as this country's greatest speech. The more conventional speech, Edward Everett's own "Gettysburg Address," is largely forgotten.

As you can see, a thesis is supported by claims, claims are supported by data, and data is supported by development. This is the logical way to use support material.

Support and Time Limits

When you read your situation and audience, you should always know how long your speech should be. Time limits are very important because they tell you how much support material you can use. Assume you're to give a four- to six-minute speech. What will you do in that time? Your introduction is likely to last one to one-and-a-half minutes. Your conclusion will probably last thirty seconds to one minute. The body of the speech will take up the remaining four minutes. It's the body that contains support material. Using these rough figures, the body of the speech will be 60 to 80 percent of the speech. Use this chart to estimate how much support material you'll need:

Speech Length	Body Length
2 minutes	1 to 1½ minutes
4 minutes	2½ to 3½ minutes
6 minutes	4 to 5 minutes
8 minutes	5 to 6½ minutes
10 minutes	6 to 8 minutes

Choosing Support Material

When you choose support material, you're really choosing your methods. The best way to select materials is to use the three guidelines you're familiar with: situation, purpose, and audience. If you've done your preliminary work, you already have a purpose statement and a thesis statement. Support material always supports the thesis, either directly (by supporting a claim) or indirectly (by developing data).

Consider this example. A speaker who is a sports psychologist has been asked to speak at your school's sports booster club. The speech will be given in August, just before school begins. The year before, your football team was very successful. The audience enthusiastically hopes for another successful year. The meeting organizers have asked the psychologist to speak for twenty to thirty minutes. The speaker has decided on the topic "Thinking Like a Winner." What kind of support material will this topic require?

Since you may know little about football or sports psychology, that question may be hard to answer. But the speaker already knows a lot. She must tie her subject to the upcoming football season. She knows the audience probably won't want to hear about complex psychological studies. Finally, she knows the audience is used to supporting winners. With that knowledge, she develops a purpose statement and a thesis statement:

Purpose Statement
The purpose of this speech is to persuade the audience that fans have an important psychological impact on athletic teams.

Thesis Statement
When your teams take the field during the upcoming season, you fans could be the difference between a successful season and an unsuccessful one, depending on whether or not you think like winners.

Her next task is to gather support material. Here are the kinds of questions she'll ask:

What characteristics separate thinking like a winner from thinking like a loser?

What factors contribute to successful athletic teams?

What can fans do to encourage thinking like a winner?

What can we learn from successful teams who haven't repeated their successes?

What examples are there of fans who helped their teams?

What have famous coaches and athletes said about the importance of fans?

What can I say to interest the audience in my topic?

What can I say to keep my audience's attention for twenty to thirty minutes?

There may be even more questions than these, but all are based on the speaker's understanding of situation, audience, and purpose.

Support comes in many forms. Knowing the types of support you can use is important for two reasons. First, knowing types of support tells you where to look and what to look for as you develop your speech. You must know what's available before you can know what you want. Second, successful speakers use a variety of support. Such variety keeps speeches lively and audiences listening.

Data

Data is evidence that you use to prove a claim. There are three kinds of data: testimony, statistics, and facts. All can be verified. That means they can be proven true. Logically, testimony, statistics, and facts are the only support that can *prove.* Without their support, the points you make in a speech will be less persuasive.

Testimony

Frequently, you'll use another's words or ideas to support a point. High-school speakers often do this, since they lack experience. If you find an authority, someone with experience and background in your topic, you can "borrow" the credibility of the expert. The statements you quote in your speech are called **testimony.**

Testimony is particularly useful in three instances. First, it's useful when you don't have much firsthand knowledge about your topic. For instance, if you were going to talk about the moon landing, you would have to quote an authority's testimony. Second, testimony is useful when the audience doubts your intentions. If you argue that Friday isn't a good day for a test, the teacher may think you're just stalling. When a school psychologist says Fridays aren't good test days, the teacher is more likely to believe it. Third, testimony is useful when the audience opposes your idea. You may be able to get them to think about your point if an authority they respect agrees with you. Here's an example of testimony:

> Few people realize it, but country music is one of the important sources of early rock and roll. Susan Agee, rock critic for *Inspire Magazine,* says that the early songs of Elvis, Bill Haley, Buddy Holly, and others were "more at home in country honky-tonks than they would be in today's rock clubs. And today's rock hits have more of Hank Williams in them than even most performers know." So, while it may not seem like it, the music that American youth likes most is directly related to country music.

Of course, you can't just throw quotes into your speech. To use testimony effectively, keep these recommendations in mind:

1. Make sure you identify your authority and, if necessary, explain why this person is an authority. Be prepared to defend your choice.

2. Avoid really long quotations. Don't be afraid to **paraphrase,** or put the authority's ideas in your own words.

3. When you paraphrase, don't misrepresent the authority by unfairly changing the words or context of the quotation.

4. Don't quote authorities who aren't fair. It's unlikely that an audience will believe such a source. Just as a speaker should have credibility, a source should have credibility.

5. Make sure your audience understands the relevance of the testimony. The old saying is: "Tell them what you're going to say—say it—then tell them what you said."

Statistics

Statistics are pieces of information presented as numbers. Always be aware of the power of statistics and of the problems they can cause when you use them. Statistics are powerful because they give the impression that they're the result of a thorough, scientific study.

Using statistics to support what you are saying can be powerfully persuasive, particularly when you use visual aids to illustrate the statistics.

Some are, of course. When a reputable source says that public approval of the president's policies has increased from 55 to 62 percent, this statistic is the result of a reliable, honest polling method. But does that mean that the statistic is a fact? Not really. The poll did get those results, but others can argue with the results.

Like testimony, statistics must be handled carefully to be effective. Follow these guidelines:

1. Make your statistics interesting and understandable with examples and illustrations. If you say, "An average high-school graduate has seen about 18,000 hours of television," you will make your point. You'll strengthen it if you add, "That is 750 solid days of TV. Over two years. Almost one-tenth of an eighteen-year-old's life."

2. Make sure your source is acceptable to your audience. Be prepared to name and defend the source of your statistics.

3. Keep the statistics as simple as you can. Don't use so many figures that the audience becomes confused or bored.

4. Whenever possible, supplement statistics with visual aids.

5. Above all, make sure your statistics say what you want them to say. It's easy to misread or misuse statistics.

6. Use recent statistics.

H. Ross Perot ran a national presidential campaign based largely on economics. One of his challenges was to make statistics persuasive. One statistic he was trying to use was the interest on the national debt, $400 billion. He knew that a figure like that was hard to comprehend. Here's how he chose to make it more understandable:

> See, the man on the street doesn't know what $400 billion is. That kind of clears his head.
>
> The interest on the national debt just this year exceeds the cost of fighting and winning World War II. Please never forget that paying interest does not buy anything for the American people. . . .
>
> . . . Let's do some strange and weird things. Just think about them.
>
> Well, I'm going to throw a really stupid one on the table. Let's just shut down the Defense Department. You don't get $400 billion.
>
> Well, that didn't work. Let's just shut down all the public schools nationwide. Sorry—that won't get me $400 billion. . . .
>
> Okay, now let's just go over and take it away from business. Let's confiscate the Fortune 500 companies' profits. I don't have half of what I need. . . .

By comparing $400 billion to spending programs and profits, Perot could impress on his audience the size of the interest on the national debt.

Facts

Facts are statements that can be proven true. Unlike testimony, a fact doesn't necessarily come from an authority. Unlike statistics, facts don't necessarily use numbers. A speaker who says, "TV has played an important role in development of modern musical taste," is making a claim. When the speaker says, "MTV is now one of the most popular cable channels in the nation," she is using a fact to help support her claim. Here is how facts can be used to support a claim:

> Released in 1967, the Beatles' album *Sgt. Pepper's Lonely Hearts Club Band* was a breakthrough in rock music [claim]. It was the first rock album critics claimed to be a unified set of songs with a common theme [fact]. It was one of the earliest to include song lyrics with the record [fact]. It cost $100,000 to produce, far more than the cost of any album up to that time [fact]. Its design was called "album art" [fact]. And the music ranged from mystical Indian tunes to old-fashioned vaudeville-style ditties [fact].

Development

Developing data is important in a speech. If you don't develop your data sufficiently, audiences may not pay attention to it, remember it, or understand it. **Development** clarifies and amplifies the claims and data in a speech. To clarify means *to make clear.* To amplify means *to enlarge or to expand.* Speakers who want to develop their claims clearly and fully can't rely on data and claims alone. Chapter 9 contains several examples of development. The more commonly used methods of development are examples, hypothetical examples, illustrations, and incidents.

Example

An **example** is a typical, specific instance of something. It's one of the most important types of support in any speech. To understand how important examples are, remember when you learned subtraction in grade school. Would you have learned if the teacher told you how to subtract but didn't show you? Weren't typical, specific examples of subtraction an important part of your learning? In fact, this paragraph uses learning subtraction as an example of the importance of examples.

Notice how often in this chapter a point is developed by using an example from a speech. Does this help your understanding of the point being made? Here is how an example might be used in a speech:

> Despite its reputation for being rebellious, rock music has done a lot of good [claim]. The music industry has frequently pulled together for good causes [data-fact]. "Concert for Bangladesh," organized by Beatle George Harrison, raised funds for a country ravaged by floods in the early 1970s [example]. Band-Aid and Live Aid, the idea of rocker Bob Geldof, raised money to buy food for starving people in North Africa [example]. "We Are the World," a project of Michael Jackson and Quincy Jones, was an all-star effort to record a song to raise money for charity [example].

To make the point, this speaker used specific names and projects. These examples help the speaker convince the audience of the claim.

Follow these recommendations for using examples in your speeches:

1. Find typical examples. Don't defeat the purpose of an example by using one that doesn't really show the point you are making.

2. Find clear examples. Make sure the audience can understand your example.

3. Find interesting examples. Dull ones can bore your audience.

4. Introduce your example. It's easy to fit an example into a speech. Just say, "For example" or "X is a good example of. . . "

5. If you have time, use more than one example.

6. Don't get into the habit of simply listing examples. Such a "laundry list" quickly gets boring.

Sometimes a speaker makes up a good example. This is a *hypothetical example*. It isn't meant to fool the audience. If you use a hypothetical example, tell your audience it's hypothetical to avoid confusion.

Illustration

Often a speaker expands an example into an **illustration,** a longer, more elaborate example. As the word implies, illustrations draw a picture for the audience. Just as pictures liven up a book, illustrations liven up a speech. Examples are important, but used alone they sound like lists. Look how the speaker talking about music uses illustrations to develop the topic:

> One reason disco music was so attractive to young people was the environment in which it was played. Even if kids just listened to it on the radio, movies like *Saturday Night Fever* gave them images of an exciting discotheque. In the mind's eye, handsome and beautiful people danced the night away. The clothes were always gorgeous. Flowing dresses billowed when the women spun around. Men wore suits, but not the kind dad or grandpa wore. These suits were white, worn over colored shirts open at the throat. Lights blazed over it all—a spinning mirrored ball on the ceiling, squares of light under the floor, spotlights from the corners, marquee lights running around the room. And behind it all, the beat—a pulsating reminder that the people, the clothes, the lights, and the music were for the young. Even if you didn't like the music, you had to admire the spectacle.

When you use an illustration, take the guidelines for examples into consideration. Follow these guidelines as well:

1. Use colorful, interesting language.

2. Treat your illustration as a word picture. Get your audience to "see" the illustration in the mind's eye.

3. Since illustrations are longer than examples, include a "tag" that ties back to the point you're making. In the example above, the tag was, "Even if you didn't like the music, you had to admire the spectacle." This reminded the audience that the speaker was illustrating music as a social force.

Incident

An **incident** (also called a *narrative* or *anecdote*) is an example in the form of a story. Everyone loves a good story. Audiences will often listen to one when they'll listen to nothing else. The story may be short or long. Be sure that the audience sees the relationship between the story and the point you're making. Otherwise, the incident is wasted. The speech on music included this incident:

> In the late 1960s, someone figured out that with enough money and the right songs, you could actually manufacture a rock-and-roll band from scratch. One day, an ad appeared telling of the need for young men who could sing and act. Thousands of people applied for the four jobs available. Requirements were related to music. The young men had to sing and/or play music. More important, they had to look the part of young rock musicians. Several musicians who were later to become very famous were rejected because they didn't look the part. The auditions went on until four likely candidates were chosen, but that was just the beginning. The TV show had to be created. The band had to be packaged, with each young man destined to acquire a catchy look and personality. Peter was goofy but sincere; Davy was cute and romantic; Mickey was creatively zany; and Mike was serious and relatively calm. The songs came next. Famous songwriters and unknowns both contributed to the band's playlist. It all paid off. The group, called the Monkees, hit number one with their first single, "Last Train to Clarksville." They were a rock force to be reckoned with and a new form of music began: Corporate Rock.

Because incidents are long, be careful about how you use them. Begin with the guidelines for examples and illustrations. Then follow these additional recommendations:

1. Treat your incident as you would a story. Tell it with enthusiasm and expect your audience to be interested.

2. Audiences respond very well to incidents, so always be on the lookout for good ones to use in speeches. Don't overuse them, however. A speech can quickly become a series of stories with no data or claims for them to support.

3. Watch your time limit. Don't let a single incident become the whole speech unless it's the topic of your speech.

Comparison and Contrast

When you point out similarities between two things, you're using **comparison.** When you point out important differences, you're using **contrast.** People use comparison and contrast all the time. When you decide what to have for lunch, you may make up your mind by comparing and contrasting a hamburger and a tuna sandwich. You'll consider cost, quantity, and taste before deciding.

Speakers often use comparison and contrast to develop their points. Sometimes an entire speech is built around the technique:

> At one time, AM radio stations were the only stations that played rock music. As FM stations gradually turned to a rock format, several differences became obvious. First, AM radio stuck to a tight, top-40 playlist. In other words, you might hear only a few tunes over and over. FM radio, on the other hand, played a broader range of music. Second, AM tunes were almost always singles, and record companies expected AM radio to boost sales of single songs. FM radio began to play album cuts, which meant they could broaden their playlists even more. Third, the AM radio dial was crowded. Static and distortion meant the music lost something in transmission. A portable AM radio's speakers didn't affect sound quality much because the quality had been hurt already in transmission. FM radio offered clear, static-free, quality sound. When young people started tuning out AM and tuning in FM, they were voting for clearer, more varied, more progressive music.

Unless you're careful, comparisons and contrasts can confuse your audience. Follow these guidelines:

1. Be sure your audience knows why you're making a comparison or a contrast. Explain what you're doing.
2. Supplement your comparison and contrast with examples.
3. Maintain a clear organization so the audience doesn't get confused. Clearly label what you're comparing or contrasting.
4. Use clear transitions.
5. Use gestures to show the two sides of the comparison and contrast.

Analogy: A Special Kind of Comparison   Sometimes a simple comparison is not enough. Speakers often use an **analogy,** or an extended comparison, to make their point. An analogy explains something the audience doesn't understand in terms of something the audience does understand. How would you explain the function of blood to a young child? You might compare the blood cells to tiny boats that carry precious cargo—the oxygen your cells need to live and work. You could then extend the comparison to include white blood cells and other important parts of blood.

Analogies come in two forms: figurative and literal. A *figurative analogy* is like the one above. Red blood cells and boats really have nothing in common. Boats are just a way to explain what the cells do. A *literal analogy* is an extended comparison of two things that actually are similar. For example, comparing the heart to a pump is a literal analogy because the heart is a pump for the body's blood. The two illustrations below demonstrate the difference between a figurative and a literal analogy:

Figurative Analogy

When the transistor radio came to the United States, it was a teen passport to another world. The young man might be at work, but he could envision Africa when he heard, ". . . the lion sleeps tonight." The young girl might be tanning on the beach, but she was also in a world of melodrama when she heard "He's a Rebel." A farmboy going to milking at 5:00 A.M. might as well have been in the big city with Dion singing "Runaround Sue." The passport could take anyone anywhere. It was small enough to put in your shirt pocket, and it even came with an earphone, so parents couldn't really tell where in the musical world their children had travelled with the "transistor passport." [Since transistor radios really have nothing literally in common with a passport, the analogy is figurative.]

Literal Analogy

The effect that the transistor radio had on young people in the 1960s is hard to imagine today. For those who were there, the change was similar to the recent boom in cellular phones. Like cellular phones, transistor radios were suddenly everywhere. They were convenient and relatively cheap. They kept people "in touch," and they had the added charm of being new and "high tech." [Since transistor radios and cellular phones are both examples of new technology with effects on culture, this analogy is literal.]

Description

A **description** provides specific physical details about the topic at hand. Speakers can give details about people, places, or things. Once again, descriptions help the audience form mental pictures. Note how vivid the following description is:

Some early rock groups went to great extremes to be noticed. The gimmicks seem pretty corny today, but they seemed successful in the '60s. Imagine going to see a rock concert and seeing the band emerge dressed as revolutionary war soldiers! All the band members would be in tight white pants—or breeches, as they were known in 1776. All would be in shirts with billowy sleeves and lacy fronts. At the start, all would wear jackets reminiscent of a revolutionary war soldier's: long tails in the rear; wide velvet lapels; double rows of brass buttons; and a three-cornered hat. The band's knee-high leather boots danced and tapped out the time to all the songs. This was the scene at a concert of Paul Revere and the Raiders, one of the hottest bands of the mid-1960s. What did the clothes have to do with music? Nothing really. But the gimmick brought this group to the public's attention. And once the attention was gained, the music sold itself.

Handle a description with the same care that you'd give an extended analogy. Otherwise, the audience may lose track of the point you're making. Follow these guidelines:

1. Use clear, colorful, exact language.

2. If a picture will help, use it (see the guidelines for using visual aids).

3. Use only relevant detail. Don't bog the audience down in unimportant description.

4. Use a "tag" to tie your description back to the point you're making. In the previous example, the tag was the statement, "The gimmick brought the group to the public's attention."

Definition

Often, you'll have to use **definition** to develop a subject. Especially in an informative speech, you may have to use a word that's unfamiliar to your audience. If you don't use the term, the audience may not be informed. If you use the term and don't define it, the audience still won't be informed. Only through definition can you make the point.

Work your definition smoothly into your speech, as this speaker did:

When the singer-songwriter took over, many thought it was the end to Tin Pan Alley, a fictional street that stood for the anonymous, professional songwriters who had been churning out most of America's pop music for decades. [This definition uses an appositive to define "Tin Pan Alley" by renaming it for people who might not know what it means.]

Be sure that your definition really clarifies rather than causing more confusion. Follow these guidelines:

1. Avoid using "according to *Webster's*" and other trite introductions to definitions.

2. Remember that there are many ways to define a term, including the dictionary definition, a synonym, a contrasting term, or an example. Don't always use the dictionary definition.

3. Don't appear to talk down to an audience when you define a term.

4. Make sure the definition is clear. Who wants to hear the word *kiss* defined as *an act of osculation?*

Integrating Types of Development

The sample speech starting on page 224 contains a variety of supportive material, both data and development. The speaker, Gene F. Jankowski, former President of CBS Broadcasting, carefully built a speech that proved his claims, developed his points, and interested his audience. Jankowski's speech contains many types of support and development. Here are some examples drawn from the speech.

Thesis	This notion [that television is the "first curriculum" for America's youth] is based on the myth that the sheer amount of time children spent on television is more important than time spent in school.
Statistics	. . . a typical child may spend 11,500 hours in school between kindergarten and high school, but spends up to 15,000 hours watching television from ages five to 18.
Fact	Total spending on education last year, including elementary and secondary schools and higher education, was $260.2 billion.
Testimony	Dr. Daniel Boorstin, the Librarian of Congress, describes the effort as "linking the pleasure, power and excitement" of books and television.
Analogy	Doing so is much the same as arguing that if men spend more time shaving than in prayer, then it follows that razors are more important than Bibles, whiskers more important than faith.
Comparison/Contrast	Unlike television, formal education takes place in institutional settings—schools and classrooms.
	Total spending on education last year, including elementary and secondary schools and higher education, was $260.2 billion. Total spending on all forms of commercial television last year was close to $20 billion, a fraction of that spent on education. Unlike schooling, television is not mandated by the state.

Example	We also recognized a need to reach out to the college campuses . . .
	. . . a unique documentary film . . .
	We have also tried to bring college professors into our day-to-day business . . .
	To that end, CBS has instituted a "Scholar-In-Residence" program . . .
Description	It is a source of constant amazement to me that the television set, an inert, immobile appliance, that does not eat, drink, or smoke, buy or sell anything, can't vote, doesn't have a job, can't think, can't turn itself on or off, and is used only at our option can be seen as the cause of so much of society's ills by so many people in education.

SAMPLE SPEECH
Television and Teachers
Gene F. Jankowski

For thirty years the Broadcast Education Association has labored to bridge the gap between the worlds of broadcasting and higher education. I am delighted to be with you today to help celebrate and encourage this most important work. To me, few tasks are more important, because misunderstandings between the worlds of education and broadcasting not only can be deep and troubling, but also can thwart productive alliances between our fields.

These misunderstandings lie at many levels. At one level there is deep confusion about the role of commercial television in the education of school children.

At other levels, the sources of confusion can be traced to deep biases against television within the academic world. It is here that the medium's central role in popular entertainment and commerce is frequently misunderstood and decried. Yet at the same time, the television industry depends upon

higher education to play an absolutely critical role in preparing young people for careers in our field. Here, too, we can encounter conflicting purposes and misunderstandings.

Let me attempt to unravel some of these misunderstandings, first by separating the facts from the myths about television and the schools in the education of young people. These roles have become so confused that television has itself been deemed to be *the* major force in educating the young. This is a preposterous myth in my view. In fact, one recent book by an NYU professor goes so far as to argue: "Television is not only a curriculum, but constitutes the major educational enterprise now being undertaken in the United States." The professor calls television the "first curriculum," school the second.

This notion is based on the *myth* that the sheer amount of time children spent on television is more important than time spent in school. The *facts* are otherwise.

This author argues that a typical child may spend 11,500 hours in school between kindergarten and high school, but spends up to 15,000 hours watching television from ages five to eighteen. Therefore, he concludes, television is the primary educational enterprise. What an incredible line of thinking!

Stating the figures that way tends to distort the fact that on average children spend over three hours a day watching television, the time increasing somewhat in the junior high school years, and then declining in high school. Of course, we know children spend much more time in school each day than that, but since they don't go to school on Saturday and Sunday, or during the summer, comparisons are misleading.

But let's not argue about the numbers, because comparing school and television based on such numbers is absurd. To do so is worse than comparing apples and oranges. When you compare totally different activities simply on the basis of the time devoted to each, you end up with meaningless numbers, and misleading conclusions. Doing so is much the same as arguing that if men spend more time shaving than in prayer, then it follows that razors are more important than Bibles, whiskers more important than faith.

Still, the *myth* persists that television and education are the same thing. But the *fact* is that schooling and television are two entirely different realms of human endeavor and experience. The differences are obvious. School is based on a formal body of knowledge organized sequentially, and is mandated by the state which supports and supervises it.

Unlike television, formal education takes place in institutional settings—schools and classrooms. Students advance through a formal sequence of courses, a curriculum. As they do, they become qualified for higher education or various professions and pursuits. The process of education is one of the most important undertakings in our society by any measure. Only health outranks education in terms of its share of Gross National Product.

Still, there is the *myth* that more money is spent on television than is spent on education. The *fact* is that's nonsense. Total spending on education last year, including elementary and secondary schools and higher education, was $260.2 billion. Total spending on all forms of commercial television last year was close to $20 billion, a fraction of that spent on education.

Then there's the *myth* that people are forced to watch television. Again the *facts* lie elsewhere. Unlike schooling, television viewing is not mandated by the state. People make viewing choices freely and independently. There is no compulsion. Television viewing takes place during leisure time, and this activity occupies a very different place in human affairs and meets very different needs.

As a primary source of entertainment, television gives the blessings of pleasure to millions of people. As the primary source of news, television is an extraordinary disseminator of information. In this respect, it undoubtedly contributes much to public knowledge and understanding. Equally important, the medium's more pervasive form, network.television, binds the nation through shared experiences—sharing the triumph of American astronauts landing on the moon; sharing the tragedy of the space shuttle exploding in disaster.

The *fact* is television can be educational, but it is not curriculum nor a school. That is a myth. Television, by design, is not an instrument of teaching. Yet, based on how it is used, the medium has much to offer in educational value.

Some academics do confuse facts and myths. And there are several answers why some of them are opposed to television. One answer is that the role of television has often been misunderstood by behavioral scientists, who have frequently attacked the medium for causing some sort of social harm. Other educators have attacked television for undermining reading and student achievement. When SAT scores went down a few years ago, television received a great deal of the blame. Now SAT scores have climbed. Young people are watching more television these days, but no one is saying our medium was only an easy scapegoat when SAT scores were low.

It is a source of constant amazement to me that the television set, an inert, immobile appliance, that does not eat, drink, or smoke, buy or sell anything, can't vote, doesn't have a job, can't think, can't turn itself on or off, and is used only at our option can be seen as the cause of so much of society's ills by so many people involved in education.

Broadcasters have been trying to improve impressions about television and to improve relationships with the academic community.

Those efforts have been to reach out to educators and to assist them wherever possible in using television to support their activities in the classroom.

At CBS, for example, such efforts include the CBS Television Reading Program, now entering its 10th year, and our partnership with the Library of Congress in the "Read More About It" project.

Dr. Daniel Boorstin, the Librarian of Congress, describes the effort as "linking the pleasure, power and excitement" of books and television.

We also recognized a need to reach out to the college campuses to talk about our business, especially where we could help demystify the process of creating television and the roles we play in it.

Central to this effort was the production of a unique documentary film, "Making Television: Inside CBS," which has now been viewed at dozens of colleges and universities, and which all of you, I hope, have had an opportunity to see during the last day or so.

We have also tried to bring college professors into our day-to-day business, so we can begin to understand each other on a more intimate basis.

To that end, CBS has instituted a "Scholar-In-Residence" program with professors in the humanities, and last summer we were pleased to have a professor from Michigan State serve as a BEA faculty intern, where he gained extensive involvement with broadcast promotion and marketing activities.

We also continue our dialogue with professors in the behavioral sciences, many of whom have been persistent and influential critics of television for many years.

While we may disagree with their conclusions, we believe it is extremely important to be aware of their concerns, and share with them our research as well. To that end, last month CBS underwrote and participated in a conference that brought together members of the Society for the Psychological Study of Social Issues. The conference provided a forum for psychologists, sociologists and various CBS executives to exchange their views.

With all these wide-ranging activities, we have not only shared our perspectives and experiences, we have listened and learned. Now, let me mention some educational experiences that have had particular relevance to many of us in the industry.

I believe that broad liberal arts training and studies in mass communications have been extremely important to a lot of us both professionally and personally. Yet when we return to college campuses today, we meet an increasing number of young people who are drawn to broadcasting through their studies, but who often receive a limited understanding of our field in the process.

That situation is underscored by the fragmentation in the field. At some schools, television is studied by broadcast or telecommunications students; at others, it's the journalism school; at others, it's mass communications; at others, it's the business school, or the film school, or the drama or speech departments.

Now this balkanization of media studies is not just untidy, it can narrow and limit the vision of young people entering our field. At CBS, managers are attempting to build on the synergies between print, broadcasting and other electronic media. We do this because economic and technological forces are causing once separate media businesses to converge and merge.

There has been no more significant year in our industry's recent history than 1985, when multi-billion dollar mergers in media business linked print, broadcasting, cable, program production and advertising firms in new and wide-ranging combinations.

Yet, for the most part, college teaching about the media field remains divided along narrow disciplines, with different disciplines claiming different pieces of media turf.

As a result, I fear we are producing jour-nalism graduates who are unprepared to be managers, programmers who have little understanding of news, and business graduates who lack knowledge of the creative process. Worse, we have graduates in all these fields who do not have a broader understanding of the society in which they live, its cultural traditions and its moral values.

As I look out across this room, I recognize that I may be preaching to the converted. I recognize that just about everywhere broadcast educators are teaching their subjects as an integral part of the humanities programs in their colleges and universities. I also realize that courses in mass communications and journalism can relate very meaningfully to other studies in the liberal arts.

For those of us who have made careers in broadcasting, the affinity between studies of telecommunications and the liberal arts is obvious. Station managers are business managers who must grapple with elements of news, public affairs and politics. They also must understand the literary, dramatic and comedic forms that underlie the programming their stations offer.

I am convinced that broadcasting and telecommunications courses can effectively contribute to a broad liberal education, but only when they are taught in a way that is intellectually rigorous. You don't have to be a Renaissance man to be a broadcaster, but it certainly helps.

Communications studies have flourished, as colleges and universities have moved away from rigid course requirements. Increasingly, students are acting as powerful consumers in selecting among liberal arts courses. This student consumerism has led to rapid expansion of journalism and broadcast offerings.

One recent survey reveals that in 1985 there were over 82,000 college students enrolled in mass communications and journalism. That reflects an increase of over 10,000 students in these fields in just five years.

Consequently, those of us who care so much about preparing young people for our field must work together to make sure that in its rapid expansion, communications coursework is not only popular, but profound; and not only abundant, but excellent.

Television and education are two different worlds, but they should not be opposing forces. Television and education should be complementary undertakings, and they will be if both broadcasters and educators work together as they have through BEA.

Business executives cannot and should not attempt to write curricula, but they can speak out on behalf of the humanities before college groups and personnel departments. If we want to assure vocationally minded college students that a liberal arts education will be valuable, then company personnel departments must be as accommodating to history majors as they are to business administration majors in their recruiting.

Let me close by noting the theme of your conference: "A Partnership of Broadcasting and Education." The word "partnership" implies working together. That's the right way to approach the relationship. There is much we can do together. There is much we can give to each other. To do so, we must continue to devote time and energy to the task of educating each other. I strongly believe that we will.

Visual Aids

Visual aids are so unlike other types of support material that they must be considered separately. Visual aids add variety to a speech. Many people in an average audience find it easier to understand what they see than what they hear. The key to using visual aids successfully is to be sure they *supplement* the speech rather than becoming the speech itself. Here are some visual aids you can use.

Chalkboard

The chalkboard is the easiest visual aid to use. You don't have to prepare much ahead of time. Just be sure a board and chalk are available and plan the kind of information you will write out on the board. These suggestions will help you. Follow them if you use an overhead projector as well:

1. Write largely enough that everyone can see. You may want to print instead of write—printing is usually easier to read.

2. Display your information from audience-left to audience-right so it follows typical page arrangement.

3. Don't write too far down the board. People in the back of the room can't see the bottom of the chalkboard.

4. Don't block the board. Stand to one side of what you've written. Use a pointer if necessary.

5. Don't speak with your back to the audience while you write on the board. Write first, then speak. (Remember, don't be afraid to be silent.)

6. Keep the things you write out simple. Use words, phrases, and abbreviations rather than complete sentences. If you spend too much time writing things on the board, the audience will lose interest.

7. Erase frequently. Don't clutter the board and make it hard to read.

Posters

Many speakers prepare visual aids ahead of time by using poster-board or newsprint. Professional speakers often have easels that hold large tablets. They write out material on several sheets of the tablet and turn the pages as necessary.

You can use posters in two ways. First, use them to preview or summarize your main ideas. Write out the words or terms that are the headings for the parts of your speech. Second, draw pictures or diagrams to clarify parts of your speech.

Posters are only helpful if everyone in the audience can see them. Follow these guidelines to use posters effectively:

1. Use dark ink—black, blue, and red are best. Yellow, pink, and light green may look pretty, but they're difficult to see from a distance.

2. Write in clear, large letters.

3. Put one idea on each sheet. Don't clutter the pages. Remember, you want the audience to focus on one idea at a time.

4. If you don't have an easel, tape posters to the chalkboard or place them on the chalk tray. Holding a poster restricts your ability to move and hides you from the audience.

5. Show a poster only when you're ready to discuss it and remove it as soon as you're finished with it. If you're going to refer to it several times, keep it out. Otherwise, you'll lose time and audience attention by taking it out several times.

6. Practice your speech with the posters. Know what you're going to say and how you're going to present the information.

Objects or Models

You may want to use an actual object or model as a part of your speech. Informative speeches that demonstrate a product or a process often are enriched by using an object or model. Real objects are powerful visual aids. Use them carefully so they don't distract from your speech. Follow these guidelines:

1. Keep it safe. Don't attempt to use objects or models that are dangerous. The risk is too great, and the audience will be uncomfortable.

2. Keep it simple. Don't use extremely complicated models or objects that are difficult for the audience to see or understand. Remember, the purpose of a visual aid is to make the speech clearer.

3. Before your speech begins, put the model somewhere out of sight. Don't bring it out until you're ready to use it. It may distract the audience.

4. Try to use only an object or model that the entire audience can see at the same time. Passing around an object or model can be a great distraction.

5. Don't block the model or object from the audience's view.

Audiovisual Equipment

A more professional way to present material is to use audiovisual equipment such as slides, movies, and videotapes. Using these sources makes giving a speech more complicated, but they can also make listening much easier and more enjoyable for the audience.

Since audiovisual resources are more complicated than other visual aids, they require more preparation. Follow these guidelines:

1. Preview the audiovisual material and practice your speech with it. This can help you avoid problems during your actual presentation.

2. Be sure you know how to use the equipment. No one wants to spend several minutes sitting in the dark while you figure out how to use a projector.

3. Be sure the equipment is in good working condition. Always test the projector before the speech. If possible, have spare bulbs for projectors.

4. Know where the electrical outlets are. Find out if the room has a movie screen. If not, arrange to have one ready.

5. Don't let audiovisual materials take over the speech. Use them as support for your speech, not as the speech itself. Gauge how much time you have. Then decide whether the materials will take too much of that time.

Handouts

Rather than prepare one poster or show a picture on a projector, many speakers prepare handouts for each member of the audience. Handouts do more than help your presentation. They also give the audience something to take home as a reminder of what you talked about. Follow these guidelines when you use handouts:

1. Plan when and how to pass out your handouts. If you pass them out at the beginning of the speech, the audience may look at them rather than listening to you. It's better to pass them out when you're ready to use them. Whenever you pass them out, do it as quickly and calmly as possible.

2. Make sure you've prepared enough handouts. It's better to have too many than too few. Ask the organizer of the occasion how many people to expect.

3. Make sure the handout is attractive and legible. It represents you and your ideas.

4. Don't pass around only one handout for everyone to see. If you can't have individual handouts, use the chalkboard or a poster instead.

Graphs

Graphs really aren't a separate type of visual aid. They can be presented on a chalkboard, a poster, AV, or handout. Graphs are very special, though. They are a good way to present statistics, especially when you use more than one or two statistics or when you compare statistics. Graphs help the audience visualize the numbers you use. Remember, when you use a graph, explain it to the audience. If you don't, many members of your audience won't understand the graph's significance. Make sure the graph is clearly labelled. Figure 12.1 (on page 232) shows three types of graphs used in public speaking.

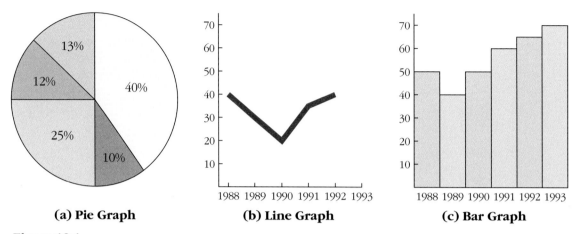

(a) Pie Graph   (b) Line Graph   (c) Bar Graph

Figure 12.1
Three Types
of Graphs

Yourself

You yourself can be a visual aid. Many topics allow you to demonstrate something to the audience. If you're giving a speech on how to hit a softball, you can use a bat and demonstrate how to use it. The sample speech on page 322 requires the speaker to demonstrate relaxation exercises.

If you're part of the visual presentation, remember the rule for all other visuals: be sure everyone can see you, and be sure your movements are large enough for everyone to tell what you're doing. Remember also that you have to demonstrate a process more than once to make sure everyone understands. Unlike a picture or poster, the audience sees what you do for only a short time.

New Technology

Like everything else in our lives, public speaking has been changed by **technology.** With new methods of projecting and generating images, doing research, and composing, speech has entered the computer age. The changes can make your speech presentation different, but the basics are always the same. A technological method is only successful if it fits situation, purpose, and audience.

Situation: Is the technology appropriate for the situation? Will you be in a location where it will be usable?

Purpose: Is the technology consistent with your purpose? For example, will the presence of a computer reduce the likelihood that your entertaining speech will actually entertain? Will it hurt the personal tone you want?

Audience: How will the audience feel about the technology? Is the technology going to call more attention to itself than it deserves? Will you spend so much time with the technology that your audience will feel left out?

Here are some examples of technology that can help speakers. Some of these items may be available to you through your class, your media center, or your local library:

1. **Overhead projector panel:** An overhead projector panel is linked to a personal computer and allows a speaker to project whatever is on the computer screen onto a wall screen. Speakers can create a series of computer screens to assist in speech delivery. Black-and-white or color is available.

2. **Projection TV:** By linking a computer or television to a TV projector, a speaker can provide an audience with color video or color computer screens. With newer computers, video and computer screens are visible simultaneously.

New technology enables speakers to project whatever is on their computer monitor onto wall screens or television screens for the audience to see.

The Overhead Projector:
A Special Audiovisual Tool

Business and professional speakers will often use an overhead projector to provide visuals for their audiences. You are probably familiar with overhead projectors from school, and you can learn a lot about their use from watching your teachers. Here are some special rules to remember when you use an overhead projector:

1. One important advantage of an overhead projector is that it allows a speaker to face the audience at all times. Don't sacrifice this advantage by turning your back on your audience and talking to the screen.

2. An overhead projector will project an image on a screen or a white wall. Practice positioning and adjusting your transparencies before your speech. This will help you get your entire visual on the screen at one time and help you realize that you must move the visual with care.

3. If you are going to use a number of transparencies prepared beforehand, number them so you can keep them in sequence. Many transparencies have an opaque strip that you can write on.

4. Don't leave a transparency on the screen after you have used it. It can take an audience's attention away from your speech.

5. If you have multiple ideas on one transparency, cover the part you don't wish to disclose with a thick piece of paper or a piece of light cardboard. The extra weight of heavy paper or cardboard will keep the projector's fan from blowing it off.

6. Remember: the projector has an on-off switch. Turn it on when you need it and off when you don't.

7. The projector runs a fan to keep itself cool. You will have to speak up to be heard over it. If questions are asked while the projector is on, you'll likely have to repeat the question so everyone can hear it.

3. **Presentation software:** To make use of overhead projection panels and projection TV (as well as 35 mm slides), presentation software allows a speaker to create visuals that are exciting and attractive. With a variety of type fonts, colors, and special effects, a speaker's visuals can look as good as those on the evening news. Some computers now come with software that can be used for presentations.

4. **Composition software:** In addition to word processing, some companies are making software to help speechwriters. Collections of quotations on floppy disks can be a handy reference source. Some software gives the user questions to help generate ideas.

5. **CD-ROM:** One problem of videotape and audiotape is that it can't be accessed readily by a speaker. If you want to see something in the middle of the tape and you are at the beginning, you have to fast forward, stop to check your place, and fast forward some more just to cue up the tape. CD-ROM (compact disk/read-only memory) technology allows immediate access to sounds and images. Access can be controlled best with a computer.

Chapter 12 Summary

Speakers create the body of a speech from support material. Support material comes in two forms: data and development. Data is evidence. It can be used to prove a claim. The three types of data are testimony, statistics, and facts. Development clarifies and amplifies the data. The most important types of development are example, illustration, incident, comparison/contrast, analogy, description, and definition. A well-developed speech uses a variety of support material. Material is chosen for its interest to the audience, its appropriateness to the situation, and its ability to support the thesis.

Often speakers supplement their speeches with visual aids. Visual aids should always be used carefully. Used incorrectly, they'll detract from the speech and make it less likely that the speaker will accomplish the speech purpose.

◆ Check Your Understanding

1. Define *support material*.

2. Explain how a speaker uses his or her understanding of situation, purpose, and audience to decide whether or not to include support material in a speech.

3. Explain the different uses of data and development.

4. Figure the suggested lengths for the bodies of speeches that are
   a. twelve minutes long
   b. sixteen minutes long
   c. twenty minutes long

5. List and define the three types of data.

6. List and define five types of development.

7. List two rules for using each of the following visual aids:
   a. chalkboard
   b. posters
   c. models/objects
   d. audiovisual equipment
   e. handouts

8. Explain some of the new types of technology.

◆ Apply Your Understanding

1. Using a speech in this book, one given in class, or one provided by your teacher, identify the kinds of support the speaker used. Your finished project should look like this chapter's list of support in Jankowski's speech. Determine if the speaker used a variety of types of support.

2. Professional public speakers often collect interesting facts, anecdotes, illustrations, and statistics to use in speech development. Start your own file. It can be in a notebook or file folder. As you read and hear interesting material, make it a part of your collection. Concentrate your efforts on subjects you find interesting or important, but don't pass up an interesting idea if it strikes you. At the end of the first week of collection, share your file in groups of four. Continue your collection for the remainder of the term.

◆ Thinking Critically about Public Speaking

1. Working in groups of four or five, select topics for research. Phrase a purpose statement and thesis statement based on situation and audience. Spending no more than one day in the library, find support material for the speech. Find (or create) at least one example for each type of data and development.

2. Before you prepare your next speech, write a prospectus—a short description of what your speech will be about. Include the following: a purpose statement, a thesis statement, a short description of audience and situation, and a list of the kind of support you wish to use. Discuss this prospectus with your teacher. After you prepare and deliver the speech, check back to see how closely you stayed to the prospectus.

◆ Speak Out!

1. Prepare a three- to five-minute informative speech, using visual aids as part of your support material. Make sure you use the visual aids according to the guidelines in this chapter. Select from the following topics or use one your teacher assigns:

   a. an interesting place to visit

    b. being an intelligent consumer (narrow the topic to one product or strategy)

    c. advertising a product

2.   Working in pairs, prepare a three- to five-minute speech on a topic of your choice. Your goal is to show the class how not to use visual aids. Provide examples from at least two types of visual aids. After the speech, discuss the mistakes you made and how to correct them.

3.   Singly or in pairs, prepare a brief speech for the class on the operation of a piece of audiovisual equipment. You may need to check with your library or media center specialist for instructions and check-out. Use the following list to guide your choice or ask your specialist for help:

a 35 mm camera	a video camera
a slide projector	an overhead projector
a videocassette recorder	a CD-ROM reader

◆ *Speech Challenge*

The relationship between claim, data, and development can be represented as a diagram:

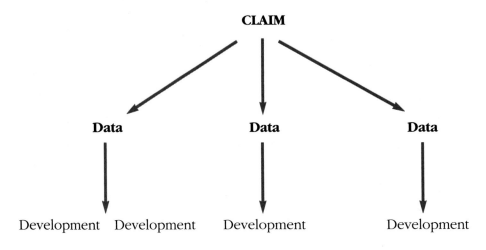

CLAIM

Data   **Data**   **Data**

Development Development   Development   Development

For example, the claim regarding Lincoln's speeches could be represented as follows:

CLAIM: Lincoln's speeches lasted
far beyond their immediate situation.

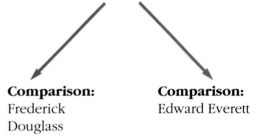

Data: Dictionaries of quotations contain far more from Lincoln than from other presidents.

Data: Lincoln's speeches have endured while others' have not.

Examples: "Of the people, by the people; with malice toward none; half slave, half free"

Comparison:
Frederick
Douglass

Comparison:
Edward Everett

Select a speech (one of your own or someone else's) and diagram how development supports data and how data supports claims.

CHAPTER ·13·

Key Terms

Attributing

Call number

Card catalog

Dewey decimal system

Journal

Keyword

Library of Congress
system

Media center

On-line catalog

Periodical

Plagiarism

Working bibliography

Chapter Objectives

After studying this chapter, you will be able to:

1. Explain the importance of research to a speaker.
2. Explain how to make efficient use of media-center time.
3. Use indexes to find information on a topic.
4. Identify reference materials useful in finding information on a topic.
5. Prepare and conduct an interview as part of the speech preparation process.
6. Explain the need to acknowledge sources used in speech preparation.

Research

When What You Know Isn't Enough

When you speak to an audience, it's natural to want to talk about things you already know. Your experiences, hobbies, or jobs are easy to speak about because to get material for the speech, you simply take inventory of the information in your memory. You use what will be effective, given the audience and the situation.

Nevertheless, people are often required to speak on topics they don't know much about. Or, speakers may want fresh, exciting material for a topic they do know about. In classes such as English, American history, government, and science, students are frequently assigned speeches so they can learn new things and share them with others. In these classes, even if you choose your topic, you probably won't find one on which you are an authority. You will have to do research.

Why is research part of speech education? Suppose you had to give a speech about I.Q. tests for a psychology class. You probably don't know much about this topic. Even if you do, you need to convince your listeners that your speech is accurate. In either case, you can borrow the authority you may lack by referring to informed, well-qualified people. After all, the audience will believe the person who invented the I.Q. test, even if they don't believe you.

To increase speech effectiveness—and your own credibility—you'll want to know the most recent information. Are there any new controversies? Knowing about them will help you understand the audience's attitudes and any situation you might face.

A quick survey of speech purposes shows how important it is to use resource materials and resource people. A speech to entertain requires interesting facts, clever sayings, or humorous anecdotes. Do you have them all stored in your memory? An informative speech must present new information to an audience. Do you always have new information ready to present in an interesting manner? A persuasive speech must try to change people's minds. Can you recall the kind of convincing, authoritative evidence that will make people think seriously about your position? The answer to these questions is probably *no*. Everyone needs help from outside sources at some time.

Using the Media Center

People now frequently call the library the **media center.** The change is an important one, for today's libraries often contain far more than

Are You Prepared for the Media Center?

1. Have you used the speaking situation to focus your research?
   a. What is your subject? Why have you chosen it?
   b. What is your purpose?
   c. What does your audience expect? What do they need to know?
2. What kinds of supportive material will you need to find to accomplish your purpose with the audience?
3. Do you have the necessary hardware for a successful trip to the media center?
   a. Pen or pencil
   b. Paper
   c. Note cards
   d. Notes already made for the speech

books. In addition to the traditional library holdings, a modern media center provides films, videotapes, compact disks, and computers. With such a storehouse of information, you must make the most efficient use of the time you spend in a media center. Of course, not every center collects the same types of material. You must learn to use the materials that are available and seek out other media centers that contain alternatives.

Focusing Your Research

However, before you can search for something, you must know what you're seeking. That means you must understand the speaking situation before you can use the media center effectively. Media center specialists would say you must *focus* your research, and the best way to do that is to use the SPAM model. Analyze your situation, purpose, and audience before beginning to select your methods.

The media center can play a part in topic selection. Think of this example: You're assigned a speech about your state. You can choose a topic about your state's history, economy, government, or geography. What are you going to do? Think about the members of your audience—what do they want or need to hear about? Think about the situation—what kinds of topics are appropriate? Think about yourself—what do you feel comfortable speaking about? Of course, you'll think about purpose—what do you want the speech to accomplish?

Once you've completed your analysis, you'll begin to think about your support materials. Is enough material available on your topic? Will the material be in the media center? Chances are, you'll have to go to the media center to find out.

Going to the media center without using the SPAM model is a serious mistake. If you're like most people, you don't have an unlimited amount of time. Thinking through your potential topic will keep you from wasting time. You may get to the media center and decide—based on what you find—to change your approach. If so, you're still in good shape because you are making an informed decision.

Narrowing Your Topic

Sometimes you will go to the media center without having narrowed your topic. For example, say that you have to speak about the environment, but you're not sure of your speech's specific topic. Here are some ways you can use the media center to help you narrow your topic, but keep in mind that the tools of the media center are supplements for your own understanding of audience and situation:

1. Read a general article in an encyclopedia. Don't ignore such entries as "environmentalism." You may want to read from a general encyclopedia or a specialized one.

2. Look in the *Readers' Guide* or some other index to periodicals. These indexes will break a complex subject down into subheadings that can be clues to narrowing a topic. In addition, indexes can give you *See* and *See also* directions that may help you think of a speech topic (for example, *"See also,* acid rain"). An article's title may help you think of related topics.

3. Find a book on the subject. Look at the table of contents and the index. Entries in either may point you to a good speech topic. Also, the number of pages devoted to a topic can give you an idea of how much material is available. If there is an entry such as "oil spills," you may have taken a step toward a speech topic you'll find interesting, and more important, one that will appeal to your audience.

Why can these sources be helpful in narrowing? Professional writers know the same rules as good public speakers. Professional writers think about situation, purpose, and audience. They also know that narrow topics are more successful than general topics. You can use their work to help you narrow your topic.

Selecting Material

The three feedback loops (Chapter 2) can help you select material from the media center. You establish the first loop when you analyze those who make up your audience and what they expect. As you research in a media center, imagine the audience is reading over your shoulder. When you read an interesting fact about your topic, ask yourself, "Is this something my audience needs to know? Will this information help me entertain, inform, or persuade?" These questions will help you choose from materials in the media center.

Here is how the process works. Suppose you've chosen to speak about your state's economy. Since your audience is composed of young people who will soon graduate, you've decided that they'll be interested in what jobs will be available in the near future. Here are your purpose statement and thesis statement:

> **Purpose Statement**
> The purpose of this speech is to inform the class about the kinds of jobs that will be available in the state when they graduate from high school.

> **Thesis Statement**
> Although some parts of the state's economy are depressed now, the demand for skilled labor and service-related jobs should be good when your class graduates from high school.

These statements will help you decide what kind of information to look for. Will you look at the state's history? Probably not. Will you look up articles about national job opportunities? Yes, since they may give a state-by-state breakdown. What happens if you see this passage in a magazine article?

> All western and southwestern states are likely to see a substantial growth in population throughout the remainder of the century. In these states, service industries will continue to need large numbers of employees to serve the needs of the growing populations. The outlook for service industries in other states is not so attractive.

Is this useful information? If you live in a western or southwestern state, it certainly says something about jobs in your area. But what if you live in a different region? This information is still useful because it explains why service jobs may not be available in your area. Without an idea of your purpose and thesis, you may not know what information is important and what isn't.

Being Prepared for Research

Using the media center successfully requires basic planning. Take along pencil, paper, and note cards, as well as any notes you've already made on your speech topic. If this is your second trip to the media center, refer to the notes from your first trip. Without them, you may look up the same sources, take down the same information, and waste time.

Preparing a Working Bibliography

When you begin to research, build a list of possible sources. This list is called a **working bibliography.** Listing sources in a working bibliography is efficient. It allows you to look up a number of sources all at once. Putting your working bibliography on note cards is helpful when you have to cite sources. Usually, a bibliography card contains the following information (see Figure 13.1).

Book	**Periodical**
Author	Author of article (if given)
Title	Title of article
Publisher	Title of periodical
Place of publication	Date of periodical
Date of publication	Volume number
	Page numbers of article

Figure 13.1
Bibliography
Card

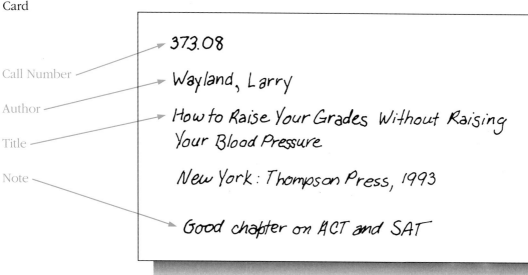

Call Number

Author

Title

Note

373.08

Wayland, Larry

How to Raise Your Grades Without Raising Your Blood Pressure

New York: Thompson Press, 1993

Good chapter on ACT and SAT

Using the Media Center Specialist

The staff of every media center can help you use its resources. If you aren't familiar with the media center, they will teach you. If you can't find information on a topic, they'll have suggestions about where to look next. They may even tell you that the information isn't available in the media center and suggest alternate sources. The media center specialist is the most important resource in the entire media center.

Researching with Books

Books in a media center usually fall into two categories: fiction and nonfiction. There also may be separate sections for paperbacks, short stories, or other groupings. Fictional works are the products of the author's imagination. Therefore, fiction isn't used for research on speeches unless you're giving a speech on one or more fictional works of a specific author. Fiction can also be a source of interesting material for introductions and examples, as well as interesting incidents and quotations. Speakers usually use nonfiction. These books are the backbone of media center research because they contain the data and development most speeches need.

How do you use the nonfiction collection efficiently? You use the card catalog. The **card catalog** is an alphabetically arranged index of all the books and other materials in the media center. Each book may appear in the card catalog many times, depending on how many subjects the book covers.

Since media centers have begun using computers to index books, catalogs have come in the traditional card format and in on-line, computerized catalogs. Either way, the catalog makes finding your books much easier.

The Card Catalog

In a card catalog, each book will have at least three entries: an author card, a title card, and a subject card. The three cards are largely the same, except for the first line. If you know an author who has written about your subject, the author cards will show you all of his or her books that the media center holds. If you know the title of a specific book, you can find it quickly by looking under the title. Usually, the subject cards will be the most useful. If your speech is about cosmetic surgery, for example, could you think of the title or author of a book right off the top of your head? Probably not. But in the card catalog, under the subject *surgery,* you'll probably find something.

Remember, if you can't find your topic, look for other subjects that might include yours. *Fishing* may be listed under *water sports. ESP* may be listed under *parapsychology.* If you have problems, ask the media specialist for help.

Subject cards have the topic printed in bold type at the top. Beneath it is information about the book. Most important, the **call number** is in the upper left corner. This number tells you where the book is stored. Figure 13.2 shows examples of the three types of cards.

Figure 13.2
Author, Title, and
Subject Cards

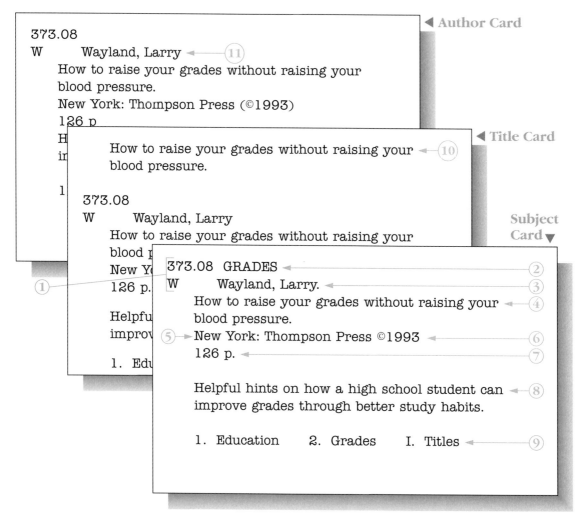

1. Call number
2. Subject heading for subject card
3. Author
4. Title of book
5. Publisher and place of publication
6. Date of copyright
7. Number of pages
8. Annotation
9. Alternate entries in card catalog
10. Title heading for title card
11. Author heading for author card

See and ***See also*** **Cards**   Often a card catalog uses *See* or *See also* entries to direct a researcher to another part of the catalog. For example, if you're researching *fossils,* a *See* or *See also* card may direct you to other topics such as *paleontology* or *prehistoric animals.*

The On-Line Catalog

When a card catalog is stored in a computer's memory and not on file cards, we say the catalog is **on-line.** That means it can be accessed through a computer terminal. Different media centers will offer different catalogs, each with its own screens and instructions. The basics, however, are almost always the same.

As with a traditional card catalog, you can look up books by title, author, and subject. The on-line catalog, however, offers an important new way to look up books: by keyword. A **keyword** is a word that is important to your search, but it may not show up in the title of a work. In fact, a keyword may be contained only in the description of the book. Right away you can see the advantage. If you are researching the topic *computers* in a card catalog, you might get some books and a *See also* card referring you to other parts of the card catalog such as *technology* or *mathematics.* A keyword search of the word *computers* will let you see the location of any book that the computer knows is about computers.

Some on-line systems go even further. You can modify your descriptions in these important ways:

1. You can tell the computer to select only books within certain dates. This can give you the most recent information, information from an important period of time, or older information.

2. You can tell the computer to select only books that mention two subjects. For example, if your speech is about how computers were used in art, you might ask for books that cover computers and art.

3. You can tell the computer to select only books that mention one subject and not another. For example, you might want to know about drawing with computers, but not if the books are about architecture or drafting. You can tell the computer to eliminate those books from your search.

4. You can modify the word in your keyword search. For example, if you want to make sure you don't eliminate possibilities, systems have ways of asking for *technology* and *technological* in one abbreviation.

Because all systems are different, you should work with your media center to find out how its on-line catalog can best be used.

On-line catalogs allow researchers to use keywords related to their topics as they search for source materials.

Call Number System

The call number on a card is a code that tells you how resources are organized in the media center. There are two systems: the Dewey decimal system and the Library of Congress system.

Dewey Decimal System   Most media centers organize nonfiction books by the **Dewey decimal system.** The word *decimal* means "ten." The ten divisions of the system are easy to learn. Figure 13.3 lists the numbers designated for each division. A book's call number in the Dewey decimal system looks like this:

808.7

Fos

This number directs you to the 800 section of the media center. It directs you to a particular part of that section: 808.7. Finally, it directs you to the specific book 808.7/Fos.

Library of Congress System   More and more, media centers arrange materials according to the **Library of Congress system,** which uses letters for primary divisions rather than the numerals of the Dewey system (see Figure 13.4). Media centers like the Library of Congress system because it provides more divisions for cataloging. Card catalog entries will look the same except for the call number.

The Dewey Decimal Categories

000–099 General Works   general reference works, journalism

100–199 Philosophy   history of philosophy, ethics, morality, psychology, parapsychology

200–299 Religion   specific religions, the Bible, history of religion, mythology

300–399 Social Studies   sociology, anthropology, political science, law, education, business, women's issues, cities, customs, folklore

400–499 Language   dictionaries, thesauruses, foreign languages, history of language

500–599 Pure Science   astronomy, physics, chemistry, geology, oceanography, weather, anthropology, biology, botany, zoology

600–699 Applied Science   medicine, engineering, agriculture, home economics, business, construction, drug and alcohol education

700–799 Arts   architecture, sculpture, drawing, handicrafts, cartooning, photography, painting, music, film, drama, recreation, sports

800–899 Literature   American literature, British literature, literature from France, Spain, Germany, and so on, literary history, criticism

900–999 History   geography, ancient history, histories of continents, biographies (920–929: many media centers have a separate biography section)

Figure 13.3
The Dewey Decimal
Categories

The Library of Congress call numbers look like this:

LN

504.2

P

The Library of Congress Categories

A General Works

B Philosophy, Religion, Psychology

C History—Auxiliary Sciences

D History—except America

E–F America

G Geography, Anthropology, Sports

H Social Sciences

J Political Sciences

K Law

L Education

M Music

N Fine Arts

P Language and Literature

Q Science

R Medicine

S Agriculture, Plant and Animal Industry

T Technology

U Military Sciences

V Naval Sciences

Z Bibliography, Libraries, Library Science

Figure 13.4
The Library of
Congress Categories

Just like a Dewey call number, the Library of Congress number directs you to a section of the media center and a particular book in that section.

Using the Index and Table of Contents

Once you've found a book, take advantage of two more research tools. A book's index and table of contents will often tell you if the book has much information on your subject. For example, imagine you're researching Native American religions, and the card catalog directs you to a book on the Apache nation. By looking for the topic *religion* in the table of contents and the index, you'll find out quickly whether the book will be useful.

Reference Books

Reference books are especially useful research tools. Reference books are collections of large amounts of information. They are the most efficient sources of information in the media center. You can find a great deal of information in a short period of time. Encyclopedias, dictionaries, almanacs, and yearbooks are examples of reference books.

Reference books can be particularly useful when you're just beginning your research. Suppose you want to speak about the Navajo Indians but you don't know enough to focus your research. Looking up *Navajo Indians* in a good general encyclopedia will give you a number of topics to choose from. You can use general information to guide you to more specific information.

Speakers also find that almanacs and yearbooks are useful. First, they store a large number of statistics, one of the speaker's most useful forms of supportive material. For example, if you wanted to know how much money the government spent fighting crime in 1993, you'd find that statistic in an almanac or yearbook. Second, almanacs also store general facts. If you need to tell an audience who won the Academy Award for best actress for the last ten years, you'd probably find that information in a good almanac. See Figure 13.5 for examples of reference books.

Figure 13.5
Examples of
Reference Books

Examples of Reference Books

General Encyclopedias
Encyclopaedia Britannica
Compton's
World Book
Americana
Academic American

Specialized Encyclopedias
International Encyclopedia of Social Sciences
Encyclopedia of Philosophy
McGraw-Hill Encyclopedia of Science and Technology

Almanacs and Yearbooks
Information Please Almanac
World Almanac and Book of Facts
Statesman's Yearbook
Statistical Abstract
Congress and the Nation

Dictionary of Quotations: A Special Resource

Often you may need a colorful phrase, a clear example, or an interesting thought about a subject. A dictionary of quotations can be very helpful in such cases. By looking up a key word, you often find just the words to build the speech. Also, if you know a quotation but not the source, a dictionary of quotations can help you find your author. If you're giving a speech on friendship and loneliness, the following quotations taken from *Bartlett's Familiar Quotations* could help you develop a speech. Each quotation could help you make a point or even encourage you to build an entire section of a speech. Some speakers especially like using quotations as their introductions, conclusions, or both.

> "Only solitary men know the full joys of friendship. Others have their family; but to a solitary and an exile his friends are everything."
>
> Willa Cather, noted American author

> "A friend is, as it were, a second self."
>
> Cicero, Roman statesman and orator

> "Lonely people talking to each other can make each other lonelier."
>
> Lillian Hellman, noted American author

Specialized Dictionaries

There are specialized dictionaries in almost every subject to help you define terms. Some subjects covered are psychology, law, American history, art, music, medicine, politics, literary terms, biography, religion, and philosophy.

Researching with Periodicals

A **periodical** is a work published at regular intervals. Magazines and newspapers are the most common periodicals in the media center, but there are others as well. A **journal,** for example, is a magazine that publishes scholarly works in particular fields of study.

Periodicals are important for two reasons. First, they contain the most recent information on a subject. For example, if your speech is about the medical uses of lasers, a magazine or medical journal will publish new information as soon as it's available. By the time a book comes out on the topic, the news is older and other breakthroughs may have occurred. Any time you're researching a rapidly changing subject, use periodicals. Even an informative speech on history should be prepared with periodicals. After all, even though history is the study of the past, new articles containing new opinions and new discoveries come out all the time.

Figure 13.6
Commonly Used
Periodicals

The second reason periodicals are so useful is the broad range of subjects they cover. Because they're supported by advertisement and subscription, you can find periodicals on almost any subject you choose (see Figure 13.6).

Commonly Used Periodicals

Periodical	Subjects
Newsweek *Time* *U.S. News & World Report*	general current events both national and international
Business Week *Forbes* *Fortune*	current topics in economics and business
Congressional Digest	important issues currently before Congress
Commonweal *The New Republic* *Atlantic Monthly* *The Nation* *New York Times Magazine* *Harper's*	politics, social issues, current events, interviews, the arts
Consumer's Digest *Consumer Reports*	consumer products, advertising, consumer affairs
Sports Illustrated	current events in sports
Psychology Today	psychology
American Heritage	American history and culture
The Wall Street Journal *New York Times* *Christian Science Monitor*	major daily newspapers covering current events both nationally and internationally

Reading a *Readers' Guide* Entry

A typical *Readers' Guide* entry is easy to read. Each edition contains a key to all abbreviations and forms. Here is a sample entry:

[1]New computer animation fools the eye.
[2]N. Shapiro. [3]il [4]Pop Mech [5]156:76-7 + [6]Ag 81

What does the entry include?

1. Title of the article: *New computer animation fools the eye.* The title is always given first. Only the first letter is capitalized. A period follows the title.

2. Author: *N. Shapiro.* The author's name is second. If the article is unsigned, there will be no author entry.

3. Special Features: *il.* This article contains illustrations (il). If the article has other special features—portraits (por), for example—this position will note them.

4. Name of Magazine: *Pop Mech.* The title of the periodical (in this case *Popular Mechanics)* is usually abbreviated. All abbreviations are listed in the front of the *Readers' Guide.*

5. Volume and page numbers: *156:76– 7 + .* The number on the left of the colon indicates the volume number. In some media centers, you must know the volume to get the periodical. The numbers to the right of the colon indicate the article's page numbers. If you forget to note the page numbers, you'll waste valuable time searching for the article once you have the periodical.

6. Date: *Ag 81.* The date of the magazine is abbreviated. For weeklies, the complete date is given (*Ag 7 81*). This, too, is essential when you request a magazine.

The *Readers' Guide*

Finding one periodical article among the millions published each year may sound difficult, but the *Readers' Guide to Periodical Literature* makes it easy. The *Readers' Guide* is arranged in alphabetical order by subject. Suppose your speech topic is *animation.* After considering your audience, situation, and your own interests, you narrow the topic to *computer animation.* Begin your periodicals search by looking in the *Readers' Guide* under *Cartoons.* This entry will tell you to look under the entry *Motion pictures—animated cartoons*. Under this subject, choose the titles that you think will be useful and request those magazines.

Other Periodical Indexes

At many media centers, computers now store other periodical indexes. There are several advantages of a periodical index on computer: many users can use one database at the same time; a computerized database can include many years in one search; and a search can be limited. Some databases are even subject specific, offering information only on health or current events, for example. Others carry many topics. You should see your media center specialist for an introduction to periodical indexes to supplement the *Readers' Guide*.

On-Line Searching

By linking computers over telephone lines, your local media center can join with many other media centers and databases. The advantages for a researcher are almost overwhelming. Going "on-line" with a search can take you to major college libraries and into government libraries. Searching in a big database can give you information (or the location of information) that high-school students could only dream about a few years ago. Searching on-line requires planning and special instruction. Media centers may have a staff person handle the search for you or may train you to search yourself. Either way, information for speeches has never been so accessible.

Taking and Using Notes

When you take notes from sources, you have to be fast and accurate. Many experienced researchers take notes on three-by-five-inch or four-by-six-inch note cards. Note cards can be filed and used easily. A typical note card contains three things. The first is a bibliographic key, which is a symbol or number that refers you to your bibliography card. A bibliographic key tells you where you found a particular note. The second element is a title or "slug." By titling each card, you won't have to read through the card every time you want to know what it is about. Third is the note itself. Try to limit each card to one idea or quotation. Figure 13.7 (on page 258) presents a note card using these elements.

Note-taking can be a fairly simple process once you master the skills and establish a routine. See the Spotlight on Speaking on page 259 for steps to follow as you research your sources.

Slug ────────────────→ SAT prep

Bibliographic Key ──→ Wayland, How to Raise Your Grades
                      P. 101

Information ────────→ Using a calculator on SAT-I
                      1. use one you're familiar with
                      2. don't use calculator on every
                         question
                      3. no question requires a calculator

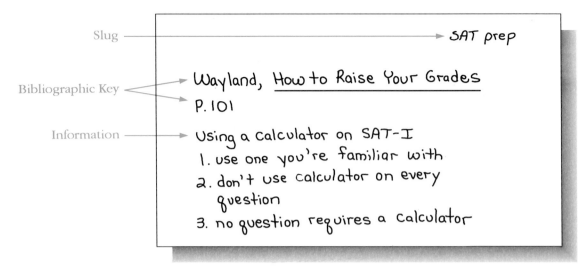

Figure 13.7
Sample Note Card

Interviewing

Sometimes the resources in a media center don't give you as much information as you need. They may not supply the personal touch you feel your audience requires. You may decide to interview someone who has special knowledge about your subject.

Interviewing someone who has special knowledge about your topic may provide the personal touch or additional information that your speech needs.

Taking Notes

Follow these guidelines to take notes most efficiently:

1. Once you locate a source, skim it to see if it has information related to your speech. If it does, immediately jot down the author, title, and date. All notes should have this information so you can tell an audience where you found the material.

2. As you read, look for key phrases that signal important information, such as *in other words, for example,* or *on the other hand.*

3. Unless you want to quote the information exactly, paraphrase it. That is, put it in your own words. In fact, writing the information in fragments is a good idea. You can put it into your own sentences later. Paraphrasing an author keeps you from unintentionally using his or her words as your own.

4. Using symbols and abbreviations can speed up your notetaking. Some symbols you might use are + for *and,* = for *the same as, w/* for *with,* and *w/o* for *without.* Words you use frequently can be shortened. If your speech is on radioactive waste, why not abbreviate the term *RAW* to save time and space?

5. Keep all notes on cards or in a folder so you won't lose important information.

6. Whenever you quote a source directly, word-for-word, be sure to put the note in quotation marks. Then you'll remember that these are the source's words, not your own.

Many people in your community know a great deal about things such as recent history, local history, careers, hobbies, community issues, and school concerns. A speech on the Great Depression of the 1930s, for example, will probably be more interesting if you interview people who lived through it. Not only can you learn facts and amusing stories unavailable in media centers, you'll also make your subject seem more immediate to your audience.

Interviewing takes time, courtesy, and work. Remember the following rules for a good interview:

1. Make an appointment. Dropping in on someone is rude. Moreover, if your resource person can prepare, you may be treated to special displays, pictures, or stories.

2. Be ready. Your resource person is doing you a favor. Show up on time. Prepare a list of questions. Know the kind of information you're looking for. Read an encyclopedia article or a magazine clipping. Going to an interview "cold" can waste your resource person's time and your own.

3. Take notes. Be sure to record information accurately and completely. If you want to tape the interview, ask the person's permission when you make the appointment. Respect the wishes of those who don't want to be taped. It makes some people uncomfortable.

4. Be courteous. By being punctual, attentive, and appreciative, your interview will go much easier. Thank the person.

Using Quoted Material

When you've compiled your materials, you must work them into your speech. You can use facts, statistics, testimony, and any of the various types of development. With your research in hand, you must decide how much to use and how to use it.

One important decision you must make is when and how to attribute material to a source. **Attributing** means identifying the original speaker of a quotation or the source of a piece of support information. You attribute material for three reasons.

First, you attribute material to build your own credibility. Just believing something's true doesn't make it so. Quoting an authority who agrees with you increases the likelihood that the audience will agree with you. It also shows the audience you have done your homework.

Second, you attribute material to build interest. If you can indicate that a famous, respected, or popular figure supports you, your audience may pay closer attention. Don't use too many attributed quotations or your speech will be dull. Audiences will suspect you of name-dropping merely to impress them.

Third, you attribute material to give credit where credit is due. If you use someone's words directly or if you borrow an original idea, it's ethical to give the source of the words or idea.

This student followed all three guidelines in a speech on freedom of the press:

> When we celebrated the bicentennial of our Constitution, we celebrated two-hundred years of freedom of the press. We cannot risk taking this cherished freedom for granted. As New York Governor Mario Cuomo stated, we must "sound the alert . . . make it clear that we *are* facing a real threat of restriction of the constitutional freedom of the press. That's not easy."

By attributing this quotation, the student showed the audience that threats to freedom of the press concern important, respected people. Cuomo is a good person to quote because he is an interesting, appealing personality. In addition, the student needed to acknowledge that the words were not his or her own.

If you take notes correctly and attribute sources, you avoid **plagiarism,** the use of someone's words or ideas without giving credit. Plagiarism is stealing words or ideas. It can occur in a speech as well as in a paper. There can be serious consequences for plagiarizing in a speech. In a recent presidential debate, for example, a candidate closed by saying:

> Why is that [I am] the first in [my] family ever to go to a university? Why is it that my wife . . . is the first in her family to ever go to college?

Later, it was discovered that a British candidate for prime minister was the first person to say these words. The controversy surrounding this and other examples of plagiarism ultimately caused the candidate to withdraw from the race.

Final Bibliography

In very formal speeches or in speeches given in school, you may sometimes have to provide a formal bibliography. The exact style or form of the bibliography varies, but the intent of all is the same: to tell your audience what sources you used. You give credit where credit is due, and the audience can look up your sources if they are interested in further research.

Chapter 13 Summary

Research enables speakers to talk about topics outside their own experience. The preliminary step is to focus your research, using the SPAM model. The next step is to prepare a working bibliography. Books in the media center are listed in the card catalog on author, title, and subject cards. The call number on the card tells where the books are stored. Call numbers refer to the cataloging system used by the center. Once the book is found, the table of contents and the index can further guide research.

Periodicals are works published at regular intervals. Journals are specialized periodicals that publish scholarly works. The information published in periodicals is usually more up-to-date than that in books. The *Readers' Guide to Periodicals* is a reference text that lists the articles published in periodicals and journals throughout the year.

Media centers also include current technology, such as computers, compact disks, microforms, films, tapes, and videotapes. When you make note cards from these or other materials, include a bibliographical key and a title for each card. Then skim the material to spot key phrases. Paraphrase material or take down direct quotes.

Attribute your sources when you use quoted materials in your speech to build your own credibility, to build interest, and to give credit where credit is due. Using someone else's ideas or words without credit is called plagiarism and is an unethical practice.

◆ Check Your Understanding

1. Explain why research is a crucial part of speech preparation.

2. Explain how using SPAM helps prepare you for research.

3. Explain how these indexes help a speaker locate a source:
   a. the card catalog   b. the *Readers' Guide*   c. on-line search

4. List three kinds of reference materials you could use to prepare a speech.

5. List three important steps to prepare for an interview.

6. Give three reasons for attributing information to a source.

◆ Apply Your Understanding

1. Using the *Readers' Guide* or another periodical index, find an interview with a famous person. Look at the questions the interviewer asked. Explain what you think the interviewer wanted the questions to accomplish. Select the best question and the worst. Add three questions you would like to ask.

2. Select a topic from the sample topics in Appendix A. Using a local media center, develop a bibliography. Include both books and periodicals. Discuss with your instructor the minimum number of sources to be listed.

◆ Thinking Critically about Public Speaking

1. Go to your school's media center to look at a journal. High-school media centers do not subscribe to many journals; they may only have journals on education. Compare an article in a journal to similar articles in a general magazine or newspaper. Explain why speakers may find journals particularly useful.

2. Select five topics of general interest to the class. Brainstorm with the class to decide what kinds of authorities would be useful if you were researching the topics for a speech. List the qualifications of the authorities. Try to think of names of specific people who meet the qualifications. If your teacher directs, find books or articles by or about these authorities.

◆ Speak Out!

1. Prepare an informative speech on one of the following research sources. Your purpose will be to educate your classmates about the source:

   Facts about the Presidents
   Oxford English Dictionary
   *Essay and General Literature
      Index*
   *Oxford Companion to
      American Literature*
   Famous First Facts
   Congressional Digest

   *Bartlett's Familiar Quota-
      tions* (or a similar work)
   Short Story Index
   Contemporary Authors
   National Geographic Index
   American Heritage Index
   Encyclopaedia Britannica
   Roget's Thesaurus

2. Using reference books only, use one class period to research a topic. On the following day, present a two- to four-minute extemporaneous speech on your subject.

◆ Speech Challenge

Interview the media specialist in your school about one of the new research technologies. Present your findings in a speech to the class. Include a sample search that you have done with the help of the media center specialist.

CHAPTER ·14·

Key Terms

Cause-effect pattern

Chronological order

Classification order

External transition

Forecast

Internal transition

Problem-solution order

Signpost

Spatial order

Subordination

Topical order
(logical order)

Transition

Chapter Objectives

After studying this chapter, you will be able to:

1. Identify the three parts of a speech and explain what should be accomplished in each.

2. Identify and explain the five major purposes of a speech introduction.

3. Identify and give an example of each of the six major types of introductions.

4. Identify and explain the six major organizational patterns used in the body of a speech.

5. Apply the principles of outlining in preparing a speech outline.

6. Explain the difference between internal and external transitions.

7. Identify and explain the three major purposes of a speech conclusion.

Speech Organization

The Purposes of an Introduction

Think about speeches you have heard that you thought were especially good. What did the speakers do to make you want to listen? Chances are in the first few sentences they gave you a reason to listen and got you involved in the topic. A good introduction does that and more. In fact, an introduction serves five major purposes:

1. **Gets the audience's attention:** A good introduction gets the audience's attention immediately. This chapter will suggest some ways to make the audience take notice.

2. **Introduces the topic:** An introduction's primary purpose is to state the topic of your speech. An audience should know what they're going to hear about. Often a speech title gives some clue. If not, it's the speaker's responsibility to make the subject matter clear in the introduction.

3. **Shows the topic's importance:** An introduction should make the members of the audience feel that the topic is important to them. They need to feel that they'll gain something by listening. If the audience doesn't believe that the topic has any meaning to them, they will be unlikely to listen. Even a speech to entertain must give the audience a reason to be entertained.

4. **Presents the thesis:** The introduction presents the thesis statement. The thesis states your purpose in a clear and concise manner. It lets the audience know what you expect of them as listeners.

5. **Forecasts the major ideas:** A good introduction also previews what is to come in specific terms. The **forecast** specifically outlines the major points of the speech. Anyone taking notes would know from the introduction how many major ideas you will cover and the order in which you'll present them.

Applying the Five Major Purposes

The following introduction to a student's speech about stress satisfies the five major purposes. See if you can identify them:

How many of you get impatient while waiting in a slow-moving line at a movie? Do you ever get behind with schoolwork because you have too many outside activities? How often do you eat a meal on the run? If you answered *yes* to the first two questions and *more than once or twice a week* to the third, you may be on your way to developing a stress-related disease by the time you're in your forties. Forty may seem a long way off, and the situations I described may seem normal for students, but some individuals are prone to creating situations that cause more stress in their lives than normal. Today, I want to discuss stress—what it is, what it can do to you, and what you can do to reduce it before it gets the better of you.

This introduction gets the members of the audience involved by asking a set of questions that are relevant to their lives. It makes the topic clear. The introduction also gives the audience a reason to listen. Young people typically don't worry about stress and high blood pressure, but the introduction suggests that the habits formed in school can affect diseases that occur later in life. This establishes the topic's importance. The last sentence in the introduction is the purpose statement. It also forecasts the speech's three major points.

In addition to the five major purposes, an introduction can, under certain circumstances, have four other purposes.

Establish Credibility

Unless speakers are well-known experts, an audience may need proof of their qualifications to speak on a subject. In situations where the audience doesn't know whether you're an expert or not, it's important to establish your credibility. If you have credibility from the outset of a speech, you're more likely to achieve your purpose.

An audience needs to feel that a speaker has credibility. A speaker who is known as an expert in a particular field has credibility when he or she speaks about that field. Student speakers generally need to establish their credibility at the beginning of each speech.

Through personal reference, you can let an audience know you have personal experience or have researched the subject. Often the person who introduces a speaker provides the background information necessary to establish credibility. If there's no introduction or if the introduction doesn't establish credibility, use the introduction of the speech to do so. In a speech on job interviewing techniques, a student established credibility with this sentence: "By following the guidelines I am going to share with you, I was able to find a summer job after spending only two days looking and interviewing."

Promote Goodwill

Occasionally, you may address hostile audiences or audiences that disagree with you. When this happens, you need to assure the audience that there will be no cause for further disagreement. For example, when U.S. presidents take office and present an inaugural address, they are trying to bring the country together after an election. Even though some voters didn't vote for the winner, the president needs everyone's support during the next four years. Thus, one goal of the inaugural speech is to promote goodwill.

President Ronald Reagan had this purpose when he gave his first inaugural address on 20 January 1981. He began by referring to President Jimmy Carter, his predecessor and the person he defeated:

> To a few of us here today this is a solemn and most momentous occasion. And, yet, in the history of our nation it is a commonplace occurrence. The orderly transfer of authority as called for in the Constitution routinely takes place as it has for almost two centuries and few of us stop to think how unique we really are.
>
> In the eyes of many in the world, this every-four-year ceremony we accept as normal is nothing less than a miracle. Mr. President, I want our fellow citizens to know how much you did to carry on this tradition. By your gracious cooperation in the transition process, you have shown a watching world that we are a united people pledged to maintaining a political system which guarantees individual liberty to a greater degree than any other. And I thank you and your people for all your help in maintaining the continuity which is the bulwark of our republic.

Establish Common Ground

There are times when we all think we have little in common with a famous speaker or even with people we know. It's important for a speaker to explain how much he or she actually does have in common with the audience. You may not think a teacher who tells you how to overcome stage fright knows how you feel. After all, he or she talks to groups every day. But the teacher probably does know how you feel, because he or she was once a beginner. By relating personal experiences, you establish a common bond with your listeners and give your speech new meaning. Consider this example, which mentions an everyday occurrence:

> If you've ever gone to the grocery store to purchase something as simple as salad dressing or laundry detergent, you know it can be a difficult task. Once you locate the correct aisle and shelf and reach out to grab a bottle or a box, you discover that there are dozens of choices. Brightly colored labels are all saying to you, "Buy me!" "Buy me!" Now what do you do?

Set a Tone

The tone or mood of a speech is important. Your introduction can establish the tone you want. If you use humor, you tell the audience that your speech will be light. If you use a serious quotation from a philosopher, you tell the audience you have an important topic to discuss. If you're to accomplish your purpose, you must use your introduction to prepare the audience for your message. Lonny Powell, a student from Idaho, used the following introduction in his speech at the national Future Farmers of America speech contest to set a tone of seriousness and immediacy for the problem he was to discuss:

> What I now hold in my hand is familiar to all of us. It is fragile—yet life-giving; simple—but unified. In fact, it is so common to each and everyone of us that we rarely think of it as having any real significance. Yes, it's an egg; but for a few brief moments I would like you to imagine it as a symbol—a symbol for a very important goal. The goal: to teach the hungry people to feed themselves. This goal is subjected to many extreme pressures. On one hand, we have such growing problems as: the forces of nature, energy shortages, and the population explosion; while on the other hand lie such deterrents as political corruption, economic crisis, and lack of education. When each problem's multiplied and combined, the pressure becomes too great and the goal soon succumbs, crumbling before our very eyes. Is our goal, to teach the hungry people to feed themselves, crumbling away? It is up to us to provide an answer.

Types of Introductions

A good speech does *not* begin in the following ways: "Today I want to talk about bicycle maintenance," "My speech is about calligraphy—the art of handwriting," or "My topic is how to buy a pet."

While the topic is clear in all of these statements, the information doesn't create excitement about the topic. Instead, the material is rather matter-of-fact and dry. There are six techniques most commonly used to fulfill your introduction purposes and to give the introduction some life: quotation; rhetorical question or series of questions; reference to history, audience, or self; humor; startling statement; and incident.

Quotation

Speakers often use a quotation to begin a speech. You can find quotable material in other speeches, novels, poetry, or books of quotations. Often, someone else has made a point better than you can. A quotation also adds credibility to your speech—not only do *you* think something, but someone famous does as well. The following opening statement uses a quotation:

> President John F. Kennedy once said: "The United States must move very fast to even stand still." Since President Kennedy made that observation over thirty years ago, the advances in technology have made it even more important for this country to prepare its students for a competitive world.

Rhetorical Question

A *rhetorical question* is a question that the speaker doesn't expect to be answered. Rather, the question is asked to stimulate the audience to think. You can use a single question or a series. The introduction to the sample speech on stress (page 322) begins with a rhetorical question.

Personal, Historical, and Audience References

References establish common ground and aid credibility. Use historical references when you're giving a speech on a special occasion. Use personal references to give the audience information about yourself or to tie yourself to a particular situation or event. Use audience reference to establish a common ground between yourself and the audience or to enhance the audience's involvement in the speech. The following excerpt is from Barbara Jordan's keynote address to the 1976 Democratic National Convention. She combines all three types of references. Jordan's personal references were that she was an African-American woman presenting a speech usually given by white males:

> One hundred and forty-four years ago, members of the Democratic Party first met in convention to select a Presidential candidate. Since that time, Democrats have continued to convene once every four years and draft a party platform and nominate a Presidential candidate. And our meeting this week is a continuation of that tradition. But there is something different about tonight. There is something special about tonight. What is different? What is special? I, Barbara Jordan, am a keynote speaker. A lot of years passed since 1832, and during that time it would have been most unusual for any national political party to ask that a Barbara Jordan deliver a keynote address . . . but tonight here I am. And I feel that notwithstanding the past that my presence here is one additional bit of evidence that the American Dream need not forever be deferred.

Humor

You can use humor to begin most kinds of speeches, even those with a serious message. It might seem contradictory, but it's possible to set a serious tone by using humor. When speakers contrast the seriousness of a problem with the lightness of a joke, they can emphasize a message quickly.

Be sure your humor is in good taste. Don't offend individuals or groups. Before you tell a joke or humorous story, ask yourself if it might offend anyone. If there's any doubt in your mind, either change the story or joke or don't use it.

A speech on male-female communication—in itself a serious topic—could begin with humor:

> Many of us often believe that men and women speak two different languages. A recent comic strip illustrated this point. It showed two men at a lunch counter talking about baseball. The waitress looked at them and said, "Can't you men ever talk about anything but sports. Can't you talk about your feelings?" The two men looked at one another somewhat confused and surprised by the question. Then one said to the other, "Okay, how do you *feel* about the Cubs?"
>
> While there may be some differences in the language patterns and topics of conversation men and women use, the real differences may be found in their perceptions of the purpose of communication. Men may view communication as a way to discuss a topic. Women, on the other hand, may see it as a way of expressing emotions and building personal relationships. It is that difference that I want to discuss with you today.

Startling Statement

A startling statement grabs the audience members' attention by shocking them or making them think about something in a way they hadn't considered. Often, you can make a topic that sounds boring into one that interests an audience through the use of a startling statement. Consider the following example:

> Look at the person on your right and the person on your left. Now look at the person behind you. Chances are that you or one of them will develop some form of cancer in your lifetime. Thirty percent of Americans will be discovered to have cancer sometime in their lifetime.

After hearing this opening, most listeners would feel vulnerable and would be more likely to listen to the remainder of the speech, which is on the warning signs of cancer. A startling statement is a good way to fulfill the purposes of getting an audience's attention and making them aware of the importance of a subject.

Incident

The final technique for starting a speech is using an incident. This introduction relates a situation to the audience and provides a concrete example directly related to the topic. By using an incident, you provide a vivid picture for the audience and involve them quickly. The following is from a speech by former San Antonio Mayor Henry Cisneros, delivered at a conference at the University of Texas on "The New Texas":

> The subject of the new Texas is at once challenging and optimistic, but it also must be grounded in some facts and some realities. Some of these are not so pleasant, so I apologize in advance for having to remind you of them. But the results, I feel, are worth the challenge. Allow me to begin by setting an important scene.

> *It is around 4 p.m. in the afternoon. An aerospace executive is describing how much of an overabundance of production lays before him. The schedule and amount of work are so heavy that it simply will not be able to be done on the site that is available to him. The number of production lines will require new buildings, new warehouses, and new people. One of the biggest problems is the hiring of engineers, because there is such a tremendous amount of work. The engineers move from plant to plant, company to company, and the executive is not able to keep enough of them on the job. A quick look at Sunday afternoon's paper which is spread on a*

nearby desk reflects that three sections of it, each 25 pages in length, are filled with classified ads. These sections are job announcements, many of them with photographs of aircraft and jet fighters, to which the engineers will be attracted to work. Technicians, welders, electricians, and construction specialists are needed. Outside the office window this afternoon, the local economy is booming. Office space is being constructed, new warehouses are under construction, cranes everywhere, traffic is congested, but the community has all the general attributes of one that is prosperous, tasteful, and well landscaped.

The foregoing is not a fanciful scene. The place was Los Angeles. The aerospace executive was talking to me, and the time was last Monday afternoon.

Cisneros used descriptive language to create a mental image of his experience. The image of a growing economy was one he could later contrast with the economic hard times his state was experiencing.

The Body of the Speech

When you prepare the body of your speech, consider your purpose, both general and specific. Your general purpose of informing, persuading, or entertaining will influence how you order your ideas.

The body of the speech is its longest part. Here you present the bulk of your information. Thus, you should give the body the greatest amount of preparation. Once you decide on a topic, narrow it, and research it, you must organize the material that you want to use. Three steps are involved in this process: (1) selecting an organizational pattern; (2) outlining the content; and (3) preparing the transitions.

Organizational Patterns

There's no single way to organize a speech. The pattern you select is determined by the information you have and your specific purpose. There are six basic patterns of organizing a speech: topical, chronological, spatial, classification, problem-solution, and cause-effect.

Topical or Logical Order   Use **topical order,** sometimes called *logical order,* when you have several ideas to present and one idea seems naturally to precede the other. This pattern is one of the most common. It's especially useful for informative and entertainment speeches. A speech about the benefit of exercise would fit this category. You might include the following ideas in this order:

I. Physical benefits of exercise
   A. Cardiovascular strength
   B. Muscle tone
   C. Weight loss
II. Mental benefits of exercise
   A. Personal alertness
   B. Improved feeling about self

Since most people think exercise is for the body, it seems logical to begin with that benefit. There's no reason, however, why you can't reverse I and II, but they seem more logical in the order here. By including an advantage not usually considered (the material in II), the speaker also builds to a climax. When a speech contains a series of related topics, you can maintain interest toward the end of the speech by presenting something new.

Chronological Order **Chronological order** uses time sequence as a framework. This pattern is useful in informative speeches or in persuasive speeches, both of which require background information. You could organize a speech on the history of baseball according to chronological sequence. Begin with the invention of the game and follow rule changes until the present day.

You can also use chronological order for a process or demonstration speech that explains how to do something. In a process speech, you explain but don't actually show how to do something. In a demonstration, you explain by showing. For either speech to make sense, you must follow the order in which things are done. The following outline from a demonstration speech illustrates:

I. How to do the spine stretcher
   A. The appropriate stance
   B. Proper breathing
   C. Bending at the waist
   D. Straightening out

Spatial Order **Spatial order** organizes material according to physical space. If you wanted to describe your classroom, you might divide your description into the front of the room, the back, the side, and the center. Dividing material according to spaces in the room is an example of spatial order. The national weather report is usually given according to regions of the country. A weather reporter doesn't randomly skip from San Francisco to Boston to Los Angeles.

You may use spatial order in informative speeches and, depending on the topic, entertainment speeches. Use this organizational pattern whenever your speech involves physical space. Divide your material into such elements as floors, parts of a room, or geographical regions. The following outline for a speech about regional foods in the United States uses spatial order as an organizing device:

   I. Northeast
      A. Beef dishes
         1. Yankee pot roast
         2. New England boiled dinner
      B. Seafood dishes
         1. Maine lobster
         2. Clam chowder
  II. South
      A. Vegetables
         1. Okra
         2. Sweet potatoes
      B. Desserts
         1. Pecan pie
         2. Bread pudding

Classification   **Classification order** puts things into categories or classes. Students are distinguished by their year in school. Athletic teams are organized by sex, grade level, experience, and ability. These are examples of classification. You can use the pattern for all three speech purposes. You can categorize solutions to problems according to type. It's easy to give information by classifying ideas. This chapter, for example, uses classification to explain organizational patterns. The following outline on athletes and superstitions classifies types of superstition:

   I. Sports superstitions come in many forms
      A. Many relate to the game itself
         1. Equipment
         2. Numbers
         3. Uniforms
      B. Others relate to the players
         1. Good-luck charms
         2. Food

Problem-Solution Order   Speakers use problem-solution order mostly for persuasive speeches. The first part of such a speech outlines a problem and the second part presents a solution. Within a problem-solution pattern, you'll find other types of organization. A speaker may organize the problem section of the speech in a logical sequence. The solution stage could involve classification. A persuader selects one solution and presents arguments that show why it's the best option. A speech about the decline of educational quality in the United States begins with a section outlining some of the problems in U.S. schools, and the next section suggests ways to solve them:

Problem-solution order

Topical order

   I. U.S. students are unprepared for a competitive world
      A. Student do not take enough math and science
      B. Only a small percentage of students take foreign languages
      C. Many graduates cannot read or write

Classification

  II. Solutions must come from a variety of sources
      A. The schools
      B. The government
      C. Parents

Cause-Effect Order   **Cause-effect order,** like problem-solution order, has two parts. The first describes the cause of a problem, and the second describes its effects. You could organize a speech on toxic waste pollution with cause-effect order. The first part of the speech would explain how and why toxic wastes cause environmental damage. The second part would discuss the effects of toxic wastes on property and health. As with the problem-solution speech, speakers often decide to incorporate other forms of organization into the two major sections:

Cause-effect order

Classification

   I. Toxic wastes are dumped into the environment
      A. Agricultural wastes affect water
          1. Seep into the groundwater
          2. Pollute lakes and streams
      B. Industrial wastes affect water

Classification

  II. Increased levels of toxin in water are harmful
      A. They harm humans
      B. They harm fish and animals

Multiple Patterns   Almost all types of speeches use more than one organizing pattern. While the total speech may use a topical pattern, each section can incorporate a separate scheme. The following outline illustrates how a speaker used multiple patterns:

   I. Superstitions are common among athletes
      A. One-third of all athletes are superstitious

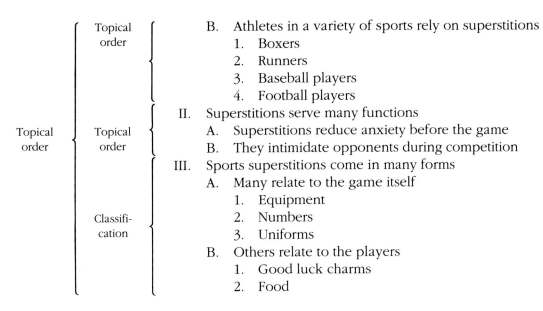

Topical order

Topical order

Topical order

Classification

B. Athletes in a variety of sports rely on superstitions
    1. Boxers
    2. Runners
    3. Baseball players
    4. Football players
II. Superstitions serve many functions
    A. Superstitions reduce anxiety before the game
    B. They intimidate opponents during competition
III. Sports superstitions come in many forms
    A. Many relate to the game itself
        1. Equipment
        2. Numbers
        3. Uniforms
    B. Others relate to the players
        1. Good luck charms
        2. Food

Organization Relates to Purpose   If you change the organization of the speech material, you can change the general purpose. Suppose your topic is exercise. Using a classification system, you can present an informative speech that describes three or four major types of exercise. A chronological sequence that explains how to perform one type of exercise would turn your speech into a process or demonstration speech. What about problem-solution order? You could begin by talking about people with health problems caused by a lack of exercise and conclude with how to make exercise a part of a daily schedule. The result is a persuasive speech. Topical order describing humorous incidents you experienced while exercising would produce a speech to entertain.

Principles of Outlining

So far in this chapter you've seen many examples of outlines or partial outlines. Although these examples give you a general idea of how to write an outline, they aren't complete. In this section, you'll learn how to write an outline and use it as a speaking guide.

Standard Subordination   The major points of a speech should be labeled with Roman numerals (I, II, III, and so on). The most general information should be the outline's first step. Items under a major point, called subpoints, should relate directly to that point and explain it. Examples, statistics, and explanations become subdivisions of the subpoint. The process of dividing material into more specific information is known as **subordination.** Here's the standard format for subordination:

I. Major point
   A. Subpoint
      1. Example (subdivision of subpoint)
         a. Additional example or explanation
         b. Additional example or explanation
            (1) Additional explanation
               (a) Additional explanation
               (b) Additional explanation

Indent each level of subordination, as shown here. As a general rule, if you have a Roman number I, you should have a II. If you have an A point, you need a B. Each level of subordination indicates you are dividing a topic to make it more specific. If you divide something, you must have more than one idea as a result. If you don't, you need to reexamine the way you've organized your material.

Your outlines will rarely go beyond the third level of subordination. The average ten-minute speech should cover from two to five major points. Three major points are about right for a five-minute speech.

One Item for a Unit of Subordination   An outline is supposed to break information down into its simplest form. Each level or unit of an outline is in its simplest form and should include only one idea, example, or illustration:

   Wrong: I. Beef and seafood

   Right: I. Beef dishes
             II. Seafood dishes

No Overlapping Items   There's more than one way to divide or classify material. Be sure your information is subdivided so each unit is distinct from other levels. Consider this example:

   Wrong: I. Specialty foods of the South
               A. Barbecue
               B. Chess pie
           II. Southern desserts
               A. Pecan pie
               B. Bread pudding

Chess pie is a type of dessert. The items listed in specialty foods shouldn't fit into another category. Or the topic of specialty foods should be abandoned, since a regional approach to dividing suggests that each region has its specialties. A more accurate outline for this topic looks like this:

Right: I. Specialty foods of the South
          A. Barbecue
          B. Cajun
     II. Southern desserts
          A. Pies
             1. pecan
             2. chess
          B. Bread pudding

Equal Value   Each level of subordination should relate consistently to a category of information. All Roman numerals should represent major points; all capital letters should represent general subdivisions; and all Arabic numerals should represent material to support a point. Don't mix types of examples as in this outline:

Wrong: A. Major industries are affected by imported cars
          1. Shipping
          2. Steel
          3. Ford Motor Company

Ford Motor Company is out of place because it isn't a major industry. It's a corporation within a major industry: automobile manufacturing. The correct subordination would follow this pattern:

Right: A. Major industries are affected by imported cars
          1. Shipping
          2. Steel
          3. Automotive
             a. Ford Motor Company
             b. Chrysler
             c. General Motors

Complete Sentences for Major Points   Many beginning speakers read large portions of an outline if they write complete sentences for every level. They speak more effectively if they use complete sentences only for major ideas. You can indicate examples, statistics, or illustrations with words or phrases. This method also produces an outline that's easier to follow during your speech.

Preparing Separate Outlines   If your speech is very long, outline the introduction, body, and conclusion with major points beginning with Roman numeral I. In most speeches, however, you'll write out the introduction and conclusion in full. Outline only the body.

VOICES OF

REFORM

Making the World Better

The voices of social reformers have been heard throughout history. Three are highlighted here.

Elizabeth Cady Stanton was among the early leaders in the women's rights and temperance movements in the nineteenth century, but she didn't live to see women get the vote in 1920.

Cesar Chavez organized farm workers in California during the 1960s and 1970s. He organized strikes and boycotts of table grapes and participated in a fast to bring attention to "La Causa."

Lech Walesa received the Nobel Peace Prize in 1983 for his work in organizing workers in Poland. Walesa founded the trade union, Solidarity, and led workers in a strike for better working conditions. His Nobel acceptance speech was read by a friend. Walesa feared that if he left Poland, he might not be allowed to return. After the fall of communism in 1989, Walesa was elected President of the Polish Republic in 1990.

WORDS TO REMEMBER

Elizabeth Cady Stanton

No matter how much women prefer to learn, to be protected and supported, nor how much men desire to have them do so, they must make the voyage of life alone, and for safety in an emergency, they must know something of the laws of navigation.

To appreciate the importance of fitting every human soul for independent action, think for a moment of the immeasurable solitude of self. We come into the world alone, unlike all who have gone before us; we leave it alone, under circumstances peculiar to ourselves.

The Solitude of Self, given at the twenty-fourth annual meeting of the National-American Woman Suffrage Association, 18 January 1892

The right is ours. Have it, we must. Use it, we will. The pens, the tongues, the fortunes, the indomitable wills of many women are already pledged to secure this right.

The voice of woman has been silenced in the state, the church, and the home, but man cannot fulfill his destiny alone, he cannot redeem his race unaided.

Speech at Seneca Falls Woman's Rights Convention, 19 July 1848

Cesar Chavez

We are poor. Our allies are few. But we have something the rich do not own. We have our own bodies and spirits and the justice of our cause as our weapons.

It is how we use our lives that determines what kind of men we are. It is my deepest belief that only by giving our lives do we find life. I am convinced that the truest act of courage, the strongest act of manliness is to sacrifice ourselves for others in a totally nonviolent struggle for justice. To be a man is to suffer for others. God help us to be men!

Speech to end his twenty-five-day fast, 10 March 1968

Lech Walesa

The sole and basic source of our strength is the solidarity of workers, peasants and intelligentsia, the solidarity of the nation, the solidarity of people who seek to live in dignity, truth, and in harmony with their consciences.

The things that have taken place in human conscience and reshaped human attitude cannot be obliterated or destroyed. They exist and will remain.

In many parts of the world the people are searching for a solution which would link the two basic values: peace and justice. The two are like bread and salt for mankind. Every nation and every community have the inalienable right to these values.

Nobel Peace Prize Acceptance Speech, 11 December 1983

Transitional Devices

Transitions are words, phrases, and sentences that tie the parts of your speech together. Transitional materials help you move smoothly from one idea to the next. They show how one idea is related to another. In doing so, they often serve as summaries for one major point in the speech. Such summaries are called *internal summaries*.

There are two types of transitions—internal and external. **Internal transitions** relate pieces of information within a section of a speech, such as the three motor companies under the general heading of automobile industry. The following words and phrases are common internal transitions:

also	for example	in addition
and	specifically	however
but	again	since
or	one other	then
another	in other words	

External transitions connect points on different levels of an outline, such as between the major points labeled with Roman numerals. External transitions usually are more than a word or phrase. They show changes in direction. They also highlight the most important points in your speech. Some common external transitions are as follows:

The final reason for change is . . .

The most important point I want to make is . . .

Now, what effect does this have on . . .

The second step in the process is . . .

Those are the problems, now what can be done about them?

One type of transition is known as a **signpost.** Signposts are markers of important divisions in the speech. They remind the audience of the original overall organization of your speech and how far you've progressed. For instance, if you forecast five rules involved in the game you're explaining, the word *second* is a signpost indicating you're now ready to explain the second rule. Signposts can serve as either internal or external transitions.

A Completed Outline

The following is the outline of a speech presented by Bret Schwarz in a public speaking class at Washburn University.

General Purpose	To inform
Purpose Statement	The purpose of this speech is to increase science fiction readers' and nonreaders' understanding of the relationship between science fiction and science.
Thesis Statement	When speaking of science fiction as a prediction of the future direction of science, two authors surface as the leaders in this art—Isaac Asimov and George Orwell.
Introduction	Why do we read science fiction? Is it because it allows us to escape from reality? Or do we read it because it is actually one of the many steps in the scientific process? Does science fiction predict what the future of science will be? I think many of us read science fiction because it does provide us with insights into the future. Our parents and grandparents remember Buck Rogers as fiction and fantasy, but we have grown up with manned flight through space and footsteps on the moon.
	When speaking of science fiction as a prediction of the future, two authors surface as the leaders in this art—Isaac Asimov and George Orwell. I would like to share with you some of their predictions and then let you determine why we read science fiction.

Body

Transition to Body	One of the most popular ideas to come out of science fiction is the robot, and Isaac Asimov is the man who told us the most about them in "I, Robot."

   I.   Isaac Asimov predicted the use of robots
      A.   Asimov predicted robots would be used in industry
      B.   Asimov predicted robots would be used in medicine
      C.   Asimov predicted robots would look like machines, not like metal people

Transition	If we look around us, we will see that Asimov wasn't far off in his predictions.

   II.   Asimov's predictions have come true
      A.   Industry uses robots
         1.   Automobile industry
         2.   Space industry
      B.   Medical technology uses computerized limbs for amputees

Transition	These are but a few uses of robotics. Scientists tell us robots will replace more and more people on assembly lines. However, not all science fiction predictions involve such intricate technology as robots. George Orwell predicted many scientific and technical changes in our everyday lives.

    III. Orwell had many valid predictions
      A. He predicted use of data banks
      B. He predicted word processors
      C. He predicted satellites
    IV. Orwell's predictions have come true
      A. Data banks know much about us
      B. Word processors are common
      C. Satellites circle the earth daily
        1. Weather
        2. Telecommunications
        3. Military

Transition   These are but a few of the science fictions that have become facts. Many others have not.

Conclusion   One scientist has estimated that only 10 percent of all science fiction can be taken as prophecy. If that is true, then why do we read science fiction? The answer is quite simple when we look at the robots, medical technology, computers, and satellites that are currently in use. That 10 percent, as Asimov and Orwell have shown us, can have a major impact on our lives.

Concluding a Speech

Just as you should begin your speech on a high note, you should also have a definite, positive ending. Don't let your speech trail off to a stop. A good speech doesn't require a speaker to say, "That's all" or "I'm finished." The audience knows when the speech is over.

Purposes of a Conclusion

A good conclusion should do three things: inform the audience you are about to close, summarize the major ideas, and leave the audience with an idea to remember.

You achieve the first objective through transitional devices. They enable you to connect the final point of the body to the conclusion. You then reinforce the major ideas of the speech with a summary. By emphasizing major ideas, you give your audience a clear understanding of your intent. Repetition is an effective way of teaching, and in speech-making it is an effective way to get a point across. A summary of major ideas is essential in a conclusion.

In addition to summarizing content, your conclusion should also make a point with the audience. You may conclude by issuing a challenge to the audience or by leaving them with a vivid picture. A memorable statement will help your audience remember the thesis of the speech long after the speech is over.

Former Secretary of Education William Bennett's conclusion to a speech encouraging the teaching of history includes all of the elements for a good conclusion. See if you can identify the transition to the conclusion, the summary, and the idea for the audience to remember:

> So in closing, I would say this: our students, our young citizens are the heirs of a precious historical legacy. Let it never be said of us that we failed as a nation because we neglected to pass on this legacy to our children, to all of them. Remember that whatever their ancestry of blood, they are all, we are all, equally heirs of the same tradition. In a fundamental sense we all have the same fathers—our founding fathers. Let it be said that we told our children their story, the whole story, the long record of our glories, our failures, our aspirations, our sins, our achievements, and our victories. Then let us leave it to them to determine their own view of it all: America in the totality of its acts. If we can dedicate ourselves to that endeavor, I'm confident that our students will discern in history and the story of their past the truth. They will cherish that truth. And that truth will keep them free, and that is yet one more reason we study history here, here in America. So let us go to it.

Types of Conclusions

You can use several techniques to conclude a speech. Generally, anything you can use to begin a speech, you can use to conclude it. A quotation can serve as a memorable statement. A rhetorical question can serve as a transition from the body to the conclusion. An incident can leave the audience with a vivid picture that illustrates your thesis one last time. A personal reference can serve as a challenge.

Most speakers try to tie the introduction to the conclusion. The person giving a speech on male-female communication differences included a reference to the introduction in the conclusion:

> It is important to remember that the differences are more in our perceptions of why we communicate and those perceptions affect what we communicate. So, the next time you and a friend of the opposite sex seem to be speaking two different languages, express your frustration as the waitress in the cartoon did. The conversation that follows hopefully will show some adaptation on both your parts and will be more productive than what she got!

Chapter 14 Summary

Every speech has three parts—introduction, body, and conclusion. Each part has specific functions. A good introduction introduces the topic, gets attention, states the thesis, forecasts the major points, and makes the audience understand the topic's importance.

A speaker can use several techniques to begin a speech. The six most common strategies are quotation, rhetorical question, references, humor, startling statement, and incident.

The body of the speech is the heart of your presentation. The material must be well-organized and clear. You can choose one of several organizational patterns: topical, chronological, spatial, classification, problem-solution, and cause-effect.

Most speeches combine organizational patterns. It's important to outline your ideas to guarantee that you're using the most effective patterns.

A completed outline should include transitions that tie your material together and make your speech flow from one idea to the next.

The conclusion can use any of the strategies used for beginning a speech. The conclusion should inform the audience the speech is drawing to a close, summarize the main points, and leave the audience with something to remember.

◆ *Check Your Understanding*

1. List the three parts of a speech and explain the purpose of each.
2. List the purposes of a good introduction and explain what each can accomplish.
3. List the six types of introductions. Give an explanation of each.
4. List the six organizational patterns for the body of a speech.
5. What are the six major principles for preparing a good outline?
6. Explain the function of internal and external transitions.
7. What are the three things a good conclusion should do?

◆ *Apply Your Understanding*

1. Select a speech from Appendix B or a speech assigned by your teacher. Outline the speech. Identify the overall organizational pattern used for the speech. Identify the organizational patterns used within the sections of the speech.

2. Select a speech from Appendix B or one assigned by your teacher. Label the internal and external transitions.

3. Rewrite the introduction and conclusion of a speech you have given previously in class. Identify the thesis and forecast in the introduction. Identify the transition, the summary, and the point for the audience to remember in the conclusion.

◆ *Thinking Critically about Public Speaking*

Select an introduction from one of the speeches in Appendix B. Identify the sentence or sentences that accomplish each of the five functions of an introduction. Are any of the functions missing? Would the introduction be better if the missing functions were included? Rewrite the introduction to include all five functions.

◆ *Speak Out!*

1. Prepare two introductions on one of the following topics:
   a. Everyone should belong to a school organization
   b. Our society puts too much emphasis on winning
   c. My favorite pastime
   d. A topic approved by your teacher
   Each introduction should include the five functions of a good introduction and should focus on a different purpose. Indicate which you are using.

2. Using one of the topics in #1, prepare a two- to three-minute speech. Justify your choice of organizational pattern.

◆ *Speech Challenge*

No one knows the organizational challenge better than those who must write a speech for another person. To experience what a speechwriter does, divide into pairs. You will write speeches for each other, so you will play the roles of both writer and speaker. Assign your speechwriter a simple topic. Tell the speechwriter what you want the speech to do (purpose) and generally what you want the speech to include. Answer the speechwriter's questions. Then, reverse roles and receive your assignment. Agree to have an outline, a rough draft, and a final draft prepared by a certain date. Each of you will give the speech prepared for you by the other.

After the speech, discuss as a class the problems encountered as a speechwriter and as a speaker. Pay specific attention to how you handled the introduction, conclusion, and transitions.

CHAPTER ·15·

Key Terms

Argumentation

Claim

Data

Deductive reasoning

Evidence

Fact

Fallacies

Inductive reasoning

Policy

Reasoning

Reservations

Support

Value

Warrant

Chapter Objectives

After studying this chapter, you will be able to:

1. Define *argumentation*.
2. Explain the three parts of the argumentation process.
3. Identify and explain the three types of claims.
4. Identify and explain the five types of reasoning.
5. Identify and explain two of the five tests of reasoning.
6. Identify and explain at least three logical fallacies.

Argumentation

The Basics of Argumentation

You have probably been in an argument with someone, so when you hear the word *argument,* you probably think of a disagreement, difference of opinion, or dispute. However, there's a difference between *having* an argument and *making* an argument. This chapter deals with making an argument.

The process of making an argument is called *argumentation.* More specifically, **argumentation** is the process of presenting reasons that support a claim. A **claim** is the conclusion, or idea, you want your audience to accept. Your claims will fall into one of three categories: fact, value, or policy. There are two steps in proving a claim: providing **support,** or **evidence** (facts, statistics, or statements by authority) used to prove a claim, and **reasoning,** the logical steps that relate the support to the claim.

Toulmin's Model

Stephen Toulmin explained the argumentation process with the following model:

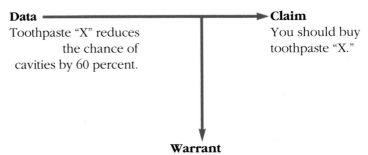

Data ──────────────────────────►**Claim**
Toothpaste "X" reduces   You should buy
the chance of   toothpaste "X."
cavities by 60 percent.

Warrant
Since you don't want cavities,

The **data** is the support, and the **warrant** is the reasoning step.

This diagram represents the ideal view of argumentation. Making arguments is not as simple as 1, 2, 3. There are occasional roadblocks, such as examples that disprove your conclusions. **Reservations** are the exceptions to your warrant. When you make an argument, be aware of reservations the audience or opponents can produce. You also need to develop responses to reservations. When reservations are considered, a Toulmin model looks like this:

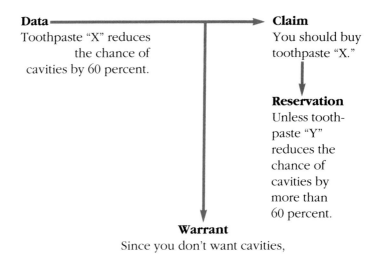

Data ──────────────────────→ **Claim**
Toothpaste "X" reduces   You should buy
the chance of   toothpaste "X."
cavities by 60 percent.

                                Reservation
                                Unless tooth-
                                paste "Y"
                                reduces the
                                chance of
                                cavities by
                                more than
                                60 percent.

Warrant
Since you don't want cavities,

Types of Claims

There are three types of claims a speaker can make: fact, value, or policy. In any given speech, you may use all three. Speeches are usually composed of a series of arguments, not just one. You may develop one claim as a step in proving another claim. The process is a complex one. By understanding each part, you can develop effective arguments.

Claims of Fact

Claims of **fact** make statements about something real. They can be proven correct or incorrect. Argumentation involving claims of fact relies on the claim's accuracy. Some claims of fact leave little room for argument. For instance, if you say, "Rainfall of 32.4 inches in 1987 was 4 inches above that for the previous year," you've told the audience members everything they need to judge your claim's validity. The validity of many other claims of fact is less obvious, however.

Suppose you argue that airline travel is more dangerous today than five years ago. This is a claim that requires support. In order to prove your claim, you'd have to cite other facts showing a decline in airline safety. You could give statistics on the number of crashes, the number of deaths and injuries, the number of near accidents, or the deteriorating condition of equipment. You'd have to compare today's statistics with those of five years ago. If the statistics support your claim, the audience will probably accept your conclusion as fact. A Toulmin model of this claim would look like this:

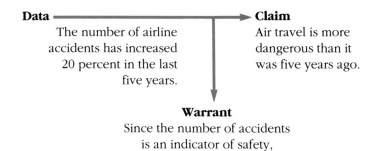

Data ⟶ **Claim**

The number of airline accidents has increased 20 percent in the last five years.

Air travel is more dangerous than it was five years ago.

Warrant
Since the number of accidents is an indicator of safety,

When making a claim of fact that requires support, be sure your support is complete. If you argue from only one perspective, opponents will be able to refute your claim. For instance, suppose you argue that airlines aren't safe because there's been an increase in *near* accidents. An opponent could dispute your claim by showing that the number of *actual* crashes and deaths is down:

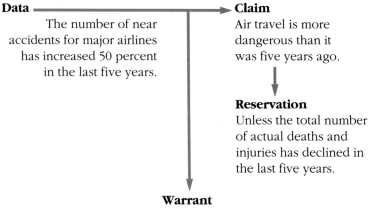

Data ⟶ **Claim**

The number of near accidents for major airlines has increased 50 percent in the last five years.

Air travel is more dangerous than it was five years ago.

Reservation
Unless the total number of actual deaths and injuries has declined in the last five years.

Warrant
Since the chance of being in an accident has increased in the last five years,

Often, you must define terms you use in claims of fact. In the airline example, you might have to define what you mean by *safety*. If you think safety includes potential as well as actual crashes, you're arguing from a different starting point than an opponent who only looks at deaths and injuries from actual crashes. You would need to

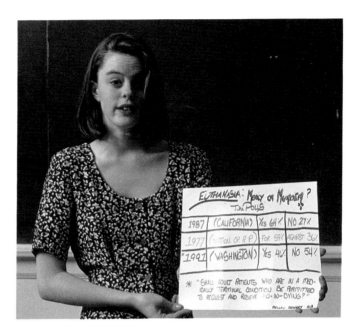

Claims of fact are often backed up with statistics. If the statistics support the claim, the audience will probably accept the claim as fact.

establish that your definition is superior in order to establish your claim of fact. One way to do that is to use definitions from experts or accepted authorities, such as government agencies.

When arguing claims of fact, you can relate them to the past, present, or future. Past facts refer to events occurring in the near or distant past. Present facts describe current conditions. Future facts make predictions. The following are examples of each:

Past: The North was responsible for starting the Civil War.

Present: Unemployment is down from six months ago.

Future: The United States will not elect a woman president or vice president before the turn of the century.

Claims of Value

Values represent judgments about the world that cannot be verified. Claims of value make relative judgments about what is good or bad, right or wrong, just or unjust, moral or immoral. Values affect judgments about people, events, ideas, and policies. There are four types of values: artistic, moral, political, and pragmatic.

Artistic values affect the way people decide things such as what is beautiful or ugly or in good taste or poor taste. In Chapter 11, artistic quality was one criterion for evaluating speeches. Such an evaluation would include making value decisions.

Moral values relate to judgments about what's right or wrong, good or bad, just or unjust. Such values affect the way people behave in society and are the basis for the laws that govern them.

Political values refer to those things that are thought to be important within the governmental structure. In the United States, people place a high value on freedom, democracy, individual rights, law, and order. Other countries have different political values. When disagreements arise between countries, it's often because they have different sets of political values guiding their actions.

Pragmatic values refer to being practical or impractical. Some values relate to how people do things. Society emphasizes time efficiency, cost efficiency, and practicality. These values often come into play when decisions are made about policies.

Values are shared by a majority of the members of a society. Researchers have found that Americans value such things as equality of opportunity, justice, freedom, and individuality. As a result, you can make arguments based on value claims because the majority of your audience can identify with the value.

You also should realize that even though people hold a large number of values in common, there are times when values come into conflict. Some values have priority over others. That doesn't mean a value is abandoned. It does mean that in given situations, one value is judged to be of greater importance than another. For instance, personal freedoms often must be sacrificed to increase the safety of society as a whole. That is why a few years ago many state governments decided to institute driver's license checks as a way to detect drunk drivers.

Because values affect behavior, claims of value play an important role when you develop many arguments. Many value claims are presented as comparisons. Thomas Paine's claim that "Liberty is more precious than life" is such a comparison. Other value claims take an absolute position on a legal policy because it either supports or contradicts a value. The claim that "capital punishment is morally wrong under any circumstance" is an example of an absolute position:

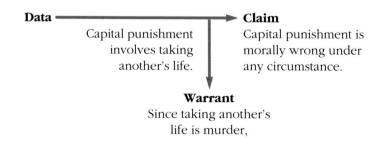

Data ——————————→ **Claim**

Capital punishment involves taking another's life.

Capital punishment is morally wrong under any circumstance.

Warrant
Since taking another's
life is murder,

Claims of Policy

Claims of **policy** make a statement about what should be done or how it should be done. These claims suggest a course of action the audience should take or should influence someone else to take. Policy claims are made in many persuasive speeches. If you gave a persuasive speech supporting an increase in the number of math, science, and language arts credits needed for high-school graduation, you would state claims of policy.

Speakers usually build claims of policy around claims of fact and value because there must be reasons for supporting or adopting a policy. The reasons are most often found in facts or values. You could build arguments in favor of increased graduation requirements on the facts that test scores in those disciplines are low, that students in other countries score better than students in the United States, and that math, science, and language arts skills are needed after graduation:

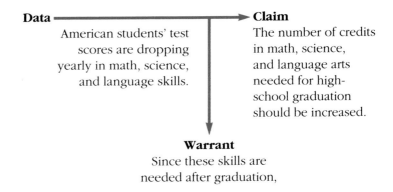

Data
American students' test scores are dropping yearly in math, science, and language skills.

Claim
The number of credits in math, science, and language arts needed for high-school graduation should be increased.

Warrant
Since these skills are needed after graduation,

Arguments supporting the policy claim that "Stricter laws are needed to preserve the environment" could appeal to values. You could appeal to a sense of responsibility to future generations. You could also appeal to pragmatic values about wastefulness.

Overlap of Claims

While there are three distinct types of claims, each type may depend on the others for support. You may support a claim of policy with a claim of fact or value that you've already established. As you can see, argumentation is a series of arguments, each building on another. Here's an example:

Claim of policy: Stricter controls on airlines are needed to increase safety.

Support: Safety has declined over the past five years as shown by an increase in near accidents, nonfatal accidents, and deteriorating equipment. (Claim of fact)

Reasoning: Safety is important to all of us, and the government has an obligation to guarantee travelers' safety. (Claim of value)

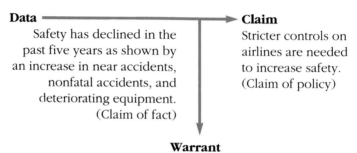

Data ──────────────────────→ **Claim**

Safety has declined in the past five years as shown by an increase in near accidents, nonfatal accidents, and deteriorating equipment. (Claim of fact)

Stricter controls on airlines are needed to increase safety. (Claim of policy)

Warrant

Safety is important to all of us, and the government has an obligation to guarantee travelers' safety. (Claim of value)

Support for Claims

To prove a claim, you must supply evidence. Chapter 12 discussed support materials and explained that evidence (or support for claims) comes in two forms: facts and testimony. Facts include statistics, examples, illustrations, comparisons/contrasts, and incidents. Hypothetical examples are not considered facts. Testimony is evidence that comments on facts and often includes opinion.

In making arguments, select the best support available. Some types of evidence suit some claims better than others. For example, claims of fact are best supported by definitions, statistics, testimony, and examples. Claims of value are best supported by definitions and testimony. Policy claims can be supported from a wide range of evidence types.

When selecting evidence, consider the members of the audience and what types of evidence they'd find most convincing. Audiences that know about your topic require more sophisticated evidence than audiences hearing about your topic for the first time.

Tests of Evidence

One way to find out if an audience will accept your evidence is to subject it to a test. You test all evidence types by determining if they are relevant, sufficient, recent, and consistent with other known information. Specific types of evidence require specific tests as well.

Relevance   Data that supports claims must relate to the issue at hand. If evidence comes from a related area rather than from your subject, or if the evidence can't be applied specifically to your claim, the evidence fails the test for relevance. If you used data about private plane accidents, the data wouldn't be relevant if you were calling for reforms in commercial aviation regulations. An example showing that an antidrug program worked in one high school would be irrelevant if that high school had resources unavailable to most other schools.

Sufficiency   You need to supply a sufficient amount of evidence to support your claim. Ask yourself if you have supplied enough examples. Do your statistics represent a wide range of situations? While it isn't necessary to read an endless list of examples, statistics, or quotations from authorities, it is important to demonstrate that claims are not based on isolated or unusual examples.

The quality of evidence is equally important to establish sufficiency. Evidence derived from well-respected sources has more authority than evidence coming from unknown or suspect sources or methods.

Sufficiency also includes whether or not you have enough evidence to counter opposing evidence. In other words, can you answer opponents' reservations to the warrants? In persuasive speeches especially, it's easy to find evidence for both sides of an argument. Your evidence must be superior to the evidence against your position.

Recency   Evidence must be up-to-date. You can't call for a change in airline regulations based on evidence collected five or ten years ago. Conditions change rapidly, and it's necessary to keep pace.

When you're establishing historical background, it's all right to use older evidence. The basic test of recency is this: does the claim require the most recent information to establish its validity? Policy claims usually require recent evidence. Some claims of fact and value can rely on older evidence.

Consistency   A final general test of the quality of evidence is its consistency with other known facts. Draw your evidence from more than one source, and be sure it's consistent with related information. For instance, if you find evidence that the number of deaths from airline accidents rose sharply but that the number of accidents was down, someone could argue that the facts are inconsistent. If you could claim that (1) travel is more dangerous, based on the death rate, and (2) there are fewer accidents, but (3) they involved bigger planes carrying more passengers, you could establish the validity of your claim.

Sometimes you shouldn't rule out evidence because it's inconsistent with previously held beliefs. In a highly technological society, information becomes outdated quickly. New breakthroughs often make previously accepted facts questionable. Remember, people once believed that the world was flat. New evidence was inconsistent with all past evidence and claims, but the new evidence turned out to be accurate.

Tests of Testimony

If evidence from authorities passes the general tests, it still requires three additional steps. You need to test authority evidence for bias, competence, and context.

Bias   It's important for you to know that authorities reach their conclusions in an objective manner. A representative of the airlines who claims that further regulations are unnecessary could be biased. He or she has a vested interest in the outcome of a policy decision. The representative's job is working for the company. His or her personal welfare is tied to the welfare of the company.

It's difficult to be objective. If an authority supports claims with appropriate facts, you can't charge him or her with bias. If any authorities are used to support conclusions, you must know how they arrived at their information.

Competence   An authority should be an expert on the topic he or she addresses. Just because a person is a well-known expert on one topic doesn't necessarily mean that he or she is knowledgeable on every subject. Suppose you're claiming that test scores are an inadequate measure of the quality of a child's education. You find two pieces of testimony supporting your claim. One is from a professor of education. The other is from a United States senator who has no background in educational testing. Which would you judge to be the better source? Why?

When you present evidence from a credible source your audience knows, you usually don't have to say a great deal about the person's qualifications. However, if the source is competent but not generally known, you must describe his or her credentials briefly.

Context   When using authority evidence, it's impossible to read every word the person said or wrote. And during your speech, time doesn't permit long quotations. That means you have to be selective. When you select a quotation, it's important to present it accurately. That means you must put the quote in context. Sometimes, when you pull one sentence out of a paragraph, it means the opposite of the paragraph as a whole. The quote is not in context. The quote doesn't reflect the authority's message. Be sure to quote fairly and accurately.

Tests for Studies   Facts and statistics are often derived from research reports or studies. When you use conclusions from studies, you must know who conducted the study. You must apply the same tests for bias and competence to studies that you apply to testimony. It's also helpful to know what techniques or methods the researchers employed to gather their data. If the researcher used sound, commonly accepted techniques, rather than untried and untested procedures, the audience will be more likely to accept the conclusions.

The Reasoning Process

Proving claims requires logic. That is how a speaker shows how and why the evidence supports the claim. Often, the speaker doesn't explain the reasoning step because it's obvious to the audience. This argument uses the audience's existing knowledge or beliefs to connect the support to the claim.

For example, suppose you're making the claim "You should use a sunscreen to avoid the risks of skin cancer." Using credible sources, you'd present evidence showing potential risks from sun exposure with and without the sunscreens. Because most audience members don't want to damage their bodies or increase the risk of skin cancer, you don't have to say "Since you should want to protect yourself from unnecessary risks to your health. . . ." The audience will supply the link for you. The logic comes from their own beliefs.

To link support to claims, you can use five types of reasoning: inductive reasoning, deductive reasoning, sign, causal relationship, and analogy.

Inductive Reasoning

Inductive reasoning draws conclusions by (1) examining specific instances or examples and (2) developing either a general rule or a specific rule. If you cite several research studies linking sun exposure with skin cancer, you would conclude that "Exposure to the sun increases a person's chances of developing skin cancer." Your conclusion would be based on inductive reasoning.

Here's another example of inductive reasoning. Suppose that your argument favors mandatory seat-belt laws for your state. You support your argument with data from five other states with mandatory laws. The data shows a decline in the number of injury-related accidents. Inductive reasoning is especially useful when you want to develop claims that predict future events based on past occurrences.

President Gerald Ford used inductive reasoning in his 1976 acceptance speech for the Republican nomination. Ford cited his past record to prove his general policy on taxes:

> Fifty-five times I vetoed extravagant and unwise legislation; forty-five times I made those vetoes stick. Those vetoes have saved American taxpayers billions and billions of dollars. I am against the big tax spender and for the little taxpayer.

Deductive Reasoning

Deductive reasoning is the opposite of inductive reasoning. It's an analytical process that (1) takes generally accepted conclusions and (2) applies them to specific instances to demonstrate that (3) the conclusion does indeed apply to the specific instance. In the seat-belt speech, you could argue for mandatory laws based on general research on seat-belt safety rather than on the specific state examples used in inductive reasoning.

To apply deductive reasoning, the conclusion must be true of any member of a particular class. In other words, seat-belt research must apply to every accident involving seat belts. Since there are exceptions to every rule, when you argue deductively, you must use qualified terms such as *most, many,* and *often,* rather than absolute terms such as *all, never,* or *always.* Remember, there are reservations to most arguments, and you must consider those reservations.

Susan B. Anthony employed deductive reasoning when she defended the fact that she had voted in an 1872 election—forty-eight years before women were given the right to vote:

It shall be my work this evening to prove to you that in thus voting, I not only committed no crime, but, instead, simply exercised my *citizen's rights,* guaranteed to me and all United States citizens by the National Constitution, beyond the power of any State to deny.

The preamble of the Federal Constitution says:

"We the people of the United States, in order to form a more perfect union, establish justice, insure domestic tranquillity, provide for the common defense, promote the general welfare, and secure the blessings of liberty to ourselves and our posterity, do ordain and establish this Constitution for the United States of America."

It was we, the people; not we, the white male citizens; nor yet we, the male citizens; but we, the whole people, who formed the Union. And we formed it, not to give the blessings of liberty, but to secure them; not to the half of ourselves and the half of our posterity, but to the whole people—women as well as men.

Sign

Reasoning from sign involves drawing conclusions about a state of affairs because of the presence of a physical sign. If you read mystery novels, you're familiar with reasoning from sign. The conclusions reached from such reasoning are often said to be based on *circumstantial evidence* because the sign isn't strong enough to support the conclusion. More information is needed.

When you reason from sign, your conclusions may be logical, but they aren't always accurate. For instance, if you call someone on the phone and no one answers, you may conclude that your friend isn't home. However, your friend may be using a hair dryer and can't hear the phone or may have switched off the phone to get some rest. Since there are limitations in reasoning from sign, don't rely on such reasoning alone when you make claims.

President Franklin Roosevelt used reasoning from sign in his speech calling for a declaration of war against Japan on 8 December 1941:

It will be recorded that the distance of Hawaii from Japan makes it obvious that the attack was deliberately planned many days or even weeks ago.

Analogy

Chapter 12 defined *analogy* as an extended comparison. It's a way to explain something the members of the audience don't understand in terms of something they do understand. Both figurative and literal analogies are acceptable forms of reasoning in making a claim.

When using literal analogies to draw a conclusion, however, the two examples must be similar in all characteristics that affect the conclusion. Suppose you're arguing for a change in a school lunch-hour policy based on a successful open lunch-hour policy at another school. If there are any major differences between the schools—if their student bodies aren't the same size, if there's a difference in access to convenient restaurants, if they aren't in similar locations (rural versus urban)—then the analogy wouldn't be valid.

In 1954, Eleanor Roosevelt used two figurative analogies in a speech in which she defended the United Nations:

> But talk can have a great value; you have to think of it as a bridge. You have to think of the General Assembly as a place where bridges are built between peoples. . . .
>
> When we look upon the failures in the United Nations, we should not be disheartened, because if we take failure and learn, eventually we will use this machinery better and better. We will also learn one important thing, and that is, no machinery works unless people make it work.

Causal Reasoning

To establish a **causal** relationship between two things, you must show that one actually causes the other. Causal reasoning is especially useful to establish claims of policy. Since policies are intended to affect a particular situation, you must show that the cause (the new policy) will actually have the desired effects that you say it will.

Suppose you're arguing for increased equipment and maintenance regulations for commercial airlines in order to reduce airline accidents. You'd have to establish a causal relationship between airline accidents and current equipment and maintenance practices. If accidents are caused by other reasons, then your claims that the policy change will make travel safer aren't valid.

When you discuss causal relationships, you must explain the difference between cause-and-effect and correlations. In a *cause-effect relationship,* one thing actually causes another. When a *correlation* exists between two things, the two simply seem to occur together or be otherwise associated. If it always seems to rain after you wash the car, that's a correlation, not a cause-effect relationship. Washing the car didn't cause the rain. Many superstitions are the result of correlations, not cause-effect.

In a televised speech on 5 February 1981, President Ronald Reagan argued for an economic package he was sending to Congress. The President used several examples of causal reasoning:

> All of you who are working know that even with cost-of-living pay raises, you can't keep up with inflation. In our progressive tax system as you increase the number of dollars you earn, you find yourself moved up into higher tax brackets, paying a higher tax rate just for trying to hold your own. The result? Your standard of living is going down.

Tests of Reasoning

As you prepare arguments and as you analyze those of others, you need to determine if the reasoning process is sound. Just as there are tests for evidence, there are also tests for the warrant or reasoning stage of the argumentation process. Each type of reasoning has its own set of tests.

Inductive Reasoning Tests

Three tests apply to inductive reasoning. First, ask if enough examples have been examined. A generalization shouldn't be based on one or two examples. If you want to convince someone that seat belts save lives, you must show that, in a significant number of accidents, people who were wearing seat belts would have died without them. If you find only a few cases out of the thousands of traffic accidents each year, you wouldn't have a valid argument.

Second, determine if examples are representative or typical. In the seat belt example, you need to show that your examples cover a wide range of accident types. What if those whose lives were saved were involved in only one type of accident? Then you must alter your conclusion to generalize for only that one type of accident. The evidence wouldn't apply to all accident types.

A final test of inductive reasoning is the test for exceptions. Does your conclusion account for exceptions? Very few conclusions apply to all instances. You must word generalizations to allow for exceptions. For example, you might learn that seat belts have little effect on safety at certain speeds. If that's the case, then your generalization should state that seat belts can save lives in the majority of accidents at speeds under (or over) a certain limit.

Tests for Deductive Reasoning

There are two tests for deductive reasoning. The first applies to the generalization—it must be true. If it isn't, then it can't be applied to the specific case. For instance, is this generalization true: someone with small, beady eyes can't be trusted. If it isn't based on any factual support, then judging a person's trustworthiness on the basis of eye size wouldn't be a valid test.

The second test is whether the generalization applies to the particular case. In other words, is the particular case you're concerned with similar in all respects to other cases that the generalization applies to? Suppose a politician argues that an opposing candidate, who is a Democrat, will raise taxes because all Democrats believe in "tax

Voters frequently must use deductive reasoning to determine whether a candidate's generalizations about his or her opponent are valid.

and spend." If the candidate can show that other Democrats did increase taxes, it's logical to assume that the Democratic candidate would also support tax increases. If, however, the Democratic candidate had a record of voting against tax increases and was a conservative on budget matters, the generalization would not apply in this particular instance. There are exceptions to every rule, and you need to know if you're dealing with an exception or not.

Tests for Arguments from Sign

The major test for arguments based on sign is whether or not the sign applies in all instances. In other words, can you draw more than one conclusion from a sign, or is it a sign only under certain circumstances? If several signs, rather than a single sign, are required to draw a conclusion, you must show the existence of the related signs.

Consider a murder investigation as an example. Suppose you walk into a room. You see a body on the floor and someone standing nearby, holding a smoking gun. The signs point to the person holding the gun as the murderer. Such circumstantial evidence wouldn't be sufficient, however, to convict the person. The police would run ballistics tests to see if that particular gun had fired the fatal bullet. To be sure the person holding the gun had fired it, the police would check for traces of gunpowder on the person's hand or clothing. All the signs must be positive before the evidence can suggest that the guilty party is identified.

Tests for Reasoning by Analogy

To test warrants based on analogy, determine if the two cases involved are similar in all major respects. Minor differences may not affect the final conclusion. However, all factors that *do* affect the conclusion must be similar. If a successful football coach takes a new job, it isn't reasonable to assume that the coaching techniques used with the old team will be equally successful with the new one. If the teams are similar in size and talent, it would seem logical to assume that what worked once will work again. But if the new team has weaknesses in basic skills, the coach's game plans might not work.

Tests for Causal Reasoning

To test conclusions based on causal reasoning, you must distinguish between cause and effect. Is an obnoxious person that way because he or she is ignored, or is the person ignored because he or she is obnoxious? The two conditions may well exist, but which is the cause and which is the effect?

A second test for causal reasoning involves the strength of the cause. You must show that the cause is sufficient to produce the effect. Suppose the president is a Republican, and the Republicans have a majority in both houses of Congress. A piece of legislation that the president supports fails. Can the president blame the Democrats for failure if the law could have been passed without any of their votes? In this situation, the answer can't be an automatic *yes* or *no*. However, a *yes* would be doubtful. Someone analyzing the president's argument would undoubtedly look for other reasons why the legislation failed.

A final test involves what are known as *alternative causes*. While a certain cause can produce an effect, other causes might also produce the same effect. In order to say that a particular cause produced an effect, you must rule out other causes. For instance, improved grades in school can result from several causes: better study habits, better teachers, better books and learning resources. To determine if a student's improvement was the result of better study habits, you'd have to show that there was no change in any other factors.

Fallacies

The tests of evidence and reasoning can be used to identify weaknesses in your own arguments or in others'. You should also look for logical **fallacies,** or flaws, in the reasoning process. Some of the more common fallacies are described here.

Hasty Generalization

You've probably met someone briefly at a party or a dance and made some quick assumptions about his or her character or personality. If your initial observations were later proved wrong, you would have been guilty of making a *hasty generalization*. In this type of fallacy, conclusions are based on incomplete evidence.

Ad Hominem Arguments

The translation for the Latin term *ad hominem* means *against the man*. *Ad hominem* arguments are made against the person, rather than against the person's arguments. If someone you don't like says something, you're likely to ignore it, saying "consider the source."

Your reason for ignoring the statement is an *ad hominem* argument. In politics, personal attacks are often called *mudslinging*. Opponents often resort to attacking a person's character instead of attacking the person's ideas. Such arguments aren't logical, since someone can make good arguments, even if his or her character isn't up to your standard. To avoid *ad hominem* arguments, examine the evidence and logical conclusions in a person's arguments.

Appeals to Popular Opinion

Appeals to popular opinion, or the bandwagon fallacy, suggest something is true because everyone thinks it is. Politicians often rely on popular opinion polls to make their decisions for them. Just because something is favored by a majority of the public does not make it the best policy. There must be other reasons.

Appeals to Tradition

When you argue against change because "we've never done it that way before," you're appealing to *tradition.* Some traditions are worth keeping. Others must change because times, technology, and knowledge change. All change isn't progress, but you shouldn't argue against change solely on the basis of tradition.

Begging the Question

Begging the question involves circular reasoning. Essentially, the warrant and the claim are the same thing. If you argue that people should support an equal rights amendment because it's the right thing to do, you're assuming that an equal rights amendment is good in and of itself. You need to prove an assumption like this before you or your audience accepts it.

Chapter 15 Summary

Regardless of your speech purpose, you'll make claims of fact, value, or policy. The process of proving claims is known as *argumentation*. In making claims, it's necessary to present support for the claim in the form of data or evidence and to explain the relationship between the data and the claim through the use of a warrant. The warrant is the reasoning step in the argumentation process. While many claims appear to be logical, it's important to examine both the evidence and reasoning behind the claims to determine if they actually prove the claim. In preparing arguments, it's also necessary to know what counterarguments, or reservations, exist. Responses to the reservations should be developed.

To test your evidence, consider its relevance, sufficiency, recency, and consistency. If you're using testimony, test it for bias and competence, and be sure to use it in context. If you're using research, check the procedures used.

The logic used in a speech to prove claims may be deductive reasoning, inductive reasoning, reasoning by sign, reasoning by analogy, or causal reasoning. Try to avoid logical fallacies.

◆ Check Your Understanding

1. Define *argumentation*.

2. Explain the three parts of the argumentation process.

3. Identify and explain the three types of claims.

4. Identify and explain the five types of reasoning.

5. Identify and explain at least two tests of reasoning.

6. Identify and explain at least three logical fallacies.

◆ Apply Your Understanding

1. Using one or more of the speeches in Appendix B, identify claims of fact, value, and policy.

2. Using one or more of the speeches in Appendix B, identify an example of each of the five types of reasoning.

◆ Thinking Critically about Public Speaking

1. Collect several ads from a newspaper or magazine. Using the Toulmin model, diagram the arguments contained in the ads. If the warrant is not given, write the assumed warrant.

2. Working in groups, examine the evidence presented in one of the speeches in Appendix B or a speech selected by your teacher. Subject the evidence to the tests of evidence described in this chapter. Present your analysis to the class.

3. Working in groups, examine the speech used in #2 to determine if the speaker uses any logical fallacies. How can the arguments be improved?

◆ *Speak Out!*

Prepare a two- to three-minute speech supporting a policy position. Use claims of fact and value to build support for your policy claim. Possible topics include:
a. Handguns should be controlled in the United States.
b. All students should be required to learn a foreign language.
c. All forms of gambling should be made illegal in the United States.

◆ *Speech Challenge*

As a class, brainstorm a series of controversial topics you would like to see debated. In pairs, select the topic you want to debate. Follow these steps:

1. Word the topic as a resolution.
   a. The resolution should contain the word *should* and propose some type of change.
   b. The resolution should be fairly and neutrally worded.
   c. The resolution should create two sides: a *pro* side and a *con* side.
   A topic should read like this: *Resolved: That the passing period between classes should be increased from five to seven minutes.*

2. Determine which of you will be pro and which con.

3. Allow the pro speaker to speak first, giving a three- to four-minute speech. The con speaker can then ask three questions.

4. Allow the con speaker to speak second, with the same time limits. The pro speaker can then ask three questions.

5. Each speaker will then give a one- to two-minute speech responding to the other side and concluding his or her position.

6. The audience will evaluate the debate according to the following guideline: Which speaker offered the best arguments in support of his or her side of the resolution?

4

Presenting
Speeches

CHAPTER

Key Terms

Demonstration speech

Oral report

Process speech

Speech to inform

Chapter Objectives

After studying this chapter, you should be able to:

1. Explain the purpose of a speech to inform.

2. List and explain the seven types of informative speeches.

3. Explain how situation, purpose, and audience affect informative speech development.

4. Apply the guidelines for developing introductions and conclusions to the speech to inform.

5. Apply the guidelines for organizing the body of a speech to the speech to inform.

6. Apply the guidelines for using supportive materials in the speech to inform.

The Speech
to Inform

Types of Speech to Inform

A speech can fulfill one of three general purposes: to inform, to persuade, or to entertain. A **speech to inform** presents information. However, its purpose goes beyond that. The speech should either give new information on a familiar topic or should introduce the audience to a new subject. Essentially, the goal of an informative speech is to make the audience more knowledgeable or to·increase their understanding of a topic and their interest in it.

Informative speeches are very common. When you hear a lecture in class, you're hearing an informative speech. When a store clerk tells you how to use the VCR you just purchased, you're listening to an informative speech. Because informative speeches are given—and heard—so often, this chapter divides them into seven types and explains how to use the SPAM model to develop them.

Speeches about Processes

The **process speech** is an informative speech that describes how something is done or how something works. A speech explaining the steps to become a black belt in karate is a process speech. A speech explaining how a science fiction film was animated is another example. A process speech relies heavily on description and explanation. Speakers often use visual aids in this type of speech. However, to give a process speech, you don't have to actually show how to do something. This type of informative speech explains a process that involves actions you generally can't show an audience.

Process speeches fall into three general categories: scientific process, historical process, and thought process. A speech on bird migration is a scientific process speech. One describing how the Battle of Gettysburg was fought is a historical process speech. A speech telling how to study a textbook for a test is an example of a thought process speech.

Demonstration Speeches

In a **demonstration speech,** you actually show the audience how to do something. If you've ever watched a cooking show on television, you saw a demonstration speech. If someone shows you how to use a socket wrench, he or she is giving a demonstration speech. If your chemistry teacher shows you the proper way to use laboratory equipment, you're watching a demonstration speech. In fact, much of what we learn comes from observing someone show us how to do something. Teachers often assign demonstration speeches as the first speech because they're common in everyday life and because they require the least research and preparation.

Speeches about Objects or Places

If you've ever visited a museum, a tour guide may have pointed out special features about the things you saw. The guide's comments were an informative speech about objects. The objects can be human-made or natural and can range from something as large as the sequoias in California to something as small as an ant. Places can also be the subjects of informative speeches. Travelogues or television specials on a country are informative presentations about a place.

Speeches about People

If your history teacher ever asked you or a classmate to make a report about a famous person, that report was an informative speech. Thousands of interesting people, both living and dead, have affected our lives. In certain situations, speeches about such people are very appropriate. When you take a job, you may find that part of the orientation process includes presentations about the founder of the company or about those who run the company. All these are examples of informative speeches. You'll find that people are good topics for speeches in a speech class.

Speeches about Events

Speeches about events can be about historical or present-day events. A speech about the Constitutional Convention would be an example of a speech about an event. So would speeches about New Orleans' Mardi Gras or the Boston Marathon.

Speeches about Ideas

Speeches about ideas make up the broadest category of informative speeches. They rely heavily on explanation and definition. Unlike other types of informative speeches, speeches about ideas deal with intangible topics. A speech that contrasts the democratic government of the United States with the Communist government of the People's Republic of China is a speech about ideas. Generally, any topic that doesn't fall into one of the earlier categories and is developed by sharing facts, examples, and definitions is a speech about an idea.

Oral Reports

A very special type of informative speech is commonly used in both the classroom and the business world. It's the **oral report,** an

An oral report is an informative speech that is a summary of facts and ideas.

informative speech in which the speaker gathers information and explains it to a particular group for a particular purpose. An oral report is a summary of facts and ideas. A book report in an English class is an example of an oral report. So is a report on a company's sales activity over the course of a year.

Some oral reports simply summarize a series of facts. Others require the presenter to interpret the information or make suggestions based on it. Suppose you belong to a club and are placed on a committee to investigate the cost of several options for a party. When the group report is made, you recommend what action the club should take. This type of oral report is an advisory report.

Oral reports require a great deal of research and preparation. They're usually brief reports, despite how much information they may have to cover. Often, it's necessary to include visual aids because they're an efficient means of presenting complex information.

The Combined Approach

Some informative speeches combine more than one of the seven types. An oral report can include a summary of a company's sales as well as an explanation of a process that could improve sales. A speech about a famous person may include information about historical events in which the person was involved. If you're using a combined approach, the combined types must complement one another. You should avoid including information that detracts from your main purpose rather than supporting it.

Developing the Speech to Inform

When you prepare a speech to inform, be aware of the situation, purpose, and audience before you select a method of development. Regardless of which of the seven types of informative speeches you are preparing, follow these general guidelines.

First, consider how relevant and useful the information will be for the audience. You must motivate an audience to listen. In a sense, this is the persuasive element in an informative speech. Before members of an audience are willing to listen, they must first be convinced they need to know the information you're sharing.

Second, be sure the information is new to the audience. If you've conducted a thorough audience analysis, this shouldn't be a problem. If the audience already knows all or most of what you're saying, you haven't achieved the purpose of an informative speech—you haven't increased the audience's knowledge or understanding of a topic.

Third, be sure that your introduction gets the audience's attention, creates interest, and makes the topic clear. It should also forecast the main ideas. Your conclusion should summarize the major points.

Fourth, avoid information overload. Remember, you can't cover everything about a topic. For an informative speech, narrowing the topic and selecting the information that's most relevant to the audience are crucial tasks. If you give the audience too much information, especially on a new topic, you'll probably lose their attention. The people in the audience will have too much to comprehend the first time they're exposed to the subject.

Developing the Process Speech

The most logical organizational pattern for a process speech is chronological. To explain a process, you must begin at the beginning and follow the steps of the process logically. If you don't know enough about the process, you'll have to conduct research. Follow the guidelines in Chapter 13.

When you organize the speech, include a clear thesis and forecast the process's major steps. The following is from the introduction to a process speech about dry cleaning:

Thesis

Contrary to its name, the dry cleaning process isn't really a "dry" process.

Forecast

The dry cleaning process involves three steps: treating the clothes with chemicals, removing the chemicals, and pressing the clothes.

When you develop the body of the process speech, you'll find the most useful supporting materials are description, definition, example, illustration, and visual aids.

Developing the Demonstration Speech

A demonstration speech is similar to a process speech except that you both explain and show the audience how to do something. Because the demonstration must provide the steps in the order that they occur, a chronological pattern is usually the most appropriate for this type of speech.

When you select and develop a topic for a demonstration speech, keep these suggestions in mind:

1. Select a topic that you can demonstrate in the room where you're giving the presentation. If you can't narrow the topic so that you can illustrate all aspects of your broad topic, then consider giving a process speech. For instance, it's impossible to demonstrate how to play basketball in a classroom. However, you can narrow the topic of how to play basketball to an explanation of how to pass and dribble the ball. Or you can give a process speech about a game plan.

2. Select a topic that you can develop within the time limits. Try to select topics that require only a short period of time. In five to seven minutes, you can demonstrate first aid procedures, sports basics, such as the proper way to swing a golf club, or simple food preparation. You can also condense a long speech by preparing some items ahead of time, without destroying the actual demonstration. For example, one student gave a speech on refinishing furniture, a process that can take several days. To meet the time limits, she used a wooden-box-type table with four sides and a top. She left one side with the old finish and showed how to apply finish remover. The next

SPOTLIGHT ON SPEAKING

Analyzing the Demonstration Speech

Use these guidelines to analyze demonstration speeches.

Situation:

1. Was the speech appropriate for a classroom setting?
2. Was the speech developed to meet the time requirements?

Purpose:

1. Did the speech meet the requirements for a demonstration speech?
2. Did the speaker fulfill the specific speech purpose?

Audience:

1. Was the speech suitable for the audience?
2. Did the speaker consider the audience's level of knowledge about the subject?
3. Was the subject of the demonstration something that the majority of the audience could do or might want to do?

Method:

1. Was the organizational pattern appropriate for a demonstration speech?
2. Did the speaker actually provide a demonstration?
3. Did the speaker provide sufficient explanation?

side had the finish removed. She used that side to show how to sand the wood. The third side was already sanded. To that side she applied a stain. The fourth side was stained. On it she showed how to apply the finishing steps. The top had all but the last step completed.

3. Select a subject the audience can see from their seats or have the audience form a circle around you.

4. Don't select a trivial topic. Remember, the purpose of an informative speech is to provide new information. Don't demonstrate something nearly everyone already knows how to do. A speech on making a peanut butter and jelly sandwich would be trivial. If you have a new twist or a gourmet recipe for peanut butter and jelly, then you would move your topic beyond what the audience already knows.

In a demonstration speech, the speaker both explains a process and shows how to do it.

As you develop the body of your demonstration speech, description, explanation, definition, illustration, and visual aids will be important supportive materials.

A Sample Demonstration Speech

Sue River gave the demonstration speech on page 322 in a basic speech course at Washburn University. The speech was to be four to six minutes long and was to include some type of visual aid. River's purpose, thesis, and outline were as follows:

Purpose
The purpose of this speech is to demonstrate exercises to the class to be used during study breaks.

Thesis
We've all experienced the physical and mental exhaustion that comes from studying, and today I'd like to talk with you about a way to break from study before study breaks you.

How to Break from Study before Study Breaks You

Introduction
    A. Description of effects of studying
    B. Thesis
    C. Forecast

  I. Benefits of exercise
    A. Relieves physical and emotional stress
    B. Replenishes vitality and energy
    C. Clears your mind
    D. Helps you make better use of time

 II. How to do the exercises
    A. Spine stretcher
        1. Purpose
        2. Stance
        3. Breathing
        4. Bend
        5. Straightening
    B. Neck saver
        1. Purpose
        2. Chin placement
        3. Chin roll
    C. Back stretcher
        1. How to sit
        2. Position of legs
        3. Bend
        4. Straightening
    D. Eye exerciser
        1. Purpose
        2. Warnings for those who wear contact lenses
        3. Widen eyes
        4. Roll eyes
        5. Close eyes

Conclusion
    A. Review benefits
    B. Ease of doing exercises
    C. Introduce handout

In presenting the speech, River's visual aids were herself and a chart containing the benefits of exercise. The notes in the margin tell you what she did during the speech to demonstrate the exercises to the class.

SAMPLE SPEECH
How to Break from Study before Study Breaks You

Thesis

Forecast

How many of you have found yourselves studying late at night with a final exam facing you in the morning? Your neck is stiff, your back hurts, your head aches, and your eyeballs feel ready to fall out of their sockets. I've had that experience, and today I'd like to talk with you about a way to break from study before study breaks you. Specifically, I'd like to explain the four benefits of exercising during study breaks, and then I will demonstrate some simple exercises you can do in just a few minutes to help release some of this built-up tension in your body. These exercises will help you return to your studies refreshed and ready to study more effectively.

The exercises I will show you can be done in five minutes, but they will have a long-lasting effect. Instead of taking a break to get some coffee, a soft drink, or something to eat, you can take a break that will benefit you four ways.

The speaker showed a chart with the four benefits listed.

First, exercise relieves physical and emotional tensions that build up while studying. Everyone is nervous before taking a test or while working on a paper. When tensions are eased, you will perform better.

Second, exercise replenishes your vitality and energy. Think about the last time you still had twenty pages of a history chapter to read and you couldn't keep your eyes open. If you had only taken a few minutes to get the blood circulating again, you would have been able to read those twenty pages and then some.

The third reason for taking an exercise break is that it clears your mind. We all are guilty of cramming before "the big exam," and things tend to get mixed up. A break will give you an opportunity to un-clutter your mind before you add new information to it.

The last reason for taking a break is that you will return to your work refreshed and will make better use of your time. By taking out five minutes, you will use the next thirty more productively.

The speaker moved away from the podium so everyone could see her.

As I said already, all these benefits can be yours with some simple exercises and five minutes of your time. I want to demonstrate four exercises for you: the spine stretcher, the neck saver, the back stretcher, and the eye exerciser.

The spine stretcher helps relieve tension in your elbows and shoulders. It releases energy locked into your spine and it brings blood into your head for your eyes and brain.

To do this exercise, stand with your hands clasped behind your back. Keep your feet a few inches apart. Breathe out and slowly bend as far down as you can go comfortably while bringing the arms up. Hold for a count of five. Slowly come up. Repeat.

Now that you have your shoulders loosened, move up to your neck. That is where a great deal of tension is centered. The neck saver and the back stretcher are designed to relieve tension in your neck, head, and back.

The neck saver is done by placing your chin on your chest. Roll your head slowly and evenly in a continuous circle all the way around until you have circled it from your right shoulder to your back, to your left shoulder, and back to the chest again. Rotate your head five times to the right and five times to the left.

The speaker paused briefly while the audience made room to do the exercise.

After completing the neck saver, you want to do the back stretcher. For this exercise, you don't even have to get out of your chair. If you have room, you might try doing this one along with me. Sit toward the edge of your chair with your legs extended outward straight in front of you with your heels on the floor. Bend forward and hold your upper calves firmly. Bend your elbows outward and very slowly and gently pull your trunk down. Relax all muscles, including those of your neck, so that your head hangs down. Hold without motion for a count of ten. Very slowly straighten up and rest a moment. Now reach forward and down farther, as far as the lower calves or the ankles, if possible. Go through the same motions and hold for a count of ten. Slowly straighten up and rest.

You should be feeling much better, but there is one last part of your body you shouldn't ignore—your eyes. This last exercise, the eye exerciser, helps remove tension from your eyes. If you wear contact lenses, don't do this one with them in place. It is also a good idea to remove your eyeglasses. This is one all of you without contacts should be able to do along with me. Begin by widening your eye sockets and holding them wide through this exercise. Move your eyes slowly to the top of the sockets. Hold for one second in that position. Slowly roll your eyes to the extreme left. Move them slowly and make the muscles work. Keep the sockets wide at all times. Hold for one second. Remember, this is not a continuous rolling of the eyes. You should hold each position. Now roll your eyes slowly to the extreme bottom. Keep the sockets wide. This wide position helps to remove tension in the muscles around the eyes. Hold for one second. Slowly roll your eyes to the extreme right. Hold for one second. Repeat this routine of the four positions and perform ten times in all. The eyes should move slowly and rhythmically and you must feel that the muscles are getting a workout by moving to the extreme positions in the sockets.

Now close your eyes and place your palms over them. Hold for a minimum count of 30. Turn your mind inward and attempt to hold it "thoughtless" for this brief interval.

Those of you who followed along with me should be ready to go to your next class refreshed. Remember, the best way to relieve tension, to replenish your energy, to clear your mind, and to make the most of your study time is to take an exercise break. The exercises I have shown you take only a few minutes, and you can do them anytime, anywhere.

Studying isn't fun and it isn't easy, but by following the procedures outlined in this handout I will give all of you, you can learn how to break from study before study breaks you.

The speaker distributed handouts at the end of her speech.

Developing Oral Reports

As mentioned earlier, an oral report is a summary. It's important to keep that characteristic in mind when you prepare an oral report. Usually, there's a set time limit for the report, and it's important to stay within it. To maximize your time for an oral report, prepare handouts before you speak so audience members can examine them after the report. Use visual aids as a means of condensing complex material.

Oral reports require research, and you need supportive material to establish your claims. Although an oral report is primarily an informative speech, it may include an element of persuasion if you're asked to give advice as well as to report facts.

Depending on the nature of the material, you can use a wide variety of organizational patterns in the body of the speech. A sales report can divide sales records according to geographical areas. A cause-effect pattern is a way to explain why sales dropped off. The key thing to remember is to select the organizational pattern (or patterns) that presents your information effectively.

When you choose support materials, you can use any type listed in Chapter 12. When giving an advisory report, be sure to include testimony or other appropriate support materials to support your claims.

Developing Other Informative Speeches

The other informative speeches—about ideas, events, and objects or places—should follow the principles of speech preparation presented in Unit 2. Consider the situation, purpose, and audience when you select a topic, narrow it, and develop it. Research the topic thoroughly, and select the best support material.

A Sample Informative Speech

The sample speech on page 326 is an example of how to combine all the speechwriting techniques discussed so far in this text. At the conclusion of the speech is an analysis of the supportive material the speaker used.

This sample speech meets a requirement for an American history class project. The assignment was for a five- to six-minute speech on a major event in twentieth-century American history. The speech was to show evidence of historical research. The audience was made up of students in the class. As you read the speech, you'll notice that it doesn't just deal with an event. It also describes the process followed. As a result, this speech combines two types of informative speeches. After choosing a topic—the invention of the atomic bomb—and conducting research, the speaker set out the specific purpose and thesis.

Purpose
The purpose of this speech is to inform the class about the exciting race from 1939 to 1945 to build the first atomic bomb.

Thesis
Although it is part science and part history, the story of the Manhattan Project is also an adventure as exciting as anything Hollywood could produce.

Since the speech is about a historical event, the developmental pattern is chronological. The student audience influenced the speaker's choice of an introduction and conclusion. Many students are interested in adventure and science fiction movies, and most students today are concerned about the potential for conflict throughout the world. The following is an outline of the speech:

Outline for "The Adventure of the Manhattan Project"
Thesis: Although it was part science and part history, the story of the Manhattan Project is also an adventure as exciting as anything Hollywood could produce.

I. Introduction
    A. Comparing the Manhattan Project to a movie script
    B. Thesis
II. The Beginning of the Adventure—1939
    A. The German research
    B. Enrico Fermi's realization
    C. Einstein's plea to President Roosevelt
III. The Development of an Atomic Pile
    A. The need for a controlled chain reaction
    B. Comparing the reaction to stacking dominoes

C. The materials used in the secret project
IV. Producing Nuclear Materials for the Bomb
    A. Three methods used
    B. Statistics on the cost
V. Los Alamos—1944–1945
    A. The purpose of the Los Alamos laboratory
    B. The first experimental blast
       1. The results
       2. 20,000 tons of TNT
       3. Oppenheimer's reaction
VI. The End of the War
    A. Truman's decision
    B. The results of the Hiroshima bomb and the Nagasaki bomb
    C. The surrender
VII. Conclusion—The Race Was Over
    A. Total cost
    B. A new kind of war
    C. First heroes of the atomic age

Research: The materials used to build this speech could be found in almost any library:

The Encyclopaedia Britannica
The Physicists by Daniel J. Kevles
The Glory and the Dream by William Manchester
Rise of the American Nation, 2nd ed., by Lewis Paul Todd and Merle Curti

---

SAMPLE SPEECH
The Adventure of the Manhattan Project

Examples   For just a moment, forget that you are a student of history. Imagine you are a Hollywood director who is responsible for a multi-million dollar movie such as *Jurassic Park* or *The Terminator.* The script you are given has this plot: A huge war is raging between an evil army

Illustration   and a good army. The war has engulfed the entire civilization. As the war continues to take millions of lives, the most brilliant scientists on each side are racing to build a top secret superweapon, a weapon so terrible and so destructive that it will guarantee victory to whoever has it—if it doesn't destroy both sides. At the end of the script, the good army achieves a breakthrough, and in a display of power unlike anything in history, the superweapon ends the war in eight days.

Does it sound like science fiction? Too far out to make a good movie? Too unrealistic? The plot may be too far out for Hollywood, but it is the true story of the Manhattan Project, America's incredible development of the first atomic bomb during World War II. Although *Thesis* it was part science and part history, the story of the Manhattan Project is also an adventure as exciting as anything Hollywood could produce.

It's hard to say where the adventure starts. Scientists throughout the first part of the twentieth century had been exploring the atom. *Incident* In the late 1930s, however, a German and an Austrian published a scientific paper which set minds in America to thinking. The Germans, who had already begun their conquest of Europe, had shown that an atomic bomb was possible. One scientist who read the paper in 1939 was Enrico Fermi, who had left Italy to escape Hitler's ally, *Incident* Mussolini. According to another scientist who shared Fermi's New York office, Fermi gazed out over New York City, spread his arms as if he held an imaginary ball, and remarked that a bomb that size could make the whole city disappear. The race to build the bomb—and possibly to win the war—was on.

But how could the scientists convince the politicians to begin the long and costly research? Into the adventure stepped the twentieth *Facts* century's greatest scientist. On August 2, 1939, Albert Einstein met with President Franklin Delano Roosevelt and warned him of the new weapon and Nazi Germany's research. F.D.R. approved spending $6,000 to begin an investigation into the possibility of building an atom bomb. Three years later the project started. It was code-named the Manhattan Project.

Before a bomb could be built, a controlled chain reaction had to take place. That means that enough atoms had to split to cause more atoms to split, and so on, until the process kept itself going. Like a *Analogy* very complicated arrangement of dominoes, one atom caused several others to split and release their energy. Fermi and the scientists working at the University of Chicago started a secret project near an aban- *Statistics* doned athletic field at the university. Using 400 tons of graphite (which is like the lead in a pencil), 12,000 pounds of uranium metal, and 100,000 pounds of uranium oxide, the scientists succeeded in creating a controlled chain reaction.

The original $6,000 investment ballooned into a $400,000,000 investment. The money was needed to fund three different plans of producing the nuclear materials for the bomb. Scientists did not know which method would work, so all three had to be tried. Each

Analogy — project worked as fast as possible. One source called the three-project competition a "nightmarish horserace." One project alone re-

Statistics — quired 28,000,000 pounds of silver worth $400,000,000. The silver was borrowed from the U.S. Treasury.

Many scientists worked in several different locations to turn out the materials for the bomb. The greatest challenge, however, lay with the scientists working in Los Alamos, New Mexico. J. Robert Oppenheimer was in charge of a staff of the most talented physicists and engineers in America. It was their job to build and test the bomb itself.

Example — The project was so secret that birth certificates of babies born to the scientists' families had no real place of birth listed.

Working on problems no scientist had ever confronted before, the staff raced to complete the bomb. The war in Europe was over, but the war in the Pacific still claimed American lives.

On July 16, 1945, before sunrise, the first experimental A-bomb

Description — was detonated. First, a flash of light brightened the darkness. Next, a shockwave and a huge roar tore at the onlookers more than 10,000 meters away. The scientists had predicted a blast equal to 5,000 tons

Statistics — of TNT. Instead, the blast was equal to 20,000 tons of TNT.

Scientists had no way of knowing exactly what was happening at

Authority — the center of the explosion, but Oppenheimer observed the scene and recalled a line from a Hindu holy work: "I am become Death, the shatterer of worlds."

President Harry Truman (who had not even been briefed on the Manhattan Project until he became President when Roosevelt died) decided that the atom bomb could force a Japanese surrender. On

Incident — August 6, 1945, a United States B-29 named *Enola Gay* dropped the first atomic bomb, code-named Little Boy, on Hiroshima, Japan. Everything in the immediate vicinity of the blast was completely de-

Statistics — stroyed. An area of 4.4 square miles was completely burned out. Between 70,000 and 80,000 people died.

On August 9, a second bomb, code-named Fat Man, was dropped

Example — on Nagasaki with similar results.

Example — On August 10, eight days after the first bomb, the Japanese surrendered. The war was over.

And the race was over. The Manhattan Project ushered in the Atomic Age.

After two billion dollars, six years, countless work hours, and more scientific genius than had ever been accumulated at one time in human history, the script was written.

And a new kind of war more horrible than ever before had been invented. In 1947, Secretary of War Henry Stimson summed up how the Manhattan Project had changed our lives:

Authority

"The face of war is the face of death. . . . War in the twentieth century has grown steadily more barbarous, more destructive, more debased in all its aspects. Now, with the release of atomic energy, man's ability to destroy himself is very nearly complete. The bombs dropped on Hiroshima and Nagasaki ended a war. They also made it wholly clear that we must never have another war."

Despite the controversy over nuclear weapons, one thing is sure. The Manhattan Project is a story of men and women committed to scientific discovery and patriotism. It is a story worth retelling.

The model speech meets the requirements of the assignment. It's also an interesting speech. How did the speaker present the information? You'll recognize the techniques from earlier chapters.

Facts

Almost all informative speeches depend on presenting facts. Facts can be proven true. Many facts are given in the speech; for example, the dates and the names are facts. How many examples of facts are in the speech?

Opinion

The difference between a fact and an opinion is that a fact can be proven or disproven. The speaker's belief that the Manhattan Project is exciting is an example of an opinion. What other opinions are presented?

Statistics

Statistics help a speech by using numbers to present information. A list of statistics can be boring. Used correctly, statistics help an audience understand your point. In the sample speech, several statistics are used to show such things as the cost of the bomb and the damage. Go back and locate several statistics in the speech.

Comparison and contrast

Comparisons show how things are alike. Contrasts show how things are different. In a way, the whole speech is a comparison between the Manhattan Project and an adventure movie.

Analogy

An analogy compares two things that are different. When the speaker compared the three projects (to a horse race or a chain reaction of dominoes), the speaker used an analogy.

Examples

An example is a typical instance of something. The speaker gives examples in the first paragraph. Rather than mentioning "a multi-million dollar movie" and going on to the next point, the speaker gives two specific examples (*Jurassic Park* and *Terminator*) to inform the audience what is meant.

Incident   An incident is usually a brief story that makes a point. Enrico Fermi's response to the possibility of the atomic bomb ("it could make the whole city disappear") is an incident. An incident may be long or short. Often, a lengthy incident is too complicated for an audience and must be shortened.

Illustration   Sometimes a speaker creates or relates incidents to make a point. Hypothetical illustrations shouldn't be presented as the truth, but only as illustrations.

Authority   When you use the words of another person or of a book or article you have researched, you're using a quotation. In the sample speech, the speaker quotes Oppenheimer and Secretary Stimson directly. Using quotations, you can also present facts, opinions, or statistics.

Presenting the Speech to Inform

As with any speech, good delivery is essential for an informative speech. As you learned in earlier chapters, the most exciting topic and well-prepared speech can be ineffective if the delivery isn't lively, sincere, and fluent. You have to rehearse to give an effective informative speech, regardless of the type.

It's especially important to practice speeches that require visual aids. Beginning speakers often have trouble coordinating visual aids with talking. Know when you want to display visuals and how you plan to display them. Always have tape or thumb tacks with you in case there's no easel or chalkboard on which to put charts. Work to maintain good eye contact with the audience, even when you're using visual aids. Remember, you're talking to the audience, not the visual.

Use your voice to create interest and to emphasize important points in the speech. By practicing your speech several times, you'll develop a fluent delivery style.

Analyzing the Speech to Inform

Use these guidelines to analyze informative speeches.

Situation:

1. Was the speech appropriate for a classroom setting?
2. Was the speech developed to fit the time limitations?

Purpose:

1. Did the speech meet the general purpose of an informative speech?
2. Did the speaker fulfill the specific speech purpose?

Audience:

1. Was the speech suitable for the audience?
2. Did the speaker consider the audience's interests, background, and knowledge levels?

Method:

1. Was the organizational pattern appropriate for the topic and purpose?
2. Did the speaker use sufficient supportive materials?
3. Did the speaker use appropriate supportive materials?

Chapter 16 Summary

The purpose of an informative speech is to present new information to an audience. There are seven types of informative speeches—process speeches, demonstration speeches, speeches about objects or places, speeches about people, speeches about events, speeches about ideas, and oral reports.

Chronological order is the logical organizational pattern for most process and demonstration speeches. Demonstration speeches must be narrowed to fit the time limits and the speech's location. When using visual aids, be sure the audience can see them. Oral reports summarize large amounts of material, so they rely heavily on hand-outs and other visual aids.

◆ Check Your Understanding

1. What's the purpose of the speech to inform?

2. What are the seven types of informative speeches?

3. How do situation, purpose, and audience affect the development of an informative speech?

4. What are the qualities of effective introductions and conclusions in the speech to inform?

5. List three guidelines for developing the body of an informative speech.

6. What types of supportive materials are appropriate for informative speeches?

◆ Apply Your Understanding

1. Generate a list of ten to fifteen topics that would make interesting informative speeches. Share the list with the class.

2. Identify five real-world occasions for informative speaking.

◆ Thinking Critically about Public Speaking

1. Working in groups, select one of the two sample speeches in this chapter and analyze it, using the guidelines for analysis supplied in the chapter. Make suggestions for improving any weaknesses in the speech.

2. Observe one of your teacher's lectures to see how well it meets the requirements for an informative speech. Prepare a written report on your teacher's strengths and weaknesses.

◆ *Speak Out!*

1. Prepare a four- to six-minute informative speech. Use the following checklist to make sure you've developed the speech completely for an audience composed of your classmates:
   a. Audience
   b. Situation
   c. Purpose
   d. Thesis
   e. Forecast
   f. Types of development
   g. Summary

2. Present a one- to three-minute impromptu demonstration or process speech on topics your teacher suggests. Be sure to include an introduction and a conclusion for the speech.

3. Select one of the speakers mentioned in this book. Prepare a four- to six-minute informative speech on the speaker. Be sure to include examples of quotations from the person's speeches.

4. Prepare an oral report of one to two minutes for a hypothetical organization. Select from one of the following:
   a. A report on expenses and supplies for the homecoming float to be given to your class
   b. A report of a study on volunteer needs to be given to a parent organization
   c. A report on student test scores and grade point averages for the school board
   d. A topic approved by your teacher

◆ *Speech Challenge*

Your teachers face an important speech challenge daily: giving informational talks to you! They compete for your attention. They are "on stage" several hours a day for nearly two-hundred days each year. The task requires planning, reading the audience, selecting appropriate speech methods—all the things you have learned about in speech class. Select a "lesson" to present from a class you are taking or have taken. Make your lesson short—seven to ten minutes. Prepare this informative speech as you would any other, using the techniques outlined in this chapter. Prepare a short "test" of one to three questions to be given after all students have given their speeches. Your goal is to get students to score as well as possible on your test.

CHAPTER ·17·

Key Terms

Attitudes

Behaviors

Belongingness needs

Fear appeal

Hierarchy

Motivated Sequence

Motivation

Persuasion

Physiological needs

Primacy effect

Recency effect

Safety needs

Self-actualization

Self-esteem

Speech to actuate

Speech to persuade

Chapter Objectives

After studying this chapter, you should be able to:

1. Define *persuasion*.
2. Explain the three purposes of a speech to persuade.
3. List and explain the two types of persuasive speeches.
4. Define *motivation* and explain its role in persuasive speaking.
5. Explain Maslow's hierarchy of needs.
6. Explain three types of persuasive strategies.
7. Explain how situation, purpose, and audience affect the development of a persuasive speech.
8. Identify and explain the five steps in Monroe's Motivated Sequence.

The Speech
to Persuade

Defining the Speech to Persuade

The purpose of the **speech to persuade** is to change, create, or reinforce attitudes or behavior. These three purposes correspond to the three types of audiences described in Chapter 8—agreeing, disagreeing, or apathetic. When your audience agrees with you, you give a speech to reinforce. When your audience disagrees with you, you give a speech to change. When your audience is apathetic or uninformed, you give a speech to create.

When you try to persuade someone, you try to change how that person thinks or acts. Because of this, it's often said that **persuasion** is intentional communication designed to produce a change in attitudes or behaviors. **Attitudes** are beliefs or feelings about people, ideas, or events. They're usually held over a long period of time. Attitudes affect much of what people do. As a result, **behaviors** are outward expressions of our attitudes. For instance, if you hold the attitude that stealing is wrong, you wouldn't shoplift, even if you didn't have enough money to buy what you need.

Changing Attitudes or Behavior

A speech that intends to produce some type of change is traditionally associated with persuasion. Because attitudes and behaviors are so closely tied, an attitude change usually produces behavioral changes, even if that isn't the primary goal of the speech. Persuasive communication relies heavily on your ability to show the listener that he or she will benefit by making the change. An example of a speech to change would be one that tried to get people to give up a habit such as smoking.

Reinforcing Attitudes or Behavior

Although attitude or behavior change is most commonly associated with persuasion, it's often designed to reinforce existing attitudes or behaviors. Sometimes attitudes change with time or with exposure to new experiences. You've probably changed brands of soft drinks or types of fast foods. Because there are so many choices available, companies try to hold on to their present customers as well as get new ones. When there's a possibility that your attitude or behavior might change, those who don't want that change must reinforce your behavior. They must counter the persuasion of their competitors. Politicians who address their supporters are reinforcing the original reasons why someone would choose to support them as well as providing additional reasons.

SPOTLIGHT ON SPEAKING

Analyzing a Speech to Change Attitudes

The following set of questions can be applied to any speech to change attitudes:

Situation:
1. Was the speech appropriate for the setting?
2. Was the speech developed to fit the time limitations?

Purpose:
1. Did the speech meet the purpose of changing attitudes?
2. Did the speaker achieve the specific purpose as stated in the thesis?

Audience:
1. Was the speech suitable for the audience?
2. Did the speech provide appropriate motivational appeals for the audience?
3. Did the speech utilize appropriate persuasive strategies for the audience?

Method:
1. Was the organizational pattern appropriate for the purpose?
2. Were the persuasive techniques appropriate for the purpose?
3. Were the persuasive appeals developed properly?
4. Were the speaker's claims supported adequately?

Creating Attitudes or Behaviors

Finally, there are times when persuasion isn't designed to change or reinforce an attitude or a behavior but to create a new one. This situation arises when the audience has no prior knowledge about a subject. This type of persuasive speech must also inform. Unless the members of the audience understand the subject, it will be difficult to get them to adopt an attitude or behavior. If you represent an organization that hopes to save whales from extinction and you're talking to people who know little about the whaling industry, you'd have to make them aware of the problem before you could expect them to support your cause.

Types of Persuasive Speeches

You are subjected to persuasion all the time. All forms of the media urge you to buy products. Friends try to persuade you to participate in various social activities. You try to persuade your parents to let you go out with friends or have the car. As a persuasive speaker, you're also attempting to get someone to do something. The two types of persuasive speeches relate to those purposes.

Speeches Affecting Attitudes

Although changing an attitude or adopting a new one most often results in behavioral changes, some speeches stop short of asking the audience to make a specific behavioral change. Because behavior is the outward expression of attitudes, a speaker might be satisfied with producing an attitude that would affect a variety of behaviors.

Propositions of Fact   Facts are often an important element in speeches that affect attitudes, because people believe what they accept as fact. When Columbus was trying to convince people that the world was round, he was attempting to change attitudes or beliefs. Essentially, he was arguing a proposition of fact, as discussed in Chapter 15. A prosecuting attorney trying to convince a jury that a defendant is guilty is attempting to persuade the jury about a fact.

As a persuasive speaker in a public speaking class, you might choose to convince your classmates about something that is factual. Examples of speech purposes dealing with facts could include the following:

> The purpose of this speech is to convince the audience that fluoridated water has no serious side effects.

> The purpose of this speech is to convince the audience that knowledge of a foreign language aids advancement in many careers.

> The purpose of this speech is to convince the audience that affirmative action has succeeded in getting more women and minorities into jobs that would have been denied them otherwise.

Propositions of Value   Persuasive speeches may address propositions of value. Values are closely related to attitudes. As Chapter 15 explained, values incorporate judgments about such things as what's good or bad, right or wrong, fair or unfair, proper or improper, best or worst. Values are related to facts, and when you give a persuasive speech on a value issue, you must incorporate facts.

Persuasive speeches are often intended to produce some change in the audience's behaviors or attitudes.

Speeches incorporating value arguments usually don't ask an audience to abandon a value. Instead, the speaker asks the audience to change a value's relative importance in relationship to another value. For instance, suppose you make the argument that individual rights are less important than societal rights when a government wants to protect people from the spread of serious diseases. You wouldn't be asking the audience to deny that individual rights are important. You'd only be asking the audience to consider them less important than society's rights in a given situation.

Here are some examples of purpose statements for values topics:

The purpose of this speech is to convince the audience that mercy killing is not justifiable under any circumstance.

The purpose of this speech is to convince the audience that basketball is a more enjoyable spectator sport than baseball.

The purpose of this speech is to convince the audience that creating jobs should be the United States' number one goal.

Propositions of Policy   Finally, speeches affecting attitudes can ask an audience to support a policy. Policy speeches propose a course of action that individuals or groups should take. Since policies are related to behaviors, these speeches also incorporate facts and values. The policies people pursue as individuals, as groups, and as a nation are guided by their values. If, for instance, people believe that mercy killing is wrong, their laws prohibit its use and penalize those who engage in it. A policy speech to affect attitudes asks the audience to support a specific policy in a given situation. The speech would stop short of asking the audience to do something, such as voting, to enact the policy.

Here are some examples of purpose statements for topics supporting policy propositions:

> The purpose of this speech is to convince the students that this high school should consider establishing a S.A.D.D. chapter.

> The purpose of this speech is to convince the audience that the United States should increase its aid to Russia.

> The purpose of this speech is to convince the audience that all high-school students should be required to take a foreign language.

Speeches Affecting Behaviors

A speech that intends to get the audience to do something is called a **speech to actuate.** This type of speech tries to change, reinforce, or create behaviors. A speech urging city council members to adopt a policy is a speech to actuate. So is a speech to convince people to develop a regular exercise program. A sales speech is a special form of a speech to actuate. Its purpose is to get the audience to purchase either a product or a service. Speeches to actuate give audiences specific suggestions about how to accomplish the action.

Here are some examples of speech purposes for topics that affect behaviors:

> The purpose of this speech is to convince audience members to wear seat belts every time they get into a car.

> The purpose of this speech is to get students to sign a petition to eliminate the closed lunch period.

> The purpose of this speech is to convince audience members to participate in the walkathon for the heart association.

Motivation and Persuasion

Regardless of your specific purpose as a persuader, you must give your listeners a *reason* to accept your arguments. In other words, you must provide **motivation**—an incentive to believe or act in a certain way.

How do you motivate someone? Think about yourself. What motivates you to clean your room, start an exercise program, say no to drugs, or drive more carefully? Sometimes the motivation is fear. Sometimes it's the possibility of a reward. In many instances, you do something because the behavior satisfies a need or desire. Whatever the specific motivation might be, you wouldn't have changed without it. When you develop a persuasive speech, you must include arguments tied to some type of motivation. The following types of motivation are common in persuasive speeches.

Maslow's Hierarchy of Human Needs

One of the most common ways to motivate a person is to appeal to a basic human need. Psychologist Abraham Maslow classified human needs into five categories. Maslow's hierarchy of needs is an arrangement of those needs in the order of their importance (see Figure 17.1). According to Maslow, the list of needs becomes increasingly more complex and more difficult to achieve. He also stated that it's difficult for someone to satisfy needs on a higher level until lower-level needs are met.

Maslow identifies the five basic human needs as these:

Physiological needs are those things that keep a person alive—food, water, and shelter are the most common. Television advertising often appeals to these needs. Think of how many commercials you've seen for food; many address nutritional needs as well as satisfaction of hunger.

Safety needs involve one's well-being or sense of security. Advertisements for smoke detectors, insurance, or car batteries often appeal to this need.

Belongingness needs involve wanting to have friends or be loved by others. Everyone needs human contact to live a healthy, well-adjusted life. Everyone needs to be accepted by others. Advertising suggesting that if you use certain products you will be

Figure 17.1
Maslow's Hierarchy
of Needs

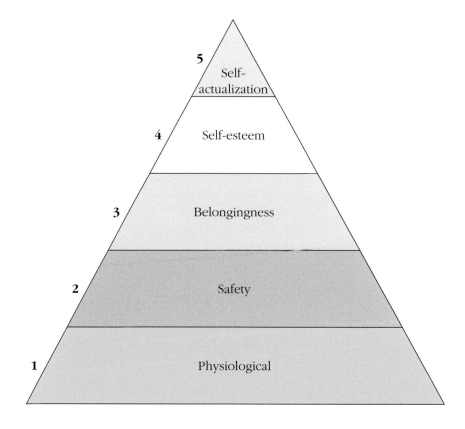

surrounded by friends or attractive members of the opposite sex appeals to this need. Watch commercials for toothpaste, mouthwash, or soap and see if they appeal to a need for affection from others.

Self-esteem refers to the feelings people have about themselves. People need to like themselves. Many public service announcements appeal to this need. For instance, advertising that encourages people to donate money to a charity is intended to make them feel good about what they've done. People feel good about helping others.

Self-actualization, the final level of need, means realizing your full potential. The U.S. Army appeal—"Be all that you can be in the Army"—is a self-actualization appeal.

Persuasive Strategies

You should select specific persuasive strategies with the situation, purpose, and audience in mind. Set realistic goals for a persuasive speech because seldom, if ever, is it possible to persuade everyone in the audience. Determine which audience members are most likely to be persuaded and develop a strategy to best appeal to that group. When you develop persuasive strategies, there are three types of appeals you can make—logical, speaker-based, and emotional.

Appeals Based on Logic

Chapter 15 discussed the basics of argumentation. The strategies discussed in that chapter are the basis for logical appeals. Review the information in that chapter before you develop persuasive speeches. Logical appeals are an important part of any persuasive speech, since you must rely on support materials when persuading.

Appeals Based on Speaker Credibility

Appeals based on a speaker's credibility are common in persuasive speaking. You can use either your own credibility as a source of persuasion or can supply evidence from other credible sources. In general, members of an audience think a speaker or quoted authority is credible if they perceive the person to be competent, knowledgeable, believable, and trustworthy.

A person may be perceived as a highly credible source before ever giving a speech or being quoted. A well-known, respected speaker can persuade largely on the basis of his or her reputation. Much can be done before a speech to advertise the speaker's expertise and to establish credibility. The introduction for a speaker often enhances the speaker's credibility by stressing competence. During the speech, a speaker can include information to establish his or her experience, knowledge, and competence.

If the speaker or source is not well-known to the audience before the speech, credibility has to be established through the speech itself. A speaker who's well organized, thorough, dynamic, and sincere is usually perceived as credible.

When using authority as a means of supporting claims, select authorities whom the audience members know and accept. If this isn't possible, be sure to include information about the authorities' credentials. You can enhance your own credibility by quoting carefully selected authorities.

It's important to remember that credibility is something you earn. You can begin your speech being perceived as highly credible. If you don't fulfill your audience's expectations, however, you may be an ineffective persuader. You can only be effective if your audience sees you as credible at the end of your speech.

Appeals Based on Emotion

All of us would like to believe that human beings are rational creatures and that logic and reasoning are the best means of persuading. While they're preferable and you should use them in most situations, you can't ignore the role of emotions when you want to motivate people. Maslow's hierarchy suggests that emotions play a large role in motivation. Belongingness needs are primarily emotional needs. In fact, some say that emotions are what make us human. While emotional appeals can be effective, you shouldn't rely on them exclusively. They can contribute to getting attention and creating a need in listeners. It's important to remember, however, that they're effective only if they're perceived as sincere.

Fear Appeals   There are several emotional appeals you can use. The most common is the fear appeal. Research has shown that under certain conditions fear is an effective persuasive device. Think about yourself. How many times have you done something (or not done something) because of fear—of physical danger, of failure, of loss of affection from a loved one?

Research on the effectiveness of varying degrees of fear appeals is inconclusive. In some situations, strong fear appeals are effective. In others, such appeals tend to make listeners rationalize that the consequences are so remote that they aren't in danger.

Whether you use strong, moderate, or weak fear appeals, remember two important points. First, for fear appeals to work, a person must feel vulnerable to the consequences. Advertising that tries to get people to wear seat belts attempts to create vulnerability by stressing that most accidents occur within twenty-five miles of home. For those who rationalize that they only need to wear seat belts on long trips, this fact should make them feel more vulnerable.

Second, fear appeals are more successful if directed at the vulnerability of a loved one. Much advertising uses this technique. Insurance advertising stresses the problems that would face a family if the major wage earner suddenly died. One brand of tires shows a baby crawling on a tire while the parents are talking about purchasing that brand of tire. When the father realizes that the baby travels more in the mother's car than his, he decides that his wife needs the best set of tires.

Humor The opposite of fear is humor. Humor by itself is not a very effective persuasive device. You can use it, however, to get attention and to create rapport with the audience. If you're trying to build credibility, humor can be effective. You can use it to make a serious point. Because people like to hear a good joke and have a good laugh, humor can emphasize ideas. After the speech, audience members are likely to remember the joke or humorous story and associate it with serious ideas.

Compassion Compassion refers to a person's ability to sympathize with others, to feel what they're feeling. When you're trying to motivate an audience to help others, appeals to compassion are effective. They are used widely by charitable organizations that aid the hungry throughout the world.

Pride Pride can be directed at self, others, or ideals. In terms of self, appeals to pride relate to self-esteem needs. People can be persuaded to do something because they'll feel good about themselves afterwards. If you've watched the Olympics, you know it's possible to feel a sense of satisfaction from others' successes. Appeals for contributions to help others succeed draw upon our sense of pride in those who represent something we admire but may not be able to achieve ourselves. Politicians frequently engage in what is known as *flag waving*, or appealing to national pride. Such speeches use national pride to gain support for a candidate or a policy.

One-Sided vs. Two-Sided Arguments

One sure thing about most persuasive topics is that they have two sides. If they didn't, there would be no need for persuasion. As a speaker, you'll have to decide whether or not to discuss only the side you support. Sometimes, especially when you're introducing new ideas or speaking to reinforce, one-sided arguments are adequate.

When your audience holds an opposing view or is likely to be exposed to the opposing view, it's important to examine both sides.

Almost all arguments have two sides. In many situations, speakers should acknowledge that there is another point of view, while at the same time showing why their position is superior.

In a two-sided speech, you acknowledge the arguments against your position and systematically show why your side is superior. When presenting two-sided arguments, especially to hostile audiences, do so in a positive manner. Acknowledge the validity of opposing arguments, but show the superiority of your own. Don't attack the intelligence, ethics, or personalities of those supporting an opposing view.

Order of Arguments

The order of your arguments can affect your success as a persuader. Research shows that the arguments at the beginning or end of a speech have more impact than those in the middle. Audiences tend to pay more attention at the beginning and end of a speech. So, put your strongest arguments in those positions.

When the arguments and evidence at the beginning have the greatest influence on the audience, there is a **primacy effect.** When those placed at the end are most persuasive, there is a **recency effect.** Research hasn't proved conclusively when primacy or recency effects are most likely to occur. However, it's possible that primacy effects are more likely when the audience is already highly interested. Recency effects are more likely when an audience is unfamiliar with a topic.

Developing the Speech to Persuade

Entire books have been written on the techniques of persuasion. While it's impossible to cover all the techniques in this chapter, keep in mind the principles stressed throughout this book.

First, consider the situation, purpose, and audience before deciding on a method. They'll determine such things as whether you'll use one-sided or two-sided arguments, what kind of motivations you'll select, and what types of evidence will be most effective in convincing your listeners.

Second, remember that a persuasive speech is primarily a speech that makes arguments or claims. You must support claims through evidence and logical analysis. Avoid logical fallacies and unsupported claims.

Third, as you organize your speech, select the pattern that presents your arguments, proofs, and reasoning most effectively. Problem-solution and cause-effect patterns are often used for persuasive speeches. However, if your goal is to change attitudes, you can use a topical arrangement. In speeches where you present two-sided arguments, present the counterarguments first, then contrast them with your own arguments.

Attitudes are enduring. It's human nature to be consistent in beliefs. As a result, attitude change isn't easy to achieve. Be realistic. People seldom completely reverse an attitude or adopt a different or new behavior after one persuasive message. Expect to give more than one speech before achieving the desired result. You also shouldn't expect to persuade every member of the audience. Select a target group and develop arguments based on that group's characteristics.

The Motivated Sequence

One persuasive method that's especially well-suited for developing any persuasive speech is the Motivated Sequence. This approach was developed by two college speech professors, Alan Monroe and Douglas Ehninger. The **Motivated Sequence** has five steps: (1) the attention step, (2) the need step, (3) the satisfaction step, (4) the visualization step, and (5) the action step.

You've already read about motivation and several methods of motivating listeners. Whether you use positive or negative motivation, the Motivated Sequence provides an organized system for approaching persuasion. Consider the logic of each step.

Attention Step   The first step in the sequence is getting the listener's attention. You must capture the audience's interest immediately, because you'll never achieve your goal unless the audience wants to hear more. Several techniques for getting attention were discussed in Chapter 14.

Need Step   This is one of the most important steps in the Motivated Sequence. Here, you give the listener a reason to accept your message. The need usually takes the form of one or more problems. Presenting problems won't guarantee a successful need step; the listener must identify with the problems. Motivational factors become important at this point in speech development.

Satisfaction Step   After presenting the need, you must tell audience members how to satisfy it. In the satisfaction or solution step, you clearly identify the behavior you want to change. In most advertising, the satisfaction step is a simple message: "Buy our product." In a speech, it usually involves suggesting a plan of action or alternative behaviors, such as exercising fifteen minutes a day.

Visualization Step   This step helps listeners understand how the solution works. If you're trying to convince someone to buy a personal computer, in the visualization step you'd explain everything the computer can do. You'd help your listener picture using it for writing reports or balancing a personal budget. Often, the visualization step is an analogy. By describing how a given solution has worked in a similar instance, it's easy for audience members to see that it will work in theirs.

Action Step   The final step tells listeners how to implement the solution. If you're trying to persuade everyone to write to a television network to express support for keeping a program on the air, you'd give specific information about the people making the decision. You'd give the names and addresses and explain how to write the letter.

   The action step provides a way for the audience to carry through with the solution. Unless listeners believe they personally can do something, you're unlikely to change their attitudes and subsequent behaviors.

The Speech to Actuate

The speech to actuate goes beyond the goal of the speech to change attitudes. This type of speech must not only get an audience to agree with the speech's premise, it must also motivate the audience to act. As a result, you must have a clear set of instructions about what needs to be done to solve a problem and what the audience can do to carry them out.

The sample speech below was given by Mary Fisher, founder of the Family AIDS Network, at the 1992 Republican National Convention. Fisher is HIV-positive. She contracted the HIV virus from her husband, who was a drug user. Fisher and her family are active in Republican politics, and she used the convention as a forum for seeking action from her party to confront the AIDS crisis. As you read Fisher's speech, see if you can identify the five steps in the Motivated Sequence.

SAMPLE SPEECH

Speech to the Republican National Convention
Mary Fisher

Less than three months ago at platform hearings in Salt Lake City, I asked the Republican party to lift the shroud of silence—that which has been draped over the issue of HIV and AIDS. I have come tonight to bring our silence to an end. I bear a message of challenge, not self-congratulation. I want your attention, not your applause. I would never have asked to be HIV-positive, but I believe that in all things there is a purpose, and I stand before you and before the nation gladly.

The reality of AIDS is brutally clear: 200,000 Americans are dead or dying. A million more are infected. Worldwide, forty million, sixty million, or a hundred million infections will be counted in the coming few years. But despite science and research, White House meetings and Congressional hearings, despite good intentions and bold initiatives, campaign slogans and hopeful promises, it is, despite it all, the epidemic which is winning tonight. In the context of an election year, I ask you here in this great hall or listening in the quiet of your home to recognize that AIDS virus is not a political creature. It does not care whether you are a Democrat or a Republican. It does not ask whether you are black or white, male or female, gay or straight, young or old.

Tonight, I represent an AIDS community whose members have been reluctantly drafted from every segment of American society. Though I am white and a mother, I am one with a black infant struggling with tubes in a Philadelphia hospital. Though I am female and contracted this disease in marriage and enjoy the warm support of my family, I am one with the lonely gay man sheltering a flickering candle from the cold wind of his family's rejection.

This is not a distant threat. It is a present danger. The rate of infection is increasing fastest among women and children. Largely unknown a decade ago, AIDS is the third leading killer of young adult Americans today. But it won't be third for long, because unlike other diseases, this one travels. Adolescents don't give each other cancer or heart disease because they believe they are in love. But HIV is different, and we have helped it along.

We have killed each other with our ignorance, our prejudice, and our silence. We may take refuge in our stereotypes, but we cannot hide there long because HIV asks only one thing of those it attacks: Are you human? And this is the right question: Are *you* human? Because people with HIV have not entered some alien state of being. They are human.

They have not earned cruelty, and they do not deserve meanness. They don't benefit from being isolated or treated as outcasts. Each of them is exactly what God made—a person, not evil, deserving of our judgment. Not victims longing for our pity. People ready for support and worthy of compassion.

My call to you, my party, is to take a public stand no less compassionate than that of the President and Mrs. Bush. They have embraced me and my family in memorable ways. In the place of judgment, they have shown affection. In difficult moments, they have raised our spirits. In the darkest hours, I have seen them reaching not only to me but also to my parents, armed with that stunning grief and special grace that comes only to parents who have themselves leaned too long over the bedside of a dying child. With the President's leadership, much good has been done. Much of the good has gone unheralded, and as the President has insisted, much remains to be done, but we do the President's cause no good if we praise the American family, but ignore a virus that destroys it.

We must be consistent if we are to be believed. We cannot love justice and ignore prejudice. Love our children and fear to teach them. Whatever our role, as parent or policy maker, we must act as eloquently as we speak, else we have no integrity.

My call to the nation is a plea for awareness. If you believe you are safe, you are in danger. Because I was not hemophiliac, I was not at risk. Because I was not gay, I was not at risk. Because I did not inject drugs, I was not at risk.

My father has devoted much of his lifetime guarding against another Holocaust. He is part of the generation who heard Pastor Niemoeller come out of the Nazi death camps to say, "They came after the Jews, and I was not a Jew, so I did not protest. They came after the trade unionists, and I was not a trade unionist, so I did not protest. Then they came after the Roman Catholics, and I was not a Roman Catholic, so I did not protest. Then they came after me, and there was no one left to protest."

The lesson history teaches is this: If you believe you are safe, you are at risk. If you do not see this killer stalking your children, look again. There is no family or community, no race or religion, no place left in America that is safe.

Until we genuinely embrace this message, we are a nation at risk. Tonight HIV marches resolutely toward AIDS in more than a million American homes, littering its pathway with the bodies of the young— young men, young women, young parents, and young children. One of the families is mine. If it is true that HIV inevitably turns to AIDS, then my children will inevitably turn to orphans. My family has been a rock of support. My 84-year-old father, who has pursued the healing of the nations, will not accept the premise that he cannot heal his daughter. My mother refuses to be broken. She still calls at midnight to tell wonderful jokes that make me laugh. Sisters and friends, and my brother Phillip, whose birthday is today, all have helped carry me over the hardest places.

I am blessed, richly and deeply blessed, to have such a family. But not all of you have been so blessed. You are HIV-positive but dare not say it. You have lost loved ones, but you dared not whisper the word *AIDS*. You weep silently. You grieve alone. I have a message for you: It is not you who should feel shame; it is we. We who tolerate ignorance and practice prejudice. We who have taught you to fear. We must lift our shroud of silence, making it safe for you to reach out for compassion. It is our task to seek safety for our children. Not in quiet denial, but in effective action.

Some day our children will be grown. My son, Max, now four, will take the measure of his mother. My son Zachary, now two, will sort through his memories. I may not be here to hear their judgments. But I know already what I hope they are.

I want my children to know that their mother was not a victim. She was a messenger. I do not want them to think, as I once did, that courage is the absence of fear. I want them to know that courage is the strength to act wisely when most we are afraid. I want them to have the courage to step forward when called by their nation or their party and give leadership no matter what the personal cost.

I ask no more of you than I ask of myself or of my children. To the millions of you who are grieving, who are frightened, who have suffered the ravages of AIDS firsthand, have courage and you will find support.

To the millions who are strong, I issue the plea: Set aside prejudice and politics to make room for compassion and sound policy. To my children I make this pledge: I will not give in, Zachary, because I draw my courage from you. Your silly giggle gives me hope. Your gentle prayers give me strength. And you, my child, give me the reason to say to America: You are at risk.

And I will not rest, Max, until I have done all I can to make your world safe. I will seek a place where intimacy is not the prelude to suffering. I will not hurry to leave you, my children, but when I go I pray that you will not suffer shame on my account.

To all within the sound of my voice, I appeal. Learn with me the lessons of history and of grace, so my children will not be afraid to say the word *AIDS* when I am gone. Then their children and yours may not need to whisper it at all. God bless the children, and God bless us all. Good night.

VOICES OF

WORLD WAR II

America, Britain, and Germany

During the 1930s and 1940s, the world witnessed some very impressive displays of oratory. The oratory came from three people whose roles in World War II changed the history of the world forever: Adolf Hitler, Winston Churchill, and Franklin Roosevelt.

Adolf Hitler was little more than a small-time politician when he began his rise to power. One of Hitler's best-known characteristics was his ability to spellbind his audiences. The impact of his messages was felt far beyond his own borders, and the free world needed someone to counter his forceful speeches.

The free world's first great defender was Prime Minister Winston Churchill of England. Churchill not only led England through the terrible attacks of the Nazi air force, he rallied his people to withstand the constant terror of night bombings, the humiliation of military defeats, and the harsh demands of wartime sacrifices. Although many thought the war was lost, he continued to lead Britain, understanding the power of his radio broadcasts to renew the fighting spirit of the British people.

A new voice joined Churchill's in defense of the Allies. When Franklin Roosevelt became convinced of the need for the U.S. to get involved in the war, his speeches helped persuade the American people to dedicate themselves to victory. Roosevelt spoke for all Americans in his insistence that the United States would not give in to the terror and violence that was coming from our enemies.

WORDS TO REMEMBER

Winston Churchill

I have nothing to offer but blood, toil, tears and sweat.

You ask, What is our aim? I can answer in one word: Victory—victory at all costs, victory in spite of all terror, victory, however long and hard the road may be; for without victory, there is no survival.

First statement as Prime Minister, 13 May 1940

We shall go on to the end, we shall fight in France, we shall fight on the seas and oceans, we shall fight with growing confidence and growing strength in the air, we shall defend our island, whatever the cost may be, we shall fight on the beaches, we shall fight on the landing grounds, we shall fight in the fields and in the streets, we shall fight in the hills; we shall never surrender . . .

Speech on Dunkirk, House of Commons, 4 June 1940

Let us therefore brace ourselves to our duties, and so bear ourselves that, if the British Empire and its Commonwealth lasts for a thousand years, men will say, "This was their finest hour."

Speech in the House of Commons, 18 June 1940

Franklin Roosevelt

No matter how long it may take us to overcome this premeditated invasion, the American people, in their righteous might, will win through to absolute victory.

Hostilities exist. There is no blinking at the fact that our people, our territory, and our interests are in grave danger. With confidence in our armed forces, with the unbounding determination of our people, we will gain the inevitable triumph. So help us God.

War Message to Congress, 8 December 1941

Books cannot be killed by fire. People die, but books never die. No man and no force can abolish memory. . . . In this war, we know, books are weapons.

Message to the American Booksellers Association, 23 April 1942

Adolf Hitler

The great masses of the people . . . will more easily fall victims to a big lie than to a small one.

Mein Kampf, 1933

The war no longer bears the characteristics of former inter-European conflicts. It is one of those elemental conflicts which usher in a new millennium and which shake the world once in a thousand years.

Speech to the Reichstag, 26 April 1942

Determining the Speech's Effectiveness

Since the ultimate goal of a persuasive speech is to affect attitudes and behaviors, you can measure a speech's effectiveness by measuring attitude change or by determining behavioral change. To determine attitude change, ask audience members to indicate their attitudes about a topic before they hear the speech. Then poll them after the speech to see if there's been any change. Use a scale such as the following for this purpose:

Circle the number that most closely resembles the strength of your opinion on the following topic:

I believe sports in junior and senior high schools should be de-emphasized.

Strongly disagree				No opinion				Strongly agree
1	2	3	4	5	6	7	8	9

You can also determine behavioral changes by noting how many people actually perform the requested action. If you've made appeals for donations, the number and size of contributions are a gauge of success. For other types of actions, you can use polls. Distribute them immediately after the speech to measure audience members' intent to pursue your recommendations. If you conduct follow-up polls a few weeks after the speech, you'll get some indication of whether or not audience members have followed through. A word of caution about polls: people often give the information they think the pollster wants to hear, rather than what they actually think or believe. Therefore, such polls are not always accurate indicators of the effectiveness of the message.

Analyzing a Speech to Actuate

Ask these questions when you analyze any speech to actuate:

Situation:

1. Was the speech appropriate for the setting?
2. Was the speech developed to fit the time limitations?

Purpose:

1. Did the speech meet the general purpose to actuate?
2. Did the speech meet the specific purpose that was stated in the thesis?

Audience:

1. Was the speech suitable for the audience?
2. Was the action step appropriate for the audience?
3. Were the motivational appeals appropriate for the audience?

Method:

1. Was the organizational pattern appropriate for a speech to actuate?
2. Did the speech employ the steps of the Motivated Sequence?
3. Were the persuasive appeals appropriate for the purpose?
4. Were the speaker's claims supported adequately?
5. Were the persuasive appeals developed adequately?

Chapter 17 Summary

In preparing a persuasive speech, you must keep the situation, purpose, and audience in mind when selecting organizational and persuasive strategies. Your listeners must feel they are affected by the problems described and that they can be a part of the solution.

You must create a motivation for change by appealing to one of the five needs identified by Maslow: physiological, safety, belongingness, self-esteem, or self-actualization. Many persuasive appeals are available to a speaker: appeals based on logic, speaker credibility, and emotion. Emotional appeals are fear appeals, humor, compassion, and pride.

Audiences tend to remember the first and last arguments more than those in the middle of the speech.

The Motivated Sequence requires that you gain the audience's attention, establish a need for change, provide a means of satisfying the need, visualize the solution, and describe how the audience can act on the solution.

A speech that tries to persuade the audience to act is a speech to actuate and must include instructions for the audience to follow.

◆ *Check Your Understanding*

1. Define *persuasion*.

2. Explain the three purposes of a speech to persuade.

3. List and explain the two types of persuasive speeches.

4. Define *motivation,* and explain its role in persuasive speaking.

5. Identify Maslow's five levels of human needs and explain how you can use them as a basis for persuasion.

6. Explain three persuasive strategies that you can use in a speech and explain when they are most appropriate.

7. Explain how situation, purpose, and audience affect the development of a persuasive speech.

8. Explain the five steps in Monroe's Motivated Sequence.

◆ *Apply Your Understanding*

1. Watch television advertisements or study advertisements in the newspaper or in magazines. Identify an advertisement that appeals to each of Maslow's five human needs. Bring the examples to class and discuss their effectiveness.

2. As a class, compile a list of persuasive messages class members have heard for each of the three persuasive goals: attitude change, reinforcement, and creation. Was Monroe's Motivated Sequence used in the speeches?

◆ *Thinking Critically about Public Speaking*

1. Working in groups, analyze Mary Fisher's speech. Find examples of appeals to Maslow's human needs. What type of introduction was used? What organizational pattern was used? What is the thesis? Is there a forecast? Identify one internal transition and one external transition. What organizational pattern is used? Outline the major ideas in the speech. Identify three types of supportive materials. Identify three types of persuasive strategies. Identify the five steps in the Motivated Sequence. Does the speech summarize?

2. Select a controversial topic from a list your teacher supplies. Prepare arguments for both sides of the issue. Outline the speech to support the side you favor. Include two-sided arguments in the outline.

◆ *Speak Out!*

Prepare a five- to seven-minute speech to persuade on a topic you feel strongly about. Use the steps in the Motivated Sequence. Analyze your audience before preparing your speech by giving them an opinion survey. Use research to support your claims. Distribute an opinion scale after your speech. Did your speech change any attitudes?

◆ *Speech Challenge*

In this speech challenge, you will be asked to do something challenging: support a position that you personally do not support. In the "real" world, this assignment may fall to you. You may have to explain or support a policy your employer stands behind and that you must back in public. Select a topic that admits to at least two sides. Choose the side you do not support. Use the methods outlined in this chapter to build your speech. Try to be as persuasive as you can be. The speech should be four to six minutes long. One of the real advantages of looking at the arguments for the side you don't support is that you will be able to better understand and defend your own position.

CHAPTER

·18·

Key Terms

After-dinner speech

Burlesque

Dramatic irony

Overstatement

Pun

Situational irony

Tone

Understatement

Verbal irony

Chapter Objectives

After studying this chapter, you should be able to:

1. Explain how to use situation, purpose, and audience to select a topic for a speech to entertain.

2. Explain the importance of an appropriate tone for the speech to entertain.

3. List criteria for using humor in a speech to entertain.

4. Identify humorous devices typically used in a speech to entertain.

5. Explain how the fundamentals of speech preparation and presentation apply to designing a speech to entertain.

6. Explain the meaning of *after-dinner speech*.

The Speech to Entertain

Defining the Speech to Entertain

The speech to entertain presents some unusual problems. Usually, the speech to entertain is short. The subject matter is often left totally up to you. Why, then, is the speech to entertain a problem?

First of all, speakers who try to entertain an audience may compare themselves to the humorous, interesting people they see on television and in motion pictures. They worry that they have to do a routine, like a nightclub comedian. Such expectations can make a speaker feel insecure.

The second problem is the type of speech. Speakers may feel that entertainment is not a strong guiding purpose. As a result, they may be confused about what to do or say.

Third, speakers worry that they won't really be very entertaining. If they give an informative speech that isn't informative or a persuasive speech that isn't persuasive, they've merely given an unsuccessful speech. But if they give an entertaining speech that isn't entertaining, they feel their speech is a flop. They worry that the audience expects more than they have to give.

Fortunately, you really don't need to worry about these problems. Audiences really don't expect you to be a polished comedian. In fact, there's quite a difference between a speech to entertain and a comedy routine. Comedy routines frequently don't have introductions and conclusions, aren't carefully organized, and frequently don't even make a point. Speeches to entertain are *speeches,* not comedy routines.

Entertaining speeches still have purpose statements and thesis statements, just like any other speech. A humorous speech uses humor to make a point. In addition, audiences often aren't very critical of speeches to entertain. Critical listening and listening for information are usually involved in listening to persuasive and informative speeches. An audience's expectations of a speech to entertain usually aren't as great as they are for other types of speeches.

Setting the Tone for a Speech to Entertain

Tone—your attitude toward subject and audience—is the first concern when you want to entertain your audience. An audience will relax and enjoy a speech to entertain only when the speaker lets them know it's okay to do so. If you set a humorous or relaxed tone early in the speech, the people in the audience know three things:

1. They know how to listen. If they expect an informative speech, they'll listen for information. If they expect a persuasive speech, they'll listen critically. By letting them know early in the speech that this speech is meant primarily to entertain, you allow them to relax and prepare to listen on a different level.

2. They know that the speaker's approach to the subject is light. Knowing this, they'll understand if you say one thing and mean another. If you don't prepare an audience by setting tone, you may find your audience believing everything you say, even if you're joking.

3. They know it's acceptable to react. Some speakers wonder why audiences don't laugh at jokes. Sometimes, audiences need a speaker whose tone says, "It's okay to laugh and smile—this speech is supposed to entertain you."

How can you set the tone for an entertainment speech? You do it by selecting the appropriate introduction and language and using appropriate nonverbal behavior.

Tone and Introduction

You have already read about introductions and their purpose. The introduction of an entertaining speech does everything any speech introduction should: it gains attention, identifies the thesis, and sets the tone. You can set the tone of the entertaining speech in any of the ways identified in Chapter 14: quotation; rhetorical question; reference to history, audience, or self; humor; startling statement; or incident. Be certain that the method you select tells the audience what the tone of the speech will be.

Tone and Language

Your word choice is very important to tone because audiences respond quickly to a speaker's language. If you use language that's informal or lighthearted, your audience will relax and expect an informal or lighthearted speech. A more difficult use of language is **burlesque,** which is treating something of minor importance as if it were very important, or vice versa. For example, if you choose to deliver an entertaining talk about fashion, a burlesque introduction might treat fashion as if it were the most important topic facing the world today:

> Ladies and gentlemen, the topic before us today is one of the most urgent facing this country since the turn of the century. In our hands is the decision that will alter the course of the United States for generations to come. It is a decision we make with great apprehension, but one that brave hearts will not pass on to another generation: Is it proper to wear a black tuxedo to the prom, or is a white evening jacket preferred?

Tone and Nonverbal Communication

There are literally hundreds of nonverbal cues that communicate your tone to an audience. A smile, a look, a wave of the hand, or a nod of the head can let the audience know that you want the audience to be entertained. Even your posture can communicate to the audience an impression of your attitude about your subject.

Preparing the Speech to Entertain

Whether you choose a humorous or a more serious approach to the speech to entertain, you still must prepare carefully. Never lose sight of your goal: to get and keep the interest of the audience. Use every skill in this book to develop an effective and entertaining speech.

The following list should remind you of some of the skills you've studied and tell you how to apply them to preparing the speech to entertain:

1. Select the topic carefully, matching it to the situation and audience. Just because your job is to entertain doesn't mean you can talk about anything you want. The audience will be far more receptive if your speech is consistent with their interests and reasons for coming together as an audience.

2. Develop the thesis for your speech and keep it in mind as you prepare. Again, the audience is more likely to listen to a unified speech than to one that's just a string of unrelated comments. Make sure your audience sees how the jokes, stories, and remarks tie back to the thesis.

3. Remember the role of feedback in speech preparation and presentation. Anticipate your audience's reactions. While you're speaking, use their responses to fine-tune your speech.

4. Remember that you can research a speech to entertain. The media center has books of quotations and anecdotes that can help you write a successful speech to entertain.

5. Pay close attention to your introduction. It's crucial in a speech to entertain because it sets the tone and gains the audience's attention. Setting tone and getting attention are especially important in the entertaining speech.

6. Remember that most speeches to entertain are fairly short. If there are time limits, respect them.

7. Vocal delivery is important. It's hard to entertain a group if your voice lacks variety in rate, pitch, or volume.

8. Gestures, posture, and facial expression also help gain and keep an audience's attention.

9. Use vivid and appealing language. You can tell a story in an entertaining way if you choose your language carefully for its audience appeal.

10. Use good judgment when you select material. The audience trusts you to give a speech that won't embarrass or offend them.

11. Rehearsal is important. Don't slight it.

The Humorous Speech

The most common type of speech to entertain is the humorous speech. Successful humorous speeches are far more than a string of jokes. Like other speeches, humorous speeches have a purpose and a thesis. They're well-organized, with strong introductions and conclusions. They use support material. Voice and nonverbal delivery are important.

If this sounds like a serious approach to a humorous speech, it is. A speech may be humorous, but it still must fit the SPAM model—situation, purpose, audience, and method. Humor is the method of accomplishing the speaker's purpose with a particular audience in a given situation.

Very few humorous speeches are only supposed to make people laugh. If your speech fits the situation and the audience, it will have something more than jokes and stories. The model speech on page 366, for example, contains an important point that the audience cares about: how we can learn from our foreign guests. The fact that the

Humorous speeches are intended to make the audience laugh, but they should still have a point to make.

situation called for a light, humorous speech didn't mean it should be silly or lacking content. Still, the speaker wasn't primarily concerned with informing or persuading. He meant to be entertaining, and he succeeded largely because he didn't lose sight of the situation and occasion.

Humor and Taste

The model speech on page 366 illustrates how a speaker used humor to develop a speech. This speech was carefully designed to suit a particular audience and situation:

S: The situation is the beginning-of-the-school-year meeting of the International Club. All the students expect a light speech on the subject that brings them together. This isn't a business meeting. It's a kick-off meeting, and everyone's to have a good time.

A: The audience is the International Club, the group that sponsors foreign exchange students at a high school. This speaker chose to show how foreign exchange students enable Americans to learn about themselves.

Having carefully thought through the situation and audience, the speaker selected the general topic: what Americans learn about America from our foreign guests. The speaker further narrowed the topic to food. Given a change in attitude—if the topic were food shortages—the speech could have been very serious.

P: Next, the speaker wrote a purpose statement and a thesis statement.

Guidelines for Using Humor

Humor can be very effective if used properly. Use the following guidelines:

1. Make sure your material is funny. To make sure, rehearse your speech with a friend. Try to think as your audience thinks.

2. Be original. Don't tell a joke or story the audience has already heard. Remember, a speech to entertain is not a comedy routine you decided to copy.

3. Don't use private jokes. A private joke is a humorous remark that only a few people understand because they have private or personal information. The rest of the audience is left out. This type of humor is most appropriate when you're with a small group of friends.

4. Pause for laughs. If you say something funny and immediately follow it with another comment, the members of the audience won't laugh. They'll be listening to your next comment. This is called *stepping on your laughs*. Effective use of pauses is part of comic timing.

5. Don't aim your humor at a single person. If you do, the audience will think you're sarcastic and mean. While some good-natured jokes about others are fine, make sure they're few and good-natured.

6. Above all, use humor that doesn't offend people. Never make jokes at another person's expense. Never use humor that makes an audience feel uncomfortable. If you suspect that a story, remark, or joke will be inappropriate, find something else to say. Follow the old rule: When in doubt, leave it out.

Purpose Statement
The purpose of this speech is to entertain the students of the International Club by describing American eating habits.

Thesis Statement
We [Americans] simply love food—in all forms, shapes, and sizes.

M: Finally, the speaker selected support material, language, and tone—the speech methods—that were light and amusing.

SAMPLE SPEECH
Food for Thought

I am very happy to be invited to talk to the International Club this afternoon. This group does so much for our school and community that I couldn't resist accepting your invitation. I'm a firm believer in better international relations. To prove it, I ate pizza with Italian sausage last night, French toast this morning, and tacos for lunch. While I might overdo eating sometimes, I'm not too unusual. Americans have a love affair with food. We simply love food in all forms, shapes, and sizes.

You've all heard the remark, "The way to a man's heart is through his stomach." That's probably a few years before modern medicine found that the way to a man's heart is to turn right at the liver. You may have heard Napoleon's famous saying, "An army marches on its stomach." Perhaps that accounts for the slowness of some armies. To these celebrated quotations, I add one more: "The way to express Americanism is through your stomach." My quote probably won't go down in history; nevertheless, it is true.

As a matter of fact, it was a foreign exchange student sponsored by your club who really first convinced me about the importance of food in understanding people. Her name was Carmen Morales, and some of you might remember her. She came from Colombia and spent a year at our school. One winter's day after school, Carmen and I had a conversation. I was having my usual after-school candy bar when I saw her. She looked a little glum, so I thought I'd cheer her up.

"What's the matter?" I asked, unwrapping my candy bar.

"Isn't it obvious?" she said. "Just look at me!"

"You look fine to me," I said. In fact, she didn't look fine. She looked as if she might cry.

"I've gained fifteen pounds since I've been in this country," she said.

"Hmmm," I mumbled through my mouthful of peanuts, thick chocolate, nougat, caramel, and crunchy peanuts. Managing to swallow, I pursued the topic. "What's the problem? Are you eating because you miss your folks back home?" She looked at me and shook her head. And I washed the candy bar down with the last swallow of Coke.

"It's you Americans," she exclaimed. "Eat, eat, eat! Wherever you go, you eat! And I'm becoming one of you."

Well, that did surprise me. I thought to be an American you had to take a citizenship test, be sworn in, and everything. I didn't know wolfing down a couple of hamburgers would do it. When I told her this, it was some time before I could calm her down. She finally told me, "You Americans love food. There are doughnuts at our club meetings before school. When I go out at night with my American sister, we almost always stop off for a snack. And a snack to her is a hamburger and fries. In my country, we have breakfast, a large afternoon meal, and a light evening meal—without all these snacks."

She was right. It took a foreign exchange

student to show me something important about us Americans. We are lips over chops in love with food. It's part of being American. As I began to think about it, I noticed the importance food has for us. What's another word used worldwide for American? *Yankee.* How do we use it? *Yankee pot roast.* Southern culture has given us some of our finest authors and our noblest traditions. What do we remember? *Southern fried chicken.* Why this kind of thing is as American as apple pie! Whoops! See what I mean?

We can build an entire meal around American-named foods. Just think: Kansas City strip steak, Maine lobster, Texas chili, New England clam chowder, and Virginia ham—and that's all out of one food group. Our fruit and vegetables could include Iowa corn (some of which has gone into this speech), Idaho potatoes, Boston baked beans, Washington apples, and Georgia peaches. For dessert, we could have baked Alaska.

Think about the important American symbols that are closely tied to food. Baseball—America's national pastime. But what's a ballgame without hot dogs, peanuts, and Cracker Jack? Or think about Hollywood. Hollywood is a symbol the world over of America's glamour and excitement, but how often do you watch a movie with your fingers glistening in the dim glow of the theater with the extra butter you asked for in the extra large tub of popcorn? How often do you watch a great American hero like Clint Eastwood with Raisinettes or Jujubes?

Even if you watch the movie at home, it's likely that food will be there. We have TV trays from which we eat our TV dinners. And do you really watch those commer-cials, or are you one of the dozen or so of us who know that commercials are put on TV so we can have an intermission during which to raid the refrigerator?

Carmen really got me to thinking. Even our nation's most important cultural heroes are identified with food. Popeye eats his spinach, usually not even stopping to cook it. Dagwood has his "hero" sandwich. Snoopy has his chocolate chip cookies. Garfield has his lasagna. Even President Reagan had his jelly beans. Our space program promises to "boldly go where no man has gone before," and what goes with them? Instant orange drink!

To Americans, food means much more than nutrition. If we allow three meals a day as the basic, then consider the rest. The tacos guiltily squeezed in during the trip to the mall. The cheeseburger you had a coupon for. The cupcake that beckoned you and pleaded until you put it out of its misery.

Some of us even have a new hobby—recreational eating. We eat at parties, meetings, brunches (a wonderful cross between breakfast and lunch), and coffee breaks. We eat to have a good time. And do we ever! Our language shows the change. We no longer simply eat, we *pig-out, chow down, snarf, dig-in,* and *grub up,* all of which are synonyms for *eat.*

We even have fad foods with absolutely no purpose other than to pass time. Bubble gum is a kind of food that serves as a toy. Even after the flavor is gone, it's there to pop, snap, stretch, and chomp. A few years ago, kids everywhere were eating "Poprocks"—small bits of flavored sugar candy that made tiny little carbonated explosions on your tongue. Now who can beat that kind of entertainment?

However, nowhere is our love affair with food more evident than in our passion for the hamburger. There are enough hamburger restaurants to feed us all three meals a day every day. We are told that we "deserve a break today." To do what? To eat, naturally! There is a great beef race. Three ounces? Four? A third of a pound? Carmen didn't understand that the simple snack of a burger and fries that her host-sister had at night was more than a snack: it was a display of patriotism.

Even those of us who diet aren't immune from the fling with food. Dieters find themselves drawn toward diet foods and health foods as a substitute for the real thing. A bean curd sandwich may be a poor substitute for a hot dog with kraut, but as Shakespeare said, "Love is blind." I believe that was in *Hamlet* or maybe *Macbeef*. American food lovers will fall for anything they can chew and swallow.

But perhaps our love affair with food isn't all bad. After all, it broadens international understanding, something the International Club really cares about. We Americans love all kinds of food: Italian, Chinese, Mexican, Greek, French, Japanese, German, and many others. We are a virtual United Nations of food.

Not only that, did you know eating keeps the crime rate down? Why, if more people were sticking ribs in their mouths instead of a gun in someone's ribs, we could solve the crime problem entirely.

Eating also keeps the farmers in business. If we weren't so intent on consuming so much, many family farms might go under.

Eating keeps teenagers employed. How many of you have worked at a fast food place—building pizzas, stuffing tacos, or flipping hamburgers?

And eating is better than fighting.

As I reflect on it, it's a good thing I talked to Carmen that day. She did make me realize something about Americans and food. Eating is part of being American. We eat because it's fun. We eat to be friendly and sociable. We eat because the world's greatest technology and most productive economic system lets us. We eat because we are free to do what we want to do. We eat what we want, when we want—and that's American. That's something we can teach the foreign exchange students we look forward to having this year—our eating habits reflect America's value on freedom.

By bringing people like Carmen Morales to America, you in the International Club help Americans like me learn about America, as well as about other countries of the world.

Now will you excuse me? I have to grab a snack. After all this talking, I'm just starved.

Sources of Humor

When you begin to develop a humorous speech, you'll probably think first of things that make you laugh. That's the logical place to start, but don't forget your audience. What will an audience usually find amusing?

Irony When a speaker uses **verbal irony,** the audience knows that what the speaker said is not what the speaker meant. Although irony isn't always funny, you can use it to develop a humorous speech. Consider this excerpt from the International Club speech:

> Even our nation's most important cultural heroes are identified with food. Popeye eats his spinach . . . Dagwood has his "hero" sandwich. Snoopy has his chocolate chip cookies. Garfield has his lasagna.

Does the speaker really mean that Popeye, Dagwood, Snoopy, and Garfield are "important cultural heroes"? Of course not. The statement is an example of verbal irony, and the audience will be amused by the idea of Snoopy as a cultural hero.

Dramatic irony is a contrast between what the audience knows and what the speaker or a character in the speaker's story knows. In the International Club speech, the speaker creates dramatic irony when he recounts the conversation with the foreign exchange student. As Carmen tells about her experience with Americans and food, the speaker says he is unthinkingly eating a candy bar and drinking a soft drink. The audience realizes that this is exactly what Carmen is talking about. The speaker pretends he was unaware of the irony.

Finally, the speaker uses **situational irony.** Situational irony occurs when there's a contrast between what someone expects and what actually happens. In fact, irony is really the basis of the speech's entire development. It's unexpected that the speaker, an American, finds out about himself and his country from a foreign student. It's supposed to be the other way around. Unexpected results, twists of fate, or surprising conclusions to stories are an important part of humorous speeches.

Overstatement Using **overstatement,** or hyperbole, also creates humor. Audiences enjoy hearing a speaker intentionally exaggerate. There are several examples of overstatement in the International Club speech:

> "Eat, eat, eat! Wherever you go, you eat!"
>
> Americans have a love affair with food.
>
> There are enough hamburger restaurants to feed us all three meals a day every day.

This speaker builds his humor by exaggerating the role of food in American life. Some of the descriptions are also exaggerated. Look at the description of the candy bar or of the "fingers glistening in the dim glow of the theater with the extra butter you asked for in the extra large tub of popcorn."

Understatement   **Understatement** is the opposite of overstatement. When the audience hears a speaker intentionally reduce or minimize the statements in a speech, they may be amused. How many people do you think go to the kitchen during the commercial? Notice what the speaker said:

> And do you really watch the commercials, or are you one of the dozen or so of us who know that commercials are put on TV so we can have an intermission during which to raid the refrigerator?

Puns   **Puns** are humorous remarks using words with two or more meanings. Here are three puns from the model speech:

> Dagwood has his "hero" sandwich. [*Hero* is also an admired person, the subject of that section of the speech.]

> . . . as Shakespeare said, "Love is blind." I believe that was in *Ham*-let or maybe Mac*beef*. [The names of the plays are really *Hamlet* and *Macbeth*. And the quotation really comes from *The Merchant of Venice*.]

Selection of Examples and Illustrations   Much of a speech's humor comes from the examples a speaker chooses. In the International Club speech, the speaker talks about diet foods. He had a wealth of examples to choose from—things such as low-calorie soft drinks, cottage cheese, and lettuce. But none of these are humorous. Instead, the speaker talks about a "bean curd sandwich." Now there's nothing wrong with bean curd. But "bean curd sandwich" is funnier than cottage cheese. The speaker goes even further, contrasting the bean curd sandwich with "a hot dog with kraut." The contrast in itself is entertaining.

As you have already learned, a long, developed example is an illustration. The model speech is built around an illustration the audience will find entertaining: American eating habits. If the speaker gave this speech to a different audience for a different purpose, he would select a different illustration. Suppose this speech were to be given to a group of businesspeople to encourage their financial support of foreign exchange programs. Would the whole speech be developed around the speaker's conversation with a student from Colombia? Not likely. This purpose requires a much more serious illustration as the basis for the speech.

Humorous speeches often contain stories—some true, some untrue. A story that entertains and makes a point is one of the public speaker's most useful tools. The story gives the audience something to remember and think about long after the speaker has finished.

Timing Timing is the correct use of rate (the speed of your speech) and pauses. Timing your delivery is part of giving a successful humorous speech. Read this passage from the International Club speech again. How should you read the speech to increase the humor? Where should you place pauses?

> As I began to think about it, I noticed the importance food has for us. What's another word used worldwide for American? *Yankee.* How do we use it? *Yankee pot roast.* Southern culture has given us some of our finest authors and our noblest traditions. What do we remember? *Southern fried chicken.* Why this kind of thing is as American as apple pie! Whoops! See what I mean?
>
> We can build an entire meal around American-named foods. Just think: Kansas City strip steak, Maine lobster, Texas chili, New England clam chowder, and Virginia ham—and that's all out of one of the four basic food groups. Our fruit and vegetables could include Iowa corn (some of which has gone into this speech), Idaho potatoes, Boston baked beans, Washington apples, and Georgia peaches. For dessert, we could have baked Alaska.

Good timing comes from practice. Rehearse your speech aloud so you can hear where you need to pause and where you can vary speed and volume effectively.

The After-Dinner Speech

Speakers are often asked to give a speech to entertain following a breakfast, luncheon, or dinner. Such a speech is usually called an **after-dinner speech.** It's usually brief. It may or may not be humorous. Unless the meal is a business meal, the speech will certainly be light. Immediately after eating, most audiences aren't ready for a serious speech that requires a great deal of attention and thought. Once again, you must carefully consider the situation, purpose, and audience as you select and prepare the topic.

The sample speech on page 372 was actually given as an after-breakfast speech by Stephen Joel Trachtenberg, President of George Washington University. The members of the audience were honor students from Newington High School, Newington, Connecticut. The speech was given at the end of the school year. As you read the speech, note how the speaker adapts his methods to accomplish his purpose with the audience in the situation.

SAMPLE SPEECH

Five Ways in Which Thinking Is Dangerous
Stephen Joel Trachtenberg

It's an honor and a pleasure for me to be here today, and to have this opportunity to address this year's Newington High School Scholars' Breakfast.

I've been giving a lot of thought in recent weeks to what I ought to be saying to you this morning. The obvious thing would be to praise you for your hard work and your accomplishments, and encourage you to continue achieving at this very high level.

But the more I thought about it, the less inclined I felt to do that. And when I asked myself why, a little voice inside my head replied as follows:

"Look, Steve, these kids are *teenagers*. And one thing we know about teenagers is that they are given to questioning the values handed them by adults. Sometimes they rebel in *not*-so-obvious ways. But if you go in there and praise them outright for their accomplishments, maybe one or two of them will reason that anything an adult tells them is good is probably bad."

Let me tell you, that voice inside my head really gave me pause. Basically it seemed to be suggesting that I use some reverse psychology. Instead of doing the obvious, I should do the *opposite* of the obvious.

In turn, that seemed to leave me only one course of action. I could come here today and *criticize* you for working so hard

and accomplishing so much. I could urge you to relax a little, to lower your standards, and to try out the pleasures of poorer grades and a generally lower academic status. Then I imagined what the local newspapers would make of my remarks, and what the chances were that I would ever again be invited to address a group of students in any high school in Connecticut.

So I found myself back at Square One. Now I *really* had to get back to basics inside my head, and, drawing on all of the studying I did at Columbia, Yale, and Harvard, I reasoned as follows:

Those of us who have studied Western history of the 19th and 20th centuries know that the Romantic movement left us with a permanent bias in favor of rebellion, risk, and generally outrageous behavior. In other words, if you can pin an *"Establishment"* label on any particular set of behaviors . . . if you can make it sound as if everybody behaving in that particular way has a pot-belly that is also bright yellow . . . then most folks in our culture will shy away from it, in favor of someone or something that is closer to Burt Reynolds or Humphrey Bogart.

Now I asked myself: Why is it that no one has considered the hypothesis that academic high achievement is actually as romantic, risky, and generally outrageous as being a pirate, or flying experimental jets, or doing any of the other things that most people are *afraid* to do? Maybe those who get high honors in a place like Newington High School are not just *smarter* than most of their contemporaries but braver too?

The more I considered this hypothesis the better I liked it, and I decided to entitle my talk today "The Five Major Risks of Academic High Achievement." An alternative and slightly broader title might be: "Five Ways in Which Thinking Is Dangerous."

Way number one, it seems to me, is that thinking—analysis—the habit of probing deeply into things—can lead to depression.

Remember that people who are regarded as not being clever aren't necessarily lacking in brain-power. They just don't make use of the brain-power that they have available. And one of the reasons for that may be that when you inquire carefully into a lot of things that go on in our world, you find that many of them fall short of perfection. In fact, quite a few of them are positively lousy.

So you can't altogether blame folks who, rather than get upsetting answers, simply don't ask questions! They stay reasonably happy by not doing too much reasoning!

A second risk of academic high achievement is that there are those who will actually hold it against you—in other words, that it can sometimes lead to a lack of popularity where particular individuals are concerned. They're the ones who will label you a—quote—"brain," and imagine that this is a deadly blow, sort of like calling you a rat or a fink.

Though I imagine that some of you have had experiences like that, I wonder if you've considered the possibility that people like that are motivated by a good deal of fear and anxiety? Once you've established your reputation as having a lot of an-

alytic capacity, *they* become nervous that you might turn that capacity in *their* direction. In other words, the person who fears your brain-power is probably a person with something to hide.

The third risk of academic high achievement lies, believe it or not, in your relationship to the adult world. I hope it won't come as a tremendous surprise when I tell you that many adults feel quite ambivalent where talented and high-achieving teenagers are concerned. On the other hand, they can't help but admire the energy and initiative teenagers like that are showing. At the same time, they can't altogether avoid the awareness that the young people they are admiring are also the—quote—"next generation" that is going to—quote—"take over the world."

In other words, a typical fear that adults have is that they are on the way to becoming obsolete. That's why dedicated teachers don't necessarily leap to their feet with enthusiasm when one of their students proves beyond a shadow of a doubt that they just made a mistake. *First* they wince. *Then* they manage to eke out a small smile. And *then*, having thought the whole thing over—then and *only* then—they leap enthusiastically to their feet!

A fourth risk of academic high achievement, in my opinion, is despair. Once you've set a high standard for yourself, there *have* to come moments when you ask yourself: "Can I keep this up?" At the age of thirteen or fourteen or fifteen, you ask whether you can keep going at this pace until you're *really* old—until you're twenty-five, say, or thirty-two. Then, when you've been doing it for thirty or forty years, you wonder whether you can keep going at this pace until retirement. And after retirement, you look at the other vigorous senior citizens—every one of them playing championship golf or giving guest lectures at a nearby college—and you wonder whether you'll *ever* be able to take it easy!

It's no accident that it was eating from the Tree of Knowledge that got Adam and Eve expelled from the easy life. Though they did with their jaws rather than their neurons, they were academic high achievers of a certain kind—and—as the Bible tells us—had to work hard and have sweat on their brows for the rest of their time on earth.

Finally, there is another risk of academic high achievement that bears some thinking about, which is that it often leads people to transform the world in which they are living, which in turn can cause a good deal of personal upset.

Let's say that you are in your teens or early twenties and you work really hard to develop a brand new concept and a brand new range of intellectual or scientific possibilities. Now the world begins to change because *you* dreamt up the microchip . . . or genetic engineering . . . or some altogether new way of looking at the human past. Well, by the time the revolution is peaking, you'll probably be thirty-five or forty years of age—ready to settle down and be a little comfortable and complacent. At that point everything around you will get shaken up, and you'll find that your teenage son or daughter is criticizing you for being so completely out of it!

Now let me tote up the risks that I've set before you in the last few minutes:

Risk number one: You may find that you sometimes get depressed.

Risk number two: Some people won't like you.

Risk number three: Grown-ups may get a little nervous when they're near you.

Risk number four: You may feel an occasional twinge of despair over "keeping up the pace."

Risk number five: You may begin to have an impact on the world around you—and you will have to live with the changes you've helped to bring about.

Looking over those five risks of academic high achievement, I realize that they look very much like the risks of maturity. When you criticize someone for being too much of a kid, you usually mean that he or she is giggly even when that's not appropriate, that he or she tries to be universally popular, that he or she wants grownups to be godlike in their complete fairness, that he or she expects life to be a nonstop party, and that he or she can't imagine things being different from the way they are right now.

What that suggests to me is that academic high achievement—the kind represented here at Newington High School today—may also be a synonym for maturity. It carries some risks—which is *always* true of maturity. It means that life gets a little more complicated—which is what true adults take for granted as they try to get through an average day. It means that life is only *sometimes* a party, and that it is full of the unexpected.

Yes, there are some risks . . . but they are risks well taken. The benefits are worth the dangers. The eagle flying high always risks being shot at by some hare-brained human with a rifle. But eagles—and young eagles like *you*—still prefer the view from that risky height to what is available flying with the turkeys far, far below.

Personally, I admire eagles. That's because I am an unreconstructed romantic. And I admire *you* for what you've accomplished. Keep up the good work! My congratulations to you all!

Trachtenberg carefully tailored his speech to fit an audience of high-school scholars. He uses some of the tools of the humorous speaker. The speech definitely has a message for the students, but the speech's light tone suits the after-dinner speech. He sets the tone early in the speech:

> It's an honor and a pleasure for me to be here today, and to have the opportunity to address this year's Newington High School Scholars' Breakfast.
>
> I've been giving a lot of thought in recent weeks to what I ought to be saying to you this morning. The obvious thing would be to praise you for your hard work and your accomplishments, and encourage you to continue achieving at this high level.
>
> But the more I thought about it, the less inclined I felt to do that. And when I asked myself why, a little voice inside my head replied as follows:
>
> "Look, Steve, these kids are *teenagers*."

As Trachtenberg begins, he acknowledges the occasion and the audience. He recognizes the reason that has brought them all together. He implies that he won't do the "obvious thing"; that is, he won't be giving the kind of speech they expect.

By the time the speaker hears the "little voice" warning him that his audience is a group of teenagers, the audience already knows he'll use irony as part of his message. He'll say one thing and mean something else. He goes on to list the reasons why thinking is dangerous. Without the clever wording and thoughtful conclusion, a listener might believe the speaker doesn't want students to think. Of course, the opposite is true, and the contrast between what the speech seems to say and what it really says is one reason for the speech's success. In building your after-dinner speech, you don't have to use irony, but you definitely need to express an attitude toward your subject, preferably a light one.

You prepare an after-dinner speech in the same way as a humorous speech. Just as the humorous speech makes a point, so should the after-dinner speech. It should be related to the situation and the audience. This will meet audience expectations and will set your speech apart from other after-dinner speeches that the audience only faintly remembers. Trachtenberg's speech certainly has its point: There are risks to thinking, but the risks are worth the rewards. The students will probably remember the speech for a long time.

In some ways, the speech to entertain makes fewer demands on a public speaker. Still, the speech must be carefully prepared to suit the audience and situation. Humor arises from many sources, including the three kinds of irony, overstatement, understatement, puns, selection of examples, and timing. Speakers should always be sensitive to audience reaction when planning humor. Speakers should also note that not all entertaining speeches are humorous, and even humorous speeches should make a point. Finally, all the skills that are used to prepare speeches to inform and persuade can be used to prepare speeches to entertain.

◆ *Check Your Understanding*

1. Explain a speaker's use of situation, purpose, and audience to select a topic for a speech to entertain.

2. Explain the importance of setting a tone in giving a speech to entertain.

3. List three things a speaker should keep in mind when using humor in a speech to entertain.

4. Identify and explain three sources of humor commonly used in speeches to entertain.

5. Select three fundamentals of speech preparation and presentation and explain how a speaker would use them in preparing a speech to entertain.

6. Define an *after-dinner speech*.

◆ *Apply Your Understanding*

1. As a class, survey the humor used in introductions of many speeches—one speech per student. You may find appropriate speeches in *Vital Speeches*. You may have to look at several speeches, since not every speech begins with a humorous remark. Compare the humor to the checklist in this chapter. Does the speaker's use of humor measure up? If the humor isn't immediately funny to you, consider situation and audience to explain why the speaker chose it for the speech.

2. Bring your favorite appropriate joke to share with the class. Tell the joke in a group. Talk about why the joke is humorous. Let each group select the best joke to be told in front of the class. Determine how the joke might be used in a speech.

◆ *Thinking Critically about Public Speaking*

1. In class discussion, list famous humorists: writers, actors, and comedians. Discuss the sources of their humor. Which kinds of humor are appropriate for public speakers? Why?

2. Select one of the speeches in this chapter. After you've read the speech again to yourself, read it aloud in class. Have several students read the same paragraph. Discuss the way vocal delivery affects the speech's appeal. Specifically analyze the different uses of timing.

◆ *Speak Out!*

1. As a class, decide on a single topic that could be the basis for a speech to entertain. Write and practice an introduction that gets the audience's attention and sets tone. Give the introduction to the class. Discuss the ways the various introductions try to establish tone.

2. Separate the class into groups of four to six. Each group should select a humorous topic. Select one student to be the host who will introduce the topic and each speaker. Each of the other students should prepare a two- to four-minute humorous speech about the topic. As they prepare, students should work together to avoid duplicating ideas. Students should also work together as they rehearse to help each other develop their speeches. Be sure to follow the guidelines on using humor in this chapter.

◆ *Speech Challenge*

Select a famous person from TV or movies. Your job is to *roast* the character. *Roast* is a pun on *toast*. A *toast* is a short speech in honor of a person or event. A *roast* is a short speech or a series of short speeches that do the opposite: good-naturedly poke fun at a person. You may roast a person by yourself or with others. Imagine that the person being roasted is present. That may help you keep your humor good-natured and in perspective. Individual speeches should be three to five minutes long.

CHAPTER ·19·

Key Terms

Ceremonial speeches

Contest speeches

Conventions

Courtesy speeches

Eulogy

Extemporaneous
   speeches

Impromptu speeches

Original oration

Specialized speeches

Chapter Objectives

After studying this chapter, you should be able to:

1. Define *specialized speech* using situation, purpose, audience, and method.

2. Define *conventions* and apply the definition to developing the specialized speech.

3. Identify conventions of various types of courtesy speeches.

4. Identify conventions of various types of ceremonial speeches.

5. Explain the use of conventions in contest speeches.

Specialized Speeches

Characteristics of Specialized Speeches

As you already know, there are three basic speech purposes: to entertain, to inform, and to persuade. Some types of speeches, however, are given so often that they stand apart from these categories. These specialized speeches are still meant to entertain, inform, and persuade. If you understand what makes these speeches special, you can more easily prepare an effective speech.

What exactly are **specialized speeches?** They're speeches given in response to situations that occur frequently. Generally speaking, specialized speeches fall into three categories: courtesy speeches, ceremonial speeches, and contest speeches. Several kinds of speeches fit into each category:

Courtesy Speeches

Accepting awards and recognition

Presenting awards and recognition

Introductions

Ceremonial Speeches

Initiations

Graduations

Dedications

Eulogies

Contest Speeches

Original orations (Original oratory)

Extemporaneous speeches

Impromptu speeches

Informative speeches

Specialized Speeches and the SPAM Model

The best way to understand specialized speeches is to use the SPAM model. Consider a graduation speech as an example.

S: Thousands of graduation speeches are given each spring. This situation is the same from year to year and from school to school.

P: Graduation speakers usually have the same general purposes. They want the members of the audience to think about the years the graduates have been in school, their common experiences and interests, and the years ahead. They want everyone to remember this very special occasion. They want to inspire the seniors to think about their time in high school and their future.

A: The audiences at graduation ceremonies have similar needs and expectations year after year. Seniors are happy to be graduating and a little anxious about leaving their friends. Parents are proud. Everyone is looking forward to the next stage in the lives of the graduating seniors.

M: Therefore, since the situation, purpose, and audience are generally the same from year to year and from school to school, graduation speakers frequently use the same methods of developing and delivering a speech. You can learn to build successful graduation speeches by studying the similarities in situation, purpose, audience, and methods in similar speeches.

This is a logical way to think about specialized speeches, but there are two warnings:

1. While specialized speeches share many significant similarities, situations, purposes, and audiences are never exactly the same. You must still consider each speech individually. Sometimes situation, purpose, or audience may call for much different methods.

2. Speakers can still be original, even though they're using similar methods to respond to similar situations, purposes, and audiences. You must always find ways to make your speech fresh and lively.

In short, even if you're giving a specialized speech, you still must study the situation, purpose, and audience and develop the appropriate methods of development.

Conventions

Characteristics that are similar in a given kind of specialized speech are called **conventions.** In other words, a convention is a practice that is traditional. Because speakers respond to similar situations, they include the same elements in their speeches. Audiences expect these conventions.

Conventions of Topic

Choose a topic that's appropriate to the situation. In the graduation speech, for example, the speaker should focus on the graduates' futures and their challenges, dreams, and responsibilities. Don't use the time to talk about a subject unrelated to graduation.

Conventions of Tone

Display an attitude toward the subject and audience that's consistent with the audience's expectations. In the graduation speech, for example, you may use humor, but ultimately most graduation speeches are dignified, hopeful, and inspiring.

Conventions of Language

Select a level of usage that's typical of speeches given in the situation. Most of the situations calling for specialized speeches are formal; that is, they're governed by a set of rules specifying what's acceptable and what isn't. In these situations, language will also be formal English. Slang isn't acceptable. In most of these situations, you should use vivid and memorable language that's consistent with the tone and topic.

Conventions of Form

Even if you're giving a specialized speech, it should be organized in a traditional, logical way. There will be an introduction, a body, and a conclusion. Your presentation will look and sound like the kind of speech the audience expects. In a graduation speech, address the majority of the speech specifically to the graduates. Conclude with congratulations to the graduates and their parents.

Conventions of Length

You should keep your speech within accepted time limits. Giving a much longer speech invites boredom. On the other hand, giving one that's too short suggests that you don't have proper regard for the audience and situation. A graduation speech usually lasts from ten to twenty minutes, and a wise speaker will stay within these limits.

Breaking Conventions

Conventions are traditions, not hard and fast rules. They may be broken. If you decide to break a convention, however, there should be a reason. Why will breaking a convention (introducing a different method) help you meet the purpose in this particular situation with this audience?

Breaking a convention could be a way of getting an audience's attention. Breaking a convention could make a speech memorable. But you also run a risk. You must consider whether the effect of breaking a convention is positive or negative. As you prepare a specialized speech, you'll quickly learn why speakers follow conventions: they've worked in the past, so they are likely to work in the present.

Room for Originality

It may sound as if you're being told to give speeches just like everyone else's. That isn't the case. Within these conventions, there's still much room for creativity. You don't need to shatter traditions to be original. In fact, skillful speakers are often those who know the conventions of specialized situations and have learned to work carefully and smoothly within those conventions. Originality, individuality, and creativity are just as important in specialized speeches as in any other speeches.

When Abraham Lincoln gave the Gettysburg Address, he didn't follow the conventions of the day. For one thing, his speech was much shorter than expected. The other speaker of the day, Edward Everett, followed the conventions and delivered a two-hour speech. Whose speech is remembered today?

Lincoln ran a risk when he broke that convention. After the Gettysburg Address, many newspapers were shocked at what they called "disrespect" in Lincoln's short remarks. They felt the serious, somber task of dedicating the battlefield as a memorial deserved more than two or three minutes.

Courtesy Speeches

Courtesy speeches are speeches that fulfill social custom. For example, it's customary to say "thank you" for a favor. One kind of courtesy speech is the thank you, or acceptance, speech. It's also customary to introduce strangers, so another kind of courtesy speech is a speech to introduce someone to a group. Courtesy speeches can be understood in terms of SPAM and conventions.

Acceptance Speech

If you receive an award or recognition of some kind, the audience often expects you to give a speech expressing your appreciation. Are their expectations reasonable? Yes. If you accept the award or recognition, you admit its worth. Out of courtesy, you owe the audience a thank you.

The type of speech you choose to give depends on you. Here are some conventions to pay attention to:

Topic: The choice of topic depends on the nature of the award. Of course, you'll mention the award and your appreciation to the group or individual giving the award. You may also want to thank people who helped you receive the award.

Tone: Let your audience know you are sincerely appreciative. While you want to appear proud of the award, this isn't the time or place for self-congratulations. The person who presents the award usually helps set the tone with a presentation speech.

Language: Formal language is usually called for. The audience probably expects language free from slang or informal, conversational expressions.

Form: In most acceptance speeches, there usually isn't time for a fully developed introduction, body, and conclusion. Many times, the award is a surprise, and your acceptance speech is impromptu. The thanks and expression of gratitude are usually all that's expected. Usually, the speaker follows this order:

1. Thank the group for the award;
2. Make a personal remark about the award's importance;
3. Thank others who helped you win the award;
4. Close by restating your appreciation.

Some acceptance speeches are longer and more involved. For example, a person who accepts a party's nomination for president is expected to give a long, persuasive speech.

Length: An acceptance speech is usually very short. In fact, since awards are frequently given in groups at banquets or large ceremonies, you may have very little time for a speech. You owe it to your audience to keep your remarks short.

Accepting for Yourself   Usually, you'll accept an award or a recognition for yourself. The following acceptance speech fulfills all the conventions identified:

> I want to thank the Booster Club for their award for Most Valuable Player. I feel very proud knowing that you who have supported us all year chose me for the award. But I want everyone to know that I could never have won an award like this without the rest of the team. This award belongs to them as much as to me. I especially want to thank Coach Greg House for his hard work. He has been an inspiration to us all. Again, thanks to the Booster Club for this beautiful plaque. It will always be important to me.

Accepting for a Group   You may have to accept awards or recognition on behalf of a group. In these cases, you speak for them.

Treat the group you speak for as another audience—make sure they'll approve of your speech. Follow the conventions of a personal acceptance speech:

> It is my pleasure to accept, on behalf of the junior class, the annual Best Homecoming Display Award. I know I speak for all the juniors when I say that this is one of the high points of our school year. As we built the display, we all hoped that the alumni and faculty on the Homecoming Committee would appreciate the spirit we wanted the whole community to see. We would like to recognize especially the donations of materials made by Hill's Hardware and Bev's Party Supply. We also wish to thank the Pep Club for their generous $50 award. With their help, the juniors met one of their goals. Thank you from all the juniors at East High School.

Presentation Speech

There are conventions for presenting an award, too.

Topic: The award and its recipient are the topics of the presentation speech. You must explain the award and what it means. You may want to explain why the recipient qualifies for the award.

In a presentation speech, the speaker needs to explain the award, what it means, and why the person receiving it is deserving.

Tone: Match the award with the tone. A very important, prestigious award deserves a more dignified, impressive presentation speech than a small award. Since the audience and the recipient will match their responses to the tone set by the presenter, this convention is very important.

Language: This convention may vary with the award and the audience. A speech giving the award for outstanding football player of the year will probably be far more formal than a speech giving the award for outstanding player in an individual game.

Form: You should usually follow the customary introduction-body-conclusion form. Many presentations are made in this order:

1. Declare the recipient of the award;
2. Explain the meaning of the award;
3. Express the appreciation of the group making the award;
4. Give the award to the recipient.

In some cases it's traditional to build suspense about the award. Use this form to build suspense:

1. Name the award;
2. Explain the award's significance;
3. Explain the qualifications for the award;
4. Name the recipient.

Length: Like the acceptance speech, the presentation speech is usually short. You may have a lengthy presentation for very special awards or very ceremonial occasions. Usually, however, the audience wants to hear and see the recipient of the award, not the presenter. This speech fulfills the requirements of presenting a speech without building suspense:

> This year's award for the Outstanding Homecoming Display goes to the junior class. The Outstanding Homecoming Display Award is given to the class, club, or organization that prepares the float or other parade entry that best promotes the spirit of East High School's Homecoming. The judges, a committee of East High alumni and faculty, were impressed with the junior class's artistry, hard work, and originality. With the plaque comes a $50 award from the Pep Club. I present the Outstanding Homecoming Display to the junior class president, Joanne Bauman.

The same speech can be constructed to build suspense, if you feel that's appropriate:

> Each year, the classes, clubs, and organizations at East High compete for the Outstanding Homecoming Display Award. The award is made by a committee of alumni and faculty members to the group that does the best job of displaying school spirit. The committee looks for artistry and originality in a display, and we all agree that this year's winner is one of the finest. This year's award—and the $50 award from the Pep Club that goes with it—goes to East High School's . . . junior class!

Speech of Introduction

One very common speaking task is to introduce another speaker to an audience. Much of what an introductory speech says depends on how much the audience already knows. Still, there are some speech conventions to pay attention to.

Topic: Obviously, the topic is the person you are presenting. Specifically, a speech of introduction will explain why the person being introduced is important. In the introduction, you can help the featured speaker by giving his or her qualifications. To find out what information you can present in an introduction, talk to the person you are introducing before you prepare the introduction.

Tone: As the introducer, you should be courteous and sincere. Even if you don't share the speaker's point of view, it's courteous to treat the speaker as a guest and to present the speaker's qualifications to the audience.

Language: The language of a speech of introduction varies with the situation. Serious, formal situations deserve serious, formal language. Lighter, informal situations deserve light, informal language. Don't let the language take away from the speech's purpose—to focus the audience's attention on the person you're introducing. Above all, *make sure you correctly pronounce the name of the person you are introducing.*

Form: Speeches of introduction use some or all of the following information:

1. Welcome the audience (if the audience hasn't already been welcomed by a previous speaker);

2. Refer to the occasion or topic that has brought the audience together;

3. Name the speaker you're about to introduce;

4. Supply information about the speaker's qualifications for speaking on the subject;

5. Provide the speech's title, if the speaker desires;

6. Model the attitude the audience should adopt toward the speaker: interest, curiosity, amusement, and so on;

7. Repeat the speaker's name;

8. Verbally or nonverbally welcome the speaker to the podium or microphone.

Anyone who's responsible for introducing a speaker should consult with him or her to see what kind of information to include in the introduction.

Length: Keep an introduction of a speaker short. The audience is really there to hear the speaker, not your introduction.

This speech fulfills the conventions listed above:

Ladies and gentlemen, welcome to the last meeting of the year of the Science Fiction and Fantasy Club. We're very lucky today to have a guest who's really in touch with what's happening now in sci-fi and fantasy literature and film. She's been to many of the local sci-fi conventions and writes a column for our local newspaper reviewing science fiction and fantasy books and films. We've asked her to speak to us on science fiction movies, a topic of interest to all of us. Since most of us read her column, we already know we're in for an interesting speech. The speech's title—"From *Star Trek* to *Star Wars*"—says it all. Please join me in welcoming Ann Nelson.

This introduction gives more background:

I am pleased so many of you have expressed your interest in nutrition and diet by coming to the first day of our "Food for Fun" workshop. The interest you show here will certainly show up in healthier families for the future.

In fact, "healthy families for the future" could be the motto of today's speaker. Charlotte Walker has worked tirelessly in our community and our state to spread the word about modern nutrition. Charlotte is called "the food lady" by countless elementary-school children throughout the state. She has appeared in workshops and conventions, both statewide and nationwide. Her own experience in diet and nutrition started at Colorado University, where she earned a Bachelor of Science degree in home economics. She pursued her education at C.U. to earn a master's degree in human development, with an emphasis on nutrition.

Her work experience has been extensive. She has been an extension agent for the state agricultural board, and she has been an adviser to several state hospitals. She has published two cookbooks, *Food for Health* and *More Food for Health.* And just in case you wondered, she practices what she knows about food nutrition on her husband and two sons, ages four and six.

The topic of her talk is "Food Myths." Please welcome Charlotte Walker.

Ceremonial Speeches

Ceremonial speeches are designed to recognize special occasions. Speeches such as graduation addresses, initiation speeches, dedications, and eulogies help the audience tie the past, present, and future together. Usually ceremonial speeches are part of a large, formal activity that may include much more than a single speech. This section emphasizes the three most common types of ceremonial speeches: graduation addresses, eulogies, and initiations.

Graduation Address

The opening section of this chapter identified some of the conventions of graduation speeches.

Topic: The topic of a graduation speech usually is the future of the graduates. You may also speak about the years the students have spent in school. Within these general guidelines, you can choose just about any topic.

Tone: Even if the future doesn't always seem bright, the graduation speaker is usually optimistic and reassuring. Even if you warn about problems in the future, remind the graduates that they can meet the challenges. Since the setting of this speech is formal and academic, speakers often use the speech to say something important to the graduates about life outside school.

Language: The language of a graduation speech will generally be formal.

Form: There's no single form recommended for the graduation address. However, most speeches will include some or all of the following items:

1. Acknowledgment of the importance of the graduation ceremonies;
2. Congratulations to the graduates for completing this stage of their education;
3. A look at the graduates' promising futures and challenges;
4. A reminder that each graduate chooses his or her own future, that is, college, career, the military, or graduate school;
5. A special congratulations to parents of graduates;
6. Some advice to the graduates.

Length: Remember that graduation ceremonies usually involve calling the names of all graduates and remarks from other speakers. The graduation address should be the longest of the speeches, but it should be short enough that the ceremony can proceed efficiently. Usually, fifteen to twenty minutes is enough.

In Barbara Bush's speech at the 1990 Wellesley College graduation, she met the conventions of commencement speeches. She also overcame a difficulty: she was not the students' first choice as graduation speaker. In fact, she was a controversial selection. Some students thought she was an inappropriate choice because her fame was the result of her marriage to George Bush, not from anything she had done in a career. Mrs. Bush handled this challenge and delivered a fine graduation speech. In the sample speech below, note how her selection of topic was one method she used to overcome audience misgivings.

SAMPLE SPEECH
Choices and Change: Your Success as a Family
Barbara Bush

Thank you President Keohane, Mrs. Gorbachev, trustees, faculty, parents, Julie Porer, Christine Bicknell and the Class of 1990. I am thrilled to be with you today, and very excited, as I know you must all be, that Mrs. Gorbachev could join us.

More than ten years ago when I was invited here to talk about our experiences in the People's Republic of China, I was struck by both the natural beauty of your campus and the spirit of this place.

Wellesley, you see, is not just a place, but

an idea, an experiment in excellence in which diversity is not just tolerated, but is embraced.

The essence of this spirit was captured in a moving speech about tolerance given last year by the student body president of one of your sister colleges. She related the story by Robert Fulghum about a young pastor who, finding himself in charge of some very energetic children, hit upon a game called "Giants, Wizards and Dwarfs." "You have to decide now," the pastor instructed the children, "which you are . . . a giant, a wizard or a dwarf?" At that, a small girl tugging on his pants leg, asked, "But where do the mermaids stand?"

The pastor told her there are *no* mermaids. "Oh yes there are," she said. "I am a mermaid."

This little girl knew what she was and she was not about to give up on either her identity *or* the game. She intended to take her place wherever mermaids fit into the scheme of things. Where *do* the mermaids stand . . . all those who are different, those who do not fit the boxes and the pigeonholes? "Answer that question," wrote Fulghum, "and you can build a school, a nation, or a whole world on it."

As that very wise young woman said . . . "Diversity, like anything worth having requires *effort.*" Effort to learn about and respect difference, to be compassionate with one another, and to cherish our own identity, and to accept unconditionally the same in all others.

You should all be very proud that this is the Wellesley spirit. Now I know your first choice for today was Alice Walker, known for *The Color Purple.* Instead you got me—known for the color of my hair! Of course, Alice Walker's book has a special resonance here. At Wellesley, each class is known by a special color, and for four years the class of '90 has worn the color purple. Today you meet on Severance Green to say goodbye to all that, to begin a new and very personal journey, a search for your own true colors.

In the world that awaits you beyond the shores of Lake Waban, no one can say what your true colors will be. But this I know: You have a first-class education from a first-class school. And so you need not, probably cannot, live a "paint-by-numbers" life. Decisions are not irrevocable. Choices do come back. As you set off from Wellesley, I hope that many of you will consider making three very special choices.

The first is to believe in something larger than yourself, to get involved in some of the big ideas of your time. I chose literacy because I honestly believe that if more people could read, write and comprehend, we would be that much closer to solving so many of the problems plaguing our society.

Early on I made another choice which I hope you will make as well. Whether you are talking about education, career or service, you are talking about life, and life must have joy. It's supposed to be fun!

One of the reasons I made the most important decision of my life, to marry George Bush, is because he made me laugh. It's true, sometimes we've laughed through our tears, but that shared laughter has been one of our strongest bonds. Find the joy in life, because as Ferris Bueller said on his day off, "Life moves pretty fast. Ya don't stop and look around once in a while, ya gonna miss it!"

The third choice that must not be missed is to cherish your human connections: your relationships with friends and family. For several years, you've had impressed upon you the importance to your career of dedication and hard work. This is true, but as important as your obligations as a doctor, lawyer or business leader will be, you are a human being first and those human connections, with spouses, with children, with friends, are the most important investments you will ever make.

At the end of your life, you will never regret not having passed one more test, not winning one more verdict or not closing one more deal. You will regret time not spent with a husband, a friend, a child or a parent.

We are in a transitional period right now, fascinating and exhilarating times, learning to adjust to the changes and the choices we, men and women, are facing. I remember what a friend said, on hearing her husband lament to his buddies that he had to babysit. Quickly setting him straight, my friend told her husband that when it's your own kids, it's not called babysitting!

Maybe we should adjust faster, maybe slower. But whatever the era, whatever the times, one thing will never change: fathers and mothers, if you have children, they must come first. Your success as a family, our success as a society, depends *not* on

what happens at the White House, but on what happens inside your house.

For over fifty years, it was said that the winner of Wellesley's annual hoop race would be the first to get married. Now they say the winner will be the first to become a C.E.O. Both of these stereotypes show too little tolerance for those who want to know where the mermaids stand. So I offer you today a new legend: the winner of the hoop race will be the first to realize her dream, not society's dream, her own personal dream. And who knows? Somewhere out in this audience may even be someone who will one day follow in my footsteps, and preside over the White House as the president's spouse. I wish him well!

The controversy ends here. But our conversation is only beginning. And a worthwhile conversation it is. So as you leave Wellesley today, take with you deep thanks for the courtesy and honor you have shared with Mrs. Gorbachev and me. Thank you. God bless you. And may your future be worthy of your dreams.

In addition to the featured graduation address, usually by an invited, outside guest, some graduation programs feature student speakers. They should follow the same guidelines established in the list of conventions. It's very important that student speakers coordinate their speeches so they aren't repetitive. In fact, speakers can team up, developing a theme for their speeches to give the ceremony unity.

Students may also give two other traditional speeches at graduation ceremonies. The salutatorian speech welcomes the audience and sets a tone for the proceedings. In this address, the student speaker traditionally looks back on the years the class has spent together. A student also gives the valedictorian's speech, which is a farewell speech. This speech follows the same general conventions for the graduation address.

The Eulogy

A **eulogy** is a speech given in response to a person's death. Since death is frequently unexpected and is always emotional, speakers often have little time and great responsibility as they develop a eulogy. Eulogies are often, but not always, given at funerals or memorial services. For this reason, you must always be sensitive to the religious beliefs of the deceased and of the friends and relatives. Use these conventions as guides as you prepare a eulogy.

Topic: The topic always centers on the deceased. Usually, a eulogy recounts the life of the deceased, stressing the deceased's strong points and the role he or she played in family and career. You must show special sensitivity to the friends and relatives of the deceased.

Tone: The tone is almost always solemn. While you may recount some lighter parts of the deceased's life, the overall tone of the eulogy will be grave and respectful.

Language: Language will be direct and sincere.

Form: The introduction of the eulogy frequently refers to those attending the services and their feelings of loss. A traditional eulogy usually covers some or all of these points:

1. A statement of grief at the passing of a loved one;
2. An extension of sympathy to close friends and relatives;
3. A chronological retelling of the life of the deceased;
4. A summary of the deceased's virtues;
5. A statement in some terms that the deceased will live on in memory, in family, in the afterlife.

Length: Like other ceremonial speeches, eulogies are part of large ceremonies. The length of the entire ceremony should determine the length of the eulogy. Often, the life of a well-known, active person cannot be summarized quickly. Be sure that a eulogy is long enough to include important information about the life of the deceased. If you don't know all the information necessary, research for the eulogy by carrying out informal interviews with other people who were close to the deceased.

Adlai Stevenson, former governor of Illinois, candidate for the presidency, and ambassador to the United Nations, was known as one of the most eloquent Americans of the mid-twentieth century. When Sir Winston Churchill, the most eloquent voice from the first half of the century, passed away, Stevenson gave the eulogy on page 394 in Washington, D.C.

SAMPLE SPEECH
Eulogy on Sir Winston Churchill
Adlai Ewing Stevenson

Today we meet in sadness to mourn one of the world's greatest citizens. Sir Winston Churchill is dead. The voice that led nations, raised armies, inspired victories and blew fresh courage into the hearts of men is silenced. We shall hear no longer the remembered eloquence and wit, the old courage and defiance, the robust serenity of indomitable faith. Our world is thus poorer, our political dialogue is diminished and the sources of public inspiration run more thinly for all of us. There is a lonesome place against the sky.

So we are right to mourn. Yet, in contemplating the life and the spirit of Winston Churchill, regrets for the past seem singularly insufficient. One rather feels a sense of thankfulness and of encouragement that throughout so long a life, such a full measure of power, virtuosity, mastery and zest played over our human scene.

Contemplating this completed career, we feel a sense of enlargement and exhilaration. Like the grandeur and the power of the masterpieces of art and music, Churchill's life uplifts our hearts and fills us with fresh revelation of the scale and the reach of human achievement. We may be sad; but we rejoice as well, as all must rejoice when they "now praise famous men" and see in their lives the full splendor of our human estate.

And regrets for the past are insufficient for another reason. Churchill, the historian, felt the continuity of past and present, the contribution which mighty men and great events make to future experience; history's

"flickering flame" lights up the past and sends its gleams into the future. So to the truth of Santayana's dictum, "Those who will not learn from the past are destined to repeat it," Churchill's whole life was witness.

It was his lonely voice that in the Thirties warned Britain and Europe of the follies of playing all over again the tragedy of disbelief and of unpreparedness. And in the time of Britain's greatest trial he mobilized the English language to inspire his people to historic valor. It was his voice again that helped assemble the great coalition that has kept peace steady throughout the last decades.

He once said: "We cannot say the past is past without surrendering the future." So today the "past" of his life and his achievements are a guide and light to the future. And we can only properly mourn and celebrate this mighty man by heeding him as a living influence in the unfolding dramas of our days ahead.

What does he tell us of this obscure future whose outlines we but dimly perceive? First, I believe, he would have us reaffirm his serene faith in human freedom and dignity. The love of freedom was not for him an abstract thing but a deep conviction that the uniqueness of man demands a society that gives his capacities full scope. It was, if you like, an aristocratic sense of the fullness and the value of life. But he was a profound democrat, and the cornerstone of his political faith, inherited from his beloved father, was the simple maxim "Trust the people." Throughout his long career, he sustained his profound concern for the well-being of his fellow citizens.

Instinctively, profoundly, the people trusted "good old Winnie," the peer's son. He could lead them in war because he had respected them in peace. He could call for their greatest sacrifices for he knew how to express their deepest dignity—citizens of equal value and responsibility in a free and democratic state.

His crucial part in the founding of the United Nations expressed his conviction that the Atlantic Charter so audaciously proclaimed by Roosevelt and Churchill at the height of Hitler's victories would have to be protected by institutions embodying the ideal of the rule of law and international cooperation.

For him, humanity, its freedom, its survival, towered above pettier interests—national rivalries, old enmities, the bitter disputes of race and creed. "In victory—magnanimity; in peace—good will" were more than slogans. His determination to continue in politics after his defeat in 1945 and to toil on in the 1950s to the limit of health and of endurance sprang from his belief that he could still "bring nearer that lasting peace which the masses of people of every race and in every land so fervently desire." The great soldier and strategist was first of all a man of peace—and for perhaps the most simple reason—his respect, his faith, his compassion for the family of man.

His career saw headlong success and headlong catastrophe. He was at the height. He was flung to the depths. He saw his worst prophecies realized, his worst forebodings surpassed. Yet throughout it all his zest for living, gallantry of spirit, wry humor and compassion for human frailty took all grimness out of his fortitude and all pomposity out of his dedication.

Churchill's sense of the incomparable value and worth of human existence never faltered, for the robust courage with which he lived to the very full never faltered. In the darkest hour, the land could still be bright, and for him hopes were not deceivers. It was forever fear that was the dupe. Victory at last would always lie with life and faith, for Churchill saw beyond the repeated miseries of human frailty the larger vision of mankind's "upward ascent towards his distant goal."

He used to say that he was half American and all English. But we put that right when the Congress made him an honorary citizen of his mother's native land and we shall always claim a part of him. I remember once years ago during a long visit at his country house he talked proudly of his American Revolutionary ancestors and happily of his boyhood visits to the United States. As I took my leave I said I was going back to London to speak to the English Speaking Union and asked if he had any message for them. "Yes," he said, "tell them that you bring greetings from an English-speaking Union." And I think that perhaps it was to the relations of the United Kingdom and the United States that he made his finest contribution.

In the last analysis, all the zest and life and confidence of this incomparable man sprang, I believe, not only from the rich endowment of his nature, but also from a profound and simple faith in God. In the prime of his powers, confronted with the apocalyptic risks of annihilation, he said serenely: "I do not believe that God has despaired of his children." In old age, as the honors and excitements faded, his resignation had a touching simplicity: "Only faith in a life after death in a brighter world where dear ones will meet again—only that and the measured tramp of time can give consolation."

The great aristocrat, the beloved leader, the profound historian, the gifted painter, the superb politician, the lord of language, the orator, the wit—yes, and the dedicated bricklayer—behind all of them was the man of simple faith, steadfast in defeat, generous in victory, resigned in age, trusting in a loving providence and committing his achievements and his triumphs to a higher power.

Like the patriarchs of old, he waited on God's judgment and it could be said of him—as of the immortals that went before him—that God "magnified him in the fear of his enemies and with his words he made prodigies to cease. He glorified him in the sight of kings and gave him commandments in the sight of his people. He showed him his Glory and sanctified him in his faith. . . . "

Initiation Speech

One frequent ceremony is an initiation, which welcomes new members into a club or organization. Initiation speeches are often formal, since informal initiations usually don't involve speeches. These conventions can guide you as you prepare an initiation speech.

Topic: The topic should be the organization into which members are being initiated. Often the speaker praises the organization and recounts its members' virtues.

Tone: Since the initiates have chosen to attend the initiation and you have accepted the offer to speak, you must express an attitude of respect and admiration for the group and its members. An initiation is important to the audience, and the speaker's attitude should reflect that importance.

Language: The speech will probably be formal.

Form: The form of the speech depends on the nature of the audience. You may use some or all of the following:

1. Express honor at being asked to speak at the initiation;
2. Acknowledge the worth of the organization;
3. Tell the initiates of the honor and importance of their membership in the organization;
4. Summarize the beliefs, goals, or attitudes that are important to the organization;

5. Congratulate the initiates for becoming members;

6. Look into the initiates' future and predict how their lives will change as members of the organization;

Length: Except for the initiation ceremony itself, this speech is often the major "entertainment" at an initiation. Its length should reflect the importance of membership in the organization. The sample speech below shows how to meet the conventions of an initiation speech.

SAMPLE SPEECH
A Mirror for You

Ladies and gentlemen, parents, and—most importantly—National Honor Society inductees. Thank you for the invitation to speak at this year's initiation ceremony. For many of the students in this room, the tables are turned: *you* have given *me* an assignment. I hope I get a passing grade from you on this speech.

At any occasion like this—one which celebrates the initiation of members into a group—I am reminded of Groucho Marx's famous quip: "I wouldn't want to be a member of any group that would have me for a member." Which leads to the topic of this speech: What kind of group would have *you* for a member? What does it mean to be a member of National Honor Society?

Well . . . you know what *national* means . . .

And . . . you know what *society* means . . .

But . . . what is *honor?* What is the *honor* in National Honor Society?

In Act One of *Julius Caesar,* a play largely about the various meanings of honor, Shakespeare has Cassius approach Brutus and ask:

"Tell me good Brutus . . . can you see your face?" Brutus responds:

"No . . . for the eye sees not itself but by reflection—by some other thing."

Cassius then proposes to become Brutus's mirror and show him what others see when they look at him. Cassius begins, "Well, *honor* is the subject of my story."

For the next few minutes, honor is the subject of *my* story. I would be your mirror and show you a truly honorable student—a member of an honor society.

The simple motto of the National Honor Society—scholarship, leadership, character, and service—will serve adequately as the dimensions of our mirror.

Scholarship is the most obvious element of this honor society. It was the first criterion for your selection. Scholarship may be measured in many ways: grades, college awards, and others. But what is honor to a scholar?

I submit it isn't *A*'s, it isn't scholarships or awards. Instead, it is the recognition of the responsibility to bring into the world fresh, original, and exciting ideas *and* to preserve for the world the ideas of yesterday.

The honorable scholar—as Emerson noted in a famous speech—acknowledges his debt to the past, but does not *live* in the past.

An honorable scholar's role is not to hoard knowledge, but to disseminate it, to let others have as much as the scholar can give. As Chaucer said of the young scholar on the trip to Canterbury, "Gladly would he learn, and gladly teach." This reflection I show to you who would be honorable scholars.

The honorable leader is another matter. Leadership is not so readily identifiable a trait as scholarship. It takes many forms and is seldom recognized in the manner of an honor roll or a grade point average. Yet leadership is a characteristic of those in National Honor Society and must be reflected in our mirror.

The vision of the leader is a glamorous vision of a single person out in front of the masses, blazing new trails, solitary, without peer.

The Chinese philosopher Lao Tzu offered a very different view of an honorable leader. Lao Tzu gave three treasures to his followers. The first was love, the second was frugality, but the third was a curious gift indeed: "the gift of not daring to be ahead of the world." NOT to be ahead of the world.

His explanation wasn't so puzzling. He said, "Because of not daring to be ahead of the world, one becomes a leader of the world."

In short, leaders cannot allow their abilities to separate them from others. An ivory tower—no matter how respected or how envied—is still an ivory tower. Honorable leaders do not lead from an ivory tower or from far in advance of their followers but from among them. A membership in an honor society is self-defeating if it serves to separate you from your fellows.

The third reflection in the mirror is character. We all learn to show two kinds of character, public and private. Since your parents know far more about your private character than I, I shall focus on your public character, which we call citizenship.

Citizenship is one of the goals of high school education. Through work in such classes as history, government, and student government, you are supposed to acquire the attributes of a good citizen, a term which requires some clarification.

When Theodore Roosevelt was called upon to define a good citizen, he said, "The first requisite of a good citizen in this Republic of ours is that he shall be willing and able to pull his own weight."

"Willing and able to pull his own weight." If this is the requirement of a good citizen, what are the requirements of an honorable citizen? There are those who would use the word *honor* as an excuse for not pulling their own weight, for putting responsibilities onto others. Rest assured that honor grants no protection from responsibility. Honor increases responsibility.

The mirror reflects honorable citizens who pull their own weight and take up the slack left by others. Honor is not retained cheaply.

The final characteristic for scrutiny is service. Again the characteristic is hard to measure, for when does service begin and self-service end? Is it not true that those things designated as service are sometimes more selfish than selfless?

There is a tendency to view service as the province of a special few: Ministers, politicians, even teachers. Service, however, takes many forms. At the beginning of World War II, Winston Churchill spoke to the Canadians on just this subject. He remarked:

"There is no room for the dilettante, the weakling, for the shirker, or the sluggard. The mine, the factory, the dockyard, or the salt sea waves, the fields to till, the house, the hospital, the chair of the scientist, the pulpit of the preacher—from the highest to the humblest tasks, all are of equal honor; all have a part to play."

All are of equal honor, the message is simple: *You* bring honor to a task; it does not bring honor to you.

And that, after all is the point of this speech. An honor society does nothing to bring honor to you, you must bring honor to it. N.H.S. is like the mirror I speak of; it only reflects what is before it. N.H.S. is a society waiting for you to give it meaning, and honor.

So, if you would know what kind of group would have you for a member, do not look at me, or to the N.H.S. manual, or even to your peers. Look to yourself. Only you can bring honor to this group—to scholarship, leadership, character, and service—and finally to yourself.

Thank you for such a pleasant assignment. I commend and congratulate both students and parents.

Contest Speeches

If you participate in speech contests, you face two kinds of conventions: (1) conventions that have developed as successful speakers are observed and used as models; and (2) conventions established by the group sponsoring the contest. Successful contest speakers pay attention to both sets of conventions. The first conventions tell a speaker what's been successful in the past. The second conventions contain rules that *must* be followed. Otherwise, the speech will be disqualified from competition.

Generally, speech contests are sponsored in one of two ways. First, a local, state, or national service organization such as the Optimists or the American Legion sponsors competitions in which all speakers speak on similar topics. In these contests you can enter only one kind of speech—usually persuasive.

The second kind of speech contest is school-sponsored, often in affiliation with a state activities association. These speech contests, also called forensics contests, include many events in addition to public speaking. This section concentrates on the four most common contest events: original oratory, extemporaneous speaking, impromptu speaking, and informative speaking.

Contest speakers must follow certain conventions, or they risk having their speech be disqualified.

SPAM and the Contest Speech

The contest speech presents you with some unique problems and opportunities. In many ways, a speech contest is a very artificial setting. You need to understand that situation, purpose, audience, and method at speech contests differ from those elements in other speeches.

Situation: At a speech contest, there is no single situation that you must consider. In fact, you may give the same speech at several different contests. As a contest speaker, you're part of a group of speakers. All of you are heard and judged, usually several times in one day. Contest speeches are compared with each other and ranked or rated. This process is much different than the informal evaluations that are given to speeches outside the contest situation.

Purpose: Contest speeches have three different purposes: First, the contest speech is a way for contestants to learn about speaking and about the topics the sponsors designate. Second, contestants enter a contest with hopes of winning the speaking event. Third, each contest speech has its own purpose, just as every speech has. Contest speeches need to meet all three purposes.

Audience: The audience is the most unusual element of a contest speech: it is a judge or a panel of judges. Frequently, these judges are experienced public speakers. They'll practice precision listening with all speeches, even those designed to entertain. Judges sit in a room, hearing several speeches in one section or round, weighing the merits of the speeches, and rating them. This kind of audience isn't listening to the speech like a typical audience. A typical audience comes together because of a common interest. Contest judges come together out of an interest in speech. They'll be interested in all aspects of speech analysis and evaluation.

Methods: Contest speakers must adjust their speech methods to the unique situation, purpose, and audience. Speech contests often don't allow visual aids. Many speech contests require memorized delivery. A student preparing for a speech contest is coached on methods that are effective and acceptable.

Original Oration

An **original oration** is a persuasive speech the student prepares. It's the most common contest speech. Not only is it one of the speeches commonly sponsored in school contests, it's the contest speech preferred by community groups. Chapter 17 gives you important information on persuasive speeches in general. Note the particular conventions of an original oration.

Topic: Selecting a good topic is crucial for an effective contest oration. Since a judge listens to many speeches in a contest round, an original topic will make your oration stand out. However, you must also consider the attitudes of judges at speech contests and avoid topics that may be too controversial. It's best to talk to a speech teacher or coach before settling on your topic.

Tone: Orations are designed to persuade—to change people's attitudes, change people's behavior, or inspire them. If you're giving a persuasive speech, you must set a tone that's sincere and concerned. You try to communicate a sense of enthusiasm and personal involvement. You must appear confident without appearing arrogant. Oration contestants can use humor, but the controlling purpose of your speech is always to persuade, not to entertain.

Language: The original oration is a memorized, highly polished speech. The speech judge expects the language to be eloquent and memorable. You should revise the manuscript several times before memorizing.

Form: Any organizational pattern may be used in an oration. Problem-solution is the most typical. You need to develop a good introduction. After all, your oration is one of several the judge must hear, so gaining the judge's attention is very important. You also must write a memorable conclusion, one that will distinguish your speech from all the others.

Length: The maximum length of an original oration is set by the contest sponsor. Sometimes the sponsor also sets a minimum. In most school-sponsored contests, the maximum length is usually ten minutes.

Because you have time to prepare an original oration, judges usually expect every part of your speech, including delivery, to be highly polished.

The sample speech below is by Joanie Tebbe. With it, she qualified for the national contest sponsored by the National Forensic League. She is currently furthering her education at the University of Texas at Austin, majoring in chemical engineering. After completing her schooling, she plans to teach.

SAMPLE SPEECH
Valuing Teachers
Joanie Tebbe

Maybe you've experienced that incredible moment. Your newborn baby sleeps gently in your arms, the innocence written on his or her face. And like all other parents, you begin to fantasize. Perhaps, she'll grow up to be the first major league female shortstop—you see it, as she races deep into the hole to make a backhand stop and then—whiz—over to first base to beat the runner by a step. Oh look! Those fine, delicate hands—a surgeon! Saving lives of other human beings. Or maybe, just maybe . . .

Best of all, he or she will use those wonderful talents locked up in that tiny little body to grow up to be the most respected of Americans—A TEACHER!

Oh no! NOT a teacher! Don't let it be true! That's not good enough for my baby! Is that how you feel?

Many Americans feel this way. A recent Gallup poll indicated more than 52 percent of all Americans would be disappointed if their son or daughter chose teaching as a profession.

In 1970, Benjamin Rush, intrigued with the role of the teacher in American society questioned our morals:

> The teacher is, next to mothers, the most important member of civil society. Why then is there so little rank connected with that occupation? Why do we treat it with so much neglect and contempt?

As in 1970, a grave injustice persists in this country. The men and women who teach our precious children are not respected for their work by the rest of society. Frankly, teaching is not honorable in the United States.

Hypothetically, let's take the case of a potentially excellent teacher. Call her or him Mr. or Ms. X. This person agrees that, next to human beings themselves, the education of these people is the most valuable resource in the U.S. The teacher-to-be knows education enhances the knowledge of a person, encourages people to believe in themselves, gives any person the opportunity to choose what to do in life, and offers the ability for our country to be a world leader. Mr. or Ms. Potential Teacher realizes the truest freedom is the pursuit of knowledge, the limitless capability to learn, to understand more. Being able to understand and build on the past work of great people and discoveries can only be revealed through education. So much is waiting to be understood, innovated, and developed. This potential teacher even feels slightly arrogant. He or she would like to be an exemplary role model for future generations of children. Influencing values such as honesty, cooperation, and respect is significant indeed. How could this person go wrong in choosing teaching as a profession?

How about salaries equal to the pay of many blue-collar, uneducated workers, no respect from society, receiving little gratitude from administrators or parents, no honor in our country, dealing with close to 150 students each day, planning lessons, teaching classes, counseling students, determining grades, correcting papers, attending meetings, sponsoring clubs or sports, discussing with parents, decorating bulletin boards, and cleaning classrooms? All this becomes quite a chore when the compliments for what these teachers have accomplished are rare. In fact, society actually condemns teachers for the poor quality of education in the United States.

I won't deny it. The education in the United States is suffering. Many critics compare our students failing scores to those of the Japanese, believing our education system just doesn't measure up. Okay, I accept that. Let's look at the differences. Japanese children study 280 days a year, where United States children study only 180. Two hours of homework each night is normal in Japan. Here, the average homework is less than thirty minutes. The reason for this division is quite simple. *Vital Speeches of the Day* quoted the United States Secretary of Education:

> In Japan, the teacher is honored. In Japan, the teacher is in the upper brackets—the upper salary brackets, and in the United States, the teacher is not honored, and is in the lower brackets. In Japan, the family respects education. In the United States, nonchalance towards education. In Japan, the students learn and the students understand that the way to success.is through education . . . We need to change that.

Revising the way society perceives teaching is the only permanent solution to our education crisis. You'll hear me say this a lot—

money determines which jobs are sought after. Salaries determine the respect, quality, and willingness to do a job. If teachers aren't paid more—respect, quality, and willingness to teach will never be regained.

In fact there's an increasing discontent spreading throughout the ivy walls. Many teachers have decided to quit. For example, according to a Kansas Speech Communication Association study, the average career of a speech and debate teacher in Kansas lasts only 3.6 years. If these teachers, the ones who teach the high-level students are discouraged, imagine the pain of dealing with students "at risk."

The term teachers use when they resign is *burnout*. The question we must ask is, "Is there burnout where there once was no fire?" Logic presents us with a dilemma that we as people concerned about our children's future cannot ignore.

Are committed, dedicated teachers truly flaming out and falling back to assume less worthwhile jobs in society? If so, shouldn't we take drastic steps to save these brilliant teachers "at risk"?

Or, on the other hand, are the teachers leaving actually easy to replace. Are there, in fact, better qualified teachers out there, who are just NOT becoming teachers. If so, what Marshall Plan of Education are we going to implement to attract these teachers to teach our future?

The answer, unfortunately, lies in a combination of both. We are losing great, caring teachers to a world of better money. The Private Business World. Now, I don't mean to offend you, but the most common background of an insurance salesman is a former teacher and the most common background of a real estate agent is elementary education. I'm not arguing whether we need insurance or real estate. But I am claiming the value to society of an exceptional, professional teacher outweighs the others.

The status of a teacher is incomprehensible. Society fails to portray the importance of the teacher. From a young age, we are taught or subconsciously notice the indignity associated with this profession. Little kids aspire to be Michael Jordan or George Washington. Who wants to be a teacher—a little old lady in front of zooey classrooms? What other picture does the media portray to us?

The movie *Dead Poets' Society* teaches us the most dangerous lesson of all—that the truly exceptional teacher will be crushed by the authority. The image rarely varies - learning is irrelevant, school is a joke, and the best thing about the place is the babes and hunks of "Beverly Hills 90210."

Yet, reality teaches us a much different, more drastic lesson.

For anyone to be successful, there must be a strong educational foundation, a dedication to learning. (Without this essential base of enriching education which allows ultimate opportunity, no one can be successful.) Our country has already felt a trend of decreased quality of teachers. Some argue that there has been a "narrowing" of education—that we are now faced with teachers for whom we must "spell out" exactly what they are to teach. Unfortunately, ignoring this crisis as it persists will achieve nothing. Make teaching more competitive. We must reverse this typical stereotype with a greater respect for teachers, which can only result from increased salaries. Without status or monetary incentives, our society can look forward to a bleak educational future, with less motivated and less qualified teachers.

Salaries are the biggest factor in determining the status of any profession. Many argue, why increase teachers' pay for the same work? Yet, teachers hold the biggest responsibility in this country—that of educating our children. They should be rewarded and motivated accordingly—with monetary substance. Right now, the low salaries are the biggest deterrent to teaching. Our "perfect" potential teacher now can't afford to even consider this profession on this account. Doctors, lawyers, and sports professionals are paid very generously and respected enormously. Subsequently, we have some of the best medical breakthroughs and sports competitions in the world. If we could transfer that status and money into the teaching profession,

excellence in education for all would follow. Where are we going to get this money? I'll answer your objection this way. Across America, we spend $2,000 per student per year. Yet, we spend $10,000 per unemployed mother on welfare and its administration. And we shell out $22,000 to imprison one societal failure. And we fall further behind our international competition and worst of all we lose that creative spark, that zest for learning and that quality of life that only education can provide.

When the day comes that all moms and dads can hold their children and dream of them in front of a classroom with other children gaining energy, knowledge and wisdom from them, then indeed we can say . . . America, you've grown up.

Extemporaneous Speeches

Interschool speech contests usually feature **extemporaneous speeches.** Also called *extemps,* these speeches are given with brief preparation about current events topics. In contests patterned after the National Forensic League's competition, students may enter domestic extemp, in which all topics are about the United States, or international extemp, in which all topics are about U.S. foreign relations or events in other countries.

In a typical contest, you draw three speech topics from a group of topics approved by the contest sponsor. You then select one of the three topics and spend thirty minutes preparing and rehearsing. During preparation, you can consult only materials approved by contest rules. Usually included are current magazines, indexes prepared by the speaker before the contest, dictionaries, and thesauruses. You can't receive help from anyone else, student or teacher. You then present the speech to a judge or judging panel. In some cases, speaking notes aren't allowed.

Judges listening to extemp speeches know you only had thirty minutes to prepare your speech. Still, they'll expect a smooth, polished delivery. Equally important are the issues you deal with. Extemp speakers must be thoroughly knowledgeable about current events. The more you know, the less time you'll need to research your topic. That gives you more time to organize and practice the speech.

These conventions can guide the extemporaneous speaker.

Topic: Since the topic changes with each speech, topic might not seem to be a convention worth considering. However, topic is one of the most important elements in an extemp speech. First, you must choose quickly from three topics, considering which topic has judge appeal and requires the least preparation.

Next, you must stick strictly to the topic. One requirement of an extemporaneous speech is *topicality*—that is, the speech deals exactly with the topic. If a topic reads, "Has recent legislation concerning foreign trade helped or hurt the United States economy?" you must answer that question. When you finish, if the judge isn't convinced that your speech has dealt with the topic, the judge may rank you low. Learning to choose a good topic is essential to successful extemporaneous speaking. Here are some suggestions:

1. Keep up with all current events so you can choose a topic based on what you know, not on what you don't know.

2. Stay away from "gimmicky" topics that don't focus on important current events.

3. Keep a file of all your speeches to help you review and practice extemporaneous speaking.

Tone: You may adopt any number of attitudes toward your topic. Most extemp speakers, however, try to convey a sense of authority. They want to assure speech judges that they know what they're talking about. Often, an extemp speaker will survey the facts of a certain topic with an objective, analytical tone. Again, your approach will depend on the topic, your own skills, and the advice of your teacher.

Language: The language of an extemp speech is direct and clear. Since the speech is prepared and rehearsed in thirty minutes, the judges don't expect the polish and eloquence of an original oration. One of the trademarks of successful extemp speakers, however, is a smooth, clear delivery with carefully selected words. Practice enables extemp speakers to think on their feet. Familiarity with current events helps speakers find the right word.

Form: Again, strong introductions and conclusions set one extemp speech apart from the competition. It's essential to state the topic in the introduction. Any organizational pattern in this book can be adapted to an extemp speech, depending on the topic. It's best to keep the form clear and simple, for two reasons. First, you must remember the organization. Some contests allow the use of a note card; others don't. Second, the judge must be able to follow your organization without confusion.

Length: Usually an extemp speech is five- to seven-minutes long. Length requirements are set by the contest sponsor.

One way to learn the conventions of the extemp speech is to attend a speech contest and listen to the competitors. Audio and video-tapes are also available.

Impromptu Speeches

In contest situations, **impromptu speeches** are speeches given with minimal preparation. Just as with an extemporaneous speech, the speaker draws a topic. Then, depending on the rules established by the contest sponsor, the speaker may have five minutes or less to prepare a speech. In some contests, the contestant must speak on the topic with no preparation.

Judges of impromptu speeches look for the speaker's ability to evaluate the topic quickly and build a speech on the spur of the moment. These conventions can help you present an impromptu speech.

Topic: Topics for impromptu speeches vary from contest to contest, from state to state. Sometimes one-word topics are used, such as *friends, clouds,* or *computers.* Other times, speakers are asked to respond to statements, questions, or quotations, such as, "Agree or disagree: 'Neither a borrower nor a lender be.'" In still other situations, the speaker must respond to current events topics. A successful impromptu speaker chooses topics about which he or she knows something or has personal experience.

Tone: Since topics differ greatly, so do the tones of various speeches. If the topic is personal, the tone will be, too. A current events topic requires a tone similar to that of an extemp speech.

Language: Impromptu speeches require you to choose words off the top of your head. The judge knows that you haven't had time to plan word choice. Speakers who practice and develop the ability to choose clear, graceful words will stand out among their competitors.

Form: Impromptu speakers have little time to plan a form. Strive for a clear, catchy introduction that states the topic. From there, try to assemble and present support material that deals with the topic. Then, strive to put together a conclusion. After you master creating the intro-body-conclusion form with minimal preparation, you can introduce other formal elements.

Length: Length is established by the contest sponsor. Usually, the impromptu speech lasts from two to five minutes.

You'll become a better impromptu speaker as you practice and observe experienced speakers.

Informative Speeches

Some speech contests ask you to prepare and deliver an informative speech. Chapter 16 gives you information on informative speeches. Some of the conventions of an informative speech in a contest are listed here.

Topic: The topic you select can be the difference between a successful and an unsuccessful speech. After listening to an informative speech, judges should feel they've learned new and important information about the topic. If you select a topic already commonly known, the speech will make less of an impact than one on a new, fresh, and exciting topic.

Tone: The tone of an informative speech may be light or serious. A speech on hot air ballooning, for example, will be light. A speech on first aid will be serious. But the judge must perceive you as interested in the topic and in telling others about the topic. If you can convey this attitude, the tone will be appropriate.

Language: Like the original oration, you prepare the informative speech well in advance of the speech contest. Consequently, the judge expects the language to be polished. Unlike the oration, the focus of the informative speech is on sharing information. The language of an informative speech should be interesting and clear. The speech should vividly present the topic. Successful speeches get the judges to "see" the topic, even though most contests do not allow visual aids.

Form: Any organizational pattern identified in this book is appropriate. Early in the speech, however, try to show the judge why he or she should be interested in the topic. The judge must see that there's a purpose for the informative speech other than to win the contest.

Length: The length is set by the contest sponsor. Typical length is five to seven minutes.

Chapter 19 Summary

Some speeches are given so often that they have a built-in set of conventions. Conventions can dictate topic, tone, language, and length. The three types of specialized speeches that high-school students encounter most often are courtesy speeches, ceremonial speeches, and contest speeches. Courtesy speeches involve accepting or giving awards and introducing speakers. Ceremonial speeches are initiations, graduations, dedications, and eulogies. Contest speeches are original orations, extemporaneous speeches, impromptu speeches, and informative speeches. The conventions of these speeches help the speaker select the correct methods of speech development.

◆ Check Your Understanding

1. What is a *specialized speech?* What makes it possible to treat specialized speeches in groups?

2. Define *conventions.* Explain the value of knowing speech conventions. Explain the two warnings to note when following speech conventions.

3. Give three conventions for each of these courtesy speeches:
   acceptance speech
   presentation speech
   introduction speech

4. Give three conventions for each of these ceremonial speeches:
   graduation speech
   eulogy
   initiation speech

5. Give three conventions for each of these contest speeches:
   original oration
   extemporaneous speech
   impromptu speech
   informative speech

◆ Apply Your Understanding

1. Use *Vital Speeches* or another source from your media center to find ceremonial and courtesy speeches, such as acceptance speeches, dedications, graduation addresses, and eulogies. Select a short (one to three minutes) section to read to the class. Before you read the selection explain the occasion to your classmates. After your presentation, discuss the conventions the speaker followed.

410

2. Make a list of the activities in your school or community that might call on someone for a ceremonial speech. List those that would require a courtesy speech.

3. Periodically, television carries award shows for sports or entertainment. Videotape three to four presenters' speeches and the same number of acceptance speeches. Show them to your classmates. Select the best speech in each category. Give reasons for your selection.

◆ Thinking Critically about Public Speaking

1. As a class, discuss the following topic: What are the risks of being tied too closely to conventions? What are the risks of ignoring the conventions?

2. If a speech contest is held in your school or close to your school, attend the contest. Observe several speakers in one category. Note the similarities. What do the speakers do alike? What do they do differently? Report back to your class on your observations.

◆ Speak Out!

1. Divide into pairs. With your partner, decide on an award that the two of you will give and receive. One of you will prepare a presentation speech; the other will prepare an acceptance speech. Present them to the class.

2. Select a famous person you would like to hear speak on a topic. Research the person's life. Be sure to know why this person is qualified to speak on the subject you are interested in. Prepare a two- to three-minute introduction of the person. Give the introduction to the class.

3. Select a famous person, living or dead. Assume you had to give a eulogy for that person. Refer to the eulogy section in this chapter and prepare a five-minute eulogy.

◆ Speech Challenge

Many speech contests are held annually. Work with your teacher to select one of the contests to participate in. Develop a speech that fits the entry requirements for the contest. If you and your teacher agree, enter the contest.

Suggested Speech Topics

The following list shows you what other students have selected as topics for their speeches. The list is not complete nor is it meant to dictate to you. Always consider your own interests and areas of knowledge when selecting a topic for classroom speeches, as well as the audience and situation.

Process or Demonstration

How to make a silk screen print
How to sculpture ice
How to apply stage make-up
How to do pantomime
How to serve a tennis ball
How to make candles
How to tie-dye a T-shirt
How to train your dog
How to decorate cakes
How to make your home more burglar proof
How to prepare a résumé
Computer basics
How to improve your listening skills
How to do calligraphy
How to use the Heimlich maneuver
How to select a personal computer
How to preserve flowers
First aid techniques to stop bleeding
How to do needlepoint
How to hold and swing a golf club
How to dissect a frog
How to refinish furniture
How to cook lasagna
How to read a road map
How to study for a test

How to begin a collection (your choice)
How to do basic country dance steps
How to use a 35mm camera
How to buy running shoes
How to reduce stress
How to get a summer job
How to perform CPR
How to improve your memory
How to change a flat tire
How to use computer graphics
How to attract and feed wild birds

Informative

Names and how they affect personality
Outdated laws
Type A personalities
Wind-powered energy
Holiday customs throughout the world
People in history
Folk medicine
Laser technology
History of space exploration
History of the Olympics
History of women's suffrage
History of rock music
History of labor unions

413

Our school's history

Our city's history

Anorexia

Learning styles

Country western music

Artificial hearts

The warning signs of cancer

Treasures of King Tut

Weather forecasting

The Great Wall of China

Ghosts

Earthquakes

Spies

Strange inventions

History of baseball

Dreams

Customs from your ethnic heritage

Tornadoes

Famous battles

Historic places

History of movie making

Folk arts

The metric system

Astrology

The Nobel Prizes

Hobbies and pastimes (specific ones)

Important event (in our state's history)

Acupuncture

I.Q. tests

History of board games (specific ones)

Sign language

Handwriting analysis

History of money

Superstitions

Fads

Energy conservation

Biofeedback

The world of Disney

Gender differences in communication

Protecting yourself from crime

World religions

Unsolved mysteries

Persuasive

Nonsmokers' rights

Child abuse

Women's rights

Government bureaucracy

Drinking and driving

Air bags

Capital punishment

Rights for left-handed people

Why college isn't for everyone

The importance of foreign language study

World hunger

Censorship

Nuclear waste disposal

Comparable worth

Preserving natural resources

Support for the arts

Medical malpractice

Gun control

Rights of the elderly

Health-care costs

Television advertising

Seat belts

Election reform

Donating blood

Say "no" to drugs

Be a volunteer

Buy American

Recycling

Juvenile crime

The need for organ donors

Poverty in the United States

Television violence

Prison reform

Frivolous lawsuits

Saving endangered species

Balancing economics and the environment

Gang violence

Rationing health care

Sample Speeches

Public speaking students know that a speech manuscript leaves out many important elements of speech: gestures, facial expression, voice, feedback, to name only a few. However, speech manuscripts do allow you to study other important elements of speech preparation and presentation—language, organization, audience analysis, support material, introductions, and conclusions.

The speeches in this appendix will help you in your study of public address. Your teacher may assign these speeches for analysis. Some of the questions at the ends of chapters in this text direct you to study speech manuscripts. As you read and study these speeches, keep the SPAM model in mind. Each speech was given in a specific situation, to a specific audience, for a specific purpose. The speaker selected methods to accomplish that purpose.

Reading these speeches aloud will help you hear the way the speeches were heard by the original audience.

Eulogy for the *Challenger* Crew

Given at a memorial service in Grace Episcopal Cathedral, Topeka, Kansas by **Governor John Carlin,** this eulogy is a tribute to the *Challenger* crew. Ron Evans, an Apollo astronaut was in attendance. The date coincided with the one hundred twenty-fifth anniversary of Kansas' statehood. Evans, Joe Engle, and Steven Hawley were all to be honored the day before at festivities. Engle and Hawley, who were space shuttle astronauts, were called back to Houston an hour after the accident.

◆ Life is a series of contrasting emotions, and yesterday, we came to realize how quickly excitement and joy can turn to shock and horror. What began as a historic event, the first teacher in space, ended as a historic tragedy—the worst disaster in our space program.

As with other tragedies this nation has experienced, we were united through our sense of disbelief, our grief, and our concern for the families of the seven crew members aboard the *Challenger.*

Today, we have an opportunity, through this service, to publicly mourn our loss. And it is a shared loss because we take pride in our nation's accomplishments, and we all admire the courage of those who are willing to chart new paths in space.

Here in Kansas, we were more deeply touched by the tragedy. We feel a part of the space program through giving it three of our native sons. Yesterday was to be a day to recognize our three Kansas space pioneers. Instead, it became a day to mourn the loss of seven others.

And it is appropriate that we take time to mourn. In a sense, our doing so motivates us to live life more fully. Yesterday's accident once again showed us how fragile and tentative life is. In a split second our dreams, ambitions, plans for contributions to society can all be ended. We are all mortal. Death does not stop because of the importance or significance of who we are or what we do.

And even with all of our modern technology, multiple backup systems, and sense of security, we cannot stop the hand of providence. So it is important that we concentrate on life during this period of mourning. All ventures have risks. Some more severe than others. But we should not let tragedy deter us from taking risks.

The pioneers who came west to Kansas did so with the knowledge they might not survive. The trails were dotted with the graves of those who did not succeed in their quest. But even with that grim reminder, others persisted and did settle this land.

The same must happen with the space program and with other new programs. We cannot let failure or tragedy deter us from our goals. We cannot let death prevent us from living. A Kansas-born poet, Edgar Lee Masters, once wrote that "you have to live life to love life."

We can take comfort in the pictures and video tapes of the smiling, expectant faces of the *Challenger* crew and know that they loved life. They loved what they were experiencing and were anticipating. They lived life fully up until the second it ended. Let us use this tragedy as a means of committing ourselves to do the same. In doing so, we will best serve their memories.

As a nation, we will again use tragedy to remind us of our common heritage. We will rely upon our faith to sustain us as it has in the past. And through that faith, we will look to the future and ensure that the work left undone by those who were taken from us will indeed be done. ◆

On Individualism and Community

Gary Lillian wrote this speech as an original oration for high school speech contests.

A student at Shawnee Mission West High School, Lillian took the speech to the National Forensic League National Speech Tournament. The speech is the national award winner from 1974. Read the speech and see how applicable it is today.

◆ Let us begin by taking some time to compile a list. At the top of that list, imagine, if you will, the name of your doctor . . . and right beside that place the first name of his or her spouse.

If you have any school age children, select one of them and picture the name of the child's teacher right below your doctor's name. If the teacher has any children, then think of their names also, and their ages if you remember them . . .

Now think of the place that you most often go to purchase your groceries, and at the bottom of the list put the grocer's name and where he or she lives . . .

Is that list just a little vague? Perhaps a bit more than vague? That is the case for the majority of us who have lost touch with the other members of our community.

There once was a time, when we lived on a smaller scale in towns and villages, that we all knew one another and rendered services to each other. Neighbors, friends, and family were often one and the same. There wasn't much choice. We lived, worked, and died among a small number of faces. We were born into a community and belonged.

As the population grew and we spread out on the land and clustered into any one of our vast American metropolises, goods and services came to be offered to the community by people detached from it. The grocers, the doctors, and the teachers of our children became less and less known to us. They were no longer of our community; they were for it. Now we face a time in which we are drawing physically closer together, but drifting toward an extreme form of individualism and privatization of social behavior which is making strangers of us, and rather than seek the paths that might unite us, we pursue the very ones that keep us separate. Three of them in particular—mobility, privacy, and individuality—have come to be the very sources of our lack of community.

Individualism, which has played a most crucial role in cutting us off from one another, was conceived as our society underwent a combination of rapid social changes coupled with a growing sense of diversity which developed the belief that we should pursue anonymously our own destinies, that we should be less aware of the social consequences of our behavior, and that we have even less concern that anyone cares how we act.

There are very few cultures which exalt privacy as does ours. The Japanese and the Arabs have not even a word for privacy. We not only have the word prominently placed between *prius* and *privado* in Mr. Webster's famous work, but have found it necessary to develop a word of ever greater intensity, *isolation,* an intentional self-withdrawal. Eventually, this withdrawal becomes habitual, and we lose the ability to let others inside our secluded world. What begins as a normal state of concern for our privacy, soon resembles a pathological state.

Our mobility more than anything else has come to sever the relationships between us and serves to breed what is emerging as a race of American nomads. In this century we have witnessed a 25 percent increase in the number of people living in a state other than the one in which they were born. With forty million Americans changing their home addresses at least once each year, we render ourselves highly vulnerable to social decay. For a community is a network of social relationships, and not just a geographical location, coming and going at a high rate may leave the physical environment of the community reasonably intact, but the personal environment collapses into disarray, and leaves the nation a fragmented society.

When caught up in highly mobile community isolated by privacy, and obsessed with individualism, the experience most often has a predictable impact upon our lifestyles. George Hormans, Harvard sociologist, has foreseen

that if our community is shattered and we fail to find another with which we can comfortably relate, we will develop disorders in thought, feeling, and behavior. A cycle is created as the loss of group membership in one generation makes us less capable of it in the next. This will leave us as well as our children alone and discontented.

Remember how neighborhoods used to be when neighbors really knew one another and friendliness was a way of life? A recent study of a group of Michigan suburbanites gives us reason to believe that this type of warmth may have been replaced. They define a good neighbor as one who is available for emergency aid; lends and can be loaned to; respects privacy; and is friendly, but not friends. Although this definition was formulated in Michigan, it finds application in New Jersey where an insurance executive apparently killed his wife, three children, and mother-in-law, then left the bodies in their $90,000 suburban home. No neighbor noticed anything amiss until the newspapers started piling up on the porch and the lights burned out over a month's time.

We would like so much to see a return to the more intimate sense of community that we once knew. As a result we often fall victim to insincere attempts by American enterprise to turn our yearning for community into dollars and cents. Their efforts have been so successful that I find it difficult to decide who loves me more, my local Shakey's Pizza Parlor or Howard Johnson's. Howard Johnson's recently conducted a campaign entitled "Howard Johnson's Loves You," complete with birthday clubs, Monday chicken fries, and Wednesday fish fries. Now Shakey's Pizza Parlor has rushed in asking "How Much Do We Love You? Enough To Give You $1.00 Off On Any Family-Sized Pizza."

But the qualities found in a mass marketed community are hardly those of a true community, for that requires elements that neither Shakey's nor Howard Johnson's can begin to offer—like a natural setting in which individuals achieve personal recognition, a group with whom to share experiences, and a place to develop enduring friendships which can contribute greatly to our self-respect and provide us with opportunities for self-fulfillment.

These, the essentials of community, we find so much lacking today, for our reasons for being together and our ways of knowing each other have declined to where they may be considered negligible. At the same time our human need for community has remained constant. The dilemma is obvious, the solution clear. You and I must make the humbling admission: I need community and I'm willing to make some sacrifices for it. They begin with our individualism, without it we have conformity. To say that we can have community without conformity is to make community that much more difficult to achieve. In this way community requires the sacrifice of part of our individuality; it means accepting the group's purpose in place of our own.

There is an inescapable relationship between privacy and community. Any of us setting out to reestablish community must anticipate that relationship and deal with it. Being in a community does little to make life more private; it takes away some of our privacy and exchanges it for the warmth of group membership. If it is community membership that we desire, then it is privacy which must be forfeited.

Mobility was once a product of economic necessity; it appears now as an alternative to commitment within a community. We have a great fear of commitment and move on in order to avoid it. As long as we seek community, that cannot be tolerated. For community is synonymous with commitment and that means a willingness to stay through friction, to work on problems when they occur, and to accept no alternatives.

The challenge before us is the delicate one of striking the right balance between community and our personal freedoms of individualism, privacy, and mobility that will do justice to us both as individuals and community members. The right combination will provide us with a special place that we can think of as our own, a living environment that we can seek to improve, and one with which we can come to feel a personal pride. To begin, each of us must take that first terrifying step; say even to one other person—"I need you." Once accomplished, it's amazing to see how many others turn out just to have been waiting their turn. Then community begins. ◆

Speech before the Virginia Convention

Patrick Henry gave many important speeches, but his "Speech before the Virginia Convention" is his most famous. In it Henry argued powerfully for preparation for a war that he thought was inevitable. His most famous words, "Give me liberty, or give me death!" remind us of the emotion of the speech. As in so many other cases, the speaker and the audience did not know that this speech would go down in history. This speech is not the precise speech Henry gave. It is compiled from the memories of those who were there who heard the speech and were moved by it.

◆ Mr. President:

No man thinks more highly than I do of the patriotism, as well as abilities, of the very worthy gentlemen who have just addressed the House. But different men often see the same subject in different lights; and, therefore, I hope it will not be thought disrespectful to those gentlemen if, entertaining as I do opinions of a character very opposite to theirs, I shall speak forth my sentiments freely and without reserve. This is no time for ceremony. The question before the House is one of awful moment to this country. For my own part, I consider it as nothing less than a question of freedom or slavery; and in proportion to the magnitude of the subject ought to be the freedom of the debate. It is only in this way that we can hope to arrive at truth, and fulfill the great responsibility which we hold to God and our country. Should I keep back my opinions at such a time, through fear of giving offense, I should consider myself as guilty of treason towards my country, and of an act of disloyalty toward the Majesty of Heaven, which I revere about all earthly kings.

Mr. President, it is natural to man to indulge in the illusions of hope. We are apt to shut our eyes against a painful truth, and listen to the song of that siren till she transforms us into beasts. Is this the part of wise men, engaged in a great and arduous struggle for liberty? Are we disposed to be of the number of those who, having eyes, see not, and, having ears, hear not, the things which so nearly concern their temporal salvation? For my part, whatever anguish of spirit it may cost, I am willing to know the whole truth; to know the worst, and to provide for it.

I have but one lamp by which my feet are guided, and that is the lamp of experience. I know of no way of judging of the future but by the past. And judging by the past, I wish to know what there has been in the conduct of the British ministry for the last ten years to justify those hopes with which gentlemen have been pleased to solace themselves and the House. Is it that insidious smile with which our petition has been lately received? Trust it not, sir; it will prove a snare to your feet. Suffer not yourselves to be betrayed with a kiss. Ask yourselves how this gracious reception of our petition comports with those warlike preparations which cover our waters and darken our land. Are fleets and armies necessary to a work of love and reconciliation? Have we shown ourselves so unwilling to be reconciled that force must be called in to win back our love? Let us not deceive ourselves, sir. These are the implements of war and subjugation; the last arguments to which kings resort. I ask gentlemen, sir, what means this martial array, if its purpose be not to force us to submission? Can gentlemen assign any other possible motive for it? Has Great Britain any enemy, in this quarter of the world, to call for all this accumulation of navies and armies? No, sir, she has none. They are meant for us: they can be meant for no other. They are sent over to bind and rivet upon us those chains which the British ministry have been so long forging. And what have we to oppose to them? Shall we try argument? Sir, we have been trying that for the last ten years. Have we anything new to offer upon the subject? Nothing. We have held

the subject up in every light of which it is capable; but it has been all in vain. Shall we resort to entreaty and humble supplication? What terms shall we find which have not been already exhausted? Let us not, I beseech you, sir, deceive ourselves longer. Sir, we have done everything that could be done to avert the storm which is now coming on. We have petitioned; we have remonstrated; we have supplicated; we have prostrated ourselves before the throne, and have implored its interposition to arrest the tyrannical hands of the ministry and Parliament. Our petitions have been slighted; our remonstrances have produced additional violence and insult; our supplications have been disregarded; and we have been spurned, with contempt, from the foot of the throne! In vain, after these things, may we indulge the fond hope of peace and reconciliation. There is no longer any room for hope. If we wish to be free—if we mean to preserve inviolate those inestimable privileges for which we have been so long contending— if we mean not basely to abandon the noble struggle in which we have been so long engaged, and which we have pledged ourselves never to abandon until the glorious object of our contest shall be obtained—we must fight! I repeat it, sir, we must fight! An appeal to arms and to the God of Hosts is all that is left us!

They tell us, sir, that we are weak; unable to cope with so formidable an adversary. But when shall we be stronger? Will it be the next week, or the next year? Will it be when we are totally disarmed, and when a British guard shall be stationed in every house? Shall we gather strength by irresolution and inaction? Shall we acquire the means of effectual resistance by lying supinely on our backs and hugging the delusive phantom of hope, until our enemies shall have bound us hand and foot? Sir, we are not weak if we make a proper use of those means which the God of nature hath placed in our power. Three millions of people, armed in the holy cause of liberty, and in such a country as that which we possess, are invincible by any force which our enemy can send against us. Besides, sir, we shall not fight our battles alone. There is a just God who presides over the destinies of nations, and who will raise up friends to fight our battles for us. The battle, sir, is not to the strong alone; it is to the vigilant, the active, the brave. Besides, sir, we have no election. If we were base enough to desire it, it is now too late to retire from the contest. There is no retreat but in submission and slavery! Our chains are forged! Their clanking may be heard on the plains of Boston! The war is inevitable—and let it come! I repeat it, sir, let it come.

It is in vain, sir, to extenuate the matter. Gentlemen may cry, Peace, Peace—but there is no peace. The war is actually begun! The next gale that sweeps from the north will bring to our ears the clash of resounding arms! Our brethren are already in the field! Why stand we here idle? What is it that gentlemen wish? What would they have? Is life so dear, or peace so sweet, as to be purchased at the price of chains and slavery? Forbid it, Almighty God! I know not what course others may take; but as for me, give me liberty or give me death! ◆

Economics 101

This speech by **Steve Dvorske,** a student at Shawnee Mission West High School, Shawnee Mission, Kansas, placed eighth at the National Forensic League National Tournament in 1986.

◆   This is Economics 101, a class that won't be found in the course description books of universities like Harvard, Yale, or even Princeton. In fact, you are lucky to have at your disposal a class not taught by some bald headed professor but by me, one that has no textbooks, but employs field study in such places as supermarkets, motels, and restaurants, a class that teaches the modern techniques of how to get things for free. Don't worry about failing for you have what it takes to pass, you're American. Economics 101 commences today, and as a graduate, you will be a bachelor in the art of getting something for nothing.

Getting something for nothing is a real desire in most Americans. Essentially, there is nothing

wrong with what Economics 101 teaches, but getting something for nothing doesn't always stop where the free trial offers do. Economics 101 has demonstrated an attitude that has set us searching for the complimentary where it sometimes wasn't meant to be found. Barbara Cashion, a professor of sociology at Georgetown University, demonstrated that it is man's natural inclination to avoid paying in situations where one can have someone else bear the cost. It is the phenomenon known as the free rider approach.

To Americans, free is a beautiful word. It not only describes our country, but it means we are getting something for nothing. In our society, nothing brightens our day more than getting our hands on a freebee or two, an after dinner mint, a free sample at the supermarket, or the quintessential freebee, the complimentary drink. We appear thrifty because of it and we are.

Unfortunately, we've gone so far in our search to get something for nothing that it doesn't matter what we get as long as it's free. So important is the free bag of peanuts or deck of cards on an airplane that it doesn't matter to us if we hate peanuts or never play cards. As long as it's free, we will devise ingenious ways of getting another freebee, whether it be asking a different stewardess or putting on dark glasses and going through the line again. We just don't seem to be happy unless we get off the plane with six bags of peanuts, three decks of cards, two motion sickness bags, and one "what to do in the case of an emergency" pamphlet.

Yet, Economics 101 doesn't stop with the end of an airplane flight. We take what we've learned and apply it to other areas. We begin to take little things—towels, pens, ashtrays, sugar packets, and make them free. Things that weren't intended to be complimentary but are made complimentary.

Motel towels really don't look that good in our pastel colored bathrooms, but they serve the purpose and so we cart them home. The *Los Angeles Times* reported that a motel chain recently lost $3 million in replacing towels alone. However, towels aren't the only things disappearing in motels. The owners have had to establish security measures to save the small items in the rooms. To keep the clothes hangers in the room is why you can't take them off the rack, to keep the televisions in the room is why they are bolted to the stand which is in turn attached to the floor, and to keep the pictures in the room is why they're bolted to the wall.

Restaurants, too, are losing a lot of items to the graduates of Economics 101. *Time* magazine reports that it is not just ashtrays, but about everything "à la cartable"—from cups and dishes to rolls and crackers. Larry Buckmaster, executive director of the Chicago and Illinois Restaurant Association states, "Restaurants are having to order twice as much sugar as they did a year ago." When we leave the restaurant, we have more sugar in our pockets than food in our stomachs. It may not be that America has rediscovered its sweet tooth, but the sugar is complimentary, isn't it?

The minor items that no one cares or worries about losing are becoming bigger and better. Roadsigns are wonderful devices for decorating rooms, and magically they are placed conveniently alongside of the road for our taking. When gangster Sam Giancana told the press, "Whatever isn't nailed down is mine, and whatever I can pry up isn't nailed down," it seems that he wasn't speaking solely for himself.

Economics 101 has allowed us to carry the get-something-for-nothing attitude from a roadsign to telephone credit cards. AT&T reports that illegal credit card use alone accounted for $71 million worth of fraudulent calls in the first nine months of 1983. Yet, Ma Bell has been charging us sky-high rates ever since Alexander Graham Bell was around. It seems only fair to get something free from her. Jane Landenberger doesn't think it's fair. Last February, the students of Economics 101 received an assignment: acquire her phone credit card number and get something free from her. That month her New York phone bill was delivered by United Parcel Services in a twenty-pound package. It consisted of 2,578 pages containing 17,000 phone calls to such places as Asia and Africa. Her bill was for $109,504.86. After weeks of hassle, she

received a phone bill made up of just the calls she herself had placed. It was for $47.03.

Economics 101's attitude has taken us beyond the complimentary gifts and into our relationships with others, where once again we attempt to get something for nothing, only this time we attempt to get it from people. Readily accepting our friends' love, appreciation, and material gifts we give nothing in return. Webster's defines friend as "a person attached to another by affection." Economics 101 is allowing us to define friend as someone who is willing and able to buy us lunch. Yet, there is no such thing as a free lunch. When we fail to give of ourselves to others, when we attempt to get something for nothing from people, when we let the attitude of Economics 101 rule our lives, we lose the one thing we all desperately need—a friend.

With all the items that Economics 101 addresses, it fails to take into account logic. Our own desire to get something for nothing makes it easy to ace the class. What we don't understand is that getting something for nothing is a fallacy. Nothing is free unless it was meant to be free. If you get something for nothing, then someone else gets nothing for something. Someone has to pay the motels' $3 million towel expense and AT&T's $71 million loss. And who's going to pay for Jane Landenberger's $109,000 phone bill?

It's difficult to fail Economics 101 and be wrong. There is nothing wrong with free things as long as they are meant to be free. We must, however, recognize what is free and what isn't, what can be taken, and what must be bought. It isn't easy to stop grabbing all that can be grabbed, but it must be done. For if we don't, we will end up like the boy in Aesop's fable who has his hand stuck in the candy jar. Removing it is so simple—let some candy go—but doing it is so difficult.

The best way to break the attitude of getting something for nothing is to stop taking and start giving. Giving is better than receiving though it is contrary to popular belief. Perhaps writer Leroy Browalor says it best, "If you have a message you can say it with a gift, and it will keep on speaking unless you prove unkind. Remember—the gift and the giver belong together. The highest type of giving is being and remaining the better part of what you gave."

It is hard to stop taking, but it must be done. What makes a person good isn't the things they receive from others, but the things they give. William Wordsworth said, "Giving is the best portion of a good man's life." With all that Economics 101 has taught us, it still cannot deny the words of Ralph Waldo Emerson, "To have a friend, one must be a friend." To be a friend, we must extend our hand when others fold theirs.

Though a towel, or a roadsign, or one free telephone call isn't the end of the world, it is an attitude that can build until we believe life is a success only when we are getting something for nothing. It isn't, though; in fact, the purpose of life is not to leave Economics 101 with an after-dinner mint or a "what to do in the case of a plane crash" pamphlet, but the purpose is in the words of William Osler, "Not to get what we can from life, but to add what we can to it." And that is not getting something for nothing. ◆

The Future of South Africa

Nelson Mandela, Deputy President of the African National Congress (ANC) in South Africa, presented this speech to a joint session of the United States Congress on 26 June 1990. Mandela's role in the anti-apartheid ANC resulted in several arrests and trials for treason. He was sentenced to life imprisonment in 1964, but was released in April 1990 as the political climate in South Africa began to change. This speech, an appeal for support for antiapartheid efforts, was only the third given to Congress by a private citizen. As you read the speech notice Mandela's use of language that is filled with vivid images.

◆ Mr. Speaker, Mr. President, esteemed Members of the United States Congress, Your Excellencies, Ambassadors, and members of the diplomatic corps, distinguished guests, ladies and gentlemen, it is a fact of the human condition that it shall, like a meteor, a mere brief passing moment in time and space, fleet across the human stage and pass out of existence. Even the golden lads and lasses, as much as the chimney sweepers, come, and tomorrow are no more. After them all they leave the people enduring, multiplying, permanent, except to the extent that the same humanity might abuse its own genius to emulate life itself.

And so we have come to Washington, in the District of Columbia, and into these hallowed chambers of the United States Congress, not as pretenders to greatness, but as a particle of a people whom we know to be noble and heroic, enduring, multiplying, permanent, rejoicing in the expectation and knowledge that their humanity will be reaffirmed and enlarged by open and unfettered communion with the nations of the world.

We have come here to tell you, and through you, your own people, who are equally noble and heroic, of the troubles and trials, the fond hopes and aspirations of the people from whom we originate.

We believe that we know it as a fact that your kind and moving invitation to ask [us] to speak here derived from your own desire to convey a message to our people. And according to your humane purposes, to give them an opportunity to say what they want of you, and what they want to make of their relationship with you.

Our people demand democracy. Our country, which continues to bleed and suffer pain, needs democracy. It cries out for the situation where the law will decree that freedom to speak of freedom constitutes the very essence of legality, and the very thing that makes for the legitimacy of the constitutional order.

It stands for the situation where those who are entitled by law to carry arms as the forces of national security and law and order, will not turn their weapons against the citizens simply because the citizens assert that equality, liberty, and the pursuit of happiness are fundamental human rights which are not only inalienable, but must if necessary be defended with the weapons of war.

We fight for and visualize a future in which all shall without regard to race, color, creed or sex have their right to vote and to be voted into all elective organs of state. We are engaged in struggle to ensure that the rights of every individual are guaranteed and protected through a democratic constitution, the rule of law, an entrenched bill of rights, which shall be enforced by an independent judiciary as well as a multi-party political system.

Mr. Speaker, we are acutely conscious of the fact that we are addressing an historic institution for whose creation and integrity many men and women lost their lives in the war of independence, the civil war, and the war against Nazism and fascism. That very history demands that we address you with respect and candor, and without any attempt to dissemble. What we have said concerning the political arrangements we seek for our country is seriously meant. It is an outcome for which many of us went to prison, for which many have died in police cells, on the gallows, in our towns and villages, and in the countries of southern Africa.

Indeed, we have even had our political representatives killed in countries as far away from South Africa as France. Unhappily, our people continue to die to this day, victims of armed agents of the state who are still determined to turn their guns against the very idea of a nonracial democracy. But this is the perspective which we will trust Congress will feel happy to support and encourage, using the enormous weight of its prestige and authority as an eminent representative of democratic practice.

To deny any person their human rights is to challenge their very humanity. To impose on them a wretched life of hunger and deprivation is to dehumanize them, but such has been the terrible fate of all black persons in our country under the system of apartheid. The extent of the deprivation of millions of people has to be seen to be believed.

The injury is made that more intolerable by the opulence of our white compatriots and the deliberate distortion of the economy to feed that opulence.

The process of the reconstruction of South African society must and will also entail the transformation of its economy. We need a strong and growing economy. We require an economy that is able to address the needs of all the people of our country, that can provide food, houses, education, health services, social security, and everything that makes human life human, that makes life joyful and not a protracted encounter with hopelessness and despair.

We believe that the fact of the apartheid structure of the South African economy and the enormous and pressing needs of the people make it inevitable that the democratic government will intervene in this economy. Acting through the elected parliament, we have put the matter to the business community of our country that the need for a public sector is one of the elements in a many sided strategy of economic development and restructuring. That has to be considered by us all, including the private sector.

The ANC holds no ideological positions which dictate that it must adopt a policy of nationalization. But, the ANC also holds the view that there is no self-regulating mechanism within the South African economy which will, on its own, insure growth with equity. At the same time, we take it as a given—as given—that the private sector is an engine of growth and development which is critical to the success of the mixed economy we hope to see in future—in the future South Africa.

We are accordingly committed to the creation of the situation in which business people, both South African and foreign, have confidence in the security of their investments, are assured of a fair rate of return on their capital, and do business in conditions of stability and peace.

We must also make the point, very firmly, that the political settlement and democracy itself cannot survive unless the material needs of the people, the bread and butter issue, are addressed as part of the process of change and as a matter of urgency.

It should never be that the anger of the poor should be the finger of accusation pointed at all of us because we failed to respond to the crisis of the people for food—to the cries of the people for food, for shelter, for the dignity of the individual.

We shall need your support to achieve the post-apartheid economic objectives, which are an intrinsic part of the process of the restoration of the human rights of the people of South Africa. We would like to approach the issue of our economic cooperation not as a relationship between donor and recipient, between a dependent and a benefactor. We would like to believe that there is a way in which we could structure this relationship so that we do indeed benefit from your enormous resources in terms of your capital, technology, all-around expertise, your enterprising spirit and your markets. This relationship should, however, be one from which your people should also derive benefit so that we who are fighting to liberate the very spirit of our entire people from the bondage of the arrogance of the ideology and practice of white supremacy do not build a relationship of subservient dependency and foreign ingratitude.

One of the benefits that should accrue to both our peoples and to the rest of the world should surely be that this complex South African society, which has known nothing but racism for three centuries, should be transformed into an oasis of good race relations where the black shall to the white be sister and brother, a fellow South African, an equal human being, both citizens of the world.

To destroy racism in the world, we together must expunge apartheid racism in South Africa. Justice and liberty must be our tools, prosperity and happiness our weapon.

Mr. Speaker, distinguished Representatives of the American people, you know this more than we do, that peace is its own reward. Our own fate, borne by a succession of generations that reach backwards into centuries, has been nothing but tension, conflict, and death.

In a sense, we do not know the meaning of peace, except in the imagination. But because we have not known true peace in its real meaning, because for centuries, generations have had to bury the victims of state violence, we have fought for the right to experience peace.

On the initiative of the ANC, a process towards the conclusion of a peaceful settlement has started. According to a logic dictated by our situation, we are engaged in an effort which includes the removal of obstacles to negotiations. This will be followed by a negotiated determination of the mechanism which will draw up the new constitution. This should lead to the formation of this constitution-making institution, and therefore the elaboration and adoption of a democratic constitution. Elections would then be held on the basis of this constitution, and for the first time South Africa would have a body of lawmakers which would, like yourselves, be mandated by the whole people.

Despite the admitted commitment of President de Klerk to walk this road with us, and despite our acceptance of his integrity and honesty of his purposes, we would be fools to believe that the road ahead of us is without major hurdles. Too many among our white compatriots are steeped in the ideology of racism to admit easily that change must come. Tragedy may yet sully the future we pray and work for if these slaves of the past take up arms in a desperate effort to resist the process which must lead to the democratic transformation of our country.

For those who care to worry about violence in our country, as we do, it is at these forces that they should focus their attention, a process in which we are engaged. We must contend still with the reality that South Africa is a country in the grip of the apartheid crime against humanity. The consequences of this continue to be felt, not only within our borders, but throughout Southern Africa, which continues to harvest the bitter fruits of conflict and war, especially in Mozambique and Angola. Peace will not come to our country and region until the apartheid system is ended.

Therefore, we say we still have a struggle on our hands. Our common and noble efforts to abolish the system of white minority domination must continue. We are encouraged and strengthened by the fact of the agreement between ourselves, this Congress, as well as President Bush and his administration, that sanctions should remain in place.

Sanctions should remain in place because the purpose for which they were imposed has not yet been achieved. We have yet to arrive at the point when we can say that South Africa is set on an irreversible course leading to its transformation into a united democratic and nonracial country. We plead that you cede the prerogative to the people of South Africa to determine the moment when it will be said that profound changes have occurred and an irreversible process achieved, enabling you and the rest of the international community to lift sanctions.

We would like to take this opportunity to thank you all for the principled struggle you waged which resulted in the adoption of the historic comprehensive Anti-apartheid Act, which made such a decisive contribution to the process of moving our country forward towards negotiations. We request that you go further and assist us with the material resources which will enable us to promote the peace process and meet other needs which arise from the changing situation you have helped to bring about.

The stand you took established the understanding among the millions of our people that here we have friends, here we have fighters against racism who feel hurt because we are hurt, who seek our success because they too seek the victory of democracy over tyranny. And here I speak not only about you, members of the United States Congress, but also of the millions of people throughout this great land who stood up and engaged the apartheid system in struggle, the masses who have given us such strength and joy by the manner in which they have received us since we arrived in this country.

Mr. Speaker, Mr. President, Senators and Representatives, we went to jail because it was impossible to sit still while the obscenity of the apartheid system was being imposed on our people. It would have been immoral to keep quiet while a racist tyranny sought to reduce an entire people into a status worse than that of the beasts of the forest.

It would have been an act of treason against the people and against our conscience to allow fear and the drive towards self-preservation to dominate our behavior, obliging us to absent ourselves from the struggle for democracy and human rights not only in our country, but throughout the world. We could not have made an acquaintance through literature with human giants such as George Washington, Abraham Lincoln, and Thomas Jefferson, and not been moved to act as they were moved to act.

We could not have had heard of and admired John Brown, Sojourner Truth, Frederick Douglass, W.E.B. DuBois, Marcus Garvey, Martin Luther King, Jr., and others, we could not have heard of these and not be moved to act as they were moved to act.

We could not have known of your Declaration of Independence and not elected to join in the struggle to guarantee the people's life, liberty, and the pursuit of happiness.

We are grateful to you all that you persisted in your resolve to have us and other political prisoners released from jail. You have given us the gift and privilege to rejoin our people, yourselves, and the rest of the international community in the common effort to transform South Africa into a united, a democratic, and nonracial country.

You have given us the power to join hands with all people of conscience to fight for the victory of democracy and human rights throughout the world. We are glad that you merged with our own people to make it possible for us to emerge from the darkness of the prison cell and join the contemporary process of the renewal of the world. We thank you most sincerely for all you have done, and count on you to persist in your noble endeavors to free the rest of our political prisoners and to emancipate our people from the life of prison that is apartheid South Africa.

The day may not be far when we will borrow the words of Thomas Jefferson and speak of the will of the South African nation. "In the exercise of that will, by this united nation of black and white people, it must surely be that there will be born a country on the Southern tip of Africa which you will be proud to call a friend and an ally because of its contribution to the universal striving towards liberty, human rights, prosperity, and peace among the peoples."

Let that day come now. Let us keep our arms locked together so that we form a solid phalanx against racism, to ensure that that day comes now. By our common actions, let us ensure that justice triumphs without delay. When that has come to pass, then shall we all be entitled to acknowledge the salute when others say of us, "Blessed are the peacemakers."

Thank you for your kind invitation to speak here today, and thank you for your welcome and the attention you have accorded our simple message. Thank you. ◆

The Beginning of Operation Desert Storm

On 2 August 1990, Iraq invaded Kuwait. The world reacted immediately and attempted to use diplomacy and economic sanctions to convince Saddam Hussein to leave Kuwait. On 16 January 1991, President George Bush and other world leaders determined that a military solution was necessary. The following speech was given by **George Bush** from the Oval Office at the White House to announce the beginning of Operation Desert Storm. As you read the speech, observe the way in which Bush constructed his arguments to support the action.

◆ Five months ago, Saddam Hussein started this cruel war against Kuwait. Tonight the battle has been joined.

This military action, taken in accord with United Nations resolutions and with the consent of the United States Congress, follows months of constant and virtually endless diplomatic activity on the part of the United Nations, the United States and many, many other countries.

Arab leaders sought what became known as an Arab solution, only to conclude that Saddam Hussein was unwilling to leave Kuwait. Others traveled to Baghdad in a variety of efforts to restore peace and justice. Our Secretary of State James Baker held an historic meeting in Geneva only to be totally rebuffed.

This past weekend, in a last-ditch effort, the Secretary General of the United Nations went to the Middle East with peace in his heart—his second such mission, and he came back from Baghdad with no progress at all in getting Saddam Hussein to withdraw from Kuwait.

Now, the twenty-eight countries with forces in the Gulf area have exhausted all reasonable efforts to reach a peaceful resolution, have no choice but to drive Saddam from Kuwait by force. We will not fail.

As I report to you, air attacks are under way against military targets in Iraq. We are determined to knock out Saddam Hussein's nuclear bomb potential. We will also destroy his chemical weapons facilities. Much of Saddam's artillery and tanks will be destroyed.

Our operations are designed to best protect the lives of all the coalition forces by targeting Saddam's vast military arsenal.

Initial reports from General Schwarzkopf are that our operations are proceeding according to plan.

Our objectives are clear. Saddam Hussein's forces will leave Kuwait. The legitimate government of Kuwait will be restored to its rightful place, and Kuwait will once again be free.

Iraq will eventually comply with all relevant United Nations resolutions, and then when peace is restored, it is our hope that Iraq will live as a peaceful and cooperative member of the family of nations, thus enhancing the security and stability of the Gulf.

Some may ask, "Why act now? Why not wait?" The answer is clear. The world could wait no longer.

Sanctions, though having some effect, showed no signs of accomplishing their objective. Sanctions were tried for well over five months, and we and our allies concluded that sanctions alone would not force Saddam from Kuwait.

While the world waited, Saddam Hussein systematically raped, pillaged, and plundered a tiny nation—no threat to his own. He subjected the people of Kuwait to unspeakable atrocities, and among those maimed and murdered—innocent children. While the world waited, Saddam sought to add to the chemical weapons arsenal he now possesses an infinitely more dangerous weapon of mass destruction, a nuclear weapon.

And while the world waited, while the world talked peace and withdrawal, Saddam Hussein dug in and moved massive forces into Kuwait. While the world waited, while Saddam stalled, more damage was being done to the fragile economies of the Third World, the emerging democracies of Eastern Europe, to the entire world, including to our own economy.

However, Saddam clearly felt that by stalling and threatening and defying the United Nations he could weaken the forces arrayed against him.

While the world waited, Saddam Hussein met every overture of peace with open contempt. While the world prayed for peace, Saddam prepared for war.

I had hoped that when the United States Congress, in historic debate, took its resolute action Saddam would realize he could not prevail and would move out of Kuwait in accord with the United Nations resolutions. He did not do that.

Instead, he remained intransigent, certain that time was on his side. Saddam was warned over and over again to comply with the will of the United Nations—leave Kuwait or be driven out. Saddam has arrogantly rejected all warnings. Instead, he tried to make this a dispute between Iraq and the United States of America.

Well, he failed. Tonight, twenty-eight nations, countries from five continents—Europe and Asia, Africa and the Arab League—have forces in the Gulf area standing shoulder-to-shoulder against Saddam Hussein. These countries had hoped the use of force could be avoided. Regrettably, we now believe that only force will make him leave.

Prior to ordering our forces into battle, I instructed our military commanders to take every necessary step to prevail as quickly as possible and with the greatest degree of protection possible for American and allied servicemen and women. I've told the American people before that this will not be another Vietnam.

And I repeat this here tonight. Our troops will have the best possible support in the entire world. And they will not be asked to fight with one hand tied behind their back.

I'm hopeful that this fighting will not go on for long and that casualties will be held to an absolute minimum. This is an historic moment. We have in this past year made great progress in ending the long era of conflict and Cold War. We have before us the opportunity to forge for ourselves and for future generations a new world order, a world where the rule of law, not the law of the jungle governs the conduct of nations. When we are successful, and we will be, we have a real chance at this new world order, an order in which a credible United Nations can use its peacekeeping role to fulfill the promise and vision of the U.N.'s founders.

We have no argument with the people of Iraq. Indeed, for the innocents caught in this conflict, I pray for their safety. Our goal is not the conquest of Iraq. It is the liberation of Kuwait.

It is my hope that somehow the Iraqi people can even now convince their dictator that he must lay down his arms, leave Kuwait, and let Iraq itself rejoin the family of peace-loving nations.

Thomas Paine wrote many years ago: "These are the times that try men's souls." Those well-known words are so very true today.

But even as planes of the multinational forces attack Iraq, I prefer to think of peace, not war. I am convinced not only that we will prevail, but that out of the horror of combat will come the recognition that no nation can stand against a world united, no nation will be permitted to brutally assault its neighbor.

No President can easily commit our sons and daughters to war. They are the nation's finest. Ours is an all-volunteer force, magnificently trained, highly motivated. The troops know why they're there. And listen to what they say, for they've said it better than any President or Prime Minister ever could. Listen to Hollywood Huddleston, Marine lance corporal.

He says, "Let's free these people so we can go home and be free again." And he's right. The terrible crimes and tortures committed by Saddam's henchmen against the innocent people of Kuwait are an affront to mankind and a challenge to the freedom of all.

Listen to one of our great officers out there, Marine Lieutenant General Walter Boomer. He said, "There are things worth fighting for. A world in which brutality and lawlessness are allowed to go unchecked isn't the kind of world we're going to want to live in."

Listen to Master Sergeant J. P. Kendall of the 82nd Airborne. "We're here for more than just the price of a gallon of gas. What we're doing is going to chart the future of the world for the next hundred years. It's better to deal with this guy now than five years from now."

And finally we should all sit up and listen to Jackie Jones, an Army lieutenant, when she says, "If we let him get away with this, who knows what's going to be next?" I've called upon Hollywood and Walter and J. P. and Jackie and all of their courageous comrades in arms to do what must be done.

Tonight America and the world are deeply grateful to them and to their families.

And let me say to everyone listening or watching tonight: When the troops we've sent in finish their work, I'm determined to bring them home as soon as possible. Tonight, as our forces fight, they and their families are in our prayers.

May God bless each and every one of them and the coalition forces at our side in the Gulf, and may He continue to bless our nation, the United States of America. ◆

Inaugural Address

On 20 January 1993, **William Jefferson Clinton** was sworn in as the forty-second president of the United States. Following the tradition of his predecessors, Clinton addressed the nation. Read Clinton's address and identify the parts of the speech that are consistent with the traditional expectations of a presidential inaugural.

◆ My fellow citizens, today we celebrate the mystery of American renewal. This ceremony is held in the depth of winter, but by the words we speak and the faces we show the world, we force the spring—a spring reborn in the world's oldest democracy that brings forth the vision and courage to reinvent America.

When our Founders boldly declared America's independence to the world and our purposes to the Almighty, they knew that America to endure would have to change; not change for change sake, but change to preserve America's ideals: life, liberty, the pursuit of happiness.

Though we marched to the music of our time, our mission is timeless. Each generation of Americans must define what it means to be an American.

On behalf of our nation, I salute my predecessor, President Bush, for his half-century of service to America. And I thank the millions of men and women whose steadfastness and sacrifice triumphed over depression, fascism, and communism.

Today, a generation raised in the shadows of the Cold War assumes new responsibilities in a world warmed by the sunshine of freedom, but threatened still by ancient hatreds and new plagues. Raised in unrivaled prosperity, we inherit an economy that is still the world's strongest, but is weakened by business failures, stagnant wages, increasing inequality, and deep divisions among our own people.

When George Washington first took the oath I have just sworn to uphold, news traveled slowly across the land by horseback and across the ocean by boat. Now, the sights and sounds of this ceremony are broadcast instantaneously to billions around the world. Communications and commerce are global. Investment is mobile. Technology is almost magical. And ambition for a better life is now universal.

We earn our livelihood in America today in peaceful competition with people all across the Earth. Profound and powerful forces are shaking and remaking our world. And the urgent question of our time is whether we can make change our friend and not our enemy.

This new world has already enriched the lives of millions of Americans who are able to compete and win in it. But when most people are working harder for less; when others cannot work at all; when the cost of health care devastates families and threatens to bankrupt our enterprises great and small; when the fear of crime robs law-abiding citizens of their freedom; and when millions of poor children cannot even imagine the lives we are calling them to lead, we have not made change our friend.

We know we have to face hard truths and take strong steps, but we have not done so; instead, we have drifted. And that drifting has eroded our resources, fractured our economy, and shaken our confidence. Though our challenges are fearsome, so are our strengths. Americans have ever been a restless, questing, hopeful people. And we must bring to our task today the vision and will of those who came before us.

From our Revolution to the Civil War, to the Great Depression, to the Civil Rights Movement, our people have always mustered the determination to construct from these crises the pillars of our history.

Thomas Jefferson believed that to preserve the very foundations of our nation, we would need dramatic change from time to time. Well, my fellow Americans, this is our time. Let us embrace it.

Our democracy must be not only the envy of the world but the engine of our own renewal. There is nothing wrong with America that cannot be cured by what is right with America. And so today we pledge an end to the era of deadlock and drift, and a new season of American renewal has begun.

To renew America we must be bold. We must do what no generation has had to do before. We must invest more in our own people, in their jobs and in their future, and at the same time cut our massive debt. And we must do so in a world in which we must compete for every opportunity. It will not be easy. It will require sacrifice, but it can be done and done fairly. Not choosing sacrifice for its own sake but for our own sake, we must provide for our nation the way a family provides for its children.

Our Founders saw themselves in the light of posterity. We can do no less. Anyone who has ever watched a child's eyes wander into sleep knows what posterity is. Posterity is the world to come—the world for whom we hold our ideals; from whom we have borrowed our planet; and to whom we bear sacred responsibility.

We must do what America does best: offer more opportunity to all and demand more responsibility from all. It is time to break the bad habit of expecting something for nothing from our government or from each other. Let us all take more responsibility not only for ourselves and our families but for our communities and our country.

To renew America, we must revitalize our democracy. This beautiful Capitol, like every capitol since the dawn of civilization, is often a place of intrigue and calculation. Powerful people maneuver for position and worry endlessly about who is in and who is out, who is up and who is down, forgetting those people whose toil and sweat sends us here and pays our way.

Americans deserve better. And in this city today there are people who want to do better. And so I say to all of you here, let us resolve to reform our politics so that power and privilege no longer shout down the voice of the people. Let us put aside personal advantage so that we can feel the pain and see the promise of America. Let us resolve to make our government a place for what Franklin Roosevelt called bold, persistent experimentation—a government for our tomorrows, not our yesterdays. Let us give this Capitol back to the people to whom it belongs.

To renew America we must meet challenges abroad as well as at home. There is no longer a clear division between what is foreign and what is domestic. The world economy, the world environment, the world AIDS crisis, the world arms race—they affect us all. Today, as an old order passes, the new world is more free but less stable. Communism's collapse has called forth old animosities and new dangers. Clearly, America must continue to lead the world we did so much to make.

While America rebuilds at home, we will not shrink from the challenges nor fail to seize the opportunities of this new world. Together with our friends and allies, we will work to shape change, lest it engulf us. When our vital interests are challenged or the will and conscience of the international community is defied, we will act—with peaceful diplomacy whenever possible, with force when necessary.

The brave Americans serving our nation today in the Persian Gulf, in Somalia, and wherever else they stand are testament to our resolve. But our greatest strength is the power of our ideas, which are still new in many lands. Across the world, we see them embraced and we rejoice. Our hopes, our hearts, our hands are with those on every continent who are building democracy and freedom. Their cause is America's cause.

The American people have summoned the change we celebrate today. You have raised your voices in an unmistakable chorus. You have cast your votes in historic numbers. And you have changed the face of Congress, the Presidency, and the political process itself. Yes, you, my fellow Americans, have forced the spring.

Now, we must do the work the season demands. To that work, I now turn with all the authority of my office. I ask the Congress to join with me. But no President, no Congress, no government can undertake this mission alone.

My fellow Americans, you, too, must play your part in our renewal. I challenge a new generation of young Americans to a season of service; to act on your idealism by helping troubled children; keeping company with those in need; reconnecting our torn communities. There is so much to be done—enough, indeed, for millions of others who are still young in spirit to give of themselves in service, too.

In serving, we recognize a simple, but powerful truth. We need each other, and we must care for one another. Today, we do more than celebrate America. We rededicate ourselves to the very idea of America, an idea born in revolution and renewed through two centuries of challenge; an idea tempered by the knowledge that, but for fate, we, the fortunate, and the unfortunate, might have been each other; an idea ennobled by the faith that our nation can summon from its myriad diversity the deepest measure of unity; an idea infused with the conviction that America's long, heroic journey must go forever upward.

And, so, my fellow Americans, as we stand at the edge of the twenty-first century, let us begin anew with energy and hope, with faith and discipline. And let us work until our work is done. The Scripture says, "and let us not be weary in well-doing, for in due season we shall reap if we faint not." From this joyful mountaintop of celebration we hear a call to service in the valley. We have heard the trumpets. We have changed the guard. And now each in our own way, and with God's help, we must answer the call.

Thank you and God bless you all. ◆

Forging an Identity and a Future

This commencement address by **Hillary Rodham Clinton** was given during the 1992 presidential campaign. In 1969, Hillary Rodham was the first student commencement speaker at Wellesley College.

The introduction of Clinton included references to the changes her class made at the college and to her accomplishments since graduation. The introduction also mentioned that she hosted numerous tea parties at the Governor's Mansion in Little Rock for potential Wellesley students. Clinton makes reference to the tea parties in her preliminary remarks. Why are the reference to the tea parties and a later one to baking cookies important to the context of the speech? Ask someone who remembers the 1992 campaign if you do not know.

◆ Thank you. That is absolutely true about all those teas, and I'm glad to have that on the public record. I must say, though, that sitting there listening to the recitation of what my class and those on both sides were responsible for was a little unsettling. But probably the only thing I would revisit, as the mother of a twelve-year-old daughter—the parental rules.

This is, as Nan says, the second chance for me to speak from this podium. The first was twenty-three years ago, when I was a graduating senior. My classmates did select me to speak, and I tried to speak for them. I can't claim that 1969 speech as my own; it reflected the hopes, values, and aspirations of my classmates. It was full of the uncompromising language you only write when you are twenty-one. But it is uncanny, to me, the degree to which those same hopes, values, and aspirations have shaped my adulthood.

We passionately rejected the notion of limitations on our abilities to make the world a better place. We saw a gap between our expectations and realities, and we were inspired, in large part by our Wellesley educations, to bridge that gap. On behalf of the class of 1969, I said then that, "The challenge now is to practice politics as the art of making what appears to be impossible, possible." That is still the challenge of politics, especially in today's far more cynical climate.

The aspiration I referred to then was "the struggle for an integrated life . . . in an atmos-

phere of . . . trust and respect." What I meant by that was a life that combines personal fulfillment in love and work with fulfilling responsibility to the larger community.

Now when the ceremonies and hoopla of my graduation were over, I commenced my adult life by heading straight for the lake. In those days, and probably still now, swimming in the lake, except at the beach and certain times, was prohibited. But it was one of my favorite rules to break. I stripped down to my swimsuit, put my clothes in a pile on the ground, took off those coke-bottle glasses that you've now seen in a hundred pictures in publications from one end of this country to the next, and waded in off Tupelo Point. While I was happily paddling around, feeling relieved, as Emily must as well, that I had survived the day, a security guard came by on his grounds, picked up my clothes and my glasses, and carried them off. Imagine my surprise when I emerged to find neither clothes nor glasses, and blind as a bat, had to feel my way back to Stone Davis. I am just so grateful that picture hasn't come back to haunt me. Because you can imagine the captions: Maybe, "Girl offers vision to classmates and then loses her own." Or better still, the tabloids might have run something like: "Girl swimming, blinded by aliens after seeing Elvis."

Well, while medical technology has allowed me to replace those glasses with contact lenses, I hope my vision today is clearer for another reason: the clarifying perspective of experience. The opportunity to share that experience with you, the honored graduates of the class of 1992, is not only a privilege but a homecoming for me. And I want to be somewhat personal. Wellesley nurtured and challenged and guided me; it instilled in me not just knowledge, but a reserve of sustaining values. I also made friends who are still among my closest friends today.

When I arrived as a freshman in 1965 from my "Ozzie and Harriet" suburb of Chicago, both the college and the country were going through a period of rapid, sometimes tumultuous change. My classmates and I felt challenged and, in turn, did challenge, from the moment we arrived everything about the college. Nothing was taken for granted. We couldn't even agree on an appropriate, politically correct cheer. To this day when we attend reunions, you can hear us cry: "1-9-6-9 Wellesley Rah, one more year, still no cheer."

But you know there often seemed little to cheer about in those days. We grew up in a decade dominated by dreams and disillusionments. Dreams of the civil rights movement, the Peace Corps, the space program. Disillusionments starting with President Kennedy's assassination, accelerated by the divisive war in Vietnam, and the deadly mixture of poverty, racism, and despair that burst into flames in the hearts of some our cities then and which is still burning today. A decade when speeches like "I Have a Dream" were followed by songs like "The Day the Music Died."

I was here on campus when Martin Luther King was murdered. My friends and I put on black armbands and went into Boston to march in anger and pain—feeling as many of you did after the acquittals in the Rodney King case. Much has changed in those intervening years— and much of it for the better—but much has also stayed the same, or at least not changed as much as we had hoped or as irrevocably.

Each new generation takes us into new territory. But while change is certain, progress is not. Change is a law of nature; progress is the challenge for both a life and a society. And what better place to speak about those challenges, particularly to women, and the challenge of leading an integrated life, than here at Wellesley, a college that not only vindicates the proposition that there is still an essential place for an all-women's college, but which defines its mission as seeking "to educate women who will make a difference in the world."

And what better time to speak about women and their concerns than in the spring of 1992. I have traveled all over America in the last months, talking and listening to women. Women who are struggling to raise their children and somehow make ends meet. Women who are battling against the persistent discrimination that still limits their opportunities for pay and promotion; women who are bumping up against the glass ceiling; who are watching the insurance premiums on themselves and their families increase; who are coping with inadequate or nonexistent child support payments after divorces which lead to precipitous drops in their standards of living. Women who are existing on shrinking welfare payments with no available jobs in sight. And women who are anguishing over the prospect that abortions will be criminalized again.

These women and their voices are there to be heard and seen and listened to by any of us. I've also talked with women about our shared values, about our common desire to educate our children, to be sure they do receive the health care they need, to protect them from the escalating violence in our streets. To wonder how we ever got to a position in our country where we have children in schools that do bullet drills instead of fire drills.

Worrying about children is something women do, and that mothers are particularly good at doing. Women who pack their children's lunch for school, who take the early bus to work, or stay out late for a PTA meeting or spend every spare minute tending to their aging parents do not need lectures from Washington about values. They don't need to hear about an idealized world that never was as righteous or carefree as some would like to think.

They, and we, need understanding and a helping hand to solve our own problems. Because most of us are doing the best we can to find whatever that right balance is for our own lives. For me, the elements of that balance are family, work, and service.

First, your personal relationships. When all is said and done, it is the people in your life, the friendships you form, and the commitments you maintain that give shape to that life. Your friends and your neighbors, the people at work, at church, wherever you come into contact with them, all who touch your daily lives. And if you choose, a marriage filled with love and respect. When I stood here before, I could never have predicted—let alone believed—that I would fall in love with someone named Bill Clinton, who grew up in the same town as Nan (that circle,

Emily, really is smaller than we think) and that I would follow my heart to a place called Arkansas. But I have to tell you, based on the years that stand between you and me, I'm very glad I had the courage to make that choice.

Second, your work. For some of you, that may overlap with your contribution to your community. For some of you, the future might not include work outside the home (and I don't mean involuntary unemployment) but most of you will at some point in your life work for pay, in jobs that used to be off-limits for women or for those that are still the backbone of the kind of nurturing and caring professions that are so important. You may choose to be a corporate executive or a rocket scientist, you may run for public office, you may choose to stay home and raise your children—but now you can make any or all of those choices and they can be the work of your life.

And the third element for me, and I hope for you, of that integrated life I alluded to all those years ago, is service. As students, we debated passionately what responsibility each individual has for the larger society. We went back and forth on just what our college's Latin motto meant: "Not to be ministered unto, but to minister."

The most eloquent explanation I have found of what I believe now and what I argued then is from Vaclav Havel, the playwright and first freely-elected President of Czechoslovakia. In a letter from prison to his wife, Olga, he wrote: "Everything meaningful in life is distinguished by a certain transcendence of individual human existence—beyond the limits of mere self-care—toward other people, toward society, toward the world. . . . Only by looking outward, by caring for things that, in terms of pure survival, you needn't bother with at all . . . and by throwing yourself over and over again into the tumult of the world, with the intention of making your voice count—only thus will you really become a person."

I first recognized what service I cared most about while I was in law school where I worked with children at the Yale New Haven Hospital and the Child Study Center and represented children through legal services. And where during my first summer I worked for the Children's Defense Fund. My experiences gave voice for me to deep feelings about what children deserved from their families and their government. I discovered that I wanted my voice to count for children.

Some of you may have already had such a life-shaping experience: the arts, the environment, other human rights issues, whatever it might be. For many of you it lies ahead. But recognize it and nurture it when it occurs.

Because my concern is making children count, I hope you will indulge me while I tell you why. The American Dream is an intergenerational compact. Or, as someone once said, one generation is supposed to leave the key under the mat for the next. We repay our parents for their love in the love we give children. And we repay our society for the opportunities we are given by expanding the opportunities given to others. That's the way it's supposed to work. You know too well that it is not. Too many of our children are being impoverished financially, socially, and spiritually. The shrinking of their futures ultimately diminishes us all. Whether you end up having children of your own or not, I hope each of you will recognize the need for a sensible national family policy that reverses the absolutely unforgivable neglect of our children in this country this year. If you have children, you will owe the highest duty to them and will confront your biggest challenges as parents.

If, like me at your age, you now know little (and maybe care less) about the mysteries of good parenting, I can promise you there is nothing like on-the-job training. I remember one very long night when my daughter, Chelsea, was about four weeks old and crying inconsolably. Nothing from my courses in my political science major seemed to help at all. Finally, I looked at her in my arms and I said, "Chelsea, you've never been a baby before, and I've never been a mother before; we are just going to have to help each other get through this."

And so far, we have. For Bill and me, she has

been the great joy of our life. And watching her grow and flourish has given even greater urgency to the task of helping all children. There are many ways of helping children. You can do it through your own personal lives by being dedicated, loving parents. You can do it in medicine or in music, social work or education, business or government service. You can do it by making policy or making cookies.

It is, though, a false choice to tell women—or men for that matter—that we must choose between caring for ourselves and our own families or caring for the larger family of humanity. In their recent Pastoral Letter, "Putting Children and Families First," the National Conference of Catholic Bishops captured this essential interplay of private and public roles: "No government can love a child and no policy can substitute for a family's care," but, "government can either support or undermine families . . . there has been an unfortunate, unnecessary, and unreal . . . polarization in discussions of how best to help families . . . the undeniable fact is that our children's future is shaped both by the values of their parents and the policies of our nation." Or, as my husband says, "Family values alone won't feed a hungry child. And material security cannot provide a moral compass. We need both."

Forty-five years ago, the biggest threat to our country came from the other side of the Iron Curtain; from the nuclear weapons that could wipe out life on our planet. While you were here at Wellesley, that threat ended. But today, our greatest threat comes not from some external Evil Empire, but from our own internal Indifferent Empire that tolerates splintered families, unparented children, embattled schools, and pervasive poverty, racism, and violence. Not for one more year can our country think of children as some asterisk on our national agenda. How we treat our children should be front and center of that agenda, or, I believe, it won't matter what else is on it. My plea is that you not only nurture the values that will determine the choices you make in your personal lives, but also insist on policies that

include those values to nurture our nation's children.

"But really Hillary," some of you may be saying to yourselves, "I've got to pay off my student loans. I can't even find a good job, let alone someone to love. How am I going to worry about the world? Our generation has fewer dreams, fewer illusions than yours."

And I hear you and millions of young women like you all over our country. As women today, you do face tough choices. And, you know, the rules are basically as follows: If you don't get married, you're abnormal. If you get married but don't have children, you're a selfish yuppie. If you get married and have children, but then go outside the home to work, you're a bad mother. If you get married and have children, but stay home, you've wasted your education. And if you don't get married, but have children and work outside the home as a fictional newscaster, you get in trouble with the Vice President. So you see, if you listen to all those people who make all those rules, you might conclude that the safest course is just to take your diploma and crawl under your bed.

But let me end by proposing an alternative. Hold onto your dreams whatever they are. Take up the challenge of forging an identity that transcends yourself. Transcend yourself, and you will find yourself. Care about something that you needn't bother with at all. Throw yourself into the world and make your voice count. Whether you make your voice count for children or for another cause, enjoy your life's journey. There is no dress rehearsal for life, and you will have to ad lib your way through every scene.

The only way to prepare is to do what you have done: get the best possible education; continue to learn from literature, scripture, and history, to understand the human experience as best you can so that you do have guideposts charting the terrain toward whatever decisions are right for you. I want you to remember this day and remember how much more you have in common with each other than with people who are trying to divide you. And I want you to stand together as you appear to me from this position: beautiful, brave, invincible. And to have a sense of celebration that you carry with you. Congratulations to each of you. Look forward and welcome the challenges ahead.

And if you'd like to meet me for a swim later, don't tell the security guards, just find me. And I hope that over the next years, you will look back on this day as a truly great opportunity that leads you to transcend and to forge an identity that is uniquely your own. Godspeed.

◆

Heroes

Katherine Menendez, a student at Topeka High School in the 1980s, presented this oration as a contest speech at tournaments in Kansas and at National Forensics League tournaments. While the speech comments on the lack of appropriate role models for youth while she was a high school student, many would make the same claim today. As you read the speech, pay particular attention to her use of examples and the support for her claims.

◆   Okay, the following thirty seconds are going to be a test. Don't get nervous. Just tell me what the following four people have in common. Ready? Okay.

Douglas MacArthur, Martin Luther King, Jr., Clark Gable, Joe DiMaggio. They are all men, true; they are all famous. What, besides their fame, do all these people have in common? These men are all the people cited by my mother and father as their heroes when they were growing up. Sadly, the youth of today aren't so sure about their idols. When most American teens are asked who they admire, they have either no idea, or they admire a character in a movie or a cartoon. Where are the MacArthurs and DiMaggios of the modern age? Where have all the heroes gone? Heroes have had a profound impact on our past and should

continue to do so in the future.

History itself is meaningless without heroes. You can tell the values of a society by the people they choose to follow. For example, the first President of the United States, George Washington, fought in some of the famous battles of the Revolutionary War and risked his life and reputation for the values he believed. He was a hero to the people of colonial America because he contained qualities important to them; qualities such as bravery and statesmanship.

Some of the more memorable heroes are those of the recent past. John F. Kennedy, Florence Nightingale, and John Wayne are some common heroes. John F. Kennedy, a former President, was admired for his youthfulness, charisma, and speaking ability. Florence Nightingale, a nurse during the Crimean War, was loved for her bravery and kindness in caring for the wounded. And, yes, even John Wayne, a movie cowboy, was admired for his ability to get the bad guy without stooping to his level. All of these are people we have heard of if not idolized at one time or another. They were all nationally known and were all good role models for our youth to follow. But, most importantly, America was not afraid to trust them. They pulled the nation together with their greatness.

This unifying force of the hero, something so commonplace in our past, is something sorely lacking from the society of the 1980s. There are few people who are admired by the entire nation. Perhaps we are afraid to trust. Sociologists have noted an absence of heroes since the late 1960s and early 1970s, around the time of such scandals as Watergate and the Vietnam War. Polls have shown that now people have a hard time finding anyone they admire, let alone find heroic. The author Sherwood Anderson put it well when he said, "Oh how Americans have wanted heroes, wanted brave, fine, simple men." In our search for brutal stark reality and absolute truth, we have killed off all our heroes. Whether on purpose or by accident, both religion and the media have taken part in the slaughter. Few people are allowed to survive as heroes in the church, and worthy people are picked apart and scrutinized by the media until their heroic pedestal comes crashing to the ground. The heroes of the past have left, taking with them the unity they brought to the nation.

Perhaps the worst part of this new lack of heroes, we have replaced formerly good role models with bad ones. Some of the people most admired by Americans today are hardly people for us to follow. Start with television. For example, Sonny Crockett, the suave detective on *Miami Vice*. Around 80 percent of the time, he's shown waving his gun around shooting at people; the remainder is filled with him destroying entire cities, wreaking havoc with his brand new Ferrari. His actions show no concern for the enemy or the innocent bystander. He makes violence seem acceptable.

Not only is TV a major influence, but consider rock music. Some of the people most seen and heard by Americans today are rock stars. For example, Ozzy Ozzbourne is known for eating live bats on stage and throwing squirming puppies in the audience to be trampled to death. His actions make violence and abusiveness seem acceptable. And yet his records are bought and listened to by people across the nation.

A third area of misplaced idolatry is in sports figures. Most generally, children and adults admire baseball players. However, these athletes are in the news almost as much for drug use as they are for their sports achievements. College football players are notorious for breaking academic rules.

The people most admired by Americans today are bad role models for us to follow, leading us in the wrong direction, so to speak. If heroes are a mirror of the times, or, to quote a book entitled, *American Heroes,* a knothole through which to view the entire ballpark, then perhaps our society is in a sorry state. Perhaps we no longer admire unifying qualities like bravery and intelligence. The heroes of today would lead us to believe that America only admires wealth, no matter how it's obtained.

Our modern lack of heroes would also lead us to believe that we no longer need heroes. However, our confused nation occasionally stumbles onto a good idol, reminding us that these leaders will always be necessary. For example, the crew of the space shuttle, *Challenger*. Soaring and majestic—blessed with the gift of life and the ability to "slip the surly bonds of Earth and touch the face of God." Truly brave, intelligent people willing to risk their lives and reputations for the good of the nation and of scientific advancement. They were good role models for the nation, young and old alike, and with their great achievements, and their tragic deaths, they pulled the nation together for a short while. The unity they brought to us reminded us that heroes will always be vital, even in this era of modern mechanization. Why? Well, you see, we as humans need a path to follow. And this path cannot be provided by computers or robotics. We, individually, need other persons to guide our actions. On the national scale, we need heroes to give the nation unity. To quote Ken Clark, former president of the American Psychological Association, "America needs heroes. People who will exhibit sufficient leadership qualities to pull various segments of our nation together."

Not only do we need heroes to guide us and give us unity, but we need them to help us become great. Democracies, like all societies and like all individuals, need a vision of greatness if they are to recognize their potential. The Athenian poet, Aristophanes, had his chorus praise Athena, the goddess of his city state, saying, "Thou great aristocrat, make this people noble, help us to excel." If we are to succeed, we need those who are successful to tread the path to greatness.

We need to begin to rediscover achievement for America. And don't despair, for it can be done. Each of us can take steps toward reinstating the hero to his or her position of leadership. First, we should assess our own heroes, think of who we truly admire, and why, and if we find them to be good role models. We should allow them to be our heroes. Secondly, we should tell our children that a hero is a good thing to have. We, as parents, teachers, siblings and friends, should help our children choose and admire the good qualities of their own heroes. If we begin to accept heroes for today, and help our children accept them for tomorrow, then, perhaps, with time, we can reinstate the glory and pride that the heroes of the past have brought to the people. Even in this age of independence at all costs, a good role model may be hard to come by, and should not be let go. It is as simple as being willing to admire those who excel in their field.

According to John Silber, the president of Boston University, "The hero is not an ideal beyond our grasp; it is relevant and compelling to each of us." Maybe now it's finally acceptable to remember that. "Now it's okay to have heroes, we are back to yearning for leadership." I hope so. Perhaps with actions like those I have suggested, the next time you are asked who your heroes are, or next time I am asked who I truly admire, we won't have to stop and think. We will be sure. ◆

The Rhetorical Tradition

The Origins of Rhetoric

Many centuries ago, in the fifth century B.C., the land of Syracuse, a part of ancient Greece, was in turmoil. Having gone through war and revolution, the confused society struggled for order. Unfortunately, these early people did not have the records and laws that a modern culture does. Even land-ownership was in question. Relying on memory only, someone would claim all the land from one stream to the next, which may have already been claimed by someone else. Somehow, the courts of Syracuse had to determine whose claim was valid.

An Early Speech Class

The rules of the courts in Syracuse required something modern courts do not. Everyone had to present his or her own case. In other words, lawyers were not allowed. This sent people scurrying to find whoever could help them prepare their cases for the courts. Since these people of 2,500 years ago knew the importance of public speaking, they searched for those who could coach them in carefully prepared speeches to present their cases.

Recognizing the need for speech teachers, a man named Corax opened a school. He promised to teach his students how to win their court cases through careful preparation and effective presentation. Corax taught public speaking for the courtroom. Not surprisingly, his school was successful.

But there is something to be learned from this brief story of the first speech class. Without teachers like Corax, without people interested in securing justice, and without judges trained to hear them, there would have been only one way to solve the land disputes in Syracuse: war.

In modern times, people equate rhetoric with trickery. Traditionally, rhetoric is a response to conflict. Without conflict, problems, or disagreements, there would have been no need for Corax's school. But because there are always conflicts of some sort, there is a need for rhetoric. Rhetoric—and speeches you or anyone else gives—is a response to a problem. Rhetoricians try to solve problems with words.

Leaders in ancient Greece, for example, knew that a democratic form of government required them to compete for the loyalty of their citizens. Rhetoric was competing by using words. It displaced weapons as a means of settling disputes. Rhetoric was born at the same time as democracy. The two depend on each other. Rhetoric functions best in a democracy, in which individuals are free to make up their minds after hearing the issues. Democracy depends on people who come forward and speak their minds.

Early Rhetoricians

Two of Greece's greatest rhetoricians were Isocrates and Aristotle. Isocrates was the most influential rhetoric teacher in Athens, Greece, about 400 B.C. Historians say he was so dedicated to his craft that he once spent ten years preparing a speech for a special ceremony at the Olympic festival. Aristotle probably wasn't as influential as a rhetoric teacher in his own time, but much of what everyone studies in speech classes today can be traced directly back to his teachings.

Why was rhetoric so important to the Greeks? From the early days of the Greek democracy in Athens and on through the days of the Republic in Rome, people recognized that an orator—a good person speaking well—could often sway an audience and gain leadership. It was natural for these scholars to analyze successful speakers to find out why they succeeded. If possible, the scholars could then teach the skills to their pupils.

Defining Rhetoric

Rhetoric has been such an important part of the culture since the days of Corax, Isocrates, and Aristotle that there are many definitions of the term. The most important are the commonsense definition and two by famous rhetoricians, Aristotle and Richard Whately.

Commonsense Definition

Just thinking about the way people use the word *rhetoric* provides one definition. Most often people use **rhetoric** in reference to public speaking, but the term can also refer to writing. Rhetoric usually refers to formal acts of communication, such as political speeches or essays. It always implies some skill or cleverness in the use of words. Based on these commonsense perceptions, the word *rhetoric* means the art of speaking and writing well. This is a suitable definition, but it does leave a few questions unanswered. For example, how can someone know when a person has written or spoken well?

Whately's Definition

One thinker who pondered this very question was Bishop Richard Whately, an Englishman writing in the early 1800s. He defined rhetoric very simply as the art of adapting discourse to its end. Discourse is public communication, either writing or speaking. Whately's definition says that people know when someone has practiced the art of speaking and writing well when they see that the speech or essay has done what it was supposed to do. In short, good rhetoric works; people who understand rhetoric get results.

Aristotle's Definition

Whately based much of his writing about rhetoric on the most famous of all thinkers on the subject, Aristotle. Aristotle lived in Greece around 350 B.C., a century after Corax and about the same time as Isocrates. He wrote one of the earliest and most important books on speech, *The Rhetoric*. As with many other subjects, Aristotle analyzed rhetoric and laid down some very important principles. His definition of rhetoric is longer than the commonsense definition, but sets down important information about speaking and writing well. "Rhetoric," wrote Aristotle, "is the art of observing in a given situation the available means of persuasion." The best way to understand this definition is to look at it one part at a time.

Situation   First, Aristotle places rhetoric in a situation, meaning that all discourse takes place at a specific time, in a specific place, and under specific circumstances. And it makes sense to say that you can understand discourse best when you take into consideration the specific situation that produced it.

It's important to remember that the situation includes the people you're talking to. Imagine a vigorous pep talk that a coach might give a football team before a game. The game is against the school's biggest rival and will decide the league championship. A coach speaks differently to football players than to history students. Even when the student in the classroom and the athlete in the locker room are the same person, that person won't behave in the same way in the two situations. Aristotle's definition reminds every speaker that the audience is an important part of the given situation.

Speakers make a serious mistake when they fail to analyze the rhetorical situation. If someone has no more reason for giving a speech than "It was required," the chances are that you won't be very interested. The speech has no goal or purpose. There was no conflict or problem—no rhetorical situation.

If the football team loses its game, no postgame speech can erase the loss. But a postgame speech can change players' attitudes about the loss and perhaps their feelings about the next game. Unless you understand the situation, you cannot fully understand the coach's speech and the tactics used to inspire the team. In other words, the football coach is involved with conflict. He or she sees an important goal: winning. He or she sees an obstacle: the opponent. Aristotle's definition reminds everyone that all rhetoric is built around conflict.

It's important that you don't interpret *conflict* too narrowly. Not all rhetoric concerns matters of life or death. Still, you must have a motive for speaking. If you want your school's student council members to vote on a new policy for school dances, you are presented with a conflict—that is, you want the rule, but not everyone feels as you do. If other students are against the rule, then you definitely have a conflict. If others just don't care, the character of the conflict changes; you have to make them care in the same way you do.

Purpose   Aristotle ties rhetoric to persuasion. This means that the purpose of rhetoric is to change people's minds and actions through the use of words and other symbols. The situation that produces a speech must be one that words can change in some way. The football coach believes words can make a difference; otherwise, he or she wouldn't waste time talking to the team. The coach has a purpose for speaking: he or she is trying to alter the players' attitudes about the game and their play on the field. Likewise, if you put in the work to prepare a speech and present it before the student council, you must feel that your speech could make a difference.

This is perhaps the most important lesson to learn about speaking and writing. You must have a purpose or a goal. Without a purpose, a speech is neither interesting nor important. You should find the purpose for each speech you give from the very beginning of this class. If you feel a purpose, so will your audience. They will sense that there is a reason to listen to you and consider what you say.

Ethics and Rhetoric

Using speech to twist facts and to confuse issues has always existed side by side with using speech to clarify and to persuade. In ancient Greece some teachers, who were called the *sophists,* encouraged this unethical behavior. To this day, using language and reasoning that is misleading and shallow is called **sophistry.**

When you listen to a speech, you must be aware that not all speakers are ethical. Sometimes, people will try to use language to obscure the truth rather than reveal it. When you give a speech, you must be aware of your ethical responsibilities.

The Five Canons of Rhetoric

Classical scholars divided rhetoric into five parts. The chart below shows you the parts and their meaning:

Invention: the identification and selection of materials

Organization: the logical arrangement of the elements of discourse

Style: the appropriate and eloquent use of language

Delivery: the use of gestures and voice in presentation

Memory: the memorization of speeches

These categories, developed 2,000 years ago by the Roman author Quintilian, aren't very different from the subjects you study in today's speech classes. The classical scholars laid the groundwork for modern study.

Classical Rhetorical Analysis

Aristotle's definition forms the basis for **rhetorical analysis**—using classical methods to understand a speech or another piece of discourse. The technique is very simple. To analyze a speech using Aristotle's principles, remember the acronym SPAM: situation, purpose, audience, methods. The principles of rhetorical analysis apply to all kinds of discourse: manuscripts of speeches, speeches on videotape, speeches by famous people and by ordinary people, speeches given hundreds of years ago or only yesterday. SPAM is even a good way to analyze essays and other nonfiction works. A short rhetorical analysis of Patrick Henry's "Speech before the Virginia House of Burgesses" is featured in Chapter 3.

The Classical Methods of Persuasion

Classical thinkers followed Aristotle's description of the methods of persuasion. His descriptions are still helpful today. First, Aristotle said there are two categories or methods of persuasion: inartistic and artistic.

Inartistic Methods

Aristotle labeled the first category *inartistic* methods of persuasion because the speaker doesn't have to think of them independently. Inartistic methods draw upon the information found in libraries, newspapers, interviews, and countless other sources.

Artistic Methods

Artistic methods of persuasion are just the opposite of inartistic methods. These methods are invented—or thought up—by the speaker. Aristotle said that artistic methods consist of three types of appeals that the speaker could make to an audience: appeals to the audience's rationality (**logos**); appeals to the audience's emotions (**pathos**); and appeals based on the speaker's character (**ethos**).

Logos: the Logical Appeal　Appealing to an audience's intellectual, rational side can be very important. Speakers who don't treat their audiences as thinkers are frequently ineffective. The logical appeal uses forceful, clear arguments to make a point.

Building a Logical Appeal　Assume that a speaker wants to persuade high school seniors to devote more of their energies to improving the community after they graduate. The speaker might use this rational argument: The community is only as good as the individuals in it. The community protects and provides for all community members. People should not take from the community if they aren't prepared to give when the community is in need.

The speaker has made a logical appeal. In essence, the message says:

Providing for and protecting individuals who cannot provide for and protect themselves is good.

The community provides for and protects such individuals.

Therefore, the community is good.

The message goes on to say:

> Individuals who desire good must become part of the community.
> The seniors desire good.
> Therefore, the seniors must become a part of the community.

The message implies:

> If people won't give to the community to make it work, they aren't entitled to the community's protection and provisions.
> Seniors who don't do as I ask won't be giving to the community.
> Therefore, seniors who don't do as I ask won't be entitled to the community's protections and provisions.

Finally, it concludes:

> All people will need some help from the community at some time.
> Seniors are people.
> Therefore, seniors will need some help some time.

Here the arguments are expressed in the form of a **syllogism:** three statements consisting of two general premises and a specific conclusion following from them. A **premise** is a statement assumed to be true and used for building this kind of logical argument:

> **Major premise:** Individuals who desire good must become part of the community.
>
> **Minor premise:** The seniors desire good.
>
> **Conclusion:** The seniors must become part of the community.

Don't think, however, that speakers making logical appeals always speak in syllogisms. Usually, a public speaker will offer only a part of a syllogism. The audience fills in the remainder. In the syllogism above, for example, the speaker needs to provide only the major premise. The audience should fill in the minor premise and the conclusion. Such a shortened syllogism is called an **enthymeme.**

Logical appeals are important because many listeners consider them the substance of a speech. Without the logical appeals, some audience members are reluctant to be persuaded.

Pathos: the Emotional Appeal   If people were 100 percent rational, no one would ever think of using emotional appeals. You know, however, that emotions play an important part in the choices that everyone makes. Sometimes people even make illogical choices for emotional reasons. Speakers must be aware that audiences are not "thinking machines." Members of an audience experience love, hate, envy, pride, jealousy, compassion, and all the other emotions humans know so well.

Emotional appeals dominate some types of speeches. The football coach might try logic with the team, but chances are everyone already understands the rational approach to the game. So, the coach will probably appeal to the team's emotions, stressing such things as school pride, personal pride, feelings of obligation to family and community, ill feelings toward an archrival, or anger over the loss to the same team last year.

Building the Emotional Appeal   Emotional appeals require the speaker to "get inside" the audience—to understand how they feel about a specific subject at a specific time. Important though they are, emotional appeals can be abused, and they sometimes don't achieve the results the speaker intends. Appeals to sentimental feelings, for example, can backfire if the audience members feel the speaker is trying to manipulate them. Appeals to anger may move an audience, but not in the direction the speaker intends. Opponents can easily attack emotional appeals that can't be supported logically.

Ethos: the Character of the Speaker   Finally, an audience may be persuaded by the way they perceive the speaker. When audience members trust a speaker, they will be more willing to be persuaded. Lack of trust means the speaker will face a difficult battle for the audience, even with logical and emotional appeals in hand. The speaker's character is traditionally judged according to three qualifications: expertise, perceived good intentions, and trustworthiness.

Expertise is another word for "qualification," or how well the speaker understands the subject of the speech. For example, you might believe a biologist who tells you soil erosion threatens the environment. You might believe a farmer who tells you soil erosion threatens the farm economy. But if a beautician tells you the same thing, you might be skeptical. Why? The beautician has no expertise in soil conservation. By the same token, you probably wouldn't believe a biologist or a farmer if they advised you to get a different kind of haircut.

Perceived good intentions is the audience's perception of the speaker's purpose or intent. If the audience thinks the speaker has good reasons for speaking and is trying to accomplish good things, the audience is more likely to listen and trust. The stress here is on *perceived* good intentions. Some audiences perceive speakers to be good people when they really aren't. Sometimes different people perceive the same speaker in different ways. Convincing an audience that you have good intentions makes it more likely that they will go along with you when you state your position.

Trustworthiness means just what the word says: Is the speaker worthy of trust? Is the speaker known to tell the truth? Can the audience believe the speaker? If the members of an audience feel a speaker's expertise is high and think the speaker has good intentions, the speaker can still fail if they feel they can't rely on the speaker to tell the truth.

Building the Ethical Appeal   It follows that if you are going to build your own ethos (personal appeal), you will want to stress your expertise, good intentions, and trustworthiness. You might wonder how you do that without seeming to be conceited. You already know how to make a good impression depending on the person you are meeting. Imagine a job interview. Don't you dress a certain way? Talk differently than you do with friends? Try to emphasize your experience and education? A speaker may do the same things because he or she is on display and, in a way, "selling" ethos.

Speakers who can provide information for their own introductions use the introduction to help build ethos. Good research and knowing your facts will encourage audiences to believe in your expertise. A good thesis statement (see Chapter 9) can help with perceived good intentions. Your trustworthiness is largely based on your reputation for telling the truth, but speakers can also build trust through audience analysis, careful preparation, and honesty in speaking and answering questions.

Speech Criticism

Speech students traditionally use these three categories—logical (logos), emotional (pathos), and ethical (ethos)—to determine why speeches are effective or ineffective. Of course, classifying the appeals found in a speech is only the first step. Next, you must think critically about those appeals and determine which were important to the speech's success or failure.

Glossary

Adrenalin—A secretion released by the adrenal glands into the bloodstream that acts as a stimulant for the heart; usually produced in situations involving fear.

After-dinner speech—A speech to entertain that usually follows a breakfast, lunch, or dinner.

Analogy—An extended comparison in which the unfamiliar is explained in terms of the familiar.

Apathy—A lack of feeling or concern, often used to describe the attitude of an audience.

Argumentation—The process of presenting the reasons that lead to support of a claim.

Articulation—The production of sounds to form words.

Artistic qualities—The manner of delivery, the language, the organization, and the overall impact of a speech.

Attitudes—The beliefs or feelings one has about other people, ideas, and events.

Attributing—Identifying the original speaker of a quotation or the original source of a piece of support information.

Audience—The people to whom a speech is directed.

Behaviors—The outward expressions of attitudes.

Belongingness needs—People's need to have friends and to be loved by others.

Call number—An identification number printed on each book and on each card in a library.

Card catalog—An alphabetical listing of the books in a library; some card catalogs are computer listings.

Categorical term—A word like *never* or *always* that allows no exceptions.

Cause-effect order—Speech organization in which the first part of a speech describes the cause of a problem and the second its effect.

Ceremonial speech—A speech delivered on a special occasion, such as a graduation or a dedication.

Channel—The means for communicating a message. It can be either verbal or nonverbal. Also called a *medium.*

Chronological order—Organizing a speech by using a time sequence.

Claim—The conclusion or idea one wants the audience to accept. See also *claim of fact, value,* and *policy.*

Claim of fact—Statement about something real. It can be proven correct or incorrect.

Claim of policy—Statement about what or how something should be done. It suggests a course of action.

Claim of value—Statement that makes a judgment about what is good or bad, right or wrong, just or unjust.

Classification order—An organizational pattern that divides items into categories or classes.

Common ground—Those experiences, beliefs, or background factors that a speaker and audience share.

Communication—The process of creating understanding through the exchange of messages.

Communication apprehension—Being fearful about participating in some form of communication.

Communication model—A diagram explaining how the parts of the communication process work and relate to one another.

Comparison/Contrast—Pointing out similarities between dissimilar subjects; pointing out differences between similar subjects.

Conclusion—A speaker's final comments that let the audience know the speech is about to close, that summarize the major points in the speech, and that leave the audience with a point to remember.

Consistency—A test of evidence to determine if more than one source supports an idea.

Contest speech—A speech designed to follow the conventions of a speaking contest sponsored by an organization or a school.

Context—The physical, social, psychological, and time elements in which communication takes place.

Controlling purpose—The dominant goal of a speech; either to persuade, to inform, or to entertain.

Conventions—Characteristics or traditions that are common to all speeches of a certain kind.

Courtesy speeches—Speeches intended to fulfill the demands of social custom, such as thanking a group for an award.

Credibility—The quality by which a speaker appears believable and sincere to an audience.

Criterion-referenced form—An evaluation form that lists specific behaviors a speaker should demonstrate to be effective.

Critical listening—A process that involves both listening for information and evaluating information.

Data—The evidence or support for a claim.

Deductive reasoning—An analysis process that takes a generally accepted conclusion and applies it to specific instances to demonstrate that the conclusion applies to the instance.

Definition—A statement expressing the meaning of a word or group of words.

Democracy—A government in which the people are free to govern themselves, usually through elected representatives.

Demographics—Statistical descriptions of the characteristics of population groups.

Demonstration speech—An informative speech in which the speaker shows the audience how to do something.

Description—Representing in words what a person or scene looks like.

Descriptive gestures—Gestures that help a speaker describe something.

Development—Amplifying and clarifying the claims and data in a speech.

Dewey decimal system—A system for organizing and arranging nonfiction books in a library.

Dynamism—The trait associated with a speech presentation style that is energetic, lively, active, or assertive.

Empathy—The ability to put oneself into another's place; to understand what and why a person feels, believes, or acts in a certain way.

Emphasis—Prominence given to key words and phrases in speaking.

Emphatic gestures—Gestures that provide emphasis for the spoken word.

Ethics—A set of beliefs about what is right and wrong.

Ethnic group—A group of people who are tied together by religion, race, culture, or national origin.

Ethos—An appeal to an audience based on the perception of the speaker's character.

Eulogy—A ceremonial speech, often given at a funeral, in memory of a person who died.

Evaluation—The process of making judgments about the strengths and weaknesses of a speech.

Evidence—Support materials, such as facts, statistics, or testimony.

Example—A typical, specific instance, used in a speech as support material.

Expertise—The qualifications of a speaker to talk on a certain subject.

Extemporaneous delivery—Delivery from an outline or notes containing key words or phrases.

External transition—Transition that connects points on different levels of an outline.

Eye contact—The speaker looking members of the audience directly in the eye to convey sincerity and establish credibility.

Fact—A statement about something real that can be proven correct or not.

Fallacy—A flaw in the reasoning process.

Fear appeal—An emotional appeal that motivates the audience to act by making them feel fearful or vulnerable.

Feedback—The process by which a receiver responds to a message, either verbally or nonverbally.

Feedback loops—The three stages of the feedback process (prespeech, presentation, and postspeech) that reinforce the idea that communication has no distinct beginning or ending.

Fluency—To flow without interruption.

Forecast—A statement that predicts the major points of a speech.

Framing—Pausing just before or just after a word or phrase to draw attention to it.

Gender—Classification according to sex; male or female.

Gesture—The use of the limbs or body to express or emphasize ideas or emotions.

Hearing—The sense through which sound is received; a passive physical process.

Hidden agenda—Concealing the real purpose of a speech; often, pretending to entertain while seeking to persuade.

Hierarchy—An arrangement of ideas, things, or people in the order of their importance.

Illustration—A long, elaborate example used in a speech as support material.

Impromptu delivery—Delivery that isn't rehearsed and doesn't involve notes or prior planning.

Incident—An example developed in the form of a story; also called *anecdote* and *narrative.*

Inductive reasoning—A process by which general conclusions are drawn through the examination of specific instances or examples.

Inflection—A change in pitch of voice.

Informative speech—See *speech to inform.*

Instance—An example developed in the form of a story.

Intensity—Conveying emotional feeling in a speech.

Interference—Anything that prevents effective communication.

Internal transition—Transition that links information within a section of a speech.

Interpersonal communication—Communication between two or three people. It can be either formal or informal.

Intrapersonal communication—Communication that takes place within oneself.

Introduction—The opening section of a speech; it draws the audience's attention, introduces the topic, shows the topic's importance, presents the thesis, and forecasts the major points in the speech.

Journal—A magazine that publishes articles of interest to specialists in a certain field.

Keyword—A word that is important to a researcher's search that may not show up in a title but only in the description of a book or article.

Library of Congress system—A system for organizing and arranging nonfiction books in a library.

Listening—Concentrating on a sound; interpreting, and reacting to it; a mental process that requires active participation by a receiver.

Logical order—See *topical order.*

Logos—An appeal made by a speaker to the rationality of an audience.

Manuscript delivery—A form of speech delivery in which every word of the speech is written out.

Mass communication—The use of electronic or print technologies to send a message to a large number of people.

Media center—A modern term for a library, especially one having audiovisual materials.

Medium—The means for communicating a message. It can be either verbal or nonverbal. Also called a *channel.*

Memorized delivery—A memorized presentation of a speech manuscript.

Message—The idea the sender wants the receiver to understand.

Method—The way in which a speaker tries to accomplish his or her speech purpose.

Motivated sequence—An approach to structuring a persuasive speech that includes five steps: attention, need, satisfaction, visualization, and action.

Motivation—An incentive to believe or act in a certain way.

Motive—A need or desire that causes a person to act.

Movement—The physical moving a speaker does to indicate to the audience that he or she is moving to a new place in a speech.

Multi-channelled—Communication that uses both verbal and nonverbal channels to communicate ideas.

Narrowing the topic—Scaling down a large, general subject to a smaller, more specific one in order to fit the time limits for a speech.

Nonverbal communication—Communication that doesn't use words; it may use facial expressions, gestures, or even silence.

Occasion—The time and circumstances in which something happens.

On-line catalog—A service provided by media centers that enables a user to obtain bibliographies on a variety of topics from a computer data bank.

Oral report—An informative speech that gathers together and explains information for a particular group or purpose; a summary of facts and ideas.

Original oration—A persuasive speech, prepared in advance and memorized, and delivered as part of a school contest.

Outline delivery—Another term for extemporaneous delivery. See *extemporaneous delivery*.

Paralinguistics—Vocal cues, such as volume, rate, or inflection, that tell a receiver how to interpret spoken words.

Paraphrase—Restating the meaning of a text or a quotation in one's own words.

Pathos—An appeal made by a speaker to the emotions of an audience.

Pause—A brief silence used in a speech to add drama or meaning.

Periodicals—Materials, such as magazines and newspapers, published at regular intervals.

Persuasion—Intentional communication designed to produce a change in attitudes or behaviors.

Physiological needs—Necessities for existence; food, water, and shelter are the most common.

Pitch—Highness or lowness of sounds, as on a musical scale.

Plagiarism—Using another person's words or ideas without giving that person credit.

Policy—A principle or set of procedures that serves to guide the actions of governments, businesses, and other organizations.

Posture—The way in which a speaker stands.

Precision—Exactness; the ability to distinguish clearly.

Primacy effect—The arrangement of arguments and evidence at the beginning of a speech so as to have the greatest persuasive impact on an audience.

Problem-solution order—Speech organization in which the first part of the speech outlines a problem and the second part gives a solution.

Process—An ongoing activity with no clear beginning or ending.

Process speech—An informative speech that describes how something is done or works.

Public speaking—One person communicating with many in a continuous, face-to-face presentation.

Purpose—The goal a speaker hopes to achieve with his or her speech.

Purpose statement—A sentence specifying the subject, the audience, and the goal of a speech.

Reading the audience—Understanding the background of the audience you are addressing.

Reasoning—The logic step in the argumentation process that relates the support to the claim.

Receiver—The object of a message.

Recency effect—Occurs when the arguments and evidence placed at the end of a speech have the greatest persuasive effect on an audience.

Reservation—The exceptions to a warrant in the reasoning process.

Resonation—The enriching and amplifying of voice sounds by the pharynx, nasal cavities, and mouth.

Respiration—The act of breathing.

Retention—The ability to remember and recall information.

Rhetoric—The art of speaking and writing well; the art of adapting discourse to its end; and the art of observing in a given situation the available means of persuasion.

Rhetorical analysis—Examining the effectiveness of a speech in terms of situation, purpose, audience, and method.

Safety needs—Human requirements that involve one's well-being or sense of security.

Selective listening—Blocking out what the listener doesn't want to hear.

Self-actualization—The realization of one's full potential.

Self-esteem—The feelings a person has about himself or herself.

Sender—The person who has a message to communicate.

Signpost—Markers for important divisions in a speech; reminders to tell the audience where a speaker is in the speech's organizational structure.

Situation—The place and time in which all communication (including public speaking) occurs.

Small group communication—Interaction among four to twelve individuals.

Sophistry—Using language to deceive and mislead.

Spatial order—Organization that divides physical space into parts.

Specialized speeches—Speeches given in response to frequently occurring occasions; courtesy speeches, ceremonial speeches, contest speeches.

Speech rate—The speed at which a person talks.

Speech to actuate—A speech designed to cause someone to change a behavior or to add a new one.

Speech to entertain—Usually a humorous speech, designed to hold the attention of the audience and amuse them.

Speech to inform—A speech that tries to make an audience more knowledgeable or to increase their understanding of a topic through presentation of information.

Speech to persuade—A speech to change, create, or reinforce attitudes or behaviors.

Stage fright—Being fearful about participating in some form of communication, especially public speaking or stage performances.

Statistics—Information presented numerically.

Subordination—The process of dividing material into more specific categories.

Support—The evidence used to prove a claim.

Technology—New methods of projecting and generating images, doing research, and composing speeches.

Teleprompter—A mechanical device that shows a speaker a manuscript, either by reflecting the image on glass plates or by using a machine similar to a television monitor.

Testimony—The opinion of others, usually experts, quoted as support material.

Thesis statement—A sentence summing up the speaker's point of view on the topic of his or her speech; usually, a part of the speech.

Topical order—An organizational pattern used when a speech contains several ideas and each seems naturally to precede the other; also referred to as *logical order*.

Transition—The words, phrases, and sentences that tie the parts of a speech together.

Values—Judgments about the world that cannot be verified as facts; relative judgments about what is good or bad, right or wrong, just or unjust.

Verbal communication—Any communication, spoken or written, that includes words.

Vibration—A motion caused by air passing over vocal cords that produces sound.

Visual aids—Support material that an audience can see.

Volume—The loudness or softness of sound.

Warrant—The reasoning step in the argumentation process.

Working bibliography—A list of possible sources compiled by a speaker during research.

Credits

Photo Credits

289 Mary Kate Denny/PhotoEdit

293 Jeff Ellis

304 David Woo/Stock, Boston

313 Paul Conklin/PhotoEdit

316 Jeff Ellis

320 Jeff Ellis

335 Bob Daemmrich/Stock, Boston

339 Jean-Claude Lejeune/Stock, Boston

346 Jim Whitmer

353 Wide World Photos

359 Jeff Greenberg/PhotoEdit

364 Ulrike Welsch

379 Russell Abraham/Stock, Boston

385 Jim Whitmer

400 Jeff Ellis

Literary Credits

Page **90** "Figure Fumble Gesture of Goodwill," by Bill Vaughn was reprinted by permission of *The Kansas City Star*, all rights reserved.

181 "Prespeech Jitters Heard on Open Mike" was taken from the *Associated Press* and appeared in *The Wichita (KS) Eagle*, 27 June 1993.

269 Excerpt from "Teach the Hungry People to Feed Themselves a Crumbling Goal?" by Lonny Powell appeared in *Speaking as a Farmer* by Dan B. Curtis and Robert S. Brewer, 1980, pages 119–122. Reprinted by permission of Kendall/Hunt Publishing Co., Dubuque, Iowa.

285 Excerpts from William J. Bennett's speech, "Once More, a Plea for History" are taken from *The London Lecture Series on Public Issues: The First Twenty Years, 1966–1986,* edited by Diana Prentice Carlin and Meredith A. Moore. Reprinted by permission of University Press of America, Lanham, Maryland.

372 "Five Ways in Which Thinking Is Dangerous," by Stephen Joel Trachtenberg, appeared in *Vital Speeches of the Day,* 15 August 1986, vol. 52, no. 21. Reprinted by permission of Vital Speeches of the Day, Mt. Pleasant, South Carolina.

390 "Choices and Change: Your Success as a Family," by Barbara Bush, appeared in *Vital Speeches of the Day,* 1 July 1990. Reprinted by permission of Vital Speeches of the Day, Mt. Pleasant, South Carolina.

416 The speech by Gary Lillian was supplied by Sally Shipley at Shawnee Mission West High School, Shawnee Mission, Kansas.

420 The speech by Steve Dvorske was supplied by Sally Shipley at Shawnee Mission West High School, Shawnee Mission, Kansas.

422 Transcripts of the speech by Nelson Mandela were made by Federal News Service and obtained from the Purdue University Public Affairs Video Archives, West Lafayette, Indiana.

430 "Wellesley Commencement Address" by Hillary Rodham Clinton was provided to Diana Carlin by the Clinton for President office in Little Rock, Arkansas, in September 1992.

Speaker Index

Subject Index